Jakob Hutter

His Life and Letters

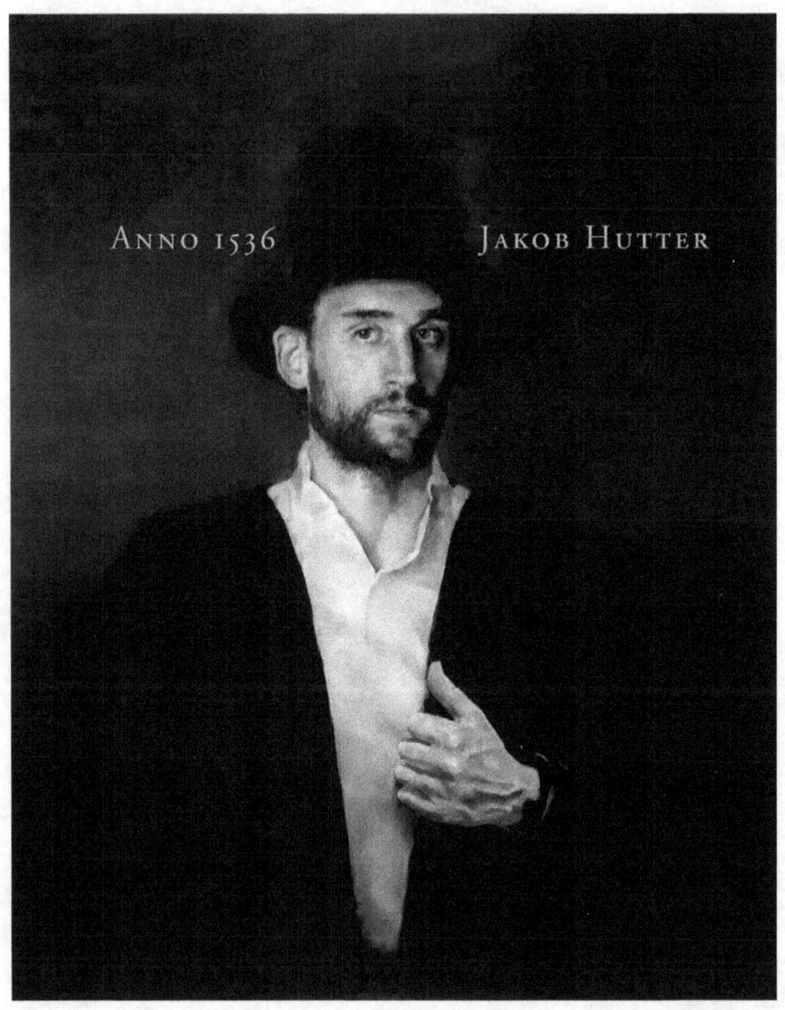

Justine Maendel, *Jakob Hutter*, oil on canvas, 2022

Jakob Hutter
His Life and Letters

Translated and edited by
Emmy Barth Maendel
and Jonathan Seiling

Plough

Published by Plough Publishing House
Walden, New York
Robertsbridge, England
Elsmore, Australia
www.plough.com

ISBN: 978-1-63608-090-1

A catalog record for this book is available from the British Library.
Library of Congress Cataloging-in-Publication Data

Names: Barth Maendel, Emmy, 1961- editor. | Seiling, Jonathan R., editor.
Title: Jakob Hutter : his life and letters / edited by Emmy Barth Maendel and Jonathan Seiling.
Description: Walden, New York : Plough Publishing House, [2024] | Series: Classics of the radical reformation; 14 | Includes bibliographical references and index. | Summary: "A scholarly biography and collection of writings by and about Jakob Hutter, an early leader of the Hutterites, a communal Anabaptist group"-- Provided by publisher.
Identifiers: LCCN 2023047269 (print) | LCCN 2023047270 (ebook) | ISBN 9781636080901 (print) | ISBN 9781636080918 (ebook)
Subjects: LCSH: Hutter, Jakob, -1536. | Anabaptists--Czech Republic--Moravia--Biography. | Hutterite Brethren--Czech Republic--Moravia--Biography.
Classification: LCC BX8143.H86 J35 2024 (print) | LCC BX8143.H86 (ebook) | DDC 284/.3--dc23/eng/20231213
LC record available at https://lccn.loc.gov/2023047269
LC ebook record available at https://lccn.loc.gov/2023047270

This is for you, Jake.
You would be so pleased.

Emmy

Classics of the Radical Reformation

Classics of the Radical Reformation is an English-language series of Anabaptist and Free Church documents translated and annotated under the direction of the Institute of Mennonite Studies, which is the research agency of the Anabaptist Mennonite Biblical Seminaries, and published by Plough Publishing House.

1. *The Legacy of Michael Sattler.* Trans., ed. John Howard Yoder.
2. *The Writings of Pilgram Marpeck.* Trans., ed. William Klassen and Walter Klaassen.
3. *Anabaptism in Outline: Selected Primary Sources.* Trans., ed. Walter Klaassen.
4. *The Sources of Swiss Anabaptism: The Grebel Letters and Related Documents.* Ed. Leland Harder.
5. *Balthasar Hubmaier: Theologian of Anabaptism.* Ed. H. Wayne Pipkin and John Howard Yoder.
6. *The Writings of Dirk Philips.* Ed. Cornelius J. Dyck, William E. Keeney, and Alvin J. Beachy.
7. *The Anabaptist Writings of David Joris: 1535–1543.* Ed. Gary K. Waite.
8. *The Essential Carlstadt: Fifteen Tracts by Andreas Bodenstein.* Trans., ed. E. J. Furcha.
9. *Peter Riedemann's Hutterite Confession of Faith.* Trans., ed. John J. Friesen.
10. *Sources of South German/Austrian Anabaptism.* Ed. C. Arnold Snyder, trans. Walter Klaassen, Frank Friesen, and Werner O. Packull.
11. *Confessions of Faith in the Anabaptist Tradition: 1527–1660.* Ed. Karl Koop.
12. *Jörg Maler's Kunstbuch: Writings of the Pilgram Marpeck Circle.* Ed. John D. Rempel.
13. *Later Writings of the Swiss Anabaptists: 1529–1592.* Ed. C. Arnold Snyder.
14. *Jakob Hutter: His Life and Letters.* Trans., ed. Emmy Barth Maendel and Jonathan Seiling

Contents

Preface

In the summer of 2003, friends of mine returned from a trip to South Tyrol, where they had toured places where sixteenth-century Anabaptists had been imprisoned and executed. They reported in lively detail on the steadfast faith of these men and women in the face of intense persecution. The story that piqued my interest was that of Katharina Hutter, wife of Jakob Hutter, after whom the Hutterian Church is named – an account of conversion, recantation, torture, pregnancy, imprisonment, and death.

In the 1980s, I had been part of the team that prepared the English translation of *The Chronicle of the Hutterian Brethren,* vol. 1. Since that time, I had worked in the Bruderhof Historical Archive and familiarized myself with its collection of Hutterite manuscripts and codices. But Katharina is not mentioned in Hutterite sources. I was determined to learn more about her.

I quickly discovered a series of German academic tomes, *Quellen zur Geschichte der Täufer* [Sources for Anabaptist History], in which transcripts of Anabaptist interrogations and government communications regarding their capture and punishment have been reproduced in the original language. As I began translating some of these texts, the life of a persecuted underground church sprang to life in sharp focus: clandestine meetings, baptisms, celebratory conferences at which a steer would be slaughtered to feed up to a hundred participants, manhunts, escapes, tortures. And there I found a transcript of Katharina Hutter's December 1535 interrogation.

In 2017 I traveled to Tyrol to look for additional information on Jakob and Katharina in the diocesan archive in Brixen (seat of the bishop in Hutter's time) and the Tiroler Landesarchiv in Innsbruck (seat of the provincial government). I hoped to find Jakob Hutter's interrogation transcript, but unfortunately it seems to have disappeared. I did find intriguing details – for instance, that Katharina's baby was probably born before her arrest, contrary to what had been assumed – but I was still looking for a description of her execution in 1538, or at least definitive confirmation of this event.

That search took me to the Styrian provincial archive to search through Johann Loserth's papers and, three years later, to Josef von Beck's papers in the Moravian state archive in Brno, Czechia. There I found the probable source: a copy of a list of martyrs (taken from a codex in Bratislava) that included her name.

The archives in Brno and Bratislava preserve a significant number of codices written by Hutterites in the late sixteenth and seventeenth centuries. These books contain copies of martyr epistles, small chronicles, sermons, doctrinal works, and song collections. I was interested in Jakob Hutter's letters and was able to make careful comparisons of the texts of his letters from various sources.

Plough had published a small book of Hutter's letters in 1979 as *Brotherly Faithfulness: Epistles from a Time of Persecution*. This book replaces that: the letters have been newly translated and differences between the various codex copies are noted. But it also goes far beyond that previous volume. Transcripts of interrogations of men and women whom Hutter had baptized, government and church correspondence concerning him and his followers, and new chronicle accounts from members of his fellowship in Moravia round out his story. In addition, a critique of Jakob Hutter by his rival Gabriel Ascherham and a description of the Hutterite communities by their opponent Christoph Andreas Fischer have been included, so that this book is a comprehensive collection of sixteenth-century texts concerning Jakob and Katharina Hutter. Apart from Hutter's letters and the excerpts from *The Chronicle of the Hutterian Brethren*, vol. 1, most of this material has not been available in English before.

My coauthor Jonathan Seiling helped organize and contextualize the material and also wrote the introduction, a noteworthy project on its own account.

It is my hope that through this book, the life and witness of Jakob Hutter and his fellow believers might be rediscovered today.

Emmy Barth Maendel
September 2023

Abbreviations

ADS — Additional Documents. See chapter 6.

CHR — Chronicle Source. See chapter 2.

Chronicle — *The Chronicle of the Hutterian Brethren,* vol. 1. Rifton, NY: Plough, 1987.

COD. 1. — Codex 1: Rkp.zv.305 in the Central Library of the Slovak Academy of Sciences in Bratislava. L-1, L-4, L-5, L-6, L-7, L-8.

COD. 2. — Codex 2: I 87.708 (Ms I 340) in the University Library in Vienna. L-3, L-4, L-6, L-8, CHR-10, CHR-11, CHR-12.

COD. 3. — Codex 3: Rkp.zv.388 in the Central Library of the Slovak Academy of Sciences in Bratislava. L-4.

COD. 4. — Codex 4: EAH 159 in Bruderhof Historical Archive, Walden, NY. L-3, L-5, L-6, L-7, L-8.

COD. 5. — Codex 5: EAH 80 in Bruderhof Historical Archive, Walden, NY. L-3, L-4, L-5.

COD. 6. — Codex 6: EAH 82 in Bruderhof Historical Archive, Walden, NY. L-3, L-4, L-7, L-8.

COD. 7. — Codex 7: HAB. 5 in Štátny archív v Bratislave in Bratislava. L-2, CHR-10, CHR-11, CHR-12.

COD. 8. — Codex 8: HAB. 6 in Štátny archív v Bratislave in Bratislava. L-3.

COD. 9. — Codex 9: HAB. 13 in Štátny archív v Bratislave in Bratislava. L-3, L-5, L-6, L-7.

COD. 10. — Codex 10: HAB. 17 in Štátny archív v Bratislave in Bratislava. L-3, L-5, L-6, L-7, L-8.

COD. 11. — Codex 11: HAB. 9 in Štátny archív v Bratislave in Bratislava. L-4, L-5 (incomplete), L-6, L-8.

COD. 12. — Codex 12: HAB. 12 in Štátny archív v Bratislave in Bratislava. L-4, CHR-10, CHR-11, CHR-12.

COD. 13: — Codex 13: HAB.16 in Štátny archív v Bratislave in Bratislava. CHR-10, CHR-11, CHR-12.

COD. 14: — Codex 14: Ab 15 in Eötvös Loránd Tudományegyetem Könyvtára in Budapest. CHR-10, CHR-11, CHR-12.

COD. 15: Codex 15: "Caspar Breitmichel Codex," Estate of Reinhold Konrath, Conrad Grebel University College, Waterloo, Ontario. CHR-10, CHR-11, CHR-12.

CRR Classics of the Radical Reformation

GAMEO *Global Anabaptist Mennonite Encyclopedia Online*

GOV Governmental Correspondence. See chapter 5.

GZOT I Müller, Lydia, *Glaubenszeugnisse oberdeutscher Taufgesinnter*, vol. 1. Leipzig: Heinsius, 1938.

HEP Hutterian Epistle. See chapter 4.

Hutt.Epist. The Hutterite Brethren in America, eds., *Die Hutterischen Epistel 1527 bis 1767*, 4 vols. Elie, MB: James Valley Book Centre, 1986–1991.

L Letter. See chapter 1.

MennLex *Mennonitisches Lexikon*

MGBL *Mennonitische Geschichtsblätter*

MQR *Mennonite Quarterly Review*

PUB. 1. Hans Fischer, *Jakob Huter: Leben, Froemmigkeit, Briefe.* Newton, KS: Mennonite Publishing, 1956.

PUB. 2. The Hutterite Brethren in America, eds., *Die Hutterischen Epistel 1527 bis 1767,* 4 vols. Elie, MB: James Valley Book Centre, 1986–1991.

PUB. 3. Rudolf Wolkan, ed. *Das grosse Geschichtsbuch der Hutterischen Brüder.* Standoff Colony, Macleod, AB., Canada, 1923.

PUB. 4. Zieglschmid, A. J. F., ed. *Die älteste Chronik der Hutterischen Brüder.* Ithaca, NY: Carl Schurz Memorial Foundation, Cayuga Press, 1943.

PUB. 5. Müller, Lydia, *Glaubenszeugnisse Oberdeutscher Taufgesinnter*, vol. 1. Leipzig: Heinsius, 1938.

PUB. 6. Zieglschmid, A. J. F., "Unpublished Sixteenth Century Letters of the Hutterian Brethren," *MQR* 15 (1941): 5–25, 118–140.

QGT *Quellen zur Geschichte der Täufer*

QGT XI Mecenseffy, Grete, ed. *Quellen zur Geschichte der Täufer*, XI Band. *Österreich I.* Gütersloh, Germany: Gerd Mohn, 1964.

QGT XIII Mecenseffy, Grete, ed. *Quellen zur Geschichte der Täufer*, XIII Band. *Österreich II*. Gütersloh, Germany: Gerd Mohn, 1972.

QGT XIV Mecenseffy, Grete, ed. *Quellen zur Geschichte der Täufer*, XIV Band. *Österreich III*. Gütersloh, Germany: Gerd Mohn, 1983.

TLA Tiroler Landesarchiv

WIT Witness. See chapter 3.

Introduction

Jakob Hutter (ca. 1500–1536)

The writer of *The Chronicle of the Hutterian Brethren,* vol. 1 (ca. 1550s), Kaspar Braitmichel (d. 1573), introduces Hutter by stating that around 1529, from Tyrol, "there came a man named Jakob, a hatter by trade. . . . He accepted the covenant of grace with a good conscience in Christian baptism, in true surrender, to follow the ways of God. When after a time it was abundantly clear that he had gifts from God, he was chosen for, and confirmed in, the service of the gospel."[1] This short paragraph aptly sums up his legacy within the Hutterite Anabaptist tradition: baptism, surrender, abundant gifts, chosen, and confirmed. It is a terse description, packed with meaning and helpful for understanding the life and legacy of this controversial figure in Anabaptist history.

Hutter's own self-assessment might best be encapsulated in a quote from his final letter in which he describes himself as

> a slave of God and apostle of Jesus Christ, and a minister of all his chosen saints, here, there, and in all territories, up [in Tyrol] and down in Moravia, called by God in his boundless grace and unspeakable mercy. He has chosen and fitted me for this task in his grace and boundless mercy, though I have in no way earned it, but only because of his overflowing faithfulness and goodness, which has reckoned me as righteous and made me worthy to serve him in the everlasting and new covenant he established and made with Abraham and his seed for eternity. He has entrusted and placed his divine, eternal word into my heart and mouth, along with the heavenly properties of his Holy Spirit . . . blessed me with his eternal, heavenly blessing . . . made his divine and eternal word alive and active in me, and in many to whom I proclaimed it

> . . . gave me this [blessing] as a sign through the dispensation and partnership of the Holy Spirit with every sort of mighty wonder and sign . . . made me a watchman, shepherd, and tender over his holy people, over his chosen, holy Christian fellowship. (L-8)

Yet some of his contemporaries disputed these claims, doubting Hutter's apostolic calling and sometimes making a caricature of him as a harsh, unwavering sectarian, like those seen elsewhere in different branches and eras of the Anabaptist movement or among other radicals.

It is not without reason that Hutter has been considered an uncompromisingly disciplined leader. The critical circumstances that confronted him did not lend themselves to a dithering guide who could not stomach controversy or the odium resulting from making unpopular decisions. He called other leaders to account in his attempt to ensure the survival of the fellowship, without abandoning authenticity or the public, missional dimension of his calling. His strict disciplinary approach clearly bore fruit in the stability and longevity of the Christian tradition that bears his name.

Hutter is a complex character whose significance for the history of Anabaptism cannot be underestimated, but given the paucity of documents and brevity of his career, sorting out the details of his life and thought remains a challenge. Gifted in many aspects of leadership, with widely recognized strengths as an orator, he apparently was envied by other "ministers of the Word," as they were called in the Hutterite tradition. In contrast to many first generation Anabaptist leaders, he had not had the benefit of higher education, but his devotion to internalizing the words of scripture is evident throughout his letters.

The conflicts into which he was drawn, as outlined in the documents in this collection, shaped the actions and decisions he believed necessary for the group's cohesion and fidelity to their calling as Christians. At times, Hutter tried desperately to mediate, a task that sometimes required a heavy hand when accusations of ministerial misconduct needed to be addressed.

Persecution in Hutter's Tyrolean context precluded the existence of a public Anabaptist movement, starting in the late 1520s. In contrast, Moravia provided a unique region for settlement of Anabaptist groups and the means to become established in a way that was nearly impossible elsewhere.

Refugees fled to Moravia from many parts of Europe as pastors could gather larger flocks there in relative security. The settlements grew rapidly and there was a constant need to manage ever-shifting leadership and group dynamics.

As a tailor of hats, Jakob was a member of the artisan-tradesman class, and although his birth date is unknown, based on the years of his professional development, it is assumed he was born around 1500. He was raised in an obscure hamlet in South Tyrol called Moos, near St. Lorenzen in present-day northern Italy, and presumably received a basic formal education.[2] In 1529, the same year he is said to have become a minister of the Word, he had become the most hunted Anabaptist leader under King Ferdinand's rule. Executed in 1536 in Innsbruck, he died as a criminal in the eyes of the state-church and as a martyr in the eyes of the Anabaptist tradition. He seemed fearless in the face of the king and bishop, eager to confront both collective and individual hypocrisy. He was indefatigable as an evangelist throughout the Tyrolean alpine regions, searching for those receptive to his interpretation of the gospel, repeatedly risking his life while spies and state officials pursued him, along with his loyal associates and their network of rebaptized followers. Unwavering under torture, he was reportedly gagged while being executed to stop him from preaching his last sermon during his execution (WIT-22). Ultimately Jakob Hutter was remembered by his tradition as one "made worthy to suffer for the name of Jesus." He was a simple man whom his followers believed was chosen by God to gather a people, to build a fellowship.

Another remarkable part of his life and legacy is the documentation concerning Hutter's wife, Katharina (née Prast). Although her interrogation records provide much detail, little is known about her personal biography. Yet her presence alongside Jakob in the years between 1533 and 1536 elucidates unique aspects of his journey as a married Anabaptist missionary who was expecting his first child when he set out on his final mission trip.

Given the rather unique trajectory of both the Tyrolean and Moravian Anabaptist communities, our study of Hutter explores longer-term contextual factors, which indelibly shaped his formative years. The rise and implementation of the community of goods as seen in the Hutterite Bruderhof was an early attempt at creating an alternative economic community, in which a covenant of faith and finance afforded Anabaptists a means of resistance against the unjust demands of the broader society.

Anti-Imperial Reform, Protest, and Tribulation

The varieties of reform undertaken in Europe contested the sacral-economic ancient regime of throne-altar-nobility already in the mid-1400s and continued unabatedly through two centuries of development until the Enlightenment breakthroughs of the 1660s, after which the stability of church-state would be forever shaken.[3] In Tyrol as in other regions, there were both steady and abrupt impulses toward revolt and reform in political and religious life; these were proposed, debated, imposed, rejected, and in some measure eventually enacted over a long and tumultuous transition.[4]

Geopolitics

Tyrol is a beautiful alpine region of rugged peaks towering over sunlit valleys. The lower slopes are covered with pine and larch trees, and above these rise the bare rock cliffs of the Dolomites. Brixen (now Bressanone) lies about 250 kilometers north of Venice and, by comparison, about 550 kilometers west of Vienna. The landscape is a spectacle, but wresting a living from it demands hard work: farming in the valleys, grazing cows on the slopes, and mining ore from the depths of the mountains themselves are hard-won means of income. A lack of mobility in terms of both transporting goods and the socioeconomic benefits therein held most Tyrolean citizens at the lower rungs of society with little room for improvement, while nobles profited from new industrial and economic developments. The seat of the territorial government of Tyrol was to the north in Innsbruck (Austria), while the ecclesiastical government for much of the region was seated in Brixen to the south of the region (Italy), where a prince-bishop ruled. The three regional districts of South Tyrol relevant to Hutter's ministry are the Italian valleys of Puster, Wipp, and Eisack.[5] North Tyrol in present-day Austria includes several districts where Innsbruck is at the central point, with the cities of Schwaz and Rattenberg further east. This northern region is wedged between Switzerland and Liechtenstein to the west, Bavaria to the north-west, and Salzburg and Carinthia to the east. From there, Moravia was 600 kilometers north and east in today's Czechia.

King Ferdinand of Austria, whom Hutter called a "cruel tyrant and enemy of divine truth" (L-4), had grown up in Spain and was neither Austrian nor familiar with common life in Tyrol. In 1521, his brother, Emperor Charles V, granted the young Ferdinand the kingship over most of modern-day Austria and South Tyrol in Italy, yet he barely spoke German. The king was therefore profoundly out of touch with a territory that had proven challenging to control or administer throughout history. Most of his subjects resented him as a foreigner, but step by step he effectively subdued all opposition – in many cases executing administrators and leaders who resisted him.[6]

The Catholic Church and the Holy Roman Empire continued the struggle for a balance of political and spiritual authority up to and throughout the sixteenth century, with many financial and economic consequences for the common folk. Georg III, bishop at Brixen from 1525 to 1538, treated the bishopric as a source of personal income rather than a pastoral charge. As a young man with no religious training, Georg was granted the ranking clerical position as the illegitimate son of Maximillian I and enjoyed traveling often to various courts of Europe, leaving the administration to others. Meanwhile, many of the small villages and hamlets had no priest of their own but were served by roving priests or chaplains. This lack of clerical stability opened opportunities to would-be reformers for a wider sphere of influence than if parishes had retained local priests. Often lacking oversight or ethical accountability, priestly misconduct was widespread. Although priests were officially forbidden to marry, it was not unusual for a priest to live in a common-law relationship and raise a family.[7] Reformers of various stripes, including Anabaptists, spoke out against this hypocrisy, calling the priests "whore mongers" and "prophets of Baal." As a prince-bishop, Georg III had secular as well as religious authority over some towns in southern Tyrol. The contest for power that ensued between religious and political authorities as a result of the vacuum left by Georg during his frequent absences led to conflicts of interest between local jurisdictions.[8]

Socioeconomics

Life for the common people was very difficult in most regions of Europe, and the imperial taxation system was a major source of resentment toward the state and church. Taxes were owed to multiple authorities, including local townships and feudal lords, the Roman Church, and the territorial king. The imminent threat of war with the Ottoman Turks gave rise to a military tax as well. With the threat of excommunication for failure to pay the tithe, it was only a matter of time before the financial advantages of an alternative spiritual community outside the Roman Church became an attractive option for the peasants. Besides having to contend with natural disasters – avalanches, floods, and poor harvests – the peasants did not own the land they worked and lived on.

In the mid-1520s, at a time of widespread unrest and revolt among peasant groups in central Europe, Michael Gaismair (1490–1532) became leader of the peasant revolution in Tyrol.[9] By 1525 – the same year that the first Anabaptists performed rebaptisms as adults – peasants throughout Europe had broken into open rebellion against oppressive authorities. Some occasions involved organized peasant armies, while others involved minor acts of terrorism. In Tyrol this revolt reached a peak in summer 1525 with the plundering and burning of churches and the homes of the rich.[10] The mob attacked the bishop's palace in Brixen on May 10, a day when the prince-bishop was absent. To this day indentation marks from the attack can be seen on the palace door. A volunteer army of several thousand miners and peasants overran castles and cities. The shocked nobles, who until then had resisted their new king, now took Ferdinand's side, mustering their own troops for a counterattack. In July 1526, the rebels moved through the Puster Valley raiding parsonages.[11] Gaismair was the son of a miner, and in his role as secretary to the bishop in Brixen, he had tried at first to moderate between the bishop and the people. But the authorities were not open to dialogue: when he traveled to Innsbruck to discuss matters, he was arrested. He managed to escape, and that same winter he wrote his famous Tyroler Landesordnung, arguably an early political manifesto of anti-imperialism, which included a few key revisions to religious life as well. He envisioned a new society that recognized the equal economic and social rights of all people, removing institutional religion as a repressive force.[12] The government was to consist of educated people as well as miners and peasants. Mines and commerce were to be run by the state and the land divided among the peasants. He proposed a type of regional healthcare for the old and sick; a university in Brixen; cultivation of olives, spices, and new types of grapes and grains; and draining of swamps.[13] Similar to the Anabaptist Balthasar Hubmaier's revolutionary vision for the church and his support for southern German peasants' revolts, Gaismair sought to impact education, health, politics, religion, and economy. Some historians see in his communal vision a model for the later Hutterian communities.[14] After Gaismair's uprising failed, he eventually fled to Venice, where he was later assassinated on the morning of April 15, 1532. Some of his earlier supporters would become Anabaptists, drawing a direct line of influence from the Tyrolean social-revolutionary movement to the search for a radically alternative society.[15]

In addition to peasant revolutions, humanist reform (both Catholic and Protestant) was oriented toward rediscovering the sources of truth in printed form, and these ideas fluidly crossed barriers of language and national context. And while artisans rarely imbibed the Latin-lettered arguments among this class of scholars, a few key theological debates were translated into the vernacular, bridging the rural-urban cultural and class divide. These anti-imperialist theological impulses extended throughout Europe, flourishing particularly in these upland regions of the Alps, where protests against clerical wealth and privilege were clear examples of the widespread anti-clericalism described so aptly by Hans-Jürgen Goertz – namely, as the root impulse toward radical reform.[16] And while humanism generally looked to the distant past, leaning on classical sources as a means to discovering truth, Zwingli and other humanists also looked to the present, leaning toward a biblicist-spiritualist hermeneutic that sought to balance a recognition of the authority of the Holy Spirit with that of the learned intellect in the task of scriptural interpretation.

Others yet would look to the future, placing their hope in apocalyptic events that would bring justice and reset the order of the world.[17] This combination of social-political radicalism with an insistence upon biblical correctives to doctrinal theology and church order may be called "Swiss-style reform," which broadly represents the initiatives of Zwingli in Zurich, along with others in the Swiss confederation; the spread of such biblical-political reformed radicalism encompassed much of the proto-Anabaptist, Anabaptist, and Swiss Reformed movements, along with other non-Lutheran reformers in Tyrol.

The key features of this radical spiritualist, anti-imperial profile thus included rejection of both clerical privilege and the feudal economic-industrial system involving the oppression of peasants by the noble class. Scripture was given priority and set up as authority over that of both the pope and ecclesiastical councils; moreover, the outer word, the Bible, was read by the faithful with guidance from the inner word, the Holy Spirit, which held priority over any other source of human authority. This quest for a future society, based on divine order rather than human tyranny or autocracy, led to attempts at enacting experimental models of communal society.

At the start of the 1520s, Dr. Jakob Strauss was another prominent early reformer active in Tyrol. He was in Innsbruck until 1521 and then gained popularity as a preacher in Hall. He appealed to miners and other citizens who rejected religious orders, the Mass, and confession and decried the exploitation of the poor.[18] The bishop of Brixen finally expelled him in May 1522, despite support for Strauss by the city council and citizens who opposed the bishop. He was forced to flee and sought refuge with Luther in Wittenberg. There he continued a prolific publishing campaign, but soon he discovered how little he held in common with the German reformer.[19] He wrote against infant baptism, veneration of saints and relics, purgatory, payment of onerous tithes and interest on debts, the accumulation of wealth in general, and the ecclesiastical ban; and he supported the marriage of priests. Strauss warned against the use of violence by peasants and urged the authorities to mitigate the situation leading to the tensions. His 1523 tract *On the Inner and Outer Baptism* requires faith as the precondition for baptism, arguing that "salvation does not depend upon the outer baptism but upon faith."[20] He died in 1532, but his whereabouts between 1527 and 1532 remain a mystery.

Following Strauss's departure from Tyrol in 1522, the drive toward social and religious reform there continued; resentment toward political and ecclesiastical authorities increased as waves of dissent passed over German territories to the northwest. After the failed peasants' revolt, Gaismair's withdrawal from the region opened a new landscape for reform leaders, some of whom came from much humbler origins.

Persecution

While the medieval Inquisition had not been officially abandoned in central Europe, there was great inconsistency as to how the church-state apparatus conducted heresy proceedings. Much of the system was being revamped in the 1520s, as Catholic humanists ridiculed inquisitors, and political resistance to Rome made the implementation of the Inquisition increasingly subject to the varied wishes of secular authorities. The emperor consorted with local ecclesiastical authorities to implement a new, more efficient means of conducting interrogations and justifying executions, based largely on civil charges rather than traditional charges of heresy. A civil proceeding was less encumbered by ecclesiastical process, and therefore, by attaching the civil charge of sedition to Anabaptism, executions became more streamlined for the state to conduct.[21] The emperor's approach to shifting the onus to civil proceedings required legislation, which he soon imposed on the entire Holy Roman Empire.[22]

On January 4, 1528, a general mandate broadly outlawed rebaptism in the Holy Roman Empire. In April 1529, the imperial estates met with a papal council at the Diet of Speyer; among other tasks relating to the suppression of internal revolt and the need for a combined strategy for defending Europe against the Ottoman Turks, the diet also mandated penalties for those who refused to present their children for baptism. That decree, the so-called *Wiedertäufermandat* issued on April 23, imposed the death penalty not only for the act of rebaptism but also for the act of refusing to present one's child for baptism – that is, rejecting or suspending the conventional practice of infant baptism. Even those who helped, abetted, or failed to report Anabaptists were subject to prosecution. In this sense, not only was the act of adult baptism as a second baptism outlawed, but the prospect that adult baptism might spread legitimately and legally through the cessation or suspension of infant baptism was effectively outlawed for all citizens of the Holy Roman Empire. Anyone who previously denounced their affiliation to Anabaptism and then returned to it would not have a second chance to denounce it but would be automatically executed as a *relapsus*. If any official was unwilling to fulfill this mandate, he would "face imperial disgrace and grave punishment."[23] Thus mandatory enforcement was introduced, and the previous requirements for an inquisitorial process for heresy were mitigated or even circumvented, using instead the more expedient and secular civil process to punish sedition.

After the vilified leader Balthasar Hubmaier was executed in Vienna on March 10, 1528, his interrogator Johann Fabri published a *Justification* document to delegitimize the entire movement. Fabri described Hubmaier's own position as advocating for a suspension of rebaptism until a time that such issues could be decided by a general council.[24] In Tyrol a secret council called the *Ketzercollegium* was also created in 1528, and local clergy were ordered to gather intelligence about those who did not participate in confession or Mass.[25] In that region there was a systematic practice of destroying the buildings where rebaptisms were conducted in an attempt to exorcise the physical spaces where Anabaptists had worshipped.

Hoping to quell the movement before it got out of hand, the authorities issued another mandate on April 1, 1528: Anyone who publicly renounced his error, performed whatever penance his priest demanded, and reported who had seduced him would receive a "light" punishment – one or two weeks imprisonment on bread and water. But those who persisted in their error would be condemned to death by fire; if they repented of their sin after being sentenced, their penalty could be reduced to death by sword; their property would be confiscated. Anyone who misled or baptized others was to be executed by fire, whether or not they recanted. All assets of an Anabaptist who was executed were taken over by the city, and the surviving family was thus deprived.[26]

But despite these threats, townspeople, farmers, miners, and even nobles continued to join the Anabaptist movement and filled the dungeons again and again, eager to "pluck the bloody rose which the faithful heart longed for."[27] Georg Kirchmayr, ecclesiastical chronicler under the bishop of Brixen, described the intensity of this time, showing great disfavor to Anabaptists, making clear the need for society to reject them (CHR-1). Although some estates in the empire argued for a mitigation of such harsh penalties, sympathy dwindled with the uprising that led to the short-lived Anabaptist kingdom of Münster in northern Germany during 1534–35.[28] That context led once again to attaching the label of sedition to Anabaptism in a new, concrete, and dramatic way, which itself led to justifying harsher persecution over the next decades in Tyrol, resulting in a disproportionately high rate of execution compared to the rest of Europe.

In response to persecution, Anabaptists developed several means to cope.[29] An alternative to becoming a martyr was the practice of "Nicodemism," whereby individuals or groups of Anabaptists would conceal their beliefs and practices, hoping that persecution would soon cease. They also used pseudonyms in some cases and often kept their identities secret from each other so that they would not be able to betray others under torture.[30] Forced underground, they would meet in secret locations for discussion and worship, such as in the forest. They developed special greetings that would reveal those who were genuine members. Perhaps the most successful safeguard against persecution was relocation or self-exile, resulting in the general exodus of Anabaptists from Tyrol to the tolerant regions of Moravia and neighboring regions.[31] Hutter wrote his followers: "We all urge you to come out of that accursed, sodomite, and murderous land. . . . Flee, flee away from those ungodly and wicked people!" (L-2).

Although Moravia became a haven for Anabaptists during the 1530s, it was not exempt from the imperial mandates. Three waves of persecution in Moravia, starting in 1528, severely compromised the initial appeal of the region; in the first phase of persecutions,[32] the optimistic climate of radical reform potential in urban settings soon fell under the shadow of repeated executions. By January 1534, Ferdinand I warned against the political dangers of the practice of community of goods, drawing comparisons between the violent revolts in Münster and communitarian settlements in Moravia.[33] In the second wave, 1535–36, the Anabaptist communities, including those under Hutter's leadership, were targeted;

at this time Hutter himself fled Moravia, only to be captured in Tyrol. Herzog Ulrich von Württemberg issued an ordinance in 1536, suspecting collaboration between Anabaptists in Münster and Moravia.[34] The third wave (1547–1552), beginning over a decade after Hutter's death, severely repressed the Hutterite communities and decimated their population.[35]

In Moravia the strong tendency toward separatism and sectarianism, in large part a result of persecution, significantly reshaped the socio-economic character of these relocated Swiss, south German, Silesian, and Tyrolean communities. Composing hymns, memorizing biblical passages consoling the faithful to remain steadfast, and collecting martyr stories were the main means of both comforting the persecuted and constructing a tradition and identity forged in the tribulation of persecution.[36]

Anabaptists' rejection of the world and their eventual embrace of an ecclesiology of separatism also emerged as a response to persecution – and with it community of goods, rejection of political office and the civic oath, and the doctrine of nonresistance. The original intention of the earliest Anabaptists had been to participate in the general reform of the church, and the social dimension of the earliest movement, with its missionary zeal and insistence on engaging the general process of reform, was more anti-imperialist than isolationist in its intent. Estimates of the number of Anabaptists executed in the 1500s in central Europe run between 2,000 and 2,500, comprising almost half of the religious martyrs in this period of European history.[37] Most of these were divided equally between the North (Netherlands, northern Germany) and the South (Switzerland, southern Germany, Austria). Women composed about one third of the martyrs within Anabaptism, a high percentage in contrast to the small number of Protestant and Catholic women martyrs for the same period.[38] In Tyrol, at least two hundred men and women were executed as Anabaptists between 1527 and 1530, with the total in subsequent years reaching about six hundred,[39] indicating a disproportionately high rate of execution compared to the rest of Europe.

Once the more theoretical threat of persecution of the mid-1520s turned into the brutal reality of executions by the hundreds at the end of the decade, the motif of God's justice and the revolutionary moment shifted to the practicality of dealing with such widespread suffering. What the famous private letter by Conrad Grebel and his cohorts to Thomas Müntzer indicated about a rejection of violence and willingness to become "sheep for the slaughter" was lived by the fledgling Anabaptist conventicles in the Tyrolean Alps. Their missionary leader Jakob Hutter was forced to confront the reality that in baptizing someone he was sentencing him to death. The revolt to demand justice turned into a posture of patience in suffering. *Gelassenheit,* denoting yieldedness or surrender, became a hallmark of Anabaptism – not only in the face of persecution. It was also an attitude of submission to one another that enabled individuals to live in close proximity, sharing their possessions.[40]

Although some individuals succumbed to torture and recanted, vast numbers of Anabaptists in Tyrol were unwavering in their faith, using the occasion of their own execution as a chance to express their convictions and convince others. This provoked the bishop of Brixen to write a proposal to Innsbruck that executions no longer take place in public, as they had the effect not only of giving a forum for the spread of Anabaptist teachings but also of souring people's regard for authorities as sympathy for Anabaptists increased. But the government in Innsbruck held fast to the king's mandate to make public the pronouncement and execution of sentences and insisted it not be violated for any reason. The Innsbruck government suggested keeping the pronouncement very short, to be immediately followed by the execution, thus limiting the opportunity to gather in crowds and communicate with the condemned. In addition, soldiers were to shout commands to those gathered, to prevent the words and preaching of condemned Anabaptists from being heard.[41]

The 1530s brought a shift from the revolutionary hopes of the 1520s, in which apocalyptic expectations of God's kingdom were pursued with force, to a renewed social-political vision in which broad-scale "Swiss-style" reform (of the Zwinglian sort) narrowed to a more "Swiss-style" sectarianism,[42] where the responsibility for broad-scale social reform was abrogated, with the emphasis shifted to an internal process aimed at purifying the "elect" as a means of exemplifying God's justice and peace in the world.

Rise of Anabaptism in Tyrol

From Zurich to Tyrol

The region was host to other key leaders in addition to the Tyrolean reformer Jakob Strauss. For example, in 1525 Andreas Karlstadt, while in Lüsen, South Tyrol, contributed significantly to the broader argument against infant baptism.[43]

The origins of the more specific practice and theology of rebaptizing, which they argued was not a rebaptism at all but the first true baptism, stem from Zurich and the consequences of the actions of Conrad Grebel, Felix Mantz, and Georg Blaurock.[44]

In Zurich, Zwingli had gathered eager young students around him in the early 1520s, independently of Luther's reform movement. He urged them to read the Bible for themselves and not to accept anything unless it could be proved from scripture. The New Testament was becoming a practical guide to Christian life. But Zwingli soon found himself at odds with some of his more radical followers – Conrad Grebel and his associates Felix Mantz and Georg Blaurock – who decided to rebaptize one another as "brethren" in January 1525.[45] In doing so, they consciously placed themselves outside the canons of the Roman Catholic Church and in opposition to the Zurich city council's statutes. As well as rejecting the practice of baptizing infants, they tested many Catholic traditions against scripture: the veneration of the Virgin Mary, prayer to saints, fasting, and transubstantiation in the Lord's Supper.

After Blaurock had been banished from Zurich, he traveled southeast to Tyrol between May and September 1527, where he found fertile ground for the theology and practice of believers' baptism. He would return to Tyrol again in the spring of 1529, to the south of the Brenner Pass, near the Puster Valley where Hutter was then active.[46] At eight years of age, the young Peter Walpot, future leader of the Hutterites, was present to witness Blaurock's execution.[47] Hans Hut and Balthasar Hubmaier were already active in Vienna and Nikolsburg, but Blaurock's missions provide the clearest possible link to the first practice of adult rebaptism in Tyrol.[48] And while there is no clear evidence that Blaurock baptized Hutter, the dates of Blaurock's appearance in Tyrol – and the degree of Hutter's clarity of his own apostolicity as a baptizer-evangelist, along with the unqualified praise heaped on Blaurock by the *Chronicle* – would certainly point to Blaurock as a possible baptizer of Jakob Hutter in either 1527 or 1529. It is equally possible, however, that a follower of Hut, Wolfgang Brandhuber, was Hutter's baptizer, as discussed below.

Blaurock was arrested in mid-August 1529 in the village of Gufidaun, in the mountains above the Eisack River, along with his companion Hans Langegger. He was questioned under torture regarding his activities and burned at the stake in Klausen[49] on September 6, 1529. After Blaurock's death, Jakob Hutter emerged as the chief Anabaptist leader in South Tyrol – in the words of his enemies, the "principal leader" (*Vorsteher*).[50] The rebaptizing movement introduced by Blaurock spread rapidly, "facilitated by the preexisting evangelical network with links to the Gaismair rebellion. . . . As the desire to transform the entire society gave way in favor of building separate communities guided by New Testament principles, the borders between Anabaptists and the rest of society became unmistakable."[51]

Early evidence points not to a clear, coherent leadership system in Tyrol but rather to the progression of an Anabaptist cell movement impacted by several influences. Few details can be said for certain concerning the relative impact of such early leaders as Blaurock, Hut, Karlstadt, Strauss, and others. In December 1527, in Sterzing, a so-called "synagogue of Anabaptists" was held at the home of Johann Kessler, which included several foreigners, prompting the regional government to order the apprehension of those who were at the meeting; however, they all escaped without a trace.[52] Soon thereafter another meeting took place in Lüsen, and again on January 15, 1528, Sterzing was host to a larger gathering of Anabaptists. In the following week, the administrative authorities in the towns were required to capture, imprison, and torture suspects until the Anabaptist participants were identified.[53] While the exact details of the earliest progenitors of Anabaptism in Tyrol are unclear, by the late 1520s there was a robust following, which spread widely between larger towns.

Another leader in Tyrol was Georg Zaunring, who in June 1528 baptized Michael Kürschner, a court clerk at Völs. Zaunring evidently appointed Kürschner as leader of the Kitzbühel congregation, a position he held until May 1529, when his capture and execution led to Blaurock briefly taking over leadership. Already by Blaurock's execution in September, Hutter had allegedly taken over "the heritage of Blaurock" as the foremost Anabaptist leader in Tyrol.[54]

Zaunring himself became a close associate of Hutter. In 1530 Hutter sent him from Tyrol to Moravia to assist Jakob Wiedemann in the leadership there. Although Zaunring was implicated in later controversies and was excommunicated for failing to bring a serious matter into the public, he was reaccepted into the fellowship, died for his faith, and is recognized in Hutterite sources as a martyr.[55]

After Hans Hut

Hans Hut traveled from Augsburg to Vienna in 1527, where he impressed Leonhard Schiemer, the former monk who would participate in the so-called Martyrs Synod that same year. Shortly after Schiemer's arrest in Rattenberg, Tyrol, in late 1527, he was executed in January 1528.[56] Similarly, Hans Schlaffer, a former parish priest in Upper Austria, was baptized by Hut and became an Anabaptist martyr shortly after Schiemer's death.[57] Each of these figures who briefly appear in the Tyrolean Anabaptist story proffered Hut's apocalypticism as a theological explanation of persecution and their times of trial.[58] Exactly how Tyrolean Anabaptism inherited separatism remains unclear, although some combination of reference to the Schleitheim Articles (1527) may be warranted.[59] Apocalyptic motifs can be noted in Hutter's letters too (esp. L-7).

What is often deemed "sectarian" or "separatist" might best be described as the rejection of a violent revolutionary apocalypticism in favor of a dispensational expectation, turning from a program of general reform in which leaders would actively engage the "magisterial" governing structures and other church leaders attempting territorial reform, to acts of resistance of different forms, and finally retreating to a socioeconomic form of existence that is in many ways the most pragmatic option after the imperial mandates against Anabaptism, resulting in a time of widespread persecution. These developments led to the socioeconomic compromise of sectarianism, the need for greater solidarity and secrecy, a consequential rejection of the civic oath and military service, and the turn to inward administration of discipline in the form of the ban.[60]

Christoph Freisleben, the schoolmaster at Wels in Upper Austria who joined Hut's rebaptizing movement in 1527, published a popular tract, *On the Genuine Baptism* (1528).[61] It has been described as "one of the more significant public statements coming out of early South German and Austrian Anabaptism."[62] Beginning with a catalog of Catholic errors concerning baptism, the argument moves from an explanation in fifteen points concerning the biblical legitimacy of the "outer baptism" to a refutation of the errors and abuses of baptismal practice. This treatise was used widely by the Hutterite tradition, as evidenced in the five handwritten copies that have survived.[63] They remain anonymous in Hutterite sources, probably because the author returned to Catholicism.

While scholars have sought to locate a linear connection of sectarian separatism from Swiss to Tyrolean Anabaptism, the clearest articulation of "evangelical sectarianism" on Tyrolean soil appears to stem from the Bavarian schoolmaster Wolfgang Brandhuber, a follower of Hans Hut and a colleague of Hans Schlaffer, Jakob Wiedemann, Peter Riedemann, and Gabriel Ascherham.[64] Previously he had been in Regensburg in 1527, where in the wake of persecution he encouraged steadfastness in the faith and labored to sustain communication between disparate Anabaptist cells. It is likely that he baptized Gabriel Ascherham, who would become a "senior leader" in Moravia and a challenge to Hutter.[65]

Originally from Burghausen (Bavaria), Brandhuber moved to Linz in 1528,[66] where other early Austrian Anabaptists promoted Hut's message of repentance and spiritual baptism.[67] In Linz, Brandhuber first established a single-household version of community of goods, and here he became a leading "re-organizer and propagator" of Anabaptism in Passau, Linz, Wels, and elsewhere, having a "tremendous" influence in Tyrol during 1528–29.[68] In addition to establishing community of goods, he emphasized modest clothing, nonresistance, and strong church discipline. Brandhuber's ideal of community of goods meant members of the fellowship who were not related would live "in a smaller single-family household," sharing property and income. A Bruderhof-style community of goods, with a single treasury and the role of treasurer for a large group of people, developed later, with the freedom to flourish in Moravia.[69]

The only surviving letter by Brandhuber is considered the "first piece of Anabaptist literature that explicitly advocates a proto-Hutterite position of communalism in very empirical terms,"[70] including keeping a common purse, which would assist the poor, and the admonition for the household to share possessions with their servants, as he himself is reported to have done (ADS-1).[71] While the exact form of economic collectivity he advocated is unclear, the *Chronicle* attests that Brandhuber's version of community of goods was more robust than that of a single household: "In the fellowship no one should be the steward of his own purse. The property of poor and rich should be distributed by the one chosen by the fellowship and everything should be held in common to serve God's glory whenever and wherever God granted it."[72]

Brandhuber's rejection of the sword was unequivocal, a position that directly countered Hubmaier's *On the Sword* (1527).[73] Thus the concrete formulation of sectarian Anabaptism becomes clearer in this proto-Hutterite leader. In an era of increasing persecution, internal division, and confusion, his vision aimed at the fulfillment of the elect as a gathered, distinct, and pure fellowship that was visible and temporal.[74] In late 1529 Brandhuber was executed in Linz, as a martyr to the steadfastness he urged in all the faithful.[75]

There is no clear documentation of a direct connection between Hutter and Brandhuber, but Hutter's own ordination as leader in Tyrolean missions roughly coincided with the death of Brandhuber and Hans Niedermayer in 1529. Peter Riedemann writes that he had worked with Brandhuber, and he became Brandhuber's immediate successor in Linz. He would later rise as a central leader of the Hutterian fellowship after Hutter's death.[76] If Brandhuber did baptize Gabriel Ascherham,[77] and even prepared Hutter and others like Riedemann for a leadership role in Tyrol, the eventual conflict between Hutter and Ascherham in 1533 may be explained as a sort of rivalry between heirs of Brandhuber's mantle in Moravia.[78] The model of nonresistant spirituality that is generally indicated by Hutter's life and ministry was not a foregone conclusion; it continued to be debated within other communities and eras of Anabaptism.[79]

Jakob Hutter's Anabaptist Journey

Jakob Hutter was born in Moos, a hamlet southwest of Bruneck (Brunico, South Tyrol) in the Puster Valley of present-day Italy. His childhood home lay in the shadows of Michelsburg Castle, where many Anabaptists would later be imprisoned. Few details of his early years are known, yet this simple leader was eventually considered by the imperial government as the foremost leader of the Anabaptists after Hubmaier. Hutter's execution was ordered as the essential means to stem the rising tide of Anabaptism in Tyrol and beyond.

The date of his birth is unknown; Hutter's name is first documented in 1529, as a missionary in Tyrol.[80] What we know about his life prior to 1529 must be inferred from other sources. After studying hatmaking in the nearby town of Prags, he settled in Spittal in Carinthia, about 140 kilometers west of Bruneck.[81]

He was renowned in two respects: as a missionary apostle in Tyrol and as the overseer, however briefly, of the Anabaptist fellowship in Auspitz, Moravia. Following his first visit to Moravia in 1529, he was summoned repeatedly to arbitrate in times of conflict, until he was given a more official position of leadership among Moravian Anabaptists in October 1533. He effectively served as leader in Moravia for only two years; in summer of 1535 he returned to Tyrol, where he was captured and then executed. Although his authority was contested at times by leaders who jockeyed for position in his absence, and despite the relative paucity of writings attesting to the particulars of his doctrines and practices, Hutter's indelible stamp on the tradition that bears his name is clearly seen in the confessions of his followers (see Chapter 3, "Witnesses"). He strove to lead a people dedicated to serving Christ alone, and he communicated this clarity of vision in more than eight letters, admonishing his flock to faithfulness and consoling them throughout harsh periods of persecution. While Hutter's writing did not aim to provide clarity in terms of confessional or doctrinal statements, Wolfgang Brandhuber's letter (1529, ADS-1), the *Ordnung*, or rule of life, found in the *Chronicle* (1529, ADS-2), the 1536 confession of Jeronimus Käls (WIT-20), and Peter Riedemann's *Account of Our Faith* (ca. 1540), were ostensibly in line with Hutter's vision. The precise details of this alignment of vision are found in the source collection of this volume. As stated repeatedly in these sources, Hutter is rightly considered the founder of the Hutterite tradition due to the leadership he provided during a time of crisis and formation.

Hutter's Conversion

In contrast to many first generation Anabaptist leaders, who were educated urbanites, Hutter came from the rural Alps, and like many leaders of the second generation, he was an artisan. Though his zeal for studying scripture is clearly evident, he was untrained in academic theology.[82] Aside from his own personal study of scripture, it appears he formed some of his particular ideas through contact with a goatherd named Wölfl, who presumably displayed similar gifts of preaching while apparently lacking formal education.

Hutter was rebaptized perhaps as early as 1526 and possibly as late as 1529. Although speculation as to the exact location and nature of Jakob's activities between 1526 and 1529 may be in vain, he is thought to have remained in Tyrol during this period, working with a presumed relative – also a hatmaker, Caspar Hueter. What little we know of his early conversion is taken from Caspar's interrogation record, given almost a decade after Jakob's employment there (GOV-27). According to Caspar, a goatherd named Wölfl began preaching throughout Tyrol in 1526, including at his home while Jakob was present.[83]

Wölfl is a highly significant but enigmatic figure, who appeared in the radical reforming movements in Tyrol quite early. Having dropped his crook already in 1525, leaving his four-legged herd in the Sarn Valley, Wölfl began to preach and to gather a different kind of flock at Bozen, using a copy of the New Testament he was given. His 1526 itinerary "maps the existence of a network of sympathizers reaching from Bozen, Klausen, and Gufidaun to the Puster and its side valleys,"[84] and subsequent travels led him through Tyrol to the Inn Valley near Innsbruck and Hall, where Jakob Strauss had preached.[85] Wherever Wölfl went, he led discussions on the Bible, and people gathered to hear him, including some noble patrons.

Wölfl also traveled to the Schnal Valley, staying in the monastery with the Carthusians, and then left Vinschgau for the Inn Valley and preached in Inzing, Hall, Oberperfuss, and Kematen. In Innsbruck a schoolmaster heard his preaching and "taught him how to read print, so that he could read God's word for himself, understand and proclaim it better, and also defend himself from attacks."[86] He again preached in Oberperfuss and Kematen at Easter in 1526 and then in Klausen. He became a popular figure especially among the miners, who in turn vowed to protect him against the magistrates. The bailiff and his wife at the castle in Gufidaun invited Wölfl to share the gospel, and they became convinced of his message. The details of his reception, not only among the peasants and miners but also by some clerics and members of lower nobility and the magistracy (Helena von Freyberg, for example), describe a period of mounting hope in Tyrol for this radical, unconventional preacher and the gospel he shared.[87]

Nothing is known of a connection of Wölfl to Hans Hut or to Georg Blaurock, nor is it clear when he began advocating rebaptism.[88] Although we might assume he was preaching against pedobaptism in 1526, he might not have advocated rebaptism until a couple years later. But we may assume that his message was broadly anti-clerical following upon the failed peasants' revolts, which provided a transition in the Puster Valley, by "feeding on the residual resentment [toward landowners] and the loss of faith in the religious establishment."[89] In 1527, Wölfl was arrested at Brixen and then again at Gufidaun where he was executed in 1533.[90] Prior to his first arrest, he had reportedly spent two weeks living with the district judge in Bozen, who bought him a New Testament and became convinced that the goatherd's beliefs were correct. While preaching at Sand in Taufers, he proclaimed, "If anyone drowns or murders me, five more will rise in my place to preach the word of God."[91] When threatened with arrest in Innsbruck by the judge, Wölfl repeated his earlier prediction: "Wherever one man is drowned or murdered, five more will arise in his place to preach the word of God."[92]

The goatherd-preacher fostered the early context in which Jakob Hutter converted to a radical version of the gospel, setting him on his own journey as a preacher and apostle. Shortly after hearing Wölfl's gospel, Hutter left Caspar's employment and moved to Spittal in Carinthia.[93] Caspar reported one curious detail about a gambling incident with Jakob, which may have precipitated Jakob's departure. Jakob, having lost, was very saddened and said, "God have mercy on me for playing away my money that I earned by such hard work. I could hang myself." Caspar then reportedly returned to Jakob the money which he had lost (GOV-27).

During the years when Jakob the journeyman was studying hatmaking in nearby Prags, many of his friends and acquaintances had become Anabaptists in the Puster Valley. By April 1529, there were several arrests of close friends, including his sister Agnes and Benedict Gamperer, who trained for the priesthood at Bruneck.[94] In June 1529, Michael Kürschner, minister of the Kitzbühel fellowship, was also executed in Innsbruck, followed by Blaurock's execution.

Hutter's early formation was marked by another lesser-known local figure, an associate of Agnes named Gregori Weber. Among the earliest martyrs of Anabaptism in Tyrol, Weber is described as a friend and teacher of Jakob Hutter. He was in the first group of Anabaptists arrested in Tyrol on April 27, 1529, and was subsequently burned at the stake with two others.[95] A crucial detail from the late 1520s is the execution of Jakob Hutter's sister Agnes. She was arrested in June 1529 in Brixen, and while the others arrested with her were executed, Agnes was released.[96] Six months later, in December, she was arrested again and shown no mercy (GOV-3).[97] Sources are silent concerning her role in Jakob's conversion, but surely the executions of close associates shaped Jakob's determination in the era of heightened persecution.

We find evidence of Jakob Hutter's activities as an Anabaptist missionary in various periods starting in May 1529. The government in Innsbruck had heard that secret meetings were taking place in the town of Welsberg in the Puster Valley. They suspected two men, Andrew Planer and Balthasar Hutter, "and possibly others yet unknown to us."[98] The police broke into Planer's house in June and discovered a group celebrating the Lord's Supper in the basement. Fourteen were captured. Ten of them admitted to having been baptized by Jakob Hutter, who had escaped (GOV-1). Neither Balthasar Hutter (probably a relative of Jakob's) nor Planer had been rebaptized, but they were interrogated under torture for the crime of hosting Anabaptists. The wives of both had joined the movement, but because they had infants at home, they were released. However, the government in Innsbruck ordered the local officials: "Follow [these women] home and if you think it is no longer necessary for them to nurse their babies, arrest them"[99] (GOV-1). In spring 1530, Jakob Hutter held the Lord's Supper at Brenner and in the Eisack and Puster valleys, where he baptized Valentin Luckner at Sand in Taufers (WIT-9). He traveled throughout Tyrol from September 1531 until March 1532, usually celebrating the Lord's Supper and baptizing.[100] On occasion he would preside at larger conference-style events.[101]

Settlements in Moravia

From all parts of the German-speaking world – most notably Switzerland, the Rhineland, the Palatinate, Swabia, Hesse, Franconia, Bavaria, Upper and Lower Austria, Tyrol, and Silesia – Anabaptists fled to Moravia. This region in modern-day Czechia had maintained greater independence from King Ferdinand I until 1536 and had a tradition of religious tolerance.[102] From 1526 until a decade after Hutter's death, the Anabaptist communities there struggled mightily to accommodate differences and achieve a form of "denominational" unity, such as the Hutterian Brethren eventually enjoyed after the early decades of leadership turmoil and division.[103]

In order to appreciate the drastically different context in Moravia as distinct from that of Tyrol and elsewhere in Europe, it is helpful to review the features of the Moravian context, including Hans Hut's legacy among many of the Anabaptist leaders in the late 1520s. Beginning in summer 1526, just prior to the defeat of Habsburg troops at the hands of the Turkish armies during the Battle of Mohács, the spread of Anabaptism to Moravia began a new era for dissident groups seeking greater tolerance and accommodation than elsewhere in Europe. Following this key battle, Ferdinand I of Habsburg succeeded to the throne of the Kingdom of Bohemia, which included the Margraviate of Moravia, where territorial lords had previously resisted the "centralizing, absolutist tendencies of Habsburg politics." The Bohemian nobles sought to defend their liberties and privileges as spelled out in the traditional estate constitution.[104]

This political tension between the local lords and the empire continued in some measure to be advantageous for such religious dissidents as the "Unity of Brethren/Bohemian Brethren" and later the Anabaptists, who were also generally considered by the noble class as industrious citizens and therefore an economic asset. Already in March of 1526, articles of "radical reform" appeared in Austerlitz following a meeting of priests, where Catholics and Hussites had already formulated an informal "bi-confessional coalition" prior to 1524, agreeing to a form of tolerance of differences.[105] The Moravian urban contexts – most notably Nikolsburg, Brünn, and Olmütz – provided relatively safe havens for broad debates on religious reform.[106]

Hans Hut's departure from Moravia in the spring of 1527 and his eventual death in December of the same year precipitated a mass migration of his followers and years of leadership tensions.[107] In late 1527, displaced Anabaptists from elsewhere in central Europe fled to southern Moravia, and these groups, in contrast to the urban-centered and state-sponsored "magisterial" reformation of Hubmaier in Nikolsburg, remained outside the public sphere, choosing to worship in private. The coupling of the ethic of nonresistance with the developing socioeconomic practice of community of goods began to orient these groups directly toward a separatist form of ecclesial maintenance and social cohesion.[108] Already in Nikolsburg, Hans Hut had challenged Hubmaier's public form of Anabaptism by attracting a following to his private meetings. Upon Hubmaier's denunciation of Hut following their disputation, the local authorities arrested Hut.[109] Aided by sympathizers, Hut managed to escape and traveled to Vienna and other parts of modern-day Austria, where he was able to convert reform-minded priests and schoolmasters to his brand of Anabaptism, also recruiting them as missionaries. After Hut's arrest, his followers gathered around Nikolsburg and elsewhere in Moravia.[110] Some of these schoolmasters became vital for the further growth of Anabaptism in Tyrol in the later 1520s, as described above.[111]

Following Hut's rejection by the territorial lords and the Nikolsburg Anabaptists who remained under Hubmaier, and also due to the Hutian fellowship's refusal to pay war taxes to support the campaign against the Turkish armies, in the winter of 1527, Hut's followers convened at Pergen, a village north of Nikolsburg. Despite the threat of a Turkish military campaign in the region, they chose to journey north toward Austerlitz where they began to form a community.[112] Based on the model of Acts 2, a form of community of goods was initiated in order to accommodate those who had no income or personal assets, differing from the example set by Brandhuber. Jakob Wiedemann – nicknamed "One-Eyed Jakob," who was originally from Memmingen (Bavaria) – led the Hutian nonresistant and war-tax-refusing Anabaptists in Nikolsburg.[113] In the spring of 1528, he brought two hundred adults (plus their children) from Nikolsburg to settle on the estates of four Kaunitz brothers in Austerlitz with the promise of exemption from war taxes.[114]

They spent their first night camping in a deserted village. In their anxious state, they turned to the Book of Acts for inspiration, as the *Chronicle* recounts: "At that time, these men laid down an overcoat in front of the people, and everyone placed their possessions onto it with a willing heart, without coercion, for the support of those in need, according to the teaching of the Prophets and Apostles."[115] The Hutian expectation of Christ's imminent return and the constant danger of persecution fueled phases of exodus from other parts of Austria as well.[116] The movement toward Austerlitz did not assume a clear uniformity of belief and practice, and attempts were made to accommodate diversity. A merger with a group of eighty to ninety Anabaptists from Tyrol and elsewhere in Austria in 1529 may have prompted the written *Ordnung* (ADS-2). Many Tyrolean communities had been deprived of their leaders, following the executions of Leonhard Schiemer, Wolfgang Brandhuber, Georg Blaurock, and others.[117]

On an economic level, the Austerlitz Anabaptist community was supported through their labor in local agriculture and various artisan trades. Hutter made reference in one letter to the "two kitchens, the school, the bath house, also the weaving room, and the bakery" already in 1530 (L-1). Starting with what appears to be Hutter's ordination as an apostle and missionary in 1529, the community in Austerlitz repeatedly called on him in times of pastoral leadership crisis – a clear testimony to their recognition of his spiritual authority. This group, which was eventually given the name "Austerlitz Brethren," was shepherded by Wiedemann from their arrival in 1528 until his execution in Vienna in or before 1536.[118] The uncertain legacy of Hans Hut became all but lost in the era of leadership controversies that followed his death in 1527.

Because of the intense persecution in Tyrol and the execution of key leaders, Jakob Hutter made a brief, exploratory trip to Moravia, traveling with Simon Schützinger and other companions in 1529. They were impressed by the community in Austerlitz, reportedly being "of one heart and soul in serving and fearing God." Thus Jakob and Simon and their companions, "in the name of the whole fellowship, united in peace with the fellowship at Austerlitz."[119] From then on, Hutter urged his converts to leave Tyrol for Moravia.

Hutter and Schützinger returned to Tyrol and enthusiastically organized a means of migration for their fellow believers. It is clear from various records that pooling money was recognized as part of the commitment to joining the Anabaptist fellowship, from which came the accusation from outsiders that Hutter and others "baptized for money" (GOV-1). A report in the governmental archival records in Innsbruck in 1529 named Jakob Hutter and Jörg Zaunring (from Rattenberg) as the foremost leaders, asserting that this group administered a common treasury in every town in the Puster Valley and on the Ritten; "everyone puts what he has into it and they care for one another from it." Zaunring held the position of "master of the purse" or treasurer (*Seckelmeister*) on the Ritten (GOV-4).[120]

At the end of May 1530, Zaunring left for Moravia with the first group, and Jakob sent along a letter (L-1).[121] He told of a meeting that had been ambushed and two brothers arrested. He also asked for prayers and encouraged those in Moravia to continue living together in love. Over the next three years, Hutter traveled tirelessly among the mountains and valleys of South Tyrol, baptizing, organizing, and exhorting the new believers. He was always in hiding, forever on the move. From time to time he gathered his flock for a fellowship meeting – sometimes as many as a hundred people in a hidden gorge or a high pasture. At such occasions Hutter and the other leaders taught the people the new faith. Baptisms were conducted along with the Lord's Supper (WIT-4, GOV-1).

Twelve Ordinances (1529)

Documents concerning the context and founding of Moravian Anabaptism, either prior to or at the time of Hutter's initial arrival, allow us to assess the degree of Hutter's early influence. It is evident that his affirmation as a leader among Tyrolean Anabaptists was accompanied by an equally strong confirmation of his authority by the other Anabaptists in Moravia in 1529. The Twelve Ordinances of 1529 as recorded in the *Chronicle* (ADS-2) formed the reference point for the fellowship, particularly for disciplinary processes in the years that immediately followed. The twelve articles clarified guidelines for a range of social-religious practices, such as meeting "at least four or five times a week if possible"; holding property in common according to the example in Acts; caring effectively for the poor among them; engaging and receiving new members; dealing with internal conflict and conducting church discipline either in public or private, according to the context for the wrongdoing. This last article, however, was put to the test during the cases of misconduct and the abuse of power by ministers.

Tensions and Conflict in Moravia

A scattered network of individual Anabaptists or "conventicles" throughout the broader regions of Tyrol and Moravia required a strong roving leader such as Jakob Hutter in order to maintain vision, communication, guidance, and solidarity under intense persecution.[122]

In late 1530 the Swiss Anabaptist leader, Wilhelm Reublin, arrived in Austerlitz, Moravia, although the Moravian group knew nothing about him, according to the *Chronicle*, and did not recognize him as having any authority.[123] However, Reublin accused Jakob Wiedemann of forcing women into marriages without their consent; likewise, concerning money, he complained that some of the ministers were supplied with delicacies while children were starving, even though their parents had donated more than enough money to the common treasury to cover their expenses. Reublin was supported by Georg Zaunring, David Burda, and a number of others. But Jakob Wiedemann refused to listen to their concerns, accusing Reublin of speaking without authority before the fellowship.

Reublin later explained the situation of his appeal process in a letter to Pilgram Marpeck, written from Auspitz: "Since I have been accused I requested to be permitted to make a reply as would be right and in accordance with imperial and divine law" (ADS-3).[124] On the Wednesday following New Year's Day, January 4, 1531, after failing to receive the desired opportunity to justify himself before the leadership, Reublin publicly denounced the leaders in the courtyard.

A second feature of Austerlitz practice and theology – namely, non-resistance and the refusal to pay war taxes – was contested by Reublin and others, notably "the Bohemian" David Burda von Schweinitz.[125] David Burda penned a line-by-line *Commentary on Romans 13*,[126] likely as a means to complement Reublin's argument, which countered the Austerlitzers' putative use of Romans 13 as an excuse for blind deference to authority. Burda's text sheds light on the controversy concerning the payment of a special war tax or "blood money." The emperor cut off finances for the burgeoning war, and these monetary demands were passed on to all levels of territories under the Holy Roman Empire. Although Moravian Anabaptists had originally gained official exemption from paying military taxes, due to imperial pressure on the lords of Austerlitz, it would appear that Wiedemann and the leaders agreed in private to pay a new, discrete tax, in lieu of the military tax. The appearance of refusing to pay war taxes allowed the leaders to save face with the fellowship, while secretly bowing to the demands of the empire, giving to Caesar his due in private.

Reublin, Burda, and others discovered what they saw as an ethical compromise, which bordered on deception, and decided to confront the matter in public. Was Romans 13 a passage that should justify an indifferent and totally deferential attitude toward governing authorities, or could authorities be questioned by their subjects? Burda declared that, for "God's elect," obedience or deference to the Habsburgs meant recognizing them as God's ordained rulers, something tantamount to blasphemy for Anabaptists in an era when their leaders and fellows had recently been martyred by those very rulers. Therefore Burda's commentary was, first, an indictment of the Anabaptist leaders whom he, Reublin, and others now opposed, and second, an admonition to the lords of Austerlitz, whose disguised military tax Burda argued should now be legitimately given to the Turks – the enemies of Charles V – as God's newly ordained governing force. Burda's argument is lengthy and playful at times, but his indictment of the Austerlitz Anabaptist leaders is unrelenting.[127]

With no hope of reconciliation, on January 8, 1531, Reublin – along with Georg Zaunring, David Burda, and Burkhard of Ofen – led a large following of more than 150 adults, plus children, to settle at Auspitz on the estate of a Cistercian convent at Alt-Brünn (Staré Brno), temporarily leaving behind forty more children and people of ill health who were unable to endure the winter journey.[128] Burda supported Reublin's exodus by hiring guards to ensure the safety of the group of children traveling to Auspitz, an act apparently unknown to the other Auspitz ministers.[129]

In connection with a visiting leader from Swabia, Reublin's teaching authority was then called into question by the other leaders in Auspitz,[130] and subsequently there came another scandalous revelation: Reublin had withheld personal funds from the common purse, for which he was then excommunicated at Auspitz. Although Reublin had played a crucial role in this emigration, which laid the foundation for what would later become the Hutterite community, the *Chronicle* would remember him as a "lying, unfaithful, crafty Ananias."

In addition to Reublin's contact with Marpeck as a leader who might influence the matter, the Austerlitz and Auspitz fellowships both appealed to Jakob Hutter, who had been absent. A report about the conflict was carried to Tyrol by Hans Amon and a companion from Auspitz, along with two members of the Austerlitz Brethren, an indication of the degree to which both communities recognized Hutter's capacity for spiritual leadership. The intent, as reported by the *Chronicle*, was for the fellowship in Tyrol to help resolve the matter and apply discipline under Hutter's and Schützinger's joint leadership.[131]

Hutter and Schützinger discerned that the Austerlitz leaders held a greater share of guilt in the schism, marking the start of a clear break between Hutter and Wiedemann. The *Chronicle* reports that Jakob Wiedemann rejected an attempt by Hutter and Schützinger to apply discipline.[132] In a reply to Wiedemann's rebuttal, Hutter asserted (1) they unjustly expelled the innocent from the fellowship; (2) they "allowed for fleshly freedom in various ways, each taking control of their own possessions, as it suited them"; and (3) there was intermarriage with unbelievers, among other matters.[133] Schützinger and Hutter entrusted Jörg Zaunring with the leadership in Auspitz and returned to Tyrol. From there Hutter began directing Anabaptists to resettle with the community in Auspitz instead of Austerlitz, making clear his allegiances.

In the large Auspitz community, David Burda was installed as one of Zaunring's assistants.[134] Then another leadership scandal visited both Zaunring and Burda when the group learned that Burda had paid for armed guards to protect the group of children as they had traveled from Austerlitz to Auspitz.[135] This was seen as a breach of their pacifist convictions; after all, the refusal of the original Austerlitz leaders to accept the armed defense offered by Leonard von Liechtenstein at Nikolsburg had been the occasion for the Wiedemann group's departure.[136]

Burda was disciplined and stripped of his leadership role. In turn, he revealed to the fellowship that recently he and Zaunring had tried to cover up a sensitive matter concerning the infidelity of Zaunring's wife. They had dealt with her affair with another member of the fellowship in private, rather than applying the public ban process, as would have been expected, presumably to allow the Zaunrings to save face. Burda, who had originally aided Zaunring in his effort to deal with it in secret, then revealed the scandal as a means of revenge. This exposé resulted in strict application of the ban, but in this case it now applied to Zaunring himself, who had not been implicated in the original affair.[137] The new scandal was the discovery of his improper application of discipline. Once again, the embattled fellowship in Auspitz turned to Hutter in Tyrol for guidance in order to settle this new crisis. He and Schützinger were dispatched immediately and arrived at Auspitz around Easter of 1532.[138] Hutter turned the spotlight back upon David Burda to condemn the very act of using blackmail, an unbrotherly tactic of revenge and a purely destructive action clearly motivated by spite.[139] In place of Zaunring, Schützinger was installed as lead pastor in Auspitz, and a union was forged with two nearby Anabaptist settlements, one also in Auspitz led by Philip Plener, nicknamed "Blauärmel,"[140] and another in Rossitz founded in 1527 under Gabriel Ascherham.[141] Trusting that the three fellowships would assist one another and counterbalance leadership challenges, Jakob Hutter once again returned to Tyrol.

Return to the Mission Field

One significant event on Hutter's resuming evangelizing activities at this time was his baptism of Katharina Prast, the woman he would later marry (WIT-18). Hutter celebrated the Lord's Supper at locations including the Inn Valley near Rattenberg, Hall, Steiner Joch, Stanser Joch, Sterzing, Pöggelhauben/Peckelhauben near present-day Franzensfeste, Lüsen, Klausen, Gufidaun, and Villnöß. On the Breitenberg above Leifers, he celebrated the Lord's Supper with a hundred people, and he celebrated it in Aicha at the entrance to the Puster Valley, Ehrenburg, and in the administrative district of St. Michelsburg, where he stayed in Hörschwang and Götzenberg. But it became increasingly difficult to use these locations as bases due to the bishop's servants and informers hunting him.

The bishop's government in Brixen hired professional spies and traitors, as evidenced in a letter from June 3, 1533 (GOV-12), in which Prince-Bishop Georg of Brixen shared secret information to all leading officials, bailiffs, and magistrates who were under his jurisdiction. Jörg Frue and Hans Mall infiltrated the ranks of the Anabaptists and joined in their meetings to discover the whereabouts of Jakob Hutter, Hans Amon, and other elders. Christof Ochs, the district judge at St. Michelsburg, received a separate letter commanding his support for the two spies in every respect, with a large sum of money as a reward. In that first month, Jörg Frue succeeded in meeting Jakob Hutter and Hans Amon at an Anabaptist gathering on the Götzenberg. After staying two days with them, Frue left to inform the bailiff and magistrate of St. Michelsburg and Schöneck. They sent soldiers to raid the Anabaptist camp, but the leaders managed to avoid capture. Eight Anabaptists were taken to Michelsburg Castle to be tortured and interrogated, but the prisoners betrayed no one, upholding the teaching of Hutter to maintain secrecy.[142]

Subsequently, Jakob Hutter escaped capture at Götzenberg and Hörschwang, withdrawing into the woods beyond St. Georgen and Gais, where he had access to Neuhaus Castle. The castle bailiff, Erhard

Zimmermann, was a friend of Anabaptists, and Anton von Wolkenstein, his wife Elsbeth, and his sons Paul and Sigmund listened to Hutter's preaching during this visit.

The Division of 1533

In summer 1533, at a gathering near the mountain village of Gufidaun, the Tyrolean fellowship decided to send Hutter to Moravia to serve the needs of the congregation at Auspitz (WIT-8). They had evidently heard rumors of continued disorder there, and they commissioned him to take over the leadership, hoping he could finally bring some stability and sending him off with prayers of intercession. Hutter brought with him a letter of recommendation from his assistant, Hans Amon, addressed to one of the leaders at Auspitz, Leonard Schmerbacher, in which he warned that Hutter's leadership might be met with resistance and resentment (HEP-1).[143] Amon's letter foreshadows the tumult that ensued, indicating that his suspicions were well-founded; a major leadership struggle would follow Hutter's arrival, eventually disintegrating the union with the communities led by Philip Plener and Gabriel Ascherham. The division remained for over a decade in which persecution from the state authorities made it even harder to sustain communal life. Hutter's perspective in this period is expressed in his letter to the fellowship in Tyrol (L-2), but the debacle is described in painstaking detail in the *Chronicle* and elsewhere (CHR-10).[144] Braitmichel's account includes many direct quotations from the verbal arguments of the leaders, offering a rich insight into this drawn-out conflict.

It began August 11, 1533, and ended on November 22, over three months later. The three communities in Auspitz and Rossitz, which had been a united fellowship, ultimately excommunicated each other; thus, the three leaders – Jakob Hutter, Philip Plener, and Gabriel Ascherham – shepherded distinctive fellowships after 1533, respectively known as the Hutterites, the Philippites, and the Gabrielites.

Two key themes of the controversy, which echo other stages of conflict in the Moravian fellowship, were the administration of the common treasury and the question of spiritual authority.[145] Concerning finances, Hutter had brought a gift from Tyrol to Moravia, in order to repay the original loan to their landlords at the abbey, on whose land they lived. Braitmichel called it a "small sum of money to repay the nuns . . . for their help in a time of need."[146] Doubtless, Hutter's presentation of a monetary gift benefiting the Auspitz fellowship would have strengthened his influence, and it certainly contrasted with Reublin's and Schützinger's dishonest hoarding.

Apart from the financial gift, Hutter was reportedly welcomed "with great joy" by "the elders and the whole fellowship." Schützinger and Hutter knew each other well as they had made the initial journey together from Tyrol to Moravia in 1529. Hutter had brought Schützinger with him the two previous times he had been called to Moravia to mediate. Hutter declared his joy that he had come to "his little children," something Schützinger and all the others echoed. They asked Jakob to help them care for the people, and he promised to do so.[147] Since Hutter had come from Tyrol to investigate rumors of disorder, Schützinger was understandably anxious. The tensions first arose when Hutter explained that he heard some dissenters hoping he would orchestrate a move to a new settlement, and he promised to punish "any selfish and inconsiderate people."[148]

Hutter began applying discipline as per the *Ordnung* in order to bring the fellowship into greater uniformity. Schützinger balked, resisting Hutter's help in this regard, to which Hutter responded, asking "whether they wanted him as a shepherd or not" because he was not "free to remain silent, not exercising his authority."[149] He then offered to serve elsewhere if he was not needed there. Afterward Hutter explained the matter to Ascherham in nearby Rossitz. Ascherham agreed he should raise the matter humbly before the fellowship, as it seemed to him that Schützinger was not prepared to resolve it amicably with Hutter.[150] Meanwhile, Schützinger had spoken with other leaders and told them he would not give Hutter much opportunity to speak to the people; these leaders questioned Schützinger's resistance to Hutter and suggested that the two should share leadership.

Shared spiritual leadership was common, so such a compromise was not a challenge to the norms of ministerial leadership in Moravia. (Later on, Peter Riedemann and Leonhard Lanzenstiel served as co-bishops until Riedemann's death.)[151] Throughout the following weeks, meetings between leaders, elders, and the entire fellowship revealed that their acceptance of Hutter was in question. Suspicions led to accusations and finally to harsh levels of slander. The involvement of Ascherham and Plener seemed only to exacerbate matters, judging from the verbal jousting reported in the *Chronicle*. When a settlement was finally reached, in which Schützinger was to maintain a degree of precedence, Hutter was left in distress and "the brotherhood separated in great anguish of heart."[152] By late September, Schützinger had fallen ill, and Hutter naturally stepped in, now "exhorting the people to the true fellowship of Jesus Christ." Not all were receptive.[153]

The next phase of the controversy involved an auditing process sanctioned by the elders, examining the various leaders' financial compliance with the community of goods – a doctrine they had all agreed to as part of joining the fellowship and that Schützinger had preached. Now it was discovered that Schützinger and his wife had withheld substantial funds from the fellowship. This infraction clarified the situation, and finally on October 12, the fellowship embraced Hutter, with Ascherham vouching for him.[154]

However, two weeks later, Plener and Ascherham challenged Hutter on his refusal to accept Burda and Bernhard Glaser back into the fellowship.[155] In addition, they questioned why Hutter claimed that Schützinger's "election did not come from God," with Plener stating it was "forever valid in his sight."[156] Additional dissenting arguments were heard among those gathered. Zaunring had already been executed as a martyr at this point,[157] but Gabriel and Philip criticized Hutter's treatment of him and Burda during the earlier controversy.[158] Despite efforts at negotiation, the breach between leaders remained. By November 22, 1533, messengers confirmed the schism, and the three fellowships remained separated for the duration of Hutter's time of leadership.[159]

Over the next years, the Hutterite group tried repeatedly to make peace with Philippite and Gabrielite groups and individuals. Gabriel Ascherham himself gave up the practice of community of goods and criticized how believers' baptism was practiced. Philip Plener evidently abandoned his people when persecution forced them out of Moravia.[160] Jakob Wiedemann and a number of his Austerlitz group died as martyrs in Vienna, as seen in a letter Jeronimus Käls wrote to Hans Amon early in 1536, shortly before his own execution.[161]

About sixty Philippites were arrested on their way back to their original homes when they were driven out of Moravia in 1535. They were imprisoned in Passau, where many of them died. They wrote a large number of songs during their imprisonment, which were included in the *Ausbund*.[162]

Peter Riedemann, who had been one of the recognized leaders of the Auspitz group, returned from four years in prison in 1537 to discover deep divisions among the fellowships that had been united when he left. He made an independent investigation, listening to the accounts of those from Plener's, Ascherham's, and Hutter's groups. Concluding that Gabriel and Philip were in the wrong, he decided to support Hans Amon and his community.[163] Riedemann wrote a letter describing his findings, and over the next years he actively sought out members of Plener's and Ascherham's groups, who were now without a shepherd, and brought many back into the fellowship.[164]

Hutter as Bishop: 1533–1535

From Tyrol and other parts of Europe, men, women, and children continued to arrive at the Anabaptist communities in Moravia. Within four weeks, 120 to 130 Anabaptists arrived from the Puster and Inn Valleys, Carinthia and Hesse (L-2). Housing had to be found for them all, and they had to find their place in the Bruderhof.

It had cost an intense battle for Hutter to be accepted as the spiritual leader and recognized as overseer of the stricter form of Anabaptist fellowship. Now he could take the reins firmly in hand, serving in Moravia for less than two years – from October 1533 to July 1535, when he set out on his last fateful mission trip in Tyrol. But within those two years he established a reputation for strict discipline and adherence to the *Ordnung*, especially in terms of community of goods, laying a foundation to sustain the fellowship that would bear his name over the ensuing centuries. The basic tenets, although owing little if anything to Hutter's own originality, were clear: no private property, strict nonviolence, adult baptism, clear spiritual leadership, mutual accountability, discipline to restore fallen members, and celebration of the Lord's Supper.[165] In addition to the spiritual order, Hutter and others established a practical organization for the daily working of the community. "Ministers of the Word" were the appointed pastors, usually on trial for a year or two before being ordained. "Ministers of temporal affairs" who served as managers and treasurers were also formally appointed.

Leadership divisions, whether due to "differing theological emphases" or the result of "charismatic leadership personalities,"[166] the influx of refugees, threats of extinction through persecution and economic devastation, and the frequent and sudden disappearance of their leaders were surely pressures that forced the fellowships to make difficult decisions between options of laxity and a harsher application of discipline.

Hutter's two years in Moravia were not without a dramatic episode, in which he confronted authorities, both those at the abbey and the governing authorities of the territory. In 1534, the abbess at Brünn, whose convent employed many of the Auspitz group, asked to borrow money from the fellowship. This was a year after the repayment of their debt, and Hutter may have suspected her request was subterfuge, a means for the convent to steal from them a part of their communal treasury during a time when persecution was increasing in Moravia. Hutter's fellowship refused, stating they would not support anything related to the Catholic Church "because all their profits come from and are used in the service of idolatry."[167] The abbess was furious and had Jakob Hutter and several of his assistants put in prison for a short time. The following year, the relationship of the community with the landowners in the abbey deteriorated even further. In April 1535, a mandate issued by the Provincial Diet in Znaim, which Ferdinand attended, expelled Anabaptists from the estates in Moravia,[168] and on Ascension Day, Hutter's fellowship was forced to move from Auspitz to Schakwitz (Sakvice), about six kilometers south. But they were soon driven from there too, with their only option being to camp in the open field at Tracht (Strachotin), another five kilometers further west.[169] "So Jakob Hutter took his bundle on his back and his assistants did the same; the brothers and sisters and all their children went in pairs, following Jakob, their shepherd. . . . They were thus driven into the meadow like a flock of sheep."[170] According to the *Chronicle*, this is when Philip Plener, whose congregation fell under the same mandate, left his people "pretending to search for a place of shelter" for them. "Not long after, a message came back that everyone should look after himself and find a place to live as best he could."[171]

Rumors spread that the Hutterite group camping in the fields carried weapons and were planning an attack. When soldiers came to investigate, they found a helpless crowd, including numerous children and sick people. Jakob Hutter pleaded with the authorities, who requested that he explain himself in a letter to the governor.[172] This was the occasion for his bold protest letter (L-4), in which he states they have no place to go, that in "every direction we would walk straight into the jaws of robbers and tyrants, like sheep cast among ravenous wolves," noting the large number of widows and orphans, those who were sick, and the helpless little children who were unable to travel any great distance. These "poor and weak ones are entrusted to us by God the Almighty, who commands us to feed, clothe, and house them, and in every way to serve them in love."[173] He further charged the lords with doing King Ferdinand's bidding, that they "fear a weak, mortal man more than the living, eternal, almighty God and are willing to expel and ruthlessly persecute the children of God, old and young, even the Lord's widows and orphans in their need and sorrow."

In response, the governor sent his servants to arrest Hutter, but he was not to be found. Instead, they took two other brethren, whom they brought to Brünn, where they racked and burned them.[174]

Katharina (Prast) Hutter

Jakob Hutter's wife is mentioned nowhere in Hutterian sources. This is not surprising as few Anabaptist women are named in the *Chronicle* or other writings of the time. We know of her existence only from court records preserved in Tyrolean archives.[175]

Her father was Laurence Prast[176] of Taufers, a village in the Ahrn Valley twelve kilometers north of Bruneck. She was probably sixteen to eighteen years old when she went to work as a maid for a wealthy family, Paul and Justina Gall. The Galls had joined the Anabaptists, and secret meetings were sometimes held in their house (WIT-9). Justina had two brothers, Paul and Leonhard Rumer, who were also active in the movement. These two young men were arrested and interrogated in September 1533 (WIT-8).

Katharina was baptized by Jakob Hutter in 1531 or 1532 at Trens (WIT-18).[177] She was evidently arrested within months of her baptism and at that time succumbed to torture and fear and recanted, as was ascertained by her captors in 1536 (GOV-35). No record of this first imprisonment has been found. However, Paul Gall was arrested in Rodeneck on December 31, 1532, along with a miller's boy, two adult women and a young girl named Sollin.[178] Katharina's association with the Gall family suggests that she may have been one of these women. Recantation was a humiliating ordeal that included standing behind the altar for three consecutive Sundays and swearing an oath never to leave the Catholic Church again. Paul Gall remained in prison for several months and was beheaded around June 25, 1533.[179] His wife Justina continued to secretly provide food for those in hiding until she fled to Moravia.[180] The government confiscated the Galls' property.

If Katharina did, indeed, recant in January 1533, she immediately regretted it and returned to the Anabaptist fellowship. Two months later she was arrested again. On March 25, 1533, the arrest was reported of four Anabaptist women in Bozen: Clara Schneider, Anna Gerber, Elspet Lippen, and Katharina, daughter of Laurence Prast of Taufers. Anna Gerber was ready to recant. Clara was possibly pregnant and would be isolated until her baby was born. But Elspet and Katharina were to be beaten with rods (GOV-10). The instructions for the women's beating was repeated on May 11 and again on June 7.[181]

Katharina must have found a way to escape after suffering these two months of cruel punishment and made her way to Moravia. She could well have traveled with Jakob Hutter that summer. In his initial role as a missionary throughout Tyrol, Jakob Hutter probably felt that there was no place for a wife, as he was unable to offer her a home. But in the community established in Moravia, he may have believed he could serve the needs of the congregation better with a woman at his side. He married Katharina sometime in the next two years in a simple service held by his assistant Hans Amon.

Although in her trial on December 3, 1535, Katharina said that the marriage took place "around last Pentecost" – that is, May 1535 (WIT-18) – it is possible that she meant the previous year. At Pentecost 1535 the community was on the run, expelled from Auspitz and then from Schackwitz, and forced to live outdoors – not an auspicious time to celebrate a wedding.[182] An additional reason for placing the marriage earlier is a report from mid-October 1535 that she was pregnant and about to give birth (GOV-18). While it may not be possible to resolve the dating of their wedding, it is evident Jakob and Katharina were married and that she was pregnant in the autumn of 1535.

Final Mission, Arrest, and Execution

Persecution in Moravia had reached unprecedented levels in the summer of 1535. Jakob Hutter was in grave danger and could no longer speak publicly, and the fellowship decided to send him to Tyrol as a missionary. From his four final letters (L-5–8) and from official records, a detailed chronology of this final mission trip can be pieced together. He set out in early summer, accompanied by Katharina and the schoolmaster Jeronimus Käls, Michel Walser, Kaspar Kränzler, and possibly Wolf Zimmermann.[183] Rather than taking the Brenner Pass, which would be closely watched, they took a trail over the Tauern range further east (WIT-18), arriving in Taufers (Katharina's hometown) in mid-July. It had been two years since Hutter was last in South Tyrol, and he had to start over to rebuild a network of trustworthy associates.[184] Slowly and cautiously Hutter learned of Anabaptists and sympathizers who had remained faithful.

On Saint James' Day (July 25), Hutter baptized several people in the woods under a spruce tree.[185] From there the Hutters departed for Sand in Taufers, where they lived in the woods, and then went on to Waldner's at Ellen to stay with a man whom Jakob had baptized earlier but who had since denied Anabaptism. On Sunday, August 5, three weeks before Saint Bartholomew's Day, Hutter called a meeting in the woods above the village of Ehrenburg. A small crowd gathered there (WIT-14). One of those who attended was probably responsible for Hutter's arrest. Anna, wife of Niclas Niderhofer, was the daughter of the local magistrate Peter Troyer, and Hutter baptized her maid, Katharina Tagwericher. A few days later he also baptized Anna and then her husband some days after the August 5 event (WIT-14). Unable to find shelter with him, they continued to the Obers' residence at Hörschwang, where Hutter baptized Hans Ober, his wife, and his daughter Dorothy, two of the servants – both named Martin – and a young man named Hans with his wife Else (WIT-14, WIT-18). From Hörschwang, Jakob and Katharina held meetings in Lüsen, also staying at times in Sterzing and again at Trens, where Hutter baptized seven or eight people.

Michel Walser carried Hutter's first letter from this trip (L-5) – in which we read of Hutter's harried yet fruitful work – the long and dangerous way back to Moravia. Throughout August and September, his presence in Tyrol was kept secret from the authorities. But eventually Peter Troyer realized his daughter was consorting with Anabaptists. On October 3, Troyer's friend Christoph Ochs, magistrate in the next district, wrote to the bishop's office in Brixen, breaking the news that Jakob Hutter had reappeared and had already baptized about twenty-five people (GOV-16).

Michel Walser had returned to Tyrol from Moravia, carrying a letter from Hans Amon.[186] In addition to increased persecution, several brothers and sisters had given in to temptation and left the fellowship. Hutter wrote in reply, resigned that "we expect that at any hour or moment the judges and henchmen . . . will come" (L-6). Added to his concern for the congregation in Moravia, for the new believers he had just baptized, and for his own safety now that the authorities were aware of his presence, he would have been anxious for Katharina and their unborn child. She was presumably in no condition to travel great distances. At this time he sent Michel Walser to help Nändl escape from prison (L-7). She may have been a friend of Katharina's from former times, and perhaps Jakob asked her to care for Katharina and the newborn child in his absence.

Another messenger arrived from Moravia – a certain Hänsel, who brought a letter with him. Hutter announced a conference at Hörschwang, a smaller gathering of about twenty people. They celebrated the Lord's Supper, aware that in such dangerous times they may not have an opportunity again. They knew that Peter Troyer had arrested his son-in-law Niclas Niderhofer and sent Anna to her brother in Carinthia (L-7). The fellowship in Moravia had asked for Hänsel to return immediately, but he was exhausted from his travels and the day after he arrived became sick with a fever. In his place, Jakob sent Christel Schmidt with his letter.

On October 15, Peter Troyer wrote again to Brixen to report how he had dealt with Niclas and Anna. He passed on the news he had heard about Jakob Hutter's activities in Bozen or Sterzing and his plans to hold a meeting in Tyrol. He described Katharina as "very pregnant, expecting the child to be born any day – if it has not happened yet. She looked in two places here in the Schöneck district for a place for her confinement, but did not stay" (GOV-18). Troyer's message was passed on to the various districts. Innsbruck responded by urging all towns to make a concerted effort. Anabaptists were known to flee from one municipality to another and were often able to shake off pursuit by crossing a border. The central government commanded magistrates to continue their hunt into districts beyond their own.

District governors ranging from Bozen to Sterzing, and Brixen to Taufers, were informed that Katharina was likely giving birth to a child somewhere. Panicked directives ensued: one to the Bishop of Brixen, a second to the authorities at Sand in Taufers, Bozen, Sterzing, and Rodeneck, and a third to the governor of the Adige Valley. These documents contained orders to search by stealth, day and night, for the whereabouts of any fugitive leaders (suspecting between five and six of them) from Moravia, especially of Jakob Hutter.

It could be that Katharina found a safe place to give birth at this time, and that Nändl stayed with her. By the end of November she was again more able to travel, perhaps leaving the baby with trusted friends.[187] Then she, Jakob, and Nändl left the Puster Valley, traveling west to Klausen.

Jakob's last letter (L-8) was probably written in early November and carried to Moravia by Jeronimus Käls. The situation in Moravia was becoming grim; brothers and sisters were no longer allowed to live in community but were forced to split into groups of eight or ten.[188] With nowhere to stay, some were returning to their former homes in other parts of Europe. Hänsel was still too sick to travel, and it was at great sacrifice that Jeronimus went.[189] Hutter sensed that his time was short. "Beloved brothers and sisters," he wrote, "consider that I . . . may no longer be able to speak to you again in this world, nor will our eyes be able to look upon you in this world . . . Yet you must not waver" (L-8).

Nändl, Katharina, and Jakob reached Trens through the woods and went on to Klausen during the night of November 30, 1535, and crossing the bridge they reached the sexton's house in Gufidaun.[190] Brixen and Innsbruck had information that Jakob Hutter was traveling disguised as a merchant, mingling with churchgoers in order to proclaim his faith to them; in Brüneck he had listened to a sermon, then shouted, "The priest actually knows the real truth, but his mouth has been gagged so that he cannot speak it."[191] Court procurator Dr. Jakob Frankfurter and the co-regent Kaspar Künigl from Ehrenburg agreed on a country-wide search between November 30 and December 1, 1535, in every suspected house in the districts of Sterzing, Steinach am Brenner, Sand in Taufers, Altrasen, Toblach, Gufidaun, Ritten, Gries bei Bozen, and Bozen. The preparations were made in secret. Those involved did not receive their orders until the evening prior to carrying it out, and, in an effort to prevent their warning anyone, these men were to be quartered in the government headquarters the night before.[192]

The night before this planned ambush, Jakob, Katharina, and Nändl arrived in Klausen. They crossed the bridge over the Eisack and, entering the town, walked up and down but found nowhere to stay. So they crossed back and went to the house of the sexton, Jakob Stainer, who had special permission to live in his house on the Gufidaun side of the river, although he was a citizen of Klausen and as sexton would have been expected to live there.[193] He and his wife Anna were sympathizers; Anna had been baptized earlier but recanted. It was midnight when they knocked on the door, and Jakob Stainer was not home. Although Anna was frightened when she saw the Hutters, she allowed them to come in and warm up, but she refused to help them further (WIT-19). At this point, Jakob and Katharina Hutter did not know where to go. "Jakob said we should go to Niclau or Jörg Müller in Villnöß or wherever God would lead us," Katharina explained later at her interrogation (WIT-18). But the ambush caught up with them before they could leave. It was still dark when the police banged on the door. Jakob, Katharina, Nändl, and their hostess, Anna, were all arrested and taken to Branzoll Castle on the hillside above Klausen. At seven o'clock in the morning, news of their capture was already on the way to Innsbruck (GOV-22).

Word came back from Innsbruck that Jakob Hutter should be brought to the capitol under guard (GOV-24). Katharina and Nändl were separated and kept in Branzoll until further notice and interrogated, and their testimonies were sent to Innsbruck. The authorities of St. Michelsburg (Hutter's home district) put together a list of questions to ask him (GOV-33); unfortunately his responses have not survived.[194] Hutter was gagged and brought to Innsbruck, where he was locked up in the Kräuterturm, a tower near the emperor's palace. Dr. Gall Müller, the court preacher, tried to convince him to recant, but Hutter remained immovable. In their report to King Ferdinand, the Innsbruck authorities wrote that instead of accepting their teaching, Hutter rebuked and cursed them (GOV-26).

Because Hutter would not reveal any names or recant, two foot soldiers were sent in the name of the king on January 1, 1536, from Kufstein to Innsbruck to scourge him (GOV-30). Yet in spite of such gruesome torture, Jakob Hutter did not betray any of his fellow believers. They put him in ice water, and then took him into a warm room and had him beaten with rods. They lacerated his body, poured brandy into the wounds, and set it on fire. Putting a hat with a tuft of feathers on his head, they mockingly led him into the cathedral. Then they tied him to a stake in the main square of Innsbruck and burned him alive. A huge crowd was present and saw his steadfast witness.[195] He persisted in his confession as an Anabaptist, as he had lived and proclaimed for ten years, and died on February 25, 1536.[196]

Katharina's Imprisonment

Meanwhile, Katharina and Nändl remained in prison. They were interrogated on December 3, probably under torture, and the names of those who had helped them and who had been baptized since they arrived in Tyrol were forced out of them (WIT-17, WIT-18). Several of these people were also arrested and interrogated; some recanted.[197] The woman in whose house they had been caught was released on paying a fine.[198] Caspar Hueter, the hatmaker for whom Jakob had worked ten years earlier, was questioned as to what he knew of Hutter's character (GOV-27).

Technically, the house where they had been captured belonged to the next township, Gufidaun.[199] Katharina was brought to Gufidaun's Summersberg Castle prison, high above Klausen on the other side of the Eisack River. There she remained for several months, and there she presumably heard of her husband's death.

On April 28, King Ferdinand sent a message to the bishop of Brixen that, since Katharina was stubbornly persisting in her error, an educated, respectable priest should see if he could persuade her (GOV-37). But before he arrived, she managed to escape from the tower, probably with the assistance of one of the guards (GOV-38). There is evidence that she returned to Moravia; a letter written by Hans Amon to Jörg Fasser describes "Jakob's Treindl" and her escape from Gufidaun with the "sister from Michelsberg" (HEP-4).[200] Two years later Katharina was executed in Schöneck.[201] Another Hutterite missionary, Onophrius Griesinger, had been sent to Tyrol; he was captured in Schöneck in August 1538, and Katharina may have been part of his group.[202]

Nändl, meanwhile, remained in Branzoll, at least until August. Then she too managed to escape. But by January 27, 1537, she had been arrested again with three other women. We can assume that she too died a martyr's death.

Although Katharina's name was not immortalized in Hutterite chronicles, she walked bravely into danger at Jakob's side. She bore the trauma of interrogation and torture, weeks of imprisonment, and the news of her husband's execution. It is perhaps appropriate to say of Katharina Hutter in phrases borrowed from a Hutterite *Denckbuch*: "This upright and brave sister in Christ, who pushed out of her mind all thoughts of her little child, husband, house and home, and all temporal things, valiantly armed her womanly heart with faith through the grace of God. She paid her Lord what she had vowed and went joyfully to meet her Bridegroom Christ with her lamp burning."[203]

Use of Scripture and Doctrinal Outlines

Hutter's eight extant letters, which also indicate that he wrote at least one more letter which is now lost (see L-3), contain his efforts to inform, admonish, and console. One letter is written to Johann Kuna von Kunstadt, governor of Moravia (L-4), and the other seven are addressed to the Anabaptist fellowships, including five letters to Moravia (L-1, L-5, L-6, L-7, L-8) and two letters to Tyrol (L-2, L-3).

Branzoll in Klausen, the castle where Jakob and Katharina Hutter were first imprisoned.

Hutter is not remembered as an original thinker. He himself might agree; his only aim was to recover a pure, faithful fellowship as attested in scripture. Therefore, to deviate from, write glosses over, or even build on those foundations would have been anathema to him. He would likely have been delighted to learn centuries later that his letters were read as consisting "mostly of ecstatic torrents of biblical passages."[204] Hutter's epistolary pastoral care aimed both to console and consolidate a suffering fellowship. He wrote his letter to the prisoners in Hohenwart (L-3) from Auspitz in his role as bishop, beginning what would evidently become the norm: for the bishop to write letters of consolation and admonition to those imprisoned for their faith, possibly awaiting execution. The Hutterites have preserved at least nine letters written by his successor Hans Amon to brethren in prison and several by Peter Riedemann.[205]

Hutter's last four letters are addressed to the congregation in Moravia from his final mission trip. Dozens of similar letters from Hutterite missionaries have been preserved, indicating the sense of accountability they had for each other: the congregation at home in intercession for those on mission, and the missionary reporting to those at home. In reading these letters it is evident that the Hutterite leadership followed such mission journeys closely, and if they heard that someone had been arrested they sent investigators to learn what had happened.[206] For example, in Hutter's last letter he writes: "The judge . . . captured five or six of our brothers and sisters and took them to Brixen. . . . At this point we do not know where they are imprisoned, but God in heaven knows. I immediately sent brothers to Lüsen and all around to visit the brothers and sisters and find out how they are. They have not returned yet, so I really do not know how matters stand" (L-8).

Regardless of the potentially formative role of other Anabaptists' writings upon Hutter, what cannot be denied on the basis of his eight letters is the indelible impact the Pauline epistles had on his self-understanding of the apostolic vocation, his phrasing and conceptual vocabulary, and the literary voice and demeanor with which he addressed the scattered communities belonging to the wider Anabaptist fellowship in Tyrol and Moravia. Theologically there is little evidence that an Augustinian-Lutheran interpretation of Pauline doctrine shaped Hutter, as it did so

The *Goldenes Dachl* above Innsbruck's main square where Hutter was burned at the stake. A plaque on the wall (not pictured) commemorates Jakob Hutter's death: "Here on February 25, 1536, Jakob Hutter, one of the most significant leaders of the Tyrolean Anabaptists, was burned at the stake, a martyr to his Christian faith."

many reformers; rather, it was the simple style of Paul's addresses to the faithful that Hutter saw as more relevant and worthy of emulation than a retranslation of concepts into sophisticated "learned" vocabulary. The personal struggle to understand the vision and authority both Paul and Hutter received from God is a key similarity in their writings.[207] Hans Fischer, who published the first complete edition of Hutter's letters in 1956, attests that Hutter's letters bespeak an "utterly exceptional passion and intimacy of the religious sentiment and experience – not just a deep internal devotion but also an austere meekness and reverence before God," and that although Hutter "was not adequately learned to write spiritual treatises, [he] was indeed filled with enough spiritual life to express in his letters the immediacy of his suffering and joy, his thoughts and feelings, his beliefs and spiritual crises."[208]

The absence of formal theological training has been an irritant to some who read Hutter as unwilling or unable to engage with concepts of higher learning; yet the reality is inescapable that he was forced to reflect in writing on the harried situation of the fellowship as they dealt with both internal and external threats to their identity, unity, or very existence. He did not have the luxury to sit in an office and devise a theological magnum opus. Given the physical distances Hutter journeyed, it is somewhat surprising that his writings are as numerous and lengthy as they are.

The lack of documentary evidence concerning Hutter's formal education has led some to suggest that Hutter's "intellectual training seems to have been limited to his reading in the Old and New Testaments."[209] While it is clear from his letters that he retained and reapplied numerous verses from scripture, it is both unnecessary and implausible to assume he would not have read popular theological tracts as well, which were in circulation among the Tyrolean and Moravian Anabaptists. Given how little Hutter directly cites scripture, preferring allusions, it is also unlikely that he would have cited other writings, even if he was alluding to their arguments. Hutter wrote letters primarily while in flight, often being pursued by authorities. Considering his clandestine trekking through the Tyrol, it is unimaginable that he could either set aside time or make space in his satchel for Melanchthon's *Loci Communes* or the *Adagia* of Erasmus; and therefore, the fact that Hutter's letters lack direct citation from any text besides scripture is entirely to be expected. He may not even have carried a Bible; the scripture passages he quotes are often not verbatim and were probably recalled from memory.

Church discipline, or the practice of the ban, became an integral aspect of Anabaptism, conceived as a means of preserving the purity of the church of believers based on the process in Matthew 18. Ulrich Stadler also wrote about it extensively in his "Cherished Instructions on Sin, Excommunication, and the Community of Goods" (ca. 1537).[210] In his *Hutterite Confession of Faith,* Peter Riedemann describes the ban as a means of restoring a fallen member.[211] It can be argued that, for Hutter too, the ban was a restorative rather than a punitive tool. He excluded and reaccepted Jörg Fasser's wife, who had withheld money (L-2), and also Georg Zaunring. However, Schützinger, Ascherham, and Plener continued in active opposition and were therefore shunned by Hutter and his fellowship in accordance with Paul's admonition in 1 Corinthians 5:11.

New Testament vs. Old Testament

While Hutter may have begun his study of scripture with a New Testament in 1526, his writing shows a clear preference for the Psalms and the Prophets, and it is possible that, in addition to his New Testament (Luther's translation), he may already have used a copy of the Worms Prophets (1529), or one of the many editions of the Psalms, and by 1531 he would have had access to an edition of the complete Bible in German, printed by Christoph Froschauer in Zurich.[212] Hutter's references to the Old Testament were more often allusions than direct citation. For his use of the New Testament, it is obvious how his preference for Paul's epistles impacted the tone and vocabulary of his own letters, yet it is notable that he also drew from other New Testament scriptures.

Hutter appropriated Paul's self-description as a "servant and slave" and as "servant and apostle" of Jesus Christ, and he also noted, as Paul did, that not only was he the author of the letter but he wrote it with his own hand (L-2, L-3). It was the letter to the Romans that Hutter cited most, especially chapter 8, which addresses how those who "walk in the Spirit" should relate to the law, the flesh, suffering, and mortality. More often though, he would allude to a wider variety of passages, similar to his use of the Old Testament.

A close analysis of his use of scripture supports Fischer's judgment that "Hutter was a master at communicating the essentials of religious thought into the thought-world of simple folks in his community, such that they could understand and grasp it. This occurred in imitating the Pauline style and in using images corresponding with biblical expression."[213] Themes that are repeated throughout his letters include his love for his brethren (expressed in almost effusive terms), intercessory prayer (L-5, L-6, L-8), eternity and salvation (L-2, L-3, L-5, L-6), and the return of Christ (L-3, L-5, L-7, L-8).[214]

Doctrinal Impacts

Through the testimonies of Hutter's followers, some of the major emphases of his teaching emerge, as evidenced in his impact on the beliefs and practices of Tyrolean Anabaptists.[215] Large gatherings were held that centered on celebrating the Lord's Supper, teaching, and baptizing. Assistants would purchase provisions including bread and wine, which were secretly deposited at the meeting place. Hutter would read from the Bible, break the bread, distribute it to those who were baptized, and then explain the basic tenets of the Anabaptist faith, imploring his listeners to embody and live out these teachings, following the will of God and the instruction of the apostle Paul. He reportedly presented ideas clearly and vividly, speaking straight from the heart.

He also made sharp attacks on clerics and political officials, aggressively condemning attendance at churches, and denouncing clergy, the Mass, and infant baptism. When Christ said to build up temples, that meant making our hearts pure, because church buildings didn't exist when Christ came to earth, only the temple that Solomon had been instructed to build in Jerusalem. The church headed by the pope, Hutter and other Anabaptist preachers claimed, was conjured up by the devil. The true church is God's fellowship, while church buildings are mere heaps of stones, accursed temples for idols of silver and gold. They are also murderers' dens where priests kill congregants' souls.

The rejection of graven images (Exod. 20:4–6) seemingly justified destroying crosses and images of saints.[216] The Mass, being an abomination and stench before God, with its sacrament on the altar, was heresy and witchcraft, a work of the devil, which cannot sanctify, for the "parish priests eat it day after day and become no better for it but are the worst of whores and adulterers." True Christians should break the bread as Christ broke it and thus affirm they are ready to die for God's sake, as Christ was ready to sacrifice his body on the cross. Just as bread is made from many grains gathered together, believers are united together in a Christian community. Breaking and eating the bread was a celebration in remembrance of Christ. In the ritual in which "a monk or parish priest holds it out over people's heads," neither the true body nor the blood of Christ were present.

Priests were false preachers and impure and therefore totally unable to proclaim the gospel, for it is written, "A bad tree does not bear good fruit"(Matt. 7:18). The worst of fornicators, "they are required not to have wives, but they certainly maintain prostitutes." Hutter taught never to make confessions to a priest. A person who sins should confess it to the whole fellowship and promise not to sin again. Anyone in the fellowship who refused to do so would be cast out. One must put trust in God alone, who made heaven and earth, for God alone receives and answers prayer. Only worship God and make intercession directly, and though saints are with God and are pure, they cannot receive prayers and act as intercessors. The same is true of Mary.

Infant baptism is a baby's bath, a form of magic. "The parish priest tries to drive the devil out of a child who is already pure," while the priest is full of devils. Since children cannot have faith, and faith should come before baptism, only those who can hear the word should be baptized, as Christ himself commanded his disciples, "Go into all the world and preach the gospel. He who believes and is baptized shall be saved"(Mark 16:15–16).

Government officials were heathen, too, and were not to be found among the Anabaptists. They ordered true Christians to be persecuted, afraid to lose power if true Christians were victorious. Luther, Zwingli, and the pope were the same, teaching nothing but manmade rules coming straight from the devil. Magistrates should be obeyed, however, if they punish evil and act justly, advancing the good. But they should not be afforded higher honor than ordinary, simple people. Rent and dues should be paid to both noblemen and officials.

Anabaptists should hold in common all things that God granted them, including both heavenly and earthly goods. Anyone owning money or property should submit it to the steward of the common purse, who would pay for all necessities. Those with more would give more than others, but if anyone fails to do this, they cannot remain in the fellowship.

Statements by Anabaptist prisoners present a "united testimony" about Hutter, who had been appointed by God's fellowship and not by the pope.[217] They attested that his words were full of power, that God spoke through him, and that he did not merely use his own strength. They submitted that the apostle Paul's teaching and Jakob Hutter's teaching were the same. Such teachings and convictions among his followers can be found scattered throughout the testimonies that were recorded by officials during interrogations.

Hutter's Significance and Legacy

Two early features of Hutterite practice – nonresistance and community of goods – arose out of the failed revolutionary attempts of peasants' revolts throughout Europe, which both predated and accompanied the development of Anabaptist ideas and practices. No scholar has done more to elucidate the historical development of nonviolence and community of goods in Anabaptism than James Stayer, in *Anabaptists and the Sword* (1976) and *The German Peasants' War and the Anabaptist Community of Goods* (1991).[218] His studies have made clear connections between the failure of peasants' uprisings and the rise of communitarian pacifism as an ultimate recourse. In the Hutterites' approach to communalism, Stayer sees a fusion of various earlier expressions of Anabaptist community of goods into a new synthesis. It was "the divine law in the Swiss manner, but it was animated by the antimaterialist piety of south German *Gelassenheit.* Above all, it made creative use of the dire poverty of Anabaptist refugees in order to transcend the social and economic limitations of the single-family household and to achieve remarkable economic productivity." Thus it was Hutterites who attained the "social goal of Michael Gaismair's Tyrolean peasants, a self-contained, relatively egalitarian society of commoners. This victory of the commons was a conditional one, however, because it did not include political independence."[219] And yet it was political, in that the authority of God's word and God's fellowship was placed far above that of both the institutional church and the imperial state, which in itself was a protest against the repressive incursions of power that had come to impact nearly every aspect of life through taxes and fealty of all sorts.

The overarching motif of resistance and revolution was manifested especially among the violent revolutionaries at the north German city of Münster, whose resistance included refusal to pay certain taxes and the attempt to create self-sufficient economic communities. The debate over taxes, which bridges both economic and political realms (especially in refusals to pay military taxes), remained a point of tension within the broader Anabaptist movement. The recourse to pacifist communalism, for which the Hutterites were one example, became a successful means of implementing a modified version of socioeconomic reform, in which the sword remained sheathed, and a more quietistic existence enabled their degree of economic decoupling from the violent society they sought to push outside their walls.[220]

While Hutter was neither the original genius of nonresistance nor the founder of community of goods, he did much to implement both in the Moravian community and in a looser form in Tyrol as well, so as to foster a pacific, communal life and ensure that economic resources were available to all those in need. It was his strict discipline and implementation of community of goods that earned him the respect of those who went on to lead the Hutterites in the following decades.[221] While Hutter might have found many of the ideals of modern communism tenable or even appealing, his concept of the state is so utterly different than that of today's political communists that any association of communism or even socialism with the economic practices of early Hutterian communities entirely misses the point of their nonparticipation in government.

Like many key leaders from the turbulent era of reforms, Hutter faced repeated controversies in which he was invited to intervene, encountering challenges to his judgments and his spiritual authority. While some may postulate that Hutter's leadership was "radical and polarizing,"[222] a closer reading of the sources reveals that Hutter did much to moderate the leadership dilemmas created by others' obvious misdemeanors and transgressions. As Hans Fischer expresses it: "How strong must have been the impression Hutter's personality made on the Anabaptists in Moravia during his first short visit, that both factions turned to him for arbitration! A total of three times – 1530, 1531, and 1533 – he traveled to Moravia, each time with the delicate task of mediation and reconciliation, each time risking his freedom and life. Through the difficult confrontations he unified the Moravian Anabaptists. His insistence on a commitment to the full practice of community of goods enabled them to survive."[223]

In terms of theological and ethical authenticity, Hans Fischer suggests that Hutter presents a standard for all subsequent Christians to compare themselves with: "For every Christian, of whatever denomination, the life and death of this disciple of Christ, Jakob Hutter, must be a challenge against which to measure his own life – that is, to learn anew, in this age of conventional Christianity, to dare again and again in Christ and with Christ to be a true Christian."[224] Such an assessment strongly concurs with that of the *Chronicle*: Jakob Hutter "had led the fellowship into its third year, gathered and built up for the Lord his people and left them to follow behind him. It is from this Jakob Hutter that the fellowship inherited the name of Hutterite, naming it the Hutterian Brethren. To this day the fellowship is not ashamed of this name, for he stood joyfully for the truth unto death and gave his body and life for it. This has been the common fate of all Christ's apostles."[225] The placement of the word "apostles" here serves the *Chronicle* as a means to solidify the claim that Jakob Hutter was an apostle of Christ.

Yet there are those who accuse Jakob Hutter of ambition and power-seeking. To this, Eberhard Arnold, a historian who collected Hutterian manuscripts and took a leading role in patterning the Bruderhof Communities on the Hutterite Church, replies:

> Jakob Hutter himself has been decisively misunderstood in his basic attitude. The history of the Hutterites, in stark contrast to that of the Gabrielites and Philippites, has borne testimony that in his struggle with these groups, with

> Simon Schützinger and the other wayward leaders, Jakob Hutter really stood before God. It makes it clear that as a prophetic figure, guided by the spirit of God, and in the strength of this spirit sensing or discerning the hidden evils, he could not possibly feel "free before God to thus keep quiet." Nor [do such accusers] correctly appreciate the task Hutter had been entrusted with. It was not suspicion and ambition but an inner leading – grounded in a task given him before God and his church – that prompted him to intervene. Without his intervention this restitution of the early Christian faith and life would, humanly seen, have foundered. Jakob Hutter's prophetic gift, just as much as his renunciation of self-defense, was rooted in the spirit of God, thus in real love to God, to his brothers, and to his enemies. His cry of "Woe to you lords of Moravia!" foretelling their doom "in the name of our Lord Jesus Christ" did not rise from vengeful feelings but from a true foresight, which found fulfillment not only in the Thirty Years' War but above all and more profoundly in the Counter-Reformation.[226]

Werner Packull, the most recent historian to assess Hutter's broader context in depth, suggests it was the clarity of Hutter's approach that led to his success, comparing Hutter's legacy to that of Gabriel and Phillip: "The memory of Hutter could not be erased. The martyrdom of this 'faithful servant of Jesus Christ, a man tested in fire,' burned itself into the consciousness of the community he led. None of those who had quarreled with him in 1533 left a testimony as clear and irrefutable."[227]

Similarly Johann Loserth writes of Hutter as a "leader of enduring great strength and great renown" (ADS-9):

> It is certain that none of [Hutter's] predecessors or successors in the eastern Anabaptist movement equaled him in importance; for none was so successful in creating and reforming. He not only afforded the cause a strong support when it had begun to waver in extremely difficult times; he was also the founder of that peculiar organization which preserved itself in Moravia with its communal character to the end, the founder of the brotherhood named for him, which still has shoots growing on the American continent. It is therefore easy to understand when the *Geschichts-Bücher* [chronicles] of the Anabaptists speak of him in highest praise.[228]

The *Chronicle* states that after 1533, "by the help and grace of God he brought the fellowship in order. For this reason we are called Hutterites still today."[229] His quality of leadership – his application of the *Ordnung* – as one unafraid to face controversy, leaves an indelible impression on those concerned with the ethics and misconduct of leaders.

Leonard Gross's assessment concurs: "Hutter walked the fine line between setting and maintaining the needed structure of the movement, with the consent of the members, and autocratic, unilateral pronouncements 'from above' which would have placed him apart from the brotherhood process itself. But this fine line Hutter seems not to have violated. For although he moved in as a leader of action, seemingly self-proclaimed, in reality the majority of the brotherhood backed his leadership – indeed, desired such a firm hand."[230]

And despite his apparent lack of theological originality, Hutter also seems in his efforts as a leader – as a commoner for the commoners – to have presented a formidable challenge to the state and church of the day by forging a communal model, which has survived nearly five centuries despite some eras of relapse and certain modifications along the way. According to Stayer, as one of the artisan class, Hutter was clearly not representative of the urban and lettered leaders of the first generation, yet he was the "dominant Anabaptist figure in the south Tyrol before coming to Moravia."[231]

Hans Kuppelwieser agrees that Hutter "was the most significant figure of Tyrolean Anabaptism." Moreover, if Hutter "had expressed his superior knowledge, organizational talent, admirable perseverance, and undaunted courage in some other way useful to the country, he would surely have gone down in history as a folk hero. However, like so many other capable [people], he was drawn into the spell of rebaptism."[232]

A historical-critical reassessment of the *Chronicle*'s view of Hutter and his legacy goes beyond our purposes here, although the documents in the source collection of this volume aim to provide the means for such a comparative study.[233] The *Martyrs Mirror* presents a rather diminutive view of Hutter. In Part 2 of the *Martyrs Mirror*, there is a passing reference to the Hutterites in Moravia in an account of the so-called Anabaptists from Thessalonica (366), and much later, in the context of describing Blaurock's role in Tyrol, Hutter is mentioned simply as "one of the overseers and teachers" in Tyrol, who brought his people to Moravia (430–31). There is a similarly perfunctory reference to Hutter in an account of the execution of "George Zaunringerad" (Zaunring).[234] Yet this perfunctory treatment of Hutterite history in the *Martyrs Mirror* fails to acknowledge that Hutterites were arguably the first established and most enduring Anabaptist group to form in Europe, whose leader was martyred the same year Menno Simons joined the Anabaptists.

The common agreement between the Catholic Loserth, the Lutheran Hans Fischer, the Bruderhof founder Eberhard Arnold, and other sympathetic Anabaptist scholars who have made a detailed study of Hutter's life and work is that the indelible impact of Hutter's leadership on the early formation of the Hutterite Church during a time of persecution accounts for its success to this day. Despite not having bequeathed systematic theological treatises, as did Hubmaier, who preceded him, or extensive church order documents, as did Riedemann, who succeeded him, the following collection demonstrates clearly how Hutter's personal involvement in the process of missions, ministry, migration, and the resolution of leadership controversies cemented his legacy as the founder of the Hutterites, who have claimed an essential consistency with their founder's vision over five centuries.

I

Jakob Hutter's Letters

Jakob Hutter did not write articles defending his beliefs, as so many of his contemporaries did. Under constant threat of arrest, he did not have the luxury of thinking through an elaborate doctrinal framework. But he did write letters to members of his fellowship (and one to the governor of Moravia). His original letters are no longer extant. But due to the Hutterites' practice of collecting and copying letters of their leaders and martyrs, eight different writings have been preserved, each appearing in multiple manuscript copies. In L-2 Hutter states that he had "written this to you twice before," implying that two letters have been lost.

In the second half of the sixteenth century, the "Golden Years," numerous large communities were established in Moravia. They evidently maintained an archive where epistles, records of martyrs, doctrinal statements, and records of the communities' daily affairs were collected, possibly in Austerlitz where chronicler Kaspar Braitmichel died in 1573.[1]

More than other Anabaptist groups, the Hutterites had a strong sense of accountability to one another. Those away on mission sent letters to the congregation at home, and the elders in Moravia wrote letters of encouragement to those in prison. Such letters or epistles were then collected and copied and bound. Some of the codices are very small, probably made to be taken on mission trips; others are large.

Although a critical edition of Hutter's letters is beyond the scope of this book, given the need to consult various manuscripts to resolve passages that are sometimes unclear or inaccurate in the published editions, we have carefully compared the available copies of each of his letters, both in manuscript and published form. No single manuscript codex contains all eight letters. The edition found in Hans Fischer, *Jakob Huter: Leben Froemmigkeit, Briefe*, contains errors and deviations from the available manuscripts. His texts were copied from the files of Josef von Beck at the Brno archives,[2] which are the likely source of the inaccuracies. Although care has been taken to preserve the Beck-Fischer version, priority has been given to manuscript copies where necessary, as the texts differ in some cases, which is indicated in the footnotes.

A listing of the manuscripts (codices) and published editions of the texts used is found in Appendix 2.

Letter 1

Written from Tyrol to the fellowship in Moravia, 1530 [3]

Hutter's first extant letter was written from Tyrol to the congregation in Moravia, probably in early summer 1530. The year prior, Hutter and his colleague Simon Schützinger had taken an exploratory journey to Moravia, in today's Czechia, as they had heard there was greater religious tolerance there. They formed a union with the group in Austerlitz, who agreed to welcome any Anabaptists who were fleeing Tyrol. In June, Georg Zaunring led a group from Tyrol to Moravia, and it can be assumed that Hutter sent this letter with them.

Summary:[4] An appeal and exhortation to persevere and become more perfect in the grace of God they had received, as they demonstrated to him when he was with them. That is, never to cease in their prayers to God, in their faith, love, and hope. Also that suffering is beneficial to the devout, a refinement for the righteous. Also a description of what they encountered in the mountains through the oppression of the godless and an appeal to fight through in faith and in such dangerous times to remain wakeful[5] in prayer to God. He commends them to the chief shepherd and gives them his greetings.

To the elect, appointed saints, and children of the living God, to my beloved and devout brothers and sisters in the Lord by God's grace, the grace we all received through the victory won by our Lord and savior, Jesus Christ:

Through our faith in his son, God has accepted us as children. He wants what is eternally beneficial for us, if we abide by him alone and grow constantly in his love; we must also be found irreproachable in all divine matters, in our obedience, yes, the customs and manners of heaven should be seen and perceived in our entire life, that our whole life and conduct is not a hindrance to the gospel of Christ.[a] That is my plea and

a. 1 Cor. 9:12.

Letter 1 (Codex 1)

admonition to you all, my beloved children and fellow members in the body of our dear Lord Jesus Christ. And during my absence I wish for you God's boundless grace, peace, and mercy, that these things may gain the victory and prevail in all of you. I wish this for all of you from God the Almighty, through Jesus Christ. Amen.

O you beloved and devout brothers and sisters in the Lord, those who were living at Butschowitz and Austerlitz when I last saw you, my beloved brothers and helpers Georg Hän and Christel, together with all those who assist in the ministry of the saints and the entire holy fellowship gathered with you: due to divine love and zeal, I cannot refrain from writing you a little about how things are with us in the Lord. For I know you are always longing for us, as we also long for you. For to us you are a living letter, written into our hearts by the Holy Spirit[a] who stirs and moves everything within us, as you demonstrated and proved to me while I was with you. Therefore, I bend my knees before the Father of all mercy and pray that you remain confident and obedient, and that your faith, love, and hope continue to grow and increase, to the glory of his great name, through Jesus Christ. Amen.

So then, I will not leave you wondering how we, I and my companions in the Lord, are faring. We are actually doing very well. Honor and praise be to the Lord alone, forever. However, tribulation, which has been the lot of all the devout from the very beginning, has also afflicted us, and yet that is both useful and good for us. Indeed, we are in great danger, yet we only stand to benefit from it. Otherwise everyone, or most people, would want to be Christians – but tribulation serves to sift them out. There are many who enjoy hearing the word of God, but if they are afflicted for the word's sake, they very quickly become frustrated and go back.

And the godless are really raging furiously wherever they know that the devout are gathered. Before long, the eagle will set out, taking the wolf, the lion, and the bear with him to destroy the work of the Lord and to tear the lambs of Christ to pieces.[b] Just now the godless have again cruelly snatched away a devout brother, along with two zealous members. On the Saturday night, eight days prior to Pentecost,[6] we wanted to meet, but the noblemen of Han[7] came with a horde of henchmen [and surrounded nine

---

a. 2 Cor. 3:3.
b. Cf. Dan. 7:4–7; Prov. 28:15.

houses].[8] But there were only two brothers inside, and the Lord helped one of them to escape. Someone had betrayed them, reporting that they had a hundred guilders in their possession. But when they found nothing, they took the brothers and the owner of the house to prison and stole whatever money and other things they could find.

And so, dear brothers and sisters, we wait for what the Lord has in store for us. Therefore, dear devout brothers and sisters, intercede for us, so that the Lord may protect us, and pray earnestly that the almighty God may keep us faithful so that his name be glorified.

Dear brothers and sisters, my desire for you is that you struggle through in faith and that you might be obedient to one another in love.[c] Contemplate the voice of God that accompanies you each day, and let it move your hearts. For I know with certainty that you do not lack any good gift,[d] therefore I do not feel the need to write to you at length. And as the anointing is teaching you daily,[e] it is thus the truth and no lie. Therefore, be true to it so that you do not lose what you have received from the Lord.

O, my fellow members, God wished that each and every one of you might take this to heart; yet dear[9] brothers and sisters, it is truly necessary to stay alert and pray! If we desire only to have a livelihood and appear before God with pure and upright hearts, and can rejoice in his advent[10] with our whole being, then we will have spared nothing. Let us keep this in mind; I wanted to remind you of it with my whole heart in a straightforward way. And I am not writing to you because of any subsistence need that I might have.

I hereby entrust you to Christ, the true chief shepherd.[11] [f] May he find pasture for you where there is plenty of nourishment and grass. May he lead you to eat and to drink at the living fountain of his Holy Spirit. May he let this stream with all its rivulets flow from there into your hearts, and into the hearts of all the children of God, so that you will become fruitful branches of Christ, the proper, true and living vine.[g] Thus I commend you to God in heaven and to the word of his grace. May he provide a powerful witness to you, in his holy work through Jesus Christ. Amen.

---

c. 1 Pet. 1:22.
d. 1 Cor. 1:7.
e. 1 John 2:27.
f. 1 Pet. 5:4.
g. John 15:1–8.

Therefore, dearly beloved brothers and sisters, we greet each one of you personally: you, my brother Kaspar, Georg Hän,[12] Christel, Hans Fleischhacker, Lorenz, Hans Plattner,[13] those of you who work in the two kitchens, in the school, in the bath house, also in the weaving room, and in the bakery – yes, each child of God personally, also those at Austerlitz – we greet you all wholeheartedly.

I, Jakob and Henn, Klaus Berk,[14] and all the devout children who are with us – we greet you with the kiss of our Lord Jesus Christ and also with his peace and embrace you with the arms of our hearts. Indeed, may the God of peace and love gain the victory in you to the glory of his great name, through Jesus Christ. Amen.

From me, Jakob, your fellow brother and minister in the tribulation of Christ.

Letter 2

Written from Moravia to the fellowship in Tyrol, 1533[15]

Jakob Hutter moved from Tyrol to Moravia in August 1533, evidently sent by the fellowship in Tyrol because of disorder and instability among the three large communities in Moravia. He came to the fellowship in Auspitz, which he had left in the care of Simon Schützinger. A second community in Auspitz was led by Philip Plener, and one in Rossitz by Gabriel Ascherham; these three were in communion with one another. Schützinger resented Hutter's arrival, and the union of the three fellowships quickly disintegrated (see CHR-9, CHR-10). Here Hutter gives his account of what transpired.

Jakob, a minister and servant of our Lord Jesus Christ and of his holy Christian fellowship through God's grace and mercy, set apart,[a] called and chosen by God our heavenly Father to preach and to proclaim his holy word and gospel and to reveal his treasure and mystery, also his glorious and magnificent riches in these last days before the magnificent and dreadful advent of our dear Lord Jesus Christ.[b] To him be praise, glory, and wholehearted honor and thanks on behalf of myself and all [holy Christian preachers, shepherds, ministers and overseers, and all][16] devout Christian hearts altogether worldwide, for all his love and faithfulness, the miracles and signs he has made manifest and shown and is still manifesting for us daily. May his holy name be praised through Jesus Christ, for ever and ever. Amen.

Grace, peace, love, faith, victory, triumph, and also eternal mercy – these I wish and desire for you from the depth of my heart, together with all the saints and children of God, my dearly beloved and coveted fellow members in the body of Jesus Christ in the Puster Valley, the Adige Valley, and the Inn Valley, in all locations wherever you are scattered for the sake of the name of God. May God also comfort and strengthen you altogether with the holy and most noble consolation[17] of his Holy Spirit, through Jesus Christ our Lord. Amen.

---

a. Rom. 1:1.
b. Joel 2:31; Acts 2:20.

An die Heilig Gmain
gottes im püstertall / Etsch
landt und Intall / Sol
diser Brieff oder Ep
istel zu hande

Ich Jacob ein diener und

Letter 2 (Codex 7)

Most dearly beloved brothers and sisters in the Lord, there is so much I would like to write to you and talk to you about, but I cannot. And no letter can properly uncover or reveal to you what is on my heart; it cannot really satisfy or fulfill the wish and longing of my heart. I would so much like to speak to you face to face. My heart is filled with an overwhelming eagerness, yearning, and heartfelt longing for you, as God in heaven knows well, as do all the children of God who are with me here. I have written this to you twice before; this is the third time, and hereafter you will hear more.[18]

Now I will let you know the situation with us here. We cannot fail to do this, out of proper, holy and godly, and even brotherly love, namely as follows: On the Thursday after the feast day of Simon and Jude[19] we took leave of and sent our dearest brothers Kuntz Maurer and Michael Schuster to you. We solemnly commissioned them with great, earnest prayer and calling upon God unceasingly, together with the whole fellowship here with us, that God might speed them on their way to you and back to us with fortuity and great joy. Through them we reported and made known to you in detail and amply, both orally and in writing, how we were faring here and how much had occurred and transpired in a short time. We hope that through God's grace and mercy this message has reached you.[20]

You ought to hear what has occurred and transpired and what God has further revealed, and that is what I want to share with you briefly in writing. The brothers will explain more thoroughly and in detail about everything. They will be our living letter to you, and you can ask them any questions.

The day after the brothers left, to our great joy, Peter Voit[21] arrived with all those you sent with him, for which we received great, heartfelt joy. We all praised and extolled God, and our hearts leapt for joy in God – they practically floated in God's love.

To the degree that I received the letters from Hans [Amon], Onophrius [Griesinger], and the other dear saints with great joy, they also brought me sadness, pain, and much heartfelt sorrow.[22] My God knows that I read aloud the letter, which dear brother Hans, my beloved and faithful assistant, had written to me: I read it with a sad and shocked heart and with tears in my eyes, and even with much weeping.

And I am also writing to you with tears in my eyes and in my heart with God as my witness, for I have learned how heavy and intense the persecution is where you are, and that the Lord has allowed evildoers to use such violence against you, namely, that they have once again captured our most dearly beloved brothers and sisters. They took Valtein,[23] the faithful brother who was so dear to me, and my devout children[a] whom I bore with pain, effort, and labor and in great anguish[b] through the grace of God: Gretel, Christina, Rüpel, Stoffl, and also Zentz[24] and others who had been captured before and had borne witness.[25] God be praised.

Many, that is, nearly all the children of God who are here with me, are also very much shocked at such news, for I lost no time in telling them, even in my great sorrow. We also earnestly cried out to God our Father for you, and you can be sure that we will continue to intercede fervently for you. Believe us in truth, and God is the truth.

A few days later, more brothers and sisters and several children came from the Puster and Inn valleys. You probably know who they are; I cannot name them all. On the same day our dear brother Klaus arrived from Carinthia and brought seven people with him. They have all found the faith here, praise be to God. Soon after that, [brother Stadler arrived with his children, and then][26] brother Peter Hueter arrived with twenty-four souls, and the day before, eighteen souls had arrived from Hesse. So we reckon that in the short time of three or four weeks the Lord added more than one hundred and twenty or thirty souls to the fellowship of God, who were baptized and inducted.[27] Those who came were from foreign lands, and from your community, both small and large. All were welcomed and taken in here with great joy, in such a manner as we would welcome the Lord himself.

We praised and thanked God from the deep depths of our hearts for these new brothers and sisters, and we will never cease to honor him for making us worthy to receive his holy children and to shelter and serve them. That is a deep, sincere, and special joy in the Lord. We hear and also know how fortunately and miraculously God prepared their journeys by water and by land, and we cannot stop marveling and praising the

a. 1 Cor. 4:15.
b. Gal. 4:19.

Lord for all the messages and letters and for all the grace-filled, loving, friendly, sweet, and comforting greetings and admonitions you have sent us in writing and also verbally. With extreme diligence, I have made these known and read them aloud for the whole fellowship of God.

These are a great comfort to all of us, and a special delight and sincere joy before God. We have all been very eager and hungry since then to hear from you and to converse. I cannot tell you enough how all of us praise God wholeheartedly for that reason. For what this has brought, through God's grace and power and through his great mercy, given that your writing and speech and all that you are doing and enabling is done in a manner that is excessively dear, loving, and sincerely pleasant, is sheer delight before God and a garland of gladness[c] [28] to me and in the hearts of all God's children, making us inwardly leap for joy. When we hear from you, whether written or in speech, we receive it as the speech of God. In truth it is so, just as though the angel Gabriel had written it, which is how we have always felt and how we feel now again about the letters from Hans [Amon] and all of you dear brothers and ministers of the Lord.

Once again it has also moved us sincerely to rejoice in hearing of those who have conquered, those who have borne witness to God's word, and with their blood have sealed it, faithfully keeping their promise to the Lord and the holy covenant they made with him. Therefore, we all praise God and his holy name, extolling and giving him the honor and fame in his highness and majesty, which properly and richly belong to him many thousand times more than we can ever offer or give to him. O, how great and inexpressible is his glory! His name be praised on account of you and all the saints and for all the signs and miracles he has done and continues to do daily through Jesus Christ, for ever and ever. Amen.

We really needed this encouragement in our great tribulation, pain, and heartfelt sorrow. It was encouraging to us; it truly came at the right time. Meanwhile, we once again are in great pain and tribulation on your account, because you are being so harshly persecuted and destroyed and we are thus robbed of seeing you face to face. Yet we have to endure sadness and pain as long as body and soul are one, as Job said.[d]

c. Ecclus. 15:6.
d. Job 14:22.

Furthermore, my most beloved children, I want to tell you that on the day after the departure of our brothers Kuntz and Michael, on a Friday, we saw three suns in the sky for a good long time, about an hour, as well as two rainbows. These had their arches turned toward each other, almost touching in the middle, and their ends pointed away from each other. And this I, Jakob, saw with my own eyes, and many brothers and sisters saw it with me. But after a while, two suns and the rainbows disappeared, and only the one sun remained. Even though the other two suns were not as bright as the one, they were clearly visible.

I feel this was no small miracle or sign from God, and perhaps God had a reason to warrant and permit it to appear. I don't want to withhold this or omit telling you about it. But the Lord alone knows what he had in mind and signified or wanted to show us by this. He knows all things which are hidden, whether present or future, in heaven or below heaven, on the earth or below the earth. May the Lord protect us from all evil and keep us holy, pure, and blameless and unblemished until the end. That is my desire and my prayer to God and my longing through Jesus Christ. Amen.

Furthermore, my chosen and dearly beloved children of the truth and of the living God, I want to tell you what else occurred and transpired among us here, namely: On the first Sunday after the brothers started on their journey to you, we gathered the fellowship together about two hours before daybreak. I wanted to speak the word of God to them, given the great need that was among us and still continues. I challenged the brothers and sisters with utmost diligence and earnestness, to be attentive and in all things maintain the right attitude toward God and toward all people, friends and enemies alike, so as not to fall into the error of rash and hasty judgments and talk, as has happened often and still occurs every day, as we have experienced, heard, and seen. There was a very good reason for giving this warning and giving this speech to the people, but it would take much too long to explain it all to you. I was greatly troubled, for I became aware, largely through God's spirit and wisdom, of things that were partly hidden, yet audible and visible in the fellowship. These things were not completely secret, and yet they had not been revealed in the fellowship.

As there are so many single brothers and sisters here, I had in mind also to speak about marriage so that they might know better how to conduct themselves. For that reason I was anxious, because if I was to speak about the truth and its proper foundation, I might say too much for some and they might seek to entangle me in my own words and accuse me or something like that. I was especially afraid of Philip and Gabriel, and not without reason. Yet I feared God even more and I prepared myself, and undertook to speak the truth with an appropriate style and modesty, trying to find the right and holy means that would allow me to stand before God and let neither Philip nor Gabriel nor any other person intimidate me. Subsequently, it was great distress, along with God's spirit and fear, which compelled me, such that I even felt forced. And so with great earnestness I admonished the people to listen sincerely and faithfully to the many words, with the greatest diligence, to be attentive to what I was saying so that they could give a witness if needed. And also I spoke in this way for various other reasons, which soon thereafter were revealed to the whole people of God who were with me.

I admonished the people to also pray, and just as we were all about to fall on our knees before God, without us knowing or wanting, Philip and Blasius [Kuhn], also Gabriel and Peter Hueter from Rossitz, entered the room. We welcomed them as brothers, although their arrival was a shock to nearly all of us, for several reasons. We had never experienced anything like this before. Nevertheless I called upon them to speak what they had on their minds.

They began by appealing to God and declaring that they had come for the sake of peace and unity and in true love, and words to that effect. They spoke like peaceful messengers and angels of God and sure enough they came in sheep's clothing and with the appearance of angels of light.[a] But in truth, inwardly, they were ravenous and fierce wolves, "who do not spare the flock," as Christ and Paul said.[b] We recognized them easily, surely, and adequately by their fruits, their words, and their actions. For God revealed them to us and let them be known with great force before I had spoken one word about marriage. For this I praise God from my heart

a. 2 Cor. 11:14.
b. Matt. 7:15; Acts 20:29.

and rejoice mightily, because otherwise they would have tried to attack me on account of my words. Others may have thought that I brought up the subject especially because of them, which was not the case. But God would no longer tolerate their craftiness and cunning. He did not want devout hearts to be deceived by them any longer, so he wanted to deliver them from the jaws and throat,[a] which had deceived them for so long with their force and poison.

That is why God allowed them to come before the whole fellowship with evil envy and hatred in their embittered hearts: they had to reveal the poisonous and crafty heart they had harbored inwardly for so long. And the entire holy fellowship of God gathered here recognized them as liars, slanderers, detractors, false shepherds and [false] prophets, for which reason they were also excluded from the entire fellowship in the power, spirit, and truth of God and they were handed over to the devil.[b]

Yet nobody should think that we acted frivolously in this matter. We did not give them any reason whatsoever to think this; rather, we acted with great earnestness and fear of God, according to God's word and command as is right and good in his sight. We acted carefully and with appropriate wisdom and discretion, and also in true humility, even having pondered all these things and having taken into consideration our courage, good sense, and reflection.

It does not bother us that they have taken offense at what is good and right, for that is what the ungodly have always done to all saints since the beginning of the world.[c] But woe to them for turning what is good into a reason for doing evil! Our conscience and heart is free and pure before God and does not accuse us[d] with regard to any part of anything, large or small, regarding this whole matter. Nor did we deal with them speedily or rashly; on the contrary, we considered everything with good measure, of course looking at it in the proper and holy light. For about five days we concerned ourselves with it, with great angst and trembling before God, together with the whole fellowship.

We also did not deal with them presumptuously or whimsically, or for the sake of quarrelling, in the manner as has often been occurring – about

a. Isa. 5:14 or 2 Tim. 4:17.
b. 1 Cor. 5:5; 1 Tim. 1:20.
c. Luke 11:50.
d. Rom. 2:15.

which a great deal could be said. But now they are also being held accountable by God and by us for these matters, because there had never been repentance or a real, genuine improvement. Rather, we spoke only of what we actually saw and heard. And everything for which they are accused or suspected, we have been able to prove by many devout and truthful witnesses, in fact, by the whole fellowship of God.

It would take too long to recount how the affair began and developed, all the causes and details of what happened from every side, with everything that was said, and how it was finally settled – the brothers will report to you as much as they know and have the gift of speaking. Besides, I hope it is not necessary, since I sense and know you have a deep trust in me and in all of us. For myself and all of us are fully revealed to you in your hearts, and I hope you trust us as if God were speaking to you, which is right, for we do speak the word of God.[29]

What follows is a complete summary: We have been living in great love, peace, and unity and in the fellowship of God grew in every holy, Christian virtue and action, ever since we separated from the evil and crafty people such as Simon [Schützinger] and others who lovingly adulated them. We were denigrated and slandered by them; all peace and unity had come to an end, and this continued as long as Simon, who was quite inept,[30] had his way. It started as soon as I arrived. In fact, without any fear of God they persecuted and slandered me and all the rest of us, more terribly than any pagan or cruel tyrant, any false prophet or false brother, has ever done. God knows this is true. Oh, how is it that I'm such a huge splinter in their eye,[e] even though, from the depth of my heart I have shown and proven to them nothing but pure love and real, genuine, Christian fidelity? God knows and recognizes this, but they talk and shout so terribly against me that it is dreadful to hear and to recount. They spread such horrible words of shame about me, saying that never has a more evil and greater rogue come into the land than me. They all clamor for vengeance and wish me evil, and their greatest longing, wish, and desire is that God may put me to shame. For they say that my arrival brought division and disunity, that previously they had lived in true peace, and that I am a cause of their division. But I am comforted by the

e. Matt. 7:3.

Lord, because "an undeserved curse or evil wish does no harm."[a] God does not hear the prayer of the unrighteous.[b] Also, I have done nothing to deserve or warrant these [accusations], whether great or small. For God knows I did not come to break the peace and unity but to increase them. This I began to do faithfully and diligently, as I can testify and prove with living and genuine witnesses. God has kept my heart pure and unblemished. In this whole matter there has never been any deceit in my heart, nor any falsehood or injustice.

Everything that happened, for which they hate, revile, and slander me, has come about through the Lord's great grace and mercy. It is on account of him alone, and I will let him alone answer for it. He will be or become strong and wise enough for them. He has made such things come to pass in me, his weak and miserable vessel,[c] as I myself am quite incapable of such things. Still, despite their many malicious and evil words about me, for the sake of the Lord and his holy people, I forebear and suffer gladly and willingly their many evil lies and the untruths they spread. And the Lord helps me loyally to endure it – otherwise, I could not do so. For they rant and rave against me more terribly than words can describe. I think they would like to stir up the heathen against me if they could, and we have already heard something to that effect from the judge here and from others. They say I bribed the people with money and that is why the people worship me – for the sake of money! They spread wicked, devilish lies like this, such as I have never heard before.

You can see that I am very much in need of your prayers, as we all are, so that God may protect me from their vengeance and jaws. The Lord will surely do this; I trust fully in his great mercy. And even if he were to give them power over my flesh, and even if my soul were gravely threatened by them, I still remain in God's hand. For as Christ and all the prophets and apostles were also reviled and persecuted, then why should it be different for me? It is for the sake of truth alone and divine justice!

They hate and antagonize [me and][31] us all without any cause. And everything that Simon, Gabriel, Philip, and others had decided and

---

a. Prov. 26:2.

b. Cf. John 9:31, "God does not hear the prayer of sinners."

c. Cf. Ps. 31:12, "like a broken vessel"; 2 Tim. 2:20–21, on honorable and dishonorable vessels.

planned to do to me has come upon them. They dug a pit for me and fell into it themselves (as the Holy Spirit declares through David);[d] the righteous judgment of God was exacted upon them, just as it was for the wicked Haman;[e] and while destroying others they themselves were destroyed (as Saint Peter points out).[f] Their folly and craftiness is evident to anyone who is willing to see and hear it.[g] That is what Saint Paul shows and writes about these end times and about wicked people such as these,[h] and such is precisely what they are! It is revealed and has been brought to light; it is no longer hidden.

They wanted to uphold Simon and make him appear to be a devout brother. Me, however, they wanted to destroy. They did all they could to support Simon with all their human strength, but the Lord stood by me throughout and helped me gain the victory.[i] He does not forsake his own. Yet right up to this day they trust Simon and all other rogues and evildoers rather than all of us. They welcome those whom we excluded for their sin and craftiness and declare boldly that these are devout and more trustworthy than all of us put together.

O brothers, what a tremendous struggle and conflict has come over the fellowship of God! How we have had to struggle and wrestle with wild beasts![j] How much we needed to be armed with the spiritual weapons, which the Holy Spirit speaks of in the scriptures![k] And if God had not stood by us with such great force, then we would certainly all have been driven apart, scattered, and even destroyed. But God has been our victory and captain; he has held us together like a strong wall and powerful fortress.

There have certainly been several frivolous souls who have left, but their hearts had never been clear in any case and were never completely content with God's people. For a long time they looked for a reason to leave, and now they have found it, and we praise God they have left. For all languid and frivolous souls must be eliminated from the fellowship of

---

d. Ps. 7: 15.
e. Esther 7:10.
f. 2 Pet. 2:1.
g. 2 Tim. 3:9.
h. 2 Tim. 3:1–9.
i. 2 Tim. 4:17.
j. 1 Cor. 15:32.
k. Rom. 13:12; 2 Cor. 10:36; Eph. 6:10–17.

God through trials and tribulation, just as dross[a] is separated from gold by fire, and chaff from wheat by the wind. But those who are devout and God-fearing have all been kept together in love, faith, peace, and unity, through the power and grace of God. Many devout Christian souls have come to the fellowship of God to take the place of the evil ones who left. This is a genuine and sure sign to us that God is with us and that everything we have done and allowed to happen was according to the will and word of God. For this reason, we have been faithfully sustained by his powerful arm.

O what a great and powerful storm, what a mighty blow, has struck the house of God! These people had such a good reputation and eminence with most people that no one could oppose them; practically everyone had to bow before and adulate[32] them. Even though someone might have had an uneasy feeling about what they said and did, one would not have had the courage or strength to admonish or contradict them. Whoever dared to do so was no longer their friend – that was quite clear. But they considered as brothers and friends anyone who flattered them, and said, "Indeed!" and "Amen!" to all they did, whether it was good or evil. I could have already brought about and created this kind of unity with many of them, but it would not have been from God. I would have been doing something inappropriate and committing a sin, instead of doing good.

There are many among them who are zealous for peace and unity, but with a total lack of understanding.[b] They do not recognize the righteousness by which God validates unity, and they want to set up their own manner of righteousness and whatever is good in their own opinion, but they are unwilling to submit to the righteousness that is valid before God. What Saint Paul said to the Jews is now true of many people. These plants are not planted by God and therefore cannot survive.[c] However long we go on patching and mending, the end will be worse than the beginning, just like putting a new patch on an old garment, as the Lord has said.[d] The arm that guided those people was a carnal one, but that which guided us was spiritual and powerful.[e] God dealt with them with

a. Isa. 1:25; Ezek. 22:18.
b. Rom. 10:2–3.
c. Matt. 15:13.
d. Matt. 9:16.
e. 2 Chron. 32:8.

firmness, wisdom, and great strength, so that they could no longer hide but had to reveal themselves and bring to light the deceitfulness of their hearts. Otherwise they would have continued to deceive us and to lead us around by the nose.

But God no longer enjoyed nor wanted to watch, and before our very eyes he established something miraculously, and with glorious power, and for that we cannot praise, honor, and glorify him enough: The gruesome devil could no longer contain or conceal himself and he appeared and burst forth in a very crude way. But that was God's doing. I think they themselves now regret to some extent that they went about it in such a crude and unwise manner. Had they been more subtle in their attack, we would not be rid of them yet and would have to put up with them still longer. But their hearts were impenitent and hardened; now in their delinquency, a deceptive party is supporting and comforting the others who have been excluded from us, and I fear that many or at least some of them may never find true repentance. That is what I am afraid of, but I certainly do not want to deny God's grace to anyone for that reason. The way they have been so far it is truly a lost cause; that much is clear to me. Simon at first wanted to repent, but now he is worse than ever, slandering and shaming us like the most wicked demon – like a raging lion[f] or a bloated dog.[g] Also David,[33] Gilg, Marx, and many others are in every way much worse than before. But that is the fate of deceptive and unfaithful hearts: they are bound to be led astray and become hardened, of which there are many examples in scripture.[h]

We tell you all this out of true love and fear of God, as a word from the Lord. We owe you this report so that you know to be on your guard around these people and all sorts of evil. Accept this warning for the sake of God's love and mercy, and lift your hearts and heads up to God, because the hour of peril, the very last hour, is at hand, as Christ and all the prophets and also all the apostles prophesied and foretold.[i] Therefore, wake up, for the Lord will come with great power and he is not far off. Let each one get ready and be armed with love, faith, and patience, with righteousness and

f. 1 Pet. 5:8.
g. Phil. 3:2, 19.
h. E.g., Exod. 7–10; Ps. 95:8; Prov. 28:14; Isa. 44:20; Rom. 16:18; Heb. 3:8,15; 4:7.
i. E.g., Matt. 24; John 5:25; 1 Cor. 15.

truth, and with total holiness and devotion so that we may be found holy and blameless before him[a] and have free and sure access to him when he comes. Then we may have joy and delight in him with all the holy, heavenly hosts. May God the Father help us toward this through Jesus Christ our Lord. To him be praise and honor, for ever and ever. Amen.

Rejoice and be comforted in the Lord, you devout and chosen, holy children of the living God, for he is with us. He is our captain and watchman, our power, strength, and also our shield. Praise be to him eternally.

Furthermore, I want to let you know, as my dearest children, my dearest fellow members in the body of Jesus Christ, that we are living and walking here in great love, in peace and in the unity of the Holy Spirit and in great justice and truth, and love toward God and our neighbor; the love we feel for one to another is increasing. The peace of God is flourishing and truth blooms, bringing forth many divine fruits. The dear, holy children of God are blossoming like the beautiful, lovely flowers in the fields, which bloom when winter and the dark season is past, when summer arrives, and when the lovely rains of May moisten the ground and make everything fruitful. As we also wrote to you before, the longer things grow, the better they become.

The Lord has taken away much power from the devil, who has constantly desired to hinder us. God will root him out of his holy fellowship, as he does daily, such as we read in the Psalms of David.[b] Such thorns or devils as these men have always prevented the good seed from sprouting and bearing fruit. And for the first time the Lord is truly freeing and unburdening the devout hearts and consciences from outward, human worries, delivering them from bondage and heavy burdens. They were previously bound by human traditions[c] and also by their commandments and whimsy – for the hearts and consciences of so many had often and for a long while been burdened, trapped, and bound, and also entangled, confused, and distressed by the false shepherds and several other misguided people. Christ has liberated them all and set them free. He was merciful to them and has led them out and is now walking ahead of them. And the lambs, the devout children of God, all rejoice in his voice and his

---

a. Eph. 1:4; Col. 1:22.
b. Cf. Pss. 3:1–7; 118:7–14.
c. Matt. 15:3–6; Mark 7:8–9.

salvation, and they follow him faithfully. They do not wish to hear the voice of a stranger, for they know and obey the voice of their shepherd and king. And they pay attention and diligently heed the king and shepherd, who is Christ.[d] This punishes, hurts, and infuriates the devil, making him roar and rave like a raging, devouring, and screaming lion.[e]

My most dearly beloved brothers, have no doubt that the only freedom we can have is the freedom of Christ, not the freedom of the flesh.[f] We are made free by God alone through Christ, redeemed and saved in our hearts, by the Holy Spirit. But our flesh and our outer nature has no freedom, no peace or security anywhere. Still we are joyful and courageous, for we know that as our outer nature diminishes and decays, our inner nature grows and increases day by day.[g] We also know that we have a building and dwelling place in heaven, made not by hands[h] but by the power of the infinite God – that remains there forever and can never be wrecked or destroyed like this mortal, bodily frame. And for this home we yearn and sigh with our whole heart; it is the goal of our longing, desires, thoughts, and hopes. Toward this we strive and labor, forgetting this mundane and perishable life and everything on earth and within it.[34]

Our hearts are full of joy. All together we exult in the Lord and thank him for his goodness, faithfulness, grace, and compassion, and for his fatherly protection and redeeming presence. Our hearts are fully at peace, completely quiet and still before God. For this we praise and glorify his most holy, all-powerful name and thank him unceasingly with our whole heart for his goodness to ourselves and to you. We wish to magnify and praise his name and not conceal his wonders and deeds in silence but to proclaim them to all the saints.[i] Even among unbelievers as well as in the fellowship we want to exult, thank, honor, and praise the Lord and declare his wonders for ever and ever. His deeds are mighty, and he has done great things for us, for he is powerful and his name is holy.[j] May his name be magnified, sanctified, exulted, and praised by us and by all the

d. John 10:3–16.
e. 1 Pet. 5:8.
f. Gal. 5:13; 1 Pet. 2:16–17.
g. 2 Cor. 4:16.
h. 2 Cor. 5:1.
i. Heb. 2:12.
j. Luke 1:49.

saints and all the heavenly hosts through Jesus Christ, from everlasting to everlasting. Amen.

You dearly beloved and holy brothers and sisters in the Lord, I want to tell you what is still our greatest concern and issue now, which saddens us, weighs on our hearts deeply, and causes us great angst and pain and much anguish. We find no rest[a] by day or by night for your sake. God is our witness concerning all that we say – as you are being laid to waste and persecuted horribly and with utmost cruelty, martyred and destroyed and secretly murdered and oppressed. May God in heaven above have mercy! It wounds and moves our hearts deeply and severely that you are being stolen from us like this, right before our very eyes.

O, dearly beloved fellow members, how we long for every one of you, that we are in sorrow and anxious for your sake. What deep compassion and heartbreak we feel for you! Yes, our hearts cry and weep for you constantly; they are heavy and sorrowful for your sake. Sometimes it seems as if our hearts will melt away with suffering, pain, and great sadness, and we sense that they are about to break. Because of you our souls continuously have no foundation or rest in our bodies; we simply cannot express ourselves, or find enough words to tell you how we feel, in truth. We now hear one sad report and tragic message after another. When I think of it, I feel more like weeping and crying my heart out than writing.

At this time, the cruel dragon, bloodhound and devil is devouring and consuming one faithful child of God and dear brother after another. Oh, dear brothers and sisters, this fills me and all of us with great pity and compassion! If it only concerned my own body, I would rather die than hear such news. Every day and every hour we are in great fear and angst for those of you who are still present, expecting to be told that you, too, have been captured. Although we know that our worrying does no good, yet we cannot stop worrying, because of the childlike, brotherly love that burns in us. And though it helps neither you nor us and drains our strength and power and all our courage, it still shows how deeply we care for you and drives us to intercede for you by day and by night in prayer and with earnest supplication and crying out to God.

---

a. Ps. 22:2.

Furthermore, I have written this to you twice already with my own hand, and now I am writing you for the third time with tears and a weeping heart: we all urge you to come out of that accursed, sodomite, and murderous land. We all wish for that. Flee, flee away from those ungodly and wicked people! Surely God has given you enough reason to do so.

O, that God might grant our prayers and wishes, and would protect you from them, those of you who are still alive, that he might send you to us, which is our hearts' wish, delight, pleasure, and desire. If this were possible, we would all willingly endure hunger and thirst, cold and heat,[b] and all kinds of tribulation, for this to happen. For your sakes we would gladly be persecuted and driven out the next day, if it were God's will, if only you would come to us. Oh, if only God would reward and fulfill our holy zeal for you, and we might be found worthy and blessed before the Lord. May the Lord's will be done according to his holy mercy and goodness, and may he fulfill your and our longing and heartfelt desire, through Jesus Christ our Lord. Amen.

My dearly beloved and chosen, holy children and fellow members, take heed of what I write to you and believe it, for truth is confirmed by the testimony of two or three witnesses.[c] Therefore, be watchful and pray to God diligently. He will teach you what is right if you are attentive and pay him heed.

In conclusion, I commend all of you to the protection of God's powerful hand. May the Lord be your guard and captain, your shelter and shield, keeping your souls and bodies safe until the great day of the Lord's revelation, through Jesus Christ. Amen.

The entire holy fellowship of God here, all ministers[35] and elders – in short, every child of God by name, small and great, brothers and sisters – they all greet you from the depths of their hearts a thousand times with a truly holy and godly, brotherly, and burning love and with the proper kiss of our Lord Jesus Christ. We greet all of you and each one personally, especially from those of us who know you so well in the Lord and who have a special love for you. I cannot pass on with pen and ink every personal greeting the brothers and sisters here would like me to; it would simply take too long. But you know their hearts well, for they are

---

b. 2 Cor. 11:27.
c. 2 Cor. 13:1; Heb. 10:28.

wide open to you in the love of God. So please accept their greetings, each one of you, and know them to be a thousand times better than anything I have written here. All the brothers and sisters you know would have liked me to put down the name of each one, but I simply cannot.

And I, Jakob, your minister and servant and brother in the Lord, an apostle and minister of God through his grace and mercy, greet every one of you a thousand times from the depth of my heart with my holy and friendly kiss, in the genuine, pure, unadulterated love of God. I think of you incessantly, every hour and every moment. With my whole heart and mind and all my soul I am thankful for and pleased with you. And I kiss you dearly in friendship from my heart and from my whole spirit, with the true, firm, and sweet kiss of Jesus Christ and of all the prophets and saints.

Although I am not with you in flesh or body,[36] my thoughts are fully and completely with all of you, all the time, and I cannot in truth put it sufficiently into spoken or written words, no matter how much my heart wishes or longs.

And give my greetings especially to all those whom I know personally and who truly love me for the sake of the Lord. They are particularly close to me, and I love them openly with my whole heart, be they brothers or sisters, shepherds or sheep, in the Puster, Adige, or Inn valleys, nobody excluded: Greet each one of them. They are well aware of the love and fidelity I feel for them, even though, for the sake of being brief, I cannot mention each one by name – they know whom I mean. Yet God wills that I still greet, comfort each one of them individually, and kiss them with my own lips and heart, and that I might serve them, educating them with much discipline and honor, myself being an example to them with all my strength and ability. That would be my greatest delight and my best and noblest joy in God, the Lord.

May my heart and mind be with you forever, as your heart, soul, and spirit are with me, and may God the Father be with us all through Jesus Christ, for ever and ever. Amen. In eternity. Amen.

I, Jakob, wrote this with my own hand, but Klaus has copied it for me, and we are sending the copy of the epistle or letter to the Puster Valley. If there is anything else you should know, brother Voit will tell you verbally. I greet you, Onophrius [Griesinger] and Hans [Amon], faithfully from a truly holy heart. Please also give my greetings a thousand times over from the depth of my heart, to the dear sisters Gretel Marbeck[37] and Ursula Brähl and to all the others. Georg Fasser's wife has been taken in through God's mercy and grace, and she is doing very well,[38] as is Bärbel from Jenbach. Your hearts will rejoice at this news. Georg Fasser, our brother and minister of the Lord, together his wife, our dear sister, greet you all faithfully, and once again, all the saints together. May the Lord be with you eternally. Amen.

Sent from Auspitz in Moravia to the Adige Valley.
Carried by brother Peter Voit.

Letter 3

Written from Moravia to prisoners in Hohenwart, 1534 [39]

Letter 3 was written in 1534 from Auspitz in Moravia to the brothers and sisters imprisoned at Hohenwart, Lower Austria.[40] *In his role as their pastor, Jakob Hutter encourages them with many passages from the Old Testament and the New Testament. By this time, persecution had driven most of the Anabaptists out of Tyrol, but it was increasing also in Moravia.*

[Summary: He wishes them grace and thanks God for his proven salvation. He speaks of his sorrow that they cannot be together; they suffer with them and remember them in prayer. With many comforting words he encourages them to remain faithful to the Lord and describes the reward of the devout and their abundance. He speaks of the tribulation he and the fellowship are experiencing and their desire for peace, the arrival of brother Offrus and those with him. He sends his greetings.][41]

Jakob, a minister of Jesus Christ, with other ministers and the whole fellowship of God, to those imprisoned at Hohenwart for the sake of Christ Jesus:

From the depths of our hearts we wish for you [without ceasing][42] the ineffable grace and mercy of God the heavenly Father, through our Lord Jesus Christ. Amen. Blessed be God the Father through Jesus Christ, our dear Lord, who has made us worthy to suffer for the sake of his most holy and almighty name, who has called us out of the terrible darkness of this evil, miserable world[a] and accepted us into the community of the elect saints, into heavenly citizenship,[b] into the hosts of many thousands of angels.[c] May God help us to reach the goal through his holy name and through our dear Lord Jesus Christ, to the praise of his glory. Amen.

You elect and most dearly beloved brothers and sisters! To our great pain and sorrow we have heard and understood that you are in prison,

---

a. 1 Pet. 2:9 (reference given in COD. 6).
b. Eph. 2:6 (reference given in COD. 6).
c. Heb. 12:22 (reference given in COD. 6).

Die Erste Epistel von de
getreuen Brüeder Jacoben
Hüeter An die gefanngnen
Des Herren Been Hohenwarth.
Im 15 . 34 Jar.

Jacob ein diener Jesu Christi

Letter 3 (Codex 10)

though it is for the sake of the [divine][43] truth. But we have no idea how you are, although we have sent brothers out to inquire. We have still not received a clear, direct message from you.

We are very sad that we cannot speak to you or see you face to face; our hearts are truly suffering with you. We pray to God faithfully and constantly for you, with great diligence and earnestness. In fact, all saints, the entire fellowship of God here at Auspitz, does not cease to intercede for you. We remember you before God without ceasing, in holy, and godly love. Therefore, we cannot refrain from writing to you in divine, brotherly love, to comfort you with the comfort we ourselves have received from God.[a] We are thus begging you to remain steadfast to the end, by the heartfelt mercy of God, in divine truth. Do not let the threats of the godless frighten you, for they cannot pluck one hair from your head unless it is God's will.[b] Revere God the Lord in your hearts, as Peter says,[c] which means, give honor to God and not to the godless people; praise God, glorify him, trust him from the very depths of your hearts, and do not doubt his help and great mercy. At times it may seem that he has abandoned you, but this will not last. Though God leads you into tribulation, [he will lead you out again.][d][44] Do not forget the comfort of the Holy Spirit,[45] with which God speaks to you and to all his children through his prophets and ministers from the beginning.

This is what God says to his own: Fear not, my servant, you poor wretched worm![e] I will be with you in fire and water[f] – that is, in all your tribulation, fear, and need – and I will be your king and captain, even your watchman and overseer. Thus David[46] proclaims, "The Lord is my shield [and weapon][47] and my light – whom shall I fear? The Lord is the strength of my life – of whom shall I be afraid, though a whole army should encamp against me, [my heart will trust in the Lord]."[g][48] Take note and consider carefully, dear brothers and sisters, what David testifies through the Holy Spirit! He says again, "I will not fear a hundred

a. 2 Cor. 1:4.
b. Luke 21:18.
c. 1 Pet. 3:15.
d. Cf. 1 Sam. 2:6.
e. Isa. 41:14.
f. Isa. 43:2.
g. Ps. 27:1, 3.

thousand people and my heart shall rely on the Lord alone, for with him I shall perform deeds and miracles."[h] Therefore, do likewise, dearly beloved brothers and sisters.

Saint Paul therefore declares, "If God is for us, who will be against us?"[i] Christ says, "No one will snatch out of my hand those who are mine, for the Father who has given them to me is stronger than all."[j] And the holy prophet Isaiah testifies, "All in heaven and on earth [and under the earth],[49] yes, all kings and princes, all lords and in general, all people and all creatures and all Gentiles are as nothing compared with God."[k]

What precious, noble, and valuable words these are for all who love God – ponder them in your hearts! For Christ said, "Whoever hears my words and diligently carries them out is like a wise and prudent man who builds his house on a good rock; even though driving rain, wind, and water come and beat upon the house, it does not fall."[l] The house represents all devout Christian hearts in whom God dwells; the rock represents Christ; the pelting rains and waters are the tribulations and persecutions and also all the threats and suffering the world inflicts, and all false teachings. All these things combined cannot turn the devout away from the truth, as Christ even says: "On this foundation [or rock][50] will I build my holy fellowship, and the gates of hell shall not overcome it."[m] The gates of hell represent the powerful people of this world: kings, princes, tyrants, all the enemies of the [divine][51] truth, yes, the princes of darkness and rulers of this world against whom we have to struggle, as Saint Paul tells us.[n]

Christ is the gate or entryway leading to eternal life, and those who follow him, who trust in him wholeheartedly, who fully and faithfully submit to him, will be saved, as he himself has said.[o] In the same way, they [the tyrants] are the gates leading to hell and eternal death. Those who trust and obey them will certainly be condemned! Yet these gates of hell cannot turn God's devout children away from the divine truth, for Christ

h. Ps. 3:6.
i. Rom. 8:31.
j. John 10:28–29.
k. Isa. 40:17, 23.
l. Matt. 7:24–25.
m. Matt. 16:18.
n. Eph. 6:12.
o. John 10:9.

promised that the gates of hell will not overcome them.[a] Saint Peter gives the same testimony [in his epistles]:[52] "Who will harm you if you diligently pursue what is right? Have no fear of their threats."[b] He also says that if we diligently perform and bring forth the works, fruits or virtues of the holy Christian faith, we shall not stumble.[c]

Saint Paul testifies similarly, saying, "The hope we have in Christ will never put us to shame, for the love [of God][53] has been poured into our hearts."[d] This love is Christ and the Father himself, as in the words of Saint John.[e] It is also the rock mentioned earlier. Saint Paul goes on to say:

> Who will separate us from the love of God? Will tribulation or distress, persecution or hunger, [nakedness,][54] peril, or sword? As it is written: For your sake we are being killed all day long; we are regarded as sheep to be slaughtered. But in all these things we are more than conquerors through him who loved us. For I am certain that neither death, nor life, nor angels, nor principalities, nor powers, nor things present, nor things to come, nor height, nor depth, nor anything else in all creation can separate us from the love of God in Christ Jesus our Lord.[f]

Dearest children of God, see what [powerful and][55] comforting words these are! Saint Paul also says, "The Lord is faithful and true and will not let you be tempted beyond your ability, but with the temptation he will always provide for you a fatherly means of grace to withstand and bear it."[g] When he says, "Have nothing to do with their [idolatry,"[h] he means to guard against all their][56] evil deeds, and whatever is laid upon you on that account, God will faithfully help you to bear it. He will aid you and stand by you in all your distress. My beloved fellow members in the body of Christ, see how wonderfully the Holy Spirit comforts us, no matter what happens. When someone who loves God ponders this and takes it to heart, it makes one leap and laugh for joy. Anyone who is sorrowful unto death should be filled with new life, for all this and much more has been written for our joy and consolation.

---

a. Matt. 16:18.
b. 1 Pet. 3:13–14.
c. Cf. 2 Pet. 1:8.
d. Rom. 5:5.
e. 1 John 4:9.
f. Rom. 8:35–39.
g. 1 Cor. 10:13.
h. 1 Cor. 10:14.

Take comfort and be at peace in your hearts, for God leads us into hell and back out again; he makes us sad and then joyful again; he gives death and also life, and after great storms he makes it beautiful once again.[i] Therefore, be long-suffering and wait patiently for the redemption of your bodies, and do not grow faint or weary in the race.[j] Do not look back either, but see to it that the love in your hearts does not grow cold[k] and die. Do not be ashamed of [the bonds and][57] suffering of Christ; rejoice in them with your whole heart, for you know that on this earth you are not promised anything but suffering and death, tribulation, anxiety, deprivation, also great persecution, pain, martyrdom, humiliation, and shame at the hand of all the godless people. This is the true sign and seal of all God's devout children; it is the sign of Christ, or the Son of Man and all his members, that must appear at the end time according to the word of the Lord. Yes, the cross and tribulation are what is befitting for all God's children. It is a beautiful honor in the sight of God the Most High and of all the saints, a lovely sign of glory and a crown of joy before them. This has been the experience of all the patriarchs and prophets, of Christ our [holy][58] Lord and all his disciples, indeed, all the elect from the beginning of the world until now, which we should well consider if such should befall us for the sake of the truth: this does not mean that we are enemies of God, but rather his friends and beloved children. As the Lord himself says, "I discipline those whom I love,"[l] and every child whom the Father receives he chastises, and he receives none who do not accept or endure discipline. Those are not children of God[m] but of the Babylonian Whore. It is written, "Happy are those who suffer the chastisement of the Lord."[n]

Throughout scripture, those who stand the test and remain steadfast are praised as blessed by the Holy Spirit and given great applause before God. "Blessed are they who mourn, for they shall be comforted."[o] Those who mourn and grieve for the Lord's sake, and those who are persecuted for the sake of truth, the kingdom of heaven is theirs.[p] "Blessed

i. 1 Sam. 2:6–7; Tob. 13:2.
j. Cf. Isa. 40:31.
k. Matt. 24:12.
l. Rev. 3:19.
m. Heb. 12:6–8.
n. Job 5:17.
o. Matt. 5:4.
p. Matt. 5:10.

are you when people revile you on my account; rejoice and be glad, for great is your reward in heaven, for in the same way they persecuted the holy prophets before you."[a] It is as if Christ were saying: By this you shall clearly notice and recognize that you are sanctified and are truly dear and pleasing to God, for he has marked and designated you with the sign of those who love him. Only of his own does Christ say that they will be crucified, persecuted, scourged, reviled, killed and put to death, robbed, hunted, captured, and tormented.[b] Therefore, Saint Paul[59] states that only through much suffering and tribulation can we enter the kingdom of God.[c] He also says that ["if we are fellow sufferers, we shall also be fellow heirs";[d] if we do not endure with Christ,[e] we shall also not reign with him. And again,][60] "It has been granted to you not only to believe in Christ but also to suffer with him and to fight the same fight which you have seen to be mine."[f] Therefore, he wants to point them toward nothing but the crucified Christ[g] and to the word of suffering and the cross. Saint Peter also says to all, "If you suffer patiently for doing right, it is a grace from God."[h] And soon thereafter, he says, "Blessed are you if you suffer for the sake of righteousness, because God's spirit rests on you and is praised in you and through you."[i] Saint James also says, "We call blessed all those who have endured chastisement."[j]

There are many more wonderful testimonies telling us not to be ashamed of, or shrink from the bonds and suffering of Christ, but to accept them from God with great thankfulness and heartfelt joy. It was not for nothing that the holy apostles thanked God when they were tortured, reviled, and beaten with rods. Joyfully they went from the council's presence, praising and thanking God from their hearts for being considered worthy to suffer shame and disgrace, and also suffering beatings for the Lord's sake.[k] They regarded it as something noble and

---

a. Matt. 5:11–12.
b. Matt. 10:17–22.
c. Acts 14:22.
d. Rom. 8:17.
e. 2 Tim. 2:12.
f. Phil. 1:29–30.
g. Cf. 1 Cor. 2:2.
h. 1 Pet.2:20.
i. 1 Pet. 4:14.
j. James 5:11.
k. Acts 5:41.

a great treasure. Saint Paul even boasted there is nothing better than the suffering and cross of Christ that he suffered in his own body.[l] Saint Peter also urges, "Let none of you suffer as an evildoer; yet if one suffers for being a Christian, then one should not be ashamed but rather praise and glorify God."[m] And Saint James pleads, "Consider it pure joy, my brethren, when you meet trials of whatever sort."[n] Take comfort in these words, my beloved brothers and sisters, and remain valiant in the truth, for Christ says, "He who endures to the end will be saved."[o] "Fight loyally unto death for God's truth, and God will fight for you."[p] Set no restrictions or time limits on the Lord's mercy; he knows the right hour; he will come at the right time, the very best time.[q]

Beloved ones, confess the Lord in complete faithfulness, and he will also acknowledge you before God his heavenly Father.[r] Do not be ashamed of him before this adulterous generation, and he will not be ashamed of you before God his heavenly Father.[s] Those who do not confess Christ before all people, but deny him and feel ashamed of him, neither will Christ acknowledge them before God and all the angels.[t] He will feel ashamed of them before all his heavenly hosts on that day. But those who overcome the devil and their own flesh and further, all unrighteousness, and valiantly fight and battle their way through this temporal death to life everlasting – on their heads God the Lord will place glorious crowns. They will receive from the Lord's hand unfading garlands.[u] God will wipe away every tear from their eyes[v] and will grant them such inexpressible joy that they will never again think of the tribulations they had to suffer. All pain will be far surpassed by glorious joy.

As Saint Paul says: "I consider that the sufferings of this time are not worth comparing with the glory that will be revealed to us."[w] He also says,

l. Col. 1:24.
m. 1 Pet. 4:15–16.
n. James 1:2.
o. Matt. 24:13.
p. Ecclus. 4:28.
q. Jth. 8:16.
r. Matt. 10:32.
s. Mark 8:38.
t. Luke 12:9.
u. Cf. Wisd. of Sol. 5:16; 1 Pet. 5:4; Rev. 2:10.
v. Rev. 7:17.
w. Rom. 8:18.

"Our suffering, which is [slight and][61] small, will bring forth a glory that is great and splendid beyond all measure."[a] Both Saint Paul and Saint John tell us that we shall be given a new heavenly nature and shall conform to the Lord, for we shall see him as he is;[b] and our bodies will be changed and will conform to his own body in its transfigured state.[c] Indeed, the chosen will be beacons and shine in their Father's kingdom like the beautiful, bright sun.[d] What a glorious kingdom God has prepared and given to his own, a kingdom such as no eye has ever seen, no ear has ever heard, and no human heart conceived.[e] The holy prophet [Ezra] and Paul tell us that the Lord will give eternal rest and peace to his own and no one shall offend them any longer;[f] they shall be with God the Father and with Jesus Christ the king; they shall sit at the table in God's kingdom with Abraham, Isaac, and Jacob,[g] and with all the prophets and saints of God; and they shall live and soar with the angels and hosts of heaven for ever and ever.

Indeed, neither I nor any of the saints can express or tell of the great and ineffable joy [and glory][62] that God will grant the chosen. The saints and prophets speak of it throughout scripture, but in my weakness I neither can nor want to explain it. Those who understand or grasp this ought to prepare and dispatch their hearts in preparation to fight and battle for this glory, with zeal and great joy, for there must be a fight for its sake! May God the Lord help you and all of us to gain the victory in this battle and win the treasure[h] through his child, Jesus Christ our Lord. To him be praise, honor, thanks, and all glory in his sovereign majesty for ever and ever. Amen.

Furthermore, beloved brothers and sisters, I want to let you know how things are with us here. The Lord is with us, although we suffer much. Yet that is right and good, and we praise and thank God for it with all our hearts. We live in deep and holy love, in the peace[63] and unity of the Holy Spirit,[i] while all the time expecting many great trials and persecution, even

a. 2 Cor. 4:17.
b. 1 Cor. 15:53–54; 1 John 3:2.
c. Cf. Phil. 3:21.
d. Cf. Matt. 13:43.
e. 1 Cor. 2:9.
f. 2 Esd. 7:91–98; Heb. 4:3, 9.
g. Matt. 8:11.
h. 1 Cor. 9:24.
i. Eph. 4:3.

greater than what we are suffering now. Whatever the Lord commands, may it be so, through his great mercy! With deep longing we wait for the redemption of our bodies,[j] for the Sabbath when we rest from all trial and labor and from all works of our own,[k] when we leave behind these earthly shelters so that our soul and spirit may at last find rest and eternal peace.[l] [64] We are working for this divine homeland with great yearning, since we have no peace or rest in this wretched wilderness. We have no lasting city here, but we are awaiting the one that is to come.[m] Brother Offrus [Griesinger] has arrived, and many other brothers and sisters.[65] Thank God, the Lord protected them and brought them safely to us. Their arrival gave us much joy, and we praised God for it with exaltation and exuberance. There are not many brothers and sisters left now in the mountains [of Tyrol].

Finally, beloved children of God, the brothers Hans [Amon], Georg Fasser, Offrus [Griesinger], Leonhart, Wilhelm,[66] and all the ministers of the church of God here greet you,[67] together with the holy fellowship, indeed every one of God's children. We greet you many hundred thousand times in holy, divine love, with our unadulterated love and the holy, heavenly kiss of our Lord and savior, Jesus Christ, from the depths of our hearts with exaltation and exuberance. [Amen.][68] And I, Jakob, an unworthy minister of our Lord Jesus Christ and of his holy [Christian][69] fellowship, greet you with all my heart many hundred thousand times with the holy kiss of my heart, in brotherly and Christian love.

I have written this to you with my own hand in the holy and pure love of God. May my simple writing and holy, faithful admonition be a comfort to you, even though I would much rather speak with you face to face, but this may not be possible now. So I commend you to God, to his gracious care and protection. May you be kept under his powerful arm and under the wings of his divine mercy. May he be with you forever, and may he gather us and bring all into his peace through his Holy Spirit. May he hold us to each other and to himself in his truth and empower us until our end, and eternally, through our Lord Jesus Christ. To him be praise, honor, and glory from our hearts, for ever and ever. Amen.

---

j. Rom. 8:23.
k. Heb. 4:9–10.
l. 2 Cor. 5:2.
m. Heb. 13:14.

Letter 4

Written from the open heath in Moravia to the governor of Moravia, 1535 [70]

Written on the open heath near Tracht after the community was driven away from Auspitz in 1535, this letter by Hutter is addressed to the governor of Moravia, Johann Kuna von Kunstadt (see last paragraph of CHR-14*). Different in style and tone from any of his other letters, it appeals to the governor on behalf of the distressed brothers and sisters and warns him of God's punishment.*

[In 1535 a great persecution took place in the Margraviate of Moravia and the true, devout believers in Christ were forcefully driven out of their houses and homes. They had to lie on the heath under the open sky with their elderly, sick, and weak, and their small children. The Moravian lords seriously ordered them, on command of King Ferdinand, to leave the land, but they were not able to obey this order (without God's command). For this reason our dear and faithful brother Jakob Hutter wrote to the Governor of Moravia, on his own and all the brethren's behalf, what he and the whole fellowship felt, earnestly yet obedient and pleading, in their pressing need, as follows:] [71]

[A copy of the letter Jakob Hutter wrote on behalf of himself and all the brethren to the governor of Moravia in 1535.] [72]

We, as those who are brothers and devotees of God and of his divine truth, and as authentic witnesses of our Lord Jesus Christ, have been driven out of many countries for the sake of God's name [and his truth]. [73] We came here to Moravia, where we have been gathered into a fellowship and are living together under the lord marshal through the care and protection of the Almighty, to whom alone we give praise and honor and declare his glory, forever.

We want to let you know, dear governor of the land of Moravia, that we received the order and message delivered by your servants, as you well know. We already answered you by word of mouth, and now want to do the same in writing, as follows: We have fled the world and all its unjust

Ein abgeschrifft od=
er Sendbrüeff so Jacob
Hüetter füre sich selbs und
an stat aller Brüeder
dem Lanndts haubt=
man im märhern züe
geschriben hat.
Anno 1.5.35. Jar.

Wier Brüeder und
lieb haber Gots und seiner Götlich=
en warhait, und warhafftige zeug=
en unsers Herren Jesu Christi, die
wier vertriben seindt aus villen
landen, und des namen gotes und
umb seiner götlichen warhait wil=
len, und hieher ins Märher=
landt komen, und versamlet un

Letter 4 (Codex 3)

and godless nature. We believe in God the Almighty and in his son, our Lord Jesus Christ. He will protect us from all such evil for evermore. We have given and devoted ourselves to God, the Lord, to live by his divine will and keep his commandments according to the example of our Lord Jesus Christ.

Because we serve him, do his will, keep his commandments, and leave behind all sin and injustice, we are therefore persecuted and despised by the whole world and robbed of all our goods. The same was done to all the saints, to the prophets, and also to Christ himself. Especially King Ferdinand, [the prince of darkness,][74] that cruel tyrant and enemy of divine truth and justice, mercilessly put many of our innocent brothers and sisters to death, murdering and killing them. He has also robbed us of house and home, all our goods, driven us out, and persecuted us terribly. But through God's grace and assistance we were able to travel or move here to Moravia, and have lived here for a time, recently under the lord marshal. We have not troubled or harmed anyone and have lived faithfully [by hard work][75] in the fear of God. Everybody will confirm this. But now even the marshal has given us notice and forced us to leave our houses and property.

So we now find ourselves out in the wilderness, in a desolate meadow under the open sky. This we accept patiently, praising God that he has made us worthy to suffer for the sake of his name. But for your sakes we feel pain and heartache, that you treat God's devout children so cruelly. We cry to him about your hardheartedness and about the enormous wrongs and injustice that increase daily. Day and night we plead with God, the Lord, to protect and keep us from evil, commending to him our cares, so that he might lead us through, according to his divine will and his [fatherly][76] mercy. And he will surely do so; he is our captain and protector and will go to battle for us. The holy prophet Isaiah and the devout prophet Ezra foretold that all who turn away from and abandon evil and all injustice, all who love and fear God from their hearts, who serve him and keep his commandments, are bound to be robbed and driven and cast away from their homes.[a] This shows that we are [children of God and that he is our father, that we are][77] fellow heirs of his glory,[b]

a. Isa. 59:15; 2 Esd. 16:70–75.
b. Rom. 8:17.

that we love him and are pleasing to him, as are all the saints. Therefore, we gladly suffer such things with great patience, and our hearts are comforted by his Holy Spirit.[c]

Behold, woe and double woe[d] to all who would persecute, exile, and hate us without cause, simply because we stand for God's truth! Their demise, punishment, and condemnation is approaching and will overtake them with terror, here and in eternity. According to his holy prophets, God wants to, and also shall, terrifyingly call them to account for all the innocent blood and all the tribulations of his saints.[e]

Now since you have commanded us to leave without delay, we give you this answer: We know of no place to go, and what burdens us especially is that we are surrounded by the king's lands. In every direction we would walk straight into the jaws of robbers and tyrants, like sheep cast among ravenous wolves and ferocious lions.[f] Besides, we have among us many ailing widows and orphans, many sick people and small, uneducated children who cannot help themselves and are unable to walk or travel. That godless tyrant Ferdinand, [that prince of darkness,][78] an enemy of divine truth and justice, had their fathers and mothers murdered. He also robbed them of their goods. These very same widows and orphans, sick people and small children, are entrusted to us by God the Almighty, who commands us to feed, clothe, and house them, and in every way to serve them from our hearts in all matters. So we cannot, and nor do we want to, abandon them or send them away – truly, may God protect and keep us forever from doing that![g] We dare not disobey God's commands for the sake of human commands, though it cost us life and limb, for we must obey God rather than humans,[h] [as Saint Peter says].[79]

We have not had time to sell our homes and possessions, which we earned by hard labor, by the sweat of our brows,[i] and which rightly belong to us before God and man. These properties are yet to be sold (though we desperately need them),[80] and in addition, we also need time because

c. Acts 3:18; Heb. 12:2.
d. Cf. Rev. 8:13.
e. Deut. 32:35–43; Joel 3:21; Jth. 8:16–23.
f. Matt. 10:16.
g. Acts 5:29.
h. Acts 4:19.
i. Gen. 3:19.

of the sick, the widows and orphans, and also the small children. Praise God, there are not just a few but many of these helpless ones among us, about as many as there are able-bodied people. Now we are out on the open meadows, with no one being harmed, as God wills. We do not want or desire to cause anyone suffering or wrong, not even our worst enemy, be it Ferdinand nor anyone else, great or small. All we do, our words and deeds, our conduct, our way of life, are there for everyone to see. Rather than knowingly wrong anybody to the value of a penny, we would let ourselves be robbed of a hundred guilders. Rather than strike our worst enemy with our hand – to say nothing of spears, swords, and halberds such as the world uses – we would die and let our own lives be taken.

As anyone can see clearly, we have no physical weapons, neither spears nor muskets. No, all in all, what we preach is what we speak, and how we live and behave: that one should live in peace and unity in God's truth and justice, as the true followers of Christ. Our words and our way of life are transparent for all to see; we are not ashamed of giving an account of ourselves to anyone. [It does not trouble us that][81] many evil things are said about us, for Christ foretold all this. Such has been the lot of all believers, of Christ himself, and of all his apostles, from the beginning.[a]

It is rumored that we took possession of the field with so many thousands, as if we were going to war, but only someone who has no knowledge of us, or someone who is up to no good, a lying scoundrel, could talk like that. We lament to God that there are so few devout people (such as we truly are). We declare our wish that all the world were like us. We would like to convince and turn all people to this faith, for that would mean the end of warfare and injustice.

Next, as a further response, we would like to say that at this time we do not know where we could go to leave the country. May God, the Lord in heaven, provide and show us where to go! We simply cannot be denied a place in this country or on earth. For the earth is the Lord's, and all that is in it belongs to our God in heaven.[b] Besides, if we agreed to depart and planned to do so, we might not be able to hold to that, for we are in God's

a. E.g., Matt. 5:10–12; Luke 6:22–23, 11:50; John 16:2; 1 Pet. 4:13–14.
b. Ps. 24:1; 1 Cor. 10:26.

hand and he does with us whatever he will. Perhaps God wills that we remain in this country to test our faith. This we do not know, but we trust in the eternal and true God.

On the other hand, we state as follows: although we are being persecuted and driven out, if almighty God in heaven showed us enough cause or gave a sufficient sign to depart from the country and move somewhere else, that he willed such, then we would do it gladly, without waiting for an ordinance. Once God's will concerning where we should go is clear to us, we will not hesitate. [We pray fervently to God day and night to lead us where he will.][82] We will not and cannot disobey his divine will. Neither can you, even if you try to hinder it. God the Almighty may suddenly reveal to us, even overnight, that we should leave you. Then we will not delay but would be prepared to live according to his will – whether to depart or to die. Perhaps you are not worthy or meritorious as to have us among you any longer.

Therefore, woe and double woe to you Moravian lords for eternity, because you have approved of, and assented to, Ferdinand, the awful tyrant and enemy of divine truth, and agreed to exile those who are devout and God-fearing from your lands; you fear a mortal, useless man more than the living, eternal, almighty God and Lord, and you are willing to expel and ruthlessly persecute the children of God, old and young, even the ailing, and afflicted widows and orphans, delivering them up mercilessly to plunder, anxiety, deprivation, with much pain, tribulation, ailment and extreme poverty. It is as if you strangled them with your own hands. It would be more considerate and preferable for us to be killed and murdered for the Lord's sake than to witness such misery being inflicted on innocent, God-fearing hearts. You will have to pay dearly for it, and you will have no excuse, even less so than Pilate, who also did not really want to crucify and kill the Lord Jesus.[c] Yet it was out of fear and dread of the emperor when the Jews threatened him (by God's direction), that Pilate condemned innocent blood. You do the same thing, using the king as your excuse. But God has made it known through the mouth of his holy prophets that he will avenge innocent blood in a terrifying and horrific way, against all who stain their hands with it.[d]

---

c. John 19:6–12.
d. Joel 3:19; 2 Esd. 15:5–27; Jth. 8:14–17.

Therefore, great misfortune, misery and distress, deprivation and great tribulation, pain and heartfelt sorrow will come upon you, even including woe, hurt, and martyrdom for this reason, and they are ordained for you by God in heaven, in this life and forever. We state and proclaim this to you in the name of our Lord Jesus Christ, that you will certainly not be spared. You will soon see and experience that we have spoken to you the divine truth in the name of our Lord Jesus Christ as a testimony against you and all who act or sin against God.

We wish all of you [to turn to the living God so that you][83] could escape such a fate. How we wish and desire that you and all people might be saved with us and inherit eternal life. So we plead with you for the sake of God to accept his word and our warning amicably, and in the best way possible, and to take them to heart. For we speak and testify to what we know, which is the truth before God.[a] We do this out of the pure, divine fear and divine love, which we feel toward God the Lord, and toward all humankind.

With this we entrust ourselves to the care and protection of the eternal Lord. May he be gracious to us and be with us forever, through Jesus Christ. Amen. As for you, may God the Lord allow you to recognize his fatherly warning and chastisement, and may he be merciful to you through our Lord Jesus Christ, according to his divine will. Amen.

[From us brothers and fellow sufferers in the suffering of Christ, driven into the fields for the sake of the word of God and the witness of Jesus Christ.][84]

---

a. John 3:32; Acts 4:20.

Letter 5

Written from Tyrol
to the fellowship in Moravia, 1535 [85]

Hutter was in Auspitz, Moravia, from August 1533 until July 1535. Forced to leave Moravia because of the letter he had written to the governor (L-4), he returned to Tyrol for what would be his final mission before his arrest. This is the first of four letters he wrote on that mission trip.[86]

[Summary: He gives his greetings and reminds them of God's grace, proven in Christ, and how the world is opposed to them. He is glad how well they are doing and speaks of his work and efforts, with thanks to God. He speaks of his sorrow in parting from them, and how the Lord has led them safely. There is much to do,[b] and few helpers. He encourages them to consult one another. He explains the delay in sending a message and says he is also waiting for news from them. He speaks of his longing for them and that he cannot forget them, of his sorrow that they are separated and that it is not his fault. He comforts them and admonishes them to remain faithful and to remember him in prayer. He boasts of Sister Nändl's faithfulness and closes with greetings.][87]

[To the chosen and appointed saints, to those who are hunted, and scattered for the Lord's sake, wherever they are throughout all Moravia, who are in tribulation, in misery and in poverty, to my most dearly beloved brothers and sisters in the Lord according to the holy faith, my dear children and fellow sufferers, to the genuine lovers of the living God – may this epistle reach you.][88]

From Jakob, an unworthy minister of God and apostle of Jesus Christ and his holy fellowship, his dear bride,[c] whom he purified and washed with his own blood: From the depth of my heart I wish grace, peace, and everlasting mercy to all the chosen saints, my dearly beloved brothers and sisters in the Lord and in the holy faith; to my coveted, beloved, and obedient children, wherever they are in all of Moravia, hunted and

---

b. Matt. 9:37.
c. Eph. 5:25–27.

204

Volgen 5. Tröstliche Epistlen. Von Unserem Lieben Und getreiwen Brueder Jacob Huetter.

Die Erste An Die Gemain Gottes In Märhern.

Letter 5 (Codex 1)

scattered by tribulation, who suffer distress and poverty for the sake of the Lord. May God our Father in the heavenly kingdom, who is the father of all grace and mercy, the God of all comfort, who consoles and strengthens you,[a] give you help in all things and stand by you in your distress and trouble, through our Lord Jesus Christ. Amen.

You holy, devout, and chosen children of the living God, my most beloved, fellow members in the body of Jesus Christ – what mighty things has God done for us in his inexpressible mercy. We shall never praise and glorify him enough for this, and can never thank him enough, even in all eternity! Through his son, Jesus Christ he redeems us from everlasting death and grants us eternal life[b] if we remain on the way of Christ to the end.

O my dear children, how great is the Father's love from the heavenly kingdom for you, because you also love him and keep his commandments, obey his holy will, and follow the footsteps of Christ,[c] living in obedience and walking according to his rule and provision! The hosts of heavenly creatures rejoice over you and constantly praise and glorify God for this reason. Given that God finds pleasure in you and has such an inexpressible love for you, which he then showed you and proved through the grace-filled act of the advent[89] and costly[90] death of his most dearly beloved son, Jesus Christ. For through him you have become dear and acceptable[91] to God, and now you are his dear, chosen children, witnesses to his holy eternal truth and fellow heirs of his almighty glory. You are partakers of his divine nature,[d] your citizenship[e] is in heaven, and your society is in God's midst,[f] with [his heavenly hosts in][92] his heavenly, eternal, future Jerusalem. God has become your gracious and merciful Father and your best friend.[g] In this way, you may expect from him nothing but pure, grand, and inexpressible grace and love and mercy, and in general, every good thing and total fatherly friendship. May his most holy and almighty name be exalted, honored, blessed, and praised in heaven above, on the

a. 2 Cor. 1:3–4.
b. Heb. 3:14.
c. 1 Pet. 2:21.
d. 2 Pet. 1:4.
e. Phil. 3:20.
f. Cf. 1 John 3 with *eure Gesellschaft ist bei Gott*, "your community is with God."
g. James 2:23.

throne of his glory. To him be praise, honor, and thanks from the depth of my heart, for you and for us and for all the saints, for his manifold, great, and boundless grace and mercy, which he has proved and demonstrated to us all, which he still does, through and through. Indeed, may he be praised and given thanks repeatedly through our dear Lord, Jesus Christ, for ever and ever. Amen.

But since you have forsaken the world and become followers of Christ and because you love God, for that reason God also loves you; and for the very reason that God loves you, the world hates you, and all godless people persecute and revile you. But rejoice[a] in that, for they did the same to all the prophets and to the Lord himself and to all saints from the beginning of the world.[b] It is a good and clear sign and seal of God's true favor.

O, my most dearly beloved brothers and sisters, please know that it was in my weakness and through his grace and acts of mercy that I have served the Lord and you up here in Tyrol and down in Moravia for quite some time. I have served faithfully among you, without any falsehood or deceit, out of divine, holy, sincere, brotherly love, day and night with great pain and heartache, even in spite of the many tribulations that I have encountered and that have befallen me in all sorts of ways. Indeed, I have cared for you as a devout and faithful father cares for his children, whom he truly, fully loves with his whole heart. This I can truthfully state before God and can very well boast about it.[c] I hope in, and entrust it to, my God and Father, for I will nevermore be ashamed as I boast of the end goal, which is nothing other than what the Lord alone seeks, who dwells in me and stands by me in all of my weaknesses, of which I have many. In that will I boast. You do know, my most dearly beloved children, what God recently permitted, and how it all occurred, namely, there was a severe and merciless persecution, which came upon me and you, for the Lord's sake. You prepared me for it, and gave me leave, sending me off with great, earnest prayer and crying out to the Lord. In general, you took leave of me in a way pleasing to God, as one who is your beloved brother, your minister and shepherd, as granted and

a. Matt. 5:12.
b. Luke 11:50.
c. 2 Cor. 10:8.

given by his grace and mercy. I consider myself quite unworthy of such respect, honor, and such heartfelt, divine, and brotherly love as you have shown me and proved in all things. May God in heaven reward you for this love and faithfulness to me and to all the saints. May he repay you here and in his eternal kingdom, through Jesus Christ. Amen. Indeed, you beloved[93] in the Lord, I cannot sufficiently thank God for the great love he has distributed into your hearts [and for the great love and faithfulness he, and you through him, have shown me].[94] O, you most dearly beloved brothers and sisters, my chosen children, I cannot [thank him enough or][95] find words to behold or express it adequately, but may God be exalted and praised in all these ways. Praise, honor, and thanks to him with our whole hearts, through Jesus Christ for ever and ever. Amen.

But now, most dearly beloved brothers and sisters, I left you at your request and wish, according to your advice and resolution, which you arrived at by the Lord's leading, with great sorrow and anguish of heart, as you know, while obeying the will of the living God in heaven. Yes, I left you with weeping and many a deep sigh, and the pain is still in my heart to this moment and will remain until God sends comfort – as I know he will surely do. May the Lord give me and all of us patience and endurance to wait for his comfort and the fulfillment of his promise. Yet the Lord has comforted me already so that the deep sorrow and pain would not be too great for me. For God is faithful and true and will not let us be tried beyond what we can bear; when temptation comes he provides a way out at the same time so that we can endure it, as Saint Paul writes.[d] These words are really true; I have experienced it many times. Experience makes one grow in wisdom and in understanding of God's ways, and it teaches hope and childlike trust in God.[e]

Now dear brothers and sisters, I want to let you know how we are. [After we left you, in the name of the Lord, as I have written, God][96] the Lord blessed our journey and hastened our way here into the Puster and Adige valleys. Here we found our brothers and sisters, who welcomed and received us with great joy and divine love [as the Lord himself].[97] We reported to one another the state of matters everywhere. Since then

d. 1 Cor. 10:13.
e. Rom. 5:4.

we have been faithfully and diligently traveling back and forth in the mountains and valleys, visiting those who hunger and thirst for the truth. We found quite a few, and they received us with joy and gratitude and with eager hearts. We proclaimed and preached the truth [and God's word] and the [holy][98] gospel and several accepted the truth and devoted themselves to God.

And the almighty God and Father has again established a fellowship here in Tyrol and increased his people daily, time and again adding to his holy fellowship here those who are being saved.[a] [We have so much work to do for the Lord],[99] day and night. We often wish we could be in many places at once and wish there were more of us, ministers and other brothers fitted for the task who are able and willing to carry out God's work. For the harvest is very ripe, but the workers are few.[b]

The resolution and counsel that I should come here was neither made in vain nor was it for naught, nor without great cause; it did not come from humans or from the flesh,[c] but from God [our Father in heaven],[100] and it was absolutely necessary. But when I have said and written that more of us from down there [i.e., Moravia] are needed up here, I do not mean that everybody should of their own volition and initiative come running here now, without the permission and knowledge and will of the devout ministers of the Lord and all his children. We will not receive anyone who comes like this, and God will also punish them from heaven. But whoever comes in divine love, in the fear of God and in the truth, with the counsel and will of God and his saints, we will receive them with much joy and deep gratitude, in divine, fire-like, holy, brotherly love, as we would receive the Lord himself.[d] They shall be welcomed a thousand times over in the Lord.

As far as we know, the godless tyrants, the enemies of the truth who have the power to kill, do not yet know that we are here. May God in heaven make them blind and unaware of it for a long time.

Yet it is not for my own sake that I wish this, as if I feared for my life; I thank and praise God for truly taking all my fear away, and I hope to

a. Acts 2:47.
b. Matt. 9:37.
c. Cf. Matt. 16:17; Gal. 1:11–12.
d. Gal. 4:14.

God that fear will never harm me. For the Lord's sake [and for the sake of his people],[101] I do not consider my life to have value. I have completely given, surrendered, and sacrificed my body and life to the Lord; with all my heart I am willing to suffer and die for his sake and for his truth. Whatever he lays upon me, whatever is a service to his glory and praise and is most useful for his holy, dear children [and of greatest benefit to his fellowship][102] – that is what I desire to do. It is for the sake of those who are weak and young and those who have not yet been edified that I hope our lives are spared until God's fire has been so brightly kindled in them and his work so well established that even great floods and torrents of rain will not be able to quench[e] that fire. Therefore, I pray to God for this to be done according to his fatherly, holy will, and ask you, my most dearly beloved fellow members, to do the same if you love us deeply. I know in my heart that you do, and of this I am certain (and I have no doubt at all that you feel complete love for us, in your hearts and in truth before God). For I know all of you deeply, just as a devoted shepherd knows his sheep,[f] and I am sure that you also know me and that it is quite apparent to you who I am.

Yet I am fully aware that tribulation and severe persecution is bound to break out before too long, perhaps immediately, unless God himself delays or alters it for his name's sake and for the sake of his people. For they are growing fierce and very bloodthirsty against the devout. There is a great hue and cry all over the country and everyone talks about you, how we have been persecuted and driven out. They spread all kinds of stories, as they usually do.

I know, most beloved ones, that you have been waiting anxiously for some news of us, and it is long overdue. I have had this in mind the whole time, that I had agreed to send you word at the earliest possible opportunity, provided that I were able to do so and that God would allow it. I have not forgotten you for a single hour, as my God in heaven knows. This is the reason for the delay: Brother Jeronimus does not know the way back, and for a long time we were not able to reach brother Kränzler, for he was ill at Sterzing.[103] He also does not know all the roads in the Puster

e. Song of Sol. 8:6–7.
f. John 10:14.

Valley, nor does he know the many and various people who have asked about God. [So we turned to the most urgent task of making visits all over the place in order to acquaint the other brothers with the trails and villages, and at the same time we did some work for the Lord.][104] That is why I was not able to easily dispense with brother Michel. Actually I still need him very badly, but out of the love which he also brings to you, I do not want to detain him any longer, so I hurried him along, sending him on his way to bring you our consolation. I am hopeful that the Lord will send me more help through you. I hope you will accept this as something good, and in the best way possible, and to recognize and grant this in the love of God.

Furthermore, beloved brothers and fellow members, I have been waiting incessantly with heartfelt yearning, with sighs and expectation, for what seems like an eternity, for a message from you. My heart has no rest, nor has my body repose, day or night. My soul and spirit long for you deeply with much yearning and sighs, for you are the true, living letter written in my heart, not with a quill and ink but by God's finger[a] – that is, by his word and spirit and his [eternal, holy][105] love. This letter, which is you, is being read incessantly, every hour, again and again, for eternity.

O, my dearest children, what great pain and constant sorrow I bear! I think of you day and night, indeed, the whole time sighing with misery and spilling many heartfelt and burning tears, which I shed for you. Not that you have given me reason to be ashamed of you but because of my deep love for you, like a devoted father thinking of his most dearly beloved, who are far from him and in great misery; not knowing how they are, he worries that they are suffering miserably in great destitution. So it is with me. My God in heaven knows I am not lying;[b] the Lord is my witness that I speak the truth before God and before you from my whole heart.

How often my eyes and my heart overflow! I pour out my grief to God in heaven and will go on crying to him in eternity until he comforts me. The greatest distress and pain I've experienced on account of you has been to hear that you are being so scattered in this way.[106] O God in heaven, I cannot cry out to you enough! With God's help I would rather suffer

a. 2 Cor. 3:2–3.
b. 2 Cor. 11:31.

another bout of persecution and great pain and martyrdom, which I could endure if only you could remain together in divine love. I am speaking of those who truly want to remain together through God's love and spirit. Yet it is not only the physical scattering or separation that worries me, but the greater and everlasting damage to the soul, which I must worry about and fear. May God protect the devout from that happening.

O you, my most beloved lambs, my brothers and sisters, where would I seek to find you again! How I enjoyed bringing this fellowship together in divine love, with such diligence, with much difficulty and labor, sometimes with great pain. And now, ravenous wolves come to scatter, to desolate, to crush with their claws; and what is left they trample underfoot, as the holy prophet Daniel says.[c] What shall I say? May God in the kingdom of heaven have pity, for my heart wants nothing more than to break in two.

God knows, my dearest children, that I am hardly able nor wanting to write, due to my pain and weeping. But that is not because my conscience accuses me of anything, nor that I feel guilt for causing the evacuation – no, I am not to be blamed for it. I have nothing to do with it, as my God well knows. Rather, it has been a complete abomination and a heartache for me, and I have always faithfully warned of it and fought against it. But whatever the Lord allows those godless rogues and enemies of truth, who persecute me and you, who have hunted and scattered us, I can do no more than endure it with patience and sorrow, accepting it and letting it happen. For that reason no one should think I am to blame. I am free of guilt and my heart is therefore free. I am innocent of all blood; it is the godless, and the children of the devil, who have made it happen with his hunting dogs or hounds of hell, and ravening wolves, as scripture says.[d] Yet the whole time my brothers and helpers and I have faithfully gathered you and held you together.

The whole time I spoke to you about such and preached through God's grace and spirit. O, so many times and incessantly I preached to you for nearly two whole years of what has now resulted and transpired! How thoroughly and diligently this was said and declared to you, so that you

c. Dan. 7:19.
d. Matt. 7:15; Acts 20:20; Phil. 3:2.

would conform yourselves to this way and live accordingly, and how it behooves you to do this, to listen to and hold onto God's word diligently, and to take it into your hearts, so that you could turn to it in times of need. For God likes to cause his word to become even dearer among you, taking us from you or you from us, in whatever way he wills, as I have said to you; also that later, even without us, you continue to believe and trust God, to serve and acknowledge him, to have him always before your eyes, and to fear and also love him with your hearts, and love one another as his devout children. If you are eager always to do God's will, keep his commandments, and endure in his truth to the end, then you will be blessed and rejoice with us eternally, and ultimately that you shall also live this way, in all respects, before God and all the saints and all peoples.

And already the hour has come. Happy are they who listened carefully to God's word, who kept it, and who now live and walk faithfully according to it! My most dearly beloved brothers and sisters, if only God would have it that I could ward off your affliction with my own body. How willingly would I present my cheeks, my back, and all my limbs to the torturers and surrender my body to whatever torment and pain, with the help of God! But why say this? We cannot change anything. May God himself be our shepherd and watchman, so that none are lost and snatched out of his hand.[a] The hour of tribulation has truly come upon us. May God give us endurance to be steadfast in our hope for comfort and joy.

Just as the prophet Jeremiah[107] said: O you, my beloved and holy city of the Most High, how shall I mourn you![b] You, the holy pleasure garden of the Lord, what great joy and pleasure I have often had in you![c] How many beautiful, dear, and fragrant flowers bloomed in you and gave great pleasure to the Lord![d] O you holy people, you heavenly and eternal Jerusalem, happy are those who speak well of you and wish you well, but woe to all who speak evil of you, who persecute and destroy you! The Lord will requite them for their deeds and their works. But those who mourn you and grieve with you, those who suffer with you will also be happy

a. John 10:28–29.
b. Jer. 9:1.
c. Cf. Isa. 51:3; Ezek. 36:35.
d. Cf. Jer. 31:12; Hos. 14:5–7.

and rejoice with you, as God says through his prophets and apostles.[e] This promise comforts and gladdens my spirit and heart, for I faithfully mourn with you, and I suffer and desire to suffer. Therefore I hope to share in your comfort too. For I am certain before God and in the Lord Jesus Christ that I must not and cannot ever forget or forsake you. About you, my most dearly beloved, I can truly say with David: If I forget you, may God also forget me; I would rather forget my right hand or my soul than forget you.[f]

O, my dearest and chosen children, may it be God's will in the kingdom of heaven that we might still see and look upon one another in divine love on this earth – you to me and me to you. O that the Almighty and merciful God and Father might still gather us in! How I long to see this; how dearly my soul and spirit yearn for it! How much I want to experience that day! I wish it for your sake, even if I would have to suffer and endure and undergo much for it. For my own sake I do not desire to live. Rather, I would much prefer to be home with my heavenly Father and with the throng of those who celebrate and rest from their labor, being freed from challenges, toil, and from all sorts of tribulation, and to live without a care, unburdened, as David says.[g]

But now, my dearest children, I could neither prevent what has happened nor the situation you and I are in at present, and I am still unable to do anything, though it breaks my heart and I could die of sorrow. How gladly and willingly I would offer my life [and endure great torture][108] if only I could change your lot! If only God would grant that I could bear all the pain for you! I know, of course, that my worries and my grief and weeping are of no gain, yet I cannot desist for it is love, the spirit of God, which compels and propels me in this way. I plead with you and admonish you, my dearest children, through the great love and sincere mercy of God, that you yearn for your actions and your lives to conform to God's will and the example and teaching of Christ Jesus. And it is just as I have been preaching and teaching you; it is thus right before God – and this you must not doubt – that is the divine truth and the righteous way,

---

e. 1 Cor. 12:26.
f. Cf. Ps. 137:5–6.
g. The reference to David is unclear, but see, e.g., Pss. 23, 127.

and you have heard from us verbally, constantly through God's grace and spirit, which has been clearly shown to you in truth, and it is my desire to testify to it with my blood, with God's help and grace.

If you love God with all your hearts and keep his commandments you will be blessed. Eagerly follow his holy will without ceasing in whatever you do, and in the midst of this godless generation, bring honor to the Lord and his saints and be a prize for them. Shine[a] like a light amidst the darkness. Let love flow among you from pure and whole hearts like newborn infants, who are reborn out of God's word and spirit. Serve each other faithfully and lovingly in all things, each one of you using the gifts you received from God, and do it willingly and gladly, without any grumbling or disagreement.[b] For it is only those who do what is right willingly and gladly, with pleasure and joy, and serve God and his people, in divine, holy love and being propelled through God's love and spirit – they are the ones God loves and helps; and whoever voluntarily, with their whole heart, chooses to serve God the Lord and to be obedient in all things, God takes pleasure and delight in them, as his beloved children.

Therefore, you must never tire of doing good[c] or weaken in your determination. Do not become lazy or sleepy in good works and in being the Lord's disciples. See to it that the love and the actual, divine light you have toward God and his saints is not extinguished in your hearts. Never look back or consider what you left behind, but always press on toward your goal[d] in order to achieve the prize and be crowned. Show each other utmost discipline and honor, and utmost mutual willingness, being generous, loving, amicable, brotherly, sincere, as children of God and disciples. Be patient in every tribulation as disciples and lambs of Christ. Remain of sound mind and alert day and night toward God and remain steadfast in the teachings of the holy apostles, which you have heard, and in the fellowship of Jesus Christ and all the saints. Continue in the breaking of bread, in which the life and love of Jesus Christ is demonstrated and the love that is and should be among us; remain in prayer to

a. Eph. 5:8.
b. Phil. 2:14.
c. Gal. 6:9; 2 Thess. 3:13.
d. Phil. 3:13–14.

God both day and night, in the Spirit and in truth,[e] with a firm faith in our gracious Father in the kingdom of heaven.

Wake up, you devout Christian, holy hearts, and lift your heads and hearts up to God our heavenly Father! Let your joy and pleasure be solely in him and in his holy law, and have your mind, soul, and spirit, and your whole heart permanently turned toward God in heaven. Watch day and night with diligence, full of holiness, in complete righteousness, truth, and with a pure, genuine, and holy heart, in order to see your bridegroom and king, your redeemer and savior, the prince of life and the genuine, chief shepherd, who is coming soon and is not far off, namely, Jesus Christ, our beloved Lord and master. Put on the wedding garment of holiness and honor, which is love, faith, hope, righteousness, and truth – yes, put on Jesus Christ, the Son of God.[f] Arm yourselves with the good works that come from a true, living, and holy faith and from a holy, God-fearing heart, so that you are found worthy of entering into his joy and glory. Amen.

O most beloved ones, wake up! Wake up for the Lord's sake, for your king is coming with great power and glory! Time is running out, and the hour has come. The great and terrible Day of the Lord, which will come upon all people, is near at hand. The signs and wonders by which we are to recognize it are here. They are gaining momentum in the most obvious way, for every kind of sin, every kind of evil and injustice, is taking over. Love has grown cold[g] or is even becoming extinguished in many people. Everywhere the holy gospel is being proclaimed abundantly, and [the sound of it][h] [109] has gone out into the whole world. Many false prophets and antichrists have arisen,[i] and much innocent blood is being shed. The godless deception knows no bounds. As the holy prophets say, the abomination of desolation reigns with great force, and one can see it coming in its evil and sin[j] – yes, everything which the holy prophets and Christ himself spoke of is now rampant and imminent.

It has also come to fruition what many people say: "See how time passes, and every vision comes to nothing."[k] And as the days pass, many

e. John 4:24.
f. Rom. 13:14; Gal. 3:27.
g. Matt. 24:12.
h. Cf. Ps. 19:4; Rom. 10:18.
i. Cf. Matt. 24.
j. Cf. Dan. 11:31; 12:11; Matt. 24:15.
k. Ezek. 12:22.

scoffers appear who say, "Where is the promise of his coming? Everything is the same as it has always been!"[a] That is what Ezekiel and Saint Peter foretold. These scoffers deliberately refuse to listen.

What I fear most is that among us there will also be some who begin to say, as many others do, "Oh, my Lord will not come for a long time."[b] And they eat and drink with the godless and associate with them, beating and tormenting their fellow servants, just as Christ says concerning the wicked servant.[c] But the Lord will come upon them on a day and at an hour when they are not expecting or thinking about him. Just when they think everything is joyful and feel most secure, destruction will suddenly come upon them. God grant that this does not happen to many of us. It is not for nothing that the Lord said he will come like a thief in the night, when everybody is fast asleep and without a care in the world.[d]

O Lord God in the kingdom of heaven, I am worried that many of you who think you are his disciples, will be found asleep and unprepared for the Lord's coming. He himself warns us: "Be ready and prepared at all times. Watch constantly, every hour of the day and night, for you do not know the day or the hour when your Lord and king will come. He will come when you do not expect him, at an hour you do not know."[e] Take note of what Christ says, how he so faithfully and adamantly warns us: Therefore, watch and be ready every moment so that you are found worthy to enter with him. Each one must hold firmly to the Lord and his word until he is taken home, so that he is found holy, pure and devout, and obedient before God.[f]

So allow the tribulation and testing to come upon you and bear them patiently. Embrace the cross with great gratitude to God, for it is a blessed and glorious thing. If you accept it in this way, it becomes a noble gift of God's great love, grace, and mercy. For Christ says, "Blessed are all who bear suffering for my sake and are persecuted for the sake of divine truth and justice. They shall be comforted. The kingdom of heaven is theirs."[g]

---

a. 2 Pet. 3:3–4.
b. Matt. 24:47–50.
c. Matt. 18:21–35.
d. Matt. 24:43; Luke 12:39–40.
e. Mark 13:32–37.
f. Cf. Matt. 24:42.
g. Matt. 5:4, 10.

He also says, "Be comforted, my children, for your misery and sorrow shall turn into joy and great glory."[h] Isaiah says, "Rejoice and be glad and be full of wonder, all you who mourn for Jerusalem, for you will also rejoice with her."[i]

David says, "When the Lord ends our captivity, we shall be full of joy and our mouths will break into laughter, and our hearts and tongues will be full of praise and glory to God. We shall sow with tears but shall reap with gladness."[j] Here we weep and are full of great sorrow as we bear the precious seed, but then with great joy shall we bring our fruits of divine righteousness before God's countenance and receive the new fruit and the reward of both eternal life and the new Jerusalem. As scripture says, distress and sorrow precede glory, honor, and joy.[k] Saint Paul writes, "If we suffer with him, we shall be fellow heirs with him. And if we are patient, we are fellow rulers with him."[l] He says more than once, "Our suffering and tribulation bear no comparison with the glory that will be revealed to us."[m] In another place he says, "Our suffering, which is temporary and slight, achieves and will bring us splendid and all-surpassing glory and joy."[n] Saint Peter says,[110] "If we remain steadfast in the Lord through all kinds of tribulation, and live according to his word, then we will also be glad with him, having inexpressible joy and glory, which no human can express."[o]

So rejoice and be comforted, you holy and devout Christian hearts, for the reward from God will be great and it is not far off. How very much the holy prophets and all the saints have said about this! For if you cling to [God and his divine truth and][111] his holy fellowship and his holy covenant, remaining in complete righteousness and truth, battling courageously in every tribulation for the eternal, divine truth, even unto death, and if you witness faithfully to God in word and deed before this godless generation, and if you serve God and his children faithfully and are obedient in your hearts in all things; and if you overcome and battle

h. John 16:20.
i. Isa. 66:10.
j. Ps. 126.
k. E.g., Rom. 8:17.
l. Rom. 8:17.
m. Rom. 8:18.
n. 2 Cor. 4:17.
o. 1 Pet. 4:13.

courageously against the whole world, the devil, sin and death, hell, and your own selves, to fight your way out of this spiteful world into the future one and through this temporal death to eternal life, then, when you do this, God will set upon you a glorious crown, which will never fade, and will give you a kingdom [that will never end].[112] He will give you rest, peace, great joy, which will never be taken from you, and such glory which shall remain in eternity. He will transfigure your body to be like the glorified body of Jesus Christ, which shines better and more brightly than the sun.[a] You too will become illumined and shine like that in God's kingdom. God will dress you in fine white silk[b] and adorn you with gold and precious jewels.[c]

The Lord will descend from the throne of his glory with hosts of many thousand angels. He will awaken and gather his own with a mighty trumpet blast.[d] In truth he is already doing it now, in the Spirit. He will take you and all the chosen to himself with the multitude of his angels, and will lead you into his kingdom in the clouds of heaven. There, you with us altogether, shall be with the Lord for ever and ever and will reign with him, living and abiding with all the heavenly hosts and all the saints, [before God in his kingdom][113] righteously and with great and eternal, unspeakable joy for ever and ever. Amen.

May the Almighty, eternal, and merciful God, Father of the heavenly kingdom, help you and us all to enter there, through his child, Jesus Christ, our beloved Lord, to whom be praise, honor, and thanks, on high, in his kingly majesty, on the throne of his all-powerful glory, for ever and ever. Amen.

For the sake of the Lord, I and all of us together ask you to pray for us day and night, without ceasing.[e] We depend on it, and we will do the same for you. We see and experience and know that God hears your prayers in heaven above. Of course we know that you already pray for us, but we urge and admonish you to continue and not slacken but rather to increase your petitions as time goes on.

---

a. Matt. 17:2.
b. Cf. Ps. 91:4.
c. Cf. Ezek. 16:11, 13.
d. 1 Thess. 4:16–17.
e. 1 Thess. 5:17.

Our dear sister Nändl is still in forced confinement.[114] Though she is allowed to walk in the house and further, they will not let her go. We hope that the Lord will set her free very soon. We are planning to work toward this, if it is God's will. She is devout and has an honest heart, and stands in great fear of the Lord and has a deep love for God and for you and all the saints. We praise and honor God in heaven, for she has found such favor in his eyes. May she and we altogether be held constantly in his truth until the end, in his divine truth through Jesus Christ. Amen.

We sent a sister to see her, and she greets you all warmly in pure, holy love, faithfully and adamantly greeting you with the holy kiss of Christ, steadfastly in the Lord. Her heart is on fire in holy, divine love, which burns for you. The same is true of the beloved brothers and sisters here, the whole fellowship of God, in every shape and form, just as it is with our dear sister Nändl and with me, Jakob, a poor, miserable little worm, yet a minister and servant of the Lord through his abundant mercy, your apostle and shepherd; and – as I hope – your dear brother and companion in the tribulation and patience of Jesus Christ and his children.[f] From the depth of my heart I greet you a thousand times over, jointly and each of you individually, all of you who fear God and love his children, with the holy, heavenly, and pure kiss of our dear Lord Jesus Christ, in holy, brotherly, fervent, inviolable, Christian love, with the eternal, fatherly peace Christ has won and given us. My heart wishes this for you constantly, and my soul and spirit also bid you greetings at all times. Before God and all people my heart remembers you and speaks nothing but good of you, and I remember you in love, for truly I hold you dearly with my whole heart before God. May God grant that I might greet each one of you in person with my mouth and with my holy kiss. May the Lord in the kingdom of heaven, our most beloved Father, and my body, soul, and spirit be with you through Jesus Christ, for ever and ever. Amen.

Carried by brother Michel.

f. Rev. 1:9.

Letter 6

Written from Tyrol to the fellowship in Moravia, 1535 [115]

When Hutter wrote this letter he realized that the authorities were aware of his presence, which dates the letter to early October (see GOV-16). He expected to be captured and executed at any moment.

[Summary: With thanks to God he expresses his longing for them and the joy he and those with him received through his message. At the same time he speaks of his sorrow for those who have abandoned the truth. He tells of his compassion and admonishes them to remain faithful to the Lord. He and the others are doing well; while they are in danger, expecting the henchmen, the people are increasing daily. He tells of two who have been banned and sends greetings.] [116]

[Jakob, an unworthy servant and minister of the Lord Jesus Christ, to the chosen saints and children of God in Moravia, who are hunted and scattered in all directions for their witness to God and for the sake of his truth and his holy name. My beloved in the Lord,] [117] may the grace, peace, and everlasting mercy and benevolence of our God in heaven and his beatitude be with you, and all who are chosen through Jesus Christ.

[Dearly beloved children of the living God, wherever you may be in Moravia, scattered about and persecuted for the sake of divine truth and justice,] [118] I constantly thank and praise my God and plead for you together with my brothers and the members who are with me. For we are very much aware of your distress and affliction, your misery and poverty, beloved brothers and sisters, and our hearts are constantly pained for you. God in heaven knows that we bear this with you, that we suffer with you and fear for you. But God in heaven, the merciful Father of all grace and mercy, who is the righteous judge of all widows and orphans[a] and the comforter of all devout, afflicted Christian hearts, wants to support us in all our distresses, and wants to protect and guard us, delivering us from all tribulation. He wishes to provide a gracious outcome for you and for

a. Cf. Luke 18:2–8.

Die Dritt Epistel des Jacoben Hüeters An die gemein gottes Im landt Merheren

Letter 6 (Codex 10)

us and wants to comfort us and rescue us from our misery. Let us give all blessing, honor, and praise to this very same God and Lord, the father and creator of mercy and grace, in heaven above, for you and for us and for all saints through Jesus Christ, for ever and ever. Amen.

Most dearly beloved brothers and sisters in the Lord, not long ago I sent our brother Michel to you. When we, in God's presence, took leave of him with earnest supplications and crying out, I begged God to lead him safely and quickly to you and to prepare his pathway, so that you could be comforted in your misery. We have also prayed and cried out to God the Almighty that we might hear and receive a message of grace from you, which we have been anxiously awaiting, sometimes with great anguish. With this same brother Michel, I sent you a written report of everything that has happened here, to let you know how we are. We trust God, our loving Father, that through his angel he has sent, led, and directed our brother to you and that you received our message of the hope that is now in the Lord.

I want to tell you and describe briefly what has resulted and transpired since then and where matters stand, to bring you up to date, as God's spirit urges me. No sooner had we said goodbye to brother Michel than a brother arrived, bringing news of your situation, both written and oral. We welcomed him joyfully and gratefully as a beloved brother sent to us by God and by you. Dear brothers and children of the living God, what you wrote has now comforted us greatly.

We have read your letter over and over and thought much about what you wrote, about your devoutness and steadfastness, your great obedience and patience, your holy, Christian life, your uprightness and courage, the manly struggle and battle of the holy martyrs and God's witnesses, who are found among you, who, even while being martyred and while under torture, remained faithful and courageously confessed the truth to the Lord and battled to the end.

We cannot adequately praise and thank, exalt, and honor God the Lord. Yes, we and many other devout Christian hearts have been sincerely comforted, revived, and strengthened, and we have found new trust in the Lord through these reports. How zealously and deeply we long in our hearts, with moans and sighs and with divine zeal, to do as they have done. For they are an inspiration and an example to us. May God grant us this through his beloved son, Jesus Christ, to whom be praise and honor and heartfelt exaltation and gratitude in his highest heaven above, for ever and ever. Amen.

At the same time we are deeply saddened and pained, yet it is a divine sadness to hear and see how such abundant indignation and great injustice have been spreading everywhere. Many who had given themselves to God, who were our brothers and sisters, have lost the way because of the injustice, persecution, and deception that is present in the world; they have become godless and have broken their covenant with the Lord and his holy people. They look back[a] and once again join the devil and the world, becoming enemies of God and his children. Alas for those people – what a severe sentence, harsh judgment and heavy punishment they will receive from God! It would surely have been better for them if they had never known the truth,[b] although in that case they would also fall under God's punishment and judgment.

We have been told of several who have lost the way and whom you banned. However, this neither hurts nor weakens us, and it should not bother or harm us when God wills it, for we know that through tribulation and persecution and all the false prophets, even through the deceit and deception of the devil and Satan, those with superficial hearts and souls must be separated from the devout and upright, just as chaff is separated from wheat by the wind and dross from silver and gold by fire.[c] The holy prophets and Christ the son of God and his holy apostles have clearly foretold and shown that many will turn away from the cross of Jesus Christ and be led astray by false prophets, that many will be deceived and fall away from the Lord, his truth, and righteousness, and will forsake and hate his holy people. This happened already at the time of the holy prophets, and at the time of Christ and his apostles. So it should not discourage or weaken or bother us, nor separate us from the love of God.

Since we have been adequately warned that this would happen and we are well aware of it through God's saints as stated above, now let us turn

a. Cf. Gen. 19:26; Luke 9:62.
b. 2 Pet. 2:21.
c. Job 21:18; Pss. 1:4; 119:119; Zech. 13:9.

our eyes all the more to the devout, upright, obedient, and God-fearing and holy children of God, those who have remained steadfast till death, though there are few such as this in our era. And let us pay no attention to the evil, godless, unrighteous, and apostate,[a] however great their number and unspeakable their mass, such as it is.

Those who are devout and upright before God, who live and carry on in the truth and remain in it, enduring to the end, who battle courageously for the truth, who witness to the Lord in martyrdom and under torture and in every temptation, and who remain true to the Lord and his people in all matters – such people are worth more in God's eyes than a hundred thousand who are godless and apostate. We should also greatly value and deeply honor such people in our hearts. Let us learn from them and follow their example in the Lord. There are those who are of the Lord, and those in whom God's spirit dwells and who bear the living word of eternal life and bear the name of God in their hearts, as Saint Peter says,[b] even if countless numbers fall away, depart, and no longer walk with the Lord. Some of those who are now revealed as false and have been excluded by you already caused me concern earlier. May God protect and preserve us from following their example by falling into the snare in which the devil has trapped them. May God grant and protect us, that these things do not continue to happen and that they do not befall us further. O God in heaven, protect those who fear and seek you!

Beloved brothers and sisters, therefore we must be all the more God-fearing and genuine in the Lord, guarding carefully against the sins that cling to us and our innate weaknesses. As the apostle Paul says, "We must no longer let sin rule our mortal bodies, no longer give in to sin and the devil; nor let our members be used as weapons of unrighteousness or any sort of sin."[c] We want to be all the more diligent, loving God and his children, and have him before our eyes in all matters. Let us also be obedient and submissive, ready and able to do his work.[d] We bear that in our minds, and it should also be our endeavor. But God in the kingdom of heaven, the father of all mercy and truth, wants to accomplish and

---

a. Cf. Luke 15:7.
b. Cf. 1 Pet. 1:22–25.
c. Rom. 6:12–13.
d. Titus 3:1.

achieve this in us[e] to the glory of his holy name through his child, Jesus Christ. Amen.

Now again, for the third time,[119] we are bearing pain and sorrow with you in holy love and such anguish in our hearts, and we are suffering with you, in order that we might see and hear and know the truth and acknowledge your great tribulation and persecution, your pain and suffering, your misery and poverty. Therefore, my heart, along with the hearts of all your members, is completely and utterly and interminably distressed, encumbered, full of pain and sadness, and my pain and anguish cannot cease and still has no end, as I had written about already. Yes, my heart weeps and mourns for you continuously, as God in heaven is my witness. He knows me, yes, he knows the thoughts of all human hearts; every secret is laid bare to him.[f] So in deep sorrow, with an anxious heart and my eyes wet with tears, I write to you again, my beloved children in the Lord. May God comfort all of us through his son, Jesus Christ, through his great mercy and with his grace-filled Holy Spirit! May he come to our aid in our distress and misery. May he be our support, that we would entrust ourselves to him in this life and in eternity. Amen.

Furthermore, dearest brothers and sisters, I admonish and request that you let the living truth, which you have been hearing, be your comfort and strength: Do not doubt or waver or lose courage, for this is the correct path, the divine truth, which is witnessed to and proven with holy, divine scripture. Many here and in other lands have shed their blood for it and have forsaken this world and all that is visible in it. You are the chosen race and royal priesthood, a holy nation, God's own people.[g] You are the fellowship of the firstborn, whose names are written in heaven;[h] and you are fellow workers[i] and children of the living God. God's heart delights in you as a father delights in his beloved children, as he is constantly proving to you in all things. Therefore, you should not doubt, for in the kingdom of heaven, God has allowed it to be sealed and proven amongst you in Moravia, through the martyrdom and agony endured by your devout

e. E.g., Rom. 15:18; 2 Cor. 4:12; Heb. 13:12.
f. 2 Esd. 16:63–64; Ecclus. 42:18.
g. 1 Pet. 2:9.
h. Heb. 12:23.
i. 1 Cor. 3:9.

knights who witnessed to it with their blood, which was a great honor to the Lord and to us. They are like a beautiful mark of distinction[120] and crown of joy for us, a loving comfort and strength from God.

Therefore, though many condemn and judge both you and us, do not be alarmed, for how can their slander, judgments, insults, and reviling hurt or concern us? As long as God our Father in the kingdom of heaven is with us and is pleased with us! So take courage. God looks upon us and you with grace and mercy. To him who sits above, upon the throne of majesty, be glory, honor, and thanks through Jesus Christ his beloved son, from us and all the saints and the heavenly hosts for ever and ever. Amen.

Furthermore, most dear children of God, I want to let you know about the situation here – out of divine love I cannot hold back: The children of God the Lord who are here, our dear brothers and sisters, are blossoming and growing in godly righteousness and truth, like beautiful, lovely, sweet-scented lilies or flowers. As a garden bursts into leaf after a lovely rain in May,[121] so they are blossoming and growing before God, in the fear of God, in God's love and peace, as said by the holy prophet Isaiah and David,[a] the holy one. Yes, their hearts burn with the fire of divine love and are constantly illuminated and kindled by God's light and eternal fire. I cannot praise, honor, and thank my God and Father enough for this. My heart rejoices before God and fills my body with leaps of great joy when I see, hear, and think of their love and faithfulness, and their devotion and obedience, such as they have received from God. How richly the almighty God has blessed them! And even though they are all very young in the Lord and have heard very little preaching of his word, still they have a wholehearted beginning in the Lord. May God help them to bring it to completion. My heart and soul have a great desire and appreciation for them. They deserve the name "pleasure garden of the Lord,"[b] or "God's paradise,"[c] as scripture says. For them I also glorify, honor, and thank God, and may his holy name be praised and exalted through Jesus Christ forever. Amen.

It is my heart's request and wish that God send down water to his garden from heaven, pouring out a shower of mercy, with the comfort of

a. E.g., Pss. 1:3; 103:15; Isa. 58:11.
b. Isa. 51:3; Ezek. 28:13.
c. Ezek. 31:8–9; Rev. 2:7.

his Holy Spirit and the oil of his mercy.[122] May he anoint all our hearts, showering them with his heavenly blessing upon his garden, so that it becomes fruitful and bears many good works. This garden is the fellowship of the living God. May he raise a fence and even lay bricks around this garden to protect and guard it from wild beasts. May he also protect it from bad thunderstorms and from evil blights so that the fruit may ripen, for the Lord's "pleasure garden" is now in full bloom. May he himself bring it to a bountiful harvest.

You should know that our being here is no longer a secret or hidden; rather, the godless people know it and are very hostile, raising a great hue and cry. For the godless, thieving priests, the watchmen and messengers of the devil and gruesome hounds of hell, are already ranting about us from their pulpits, warning people that we are in the country and up in the mountains, ordering them to attend to their accursed idols and sacrament. For the holy city, built on the holy mountain of Zion, cannot be hidden. The light shines out and illuminates brightly, and is not covered up, but it burns and shines like a lamp in the darkness.[d] This light is the children of the living God, for God ignited his flame in them. For "there is nothing secret or hidden that will not be revealed," as Christ says.[e]

They threaten us with their judges, henchmen, and executioners. That godless, sodomite sea is roaring and raging, and is beginning to churn. I am afraid it will not rest until the devout Jonah is cast in and the great Leviathan or whale (according to the flesh) has swallowed him.[f] [123] This is Ferdinand, the cruel tyrant and enemy of truth, with all his followers, and the accursed pope with his accursed hounds of hell. But God will command the sea to give back his own and they once again will be released from the belly of the earth and from the violence of the godless; they will be raised up with the devout Jonah and will be resurrected with Christ Jesus through God's mighty power and glory to eternal joy and glory. May God grant this and help us all. Amen!

Beloved brothers and sisters, day in and out we expect that at any hour or moment the judges and henchmen and executioners and great tribulation will come. We have resigned ourselves to it and expect nothing else.

---

d. Matt. 5:15.
e. Matt. 10:26.
f. Jon. 1:17.

May the Lord give us strength, might, love, and faith and persistence to remain in his divine truth to our end, witnessing to the truth, and fighting for it unto our death. We hope to be a resource for you and all the devout, and offer a good example, leaving behind a model for how to serve God and follow his word; we would like to give this as a reflection of integrity and devotion and a good reputation of virility for all people, and to leave this behind concerning all matters. For this we struggle, battle, and labor. May God in heaven fulfill this intention and longing and complete it in us to the end, through Christ. Amen.

Furthermore, dear brothers and sisters, everyday the Lord is still increasing his holy, Christian fellowship with those who are saved. "The harvest is ripe and there is much work to do, but devout, faithful laborers are very scarce."[a] As Christ says, therefore, we need to insistently "call upon the Lord of the harvest, begging him to send workers into his vineyard."[b] Many of the people we were told about as those seeking the truth do not amount to anything, but many we knew nothing about come forward and they are devout and join us. One child of God awakens another and thus one is revealed by another and led to God. There is so much of God's work for us to do [among the brothers and sisters and those who are asking after God].[124] We cannot do it all at once. But we will do as much as we can and will not spare our effort. We are really needed everywhere at once; the urgency and scale of the task weigh heavily upon us.

Therefore, dearest brothers and sisters, I would have liked to write more, but I do not have time, and so I pass on to you now what I have hurriedly put on paper. Therefore, dearest brothers and sisters, remember us faithfully before God in all matters.

I want to let you know regarding Martin Nieder and Christel Bühler,[125] who fell away from God and his people and are now excluded and separated, as you know; they are now up here in Sterzing.[126] They are horrible, godless, wicked men in an alliance with the devil, and they are dreadful, spiteful young men. They were in Innsbruck before the government, betraying and explaining everything they know; they have told many terrible lies and untruths and keep on doing it repeatedly. They slander

a. Matt. 9:37.
b. Matt. 9:38.

and denigrate God and the divine truth. Of their vices and the sins they are committing, quite a lot more could be said, but I will write more about that to the ministers. I am telling you this most briefly because they plan to depart from there in a few days. They have no good intentions; they are only out to make trouble. Their designs are very evil. The godless are partly responsible for their journey. Therefore, do not trust them; guard yourselves and be wary of them, for they will come like thieves and murderers, sent out to rob, steal, cheat, and murder. Guard yourselves.

Finally and in closing, I commend you to God the Almighty, to his merciful shelter and protection, and to the word of his grace. May he comfort and strengthen you, stand by you on all occasions, and be with you always through our Lord Jesus Christ, both here and forever in eternity. Amen.

To you, most dearly beloved children of the living God: all the saints, the entire fellowship of God who are here, send you altogether warmest greetings, in fidelity and constancy, from the depths of their hearts, in divine, flaming, fraternal, and Christian love, a thousand times over, with the peace of the Lord and with the holy kiss of Jesus Christ. They long for you faithfully and wish they could see you face to face in the love of God. And I, Jakob, your minister and apostle, your true, loving brother and friend in the Lord (for I believe you love me), I also greet you with my own hand in divine, holy, incorruptible, brotherly love, a thousand times over, and to each individually, with a rightful kiss from Jesus Christ. I embrace you with the arms of my heart and mind. I send you greetings for ever and ever, without ceasing, in God's love and spirit. May the peace, love, and spirit of the Lord and God, and my soul and spirit and heart be with you forever and eternally through Jesus Christ. Amen. [From me, Jakob, a minister and unworthy servant and apostle of the Lord and his children, your faithful brother and friend in the Lord.][127]

Carried by Wolf Zimmermann.

Letter 7

Written from Tyrol to the fellowship in Moravia, 1535 [128]

This letter must have been written shortly after Letter 6 had been sent. A messenger (Brother Hänsel) had arrived, bringing news of increased persecution in Moravia. In Tyrol, some of Hutter's new converts had been arrested. His letter is filled with foreboding.

[Summary: He wishes them grace from God and prays earnestly that they remain firm. He speaks of the joy he and those with him received through their message and that they were well in the Lord. He speaks of the tribulation on both sides, that some have been imprisoned and a sister was released unstained. He speaks of the judgment of the flesh and warns of superficiality. He mentions that their message was hindered. He admonishes them to remain firm and desires prayers for himself and all the devout and sends greetings.][129]

[Jakob, a minister of the Lord and his holy fellowship, with all the saints and children of God who are here in the Puster and Adige valleys,][130] [to the elect saints and children of God, the beloved guests, foreigners, pilgrims of the Lord, our beloved brothers, wherever they are in all of Moravia, hunted and scattered in misery and poverty, our beloved in Christ:][131]

May the ineffable grace and compassion, eternal peace, blessing, benevolence, and help of our heavenly Father, and the balm and consolation of the Holy Spirit from on high be with you, beloved and chosen brothers, together with all distressed, devout, Christian hearts. Indeed, may God in heaven comfort and strengthen you, assist and stand by you in your great distress and worries, your misery and tribulation. May God in heaven send down wine from heaven for you to drink, to strengthen you and give you joy even in your tribulation – the comfort of his Holy Spirit. May God in heaven be your captain, your protector and safeguard, your castle and fortress against your enemies and adversaries! May God in the kingdom of heaven have mercy on you and look upon you with

Jacob Huetters Liebe. Dann Jr seit mir In der warhait von gantzem hertzen vor Gott lieb. Wolte Gott, daß möcht ein Jdlichs Jn Sunderhait grüessen mit meinem mundt, vnd mit meiner gegenwertigen person. etc. Der Herr von himelreich, vnser aller liebster vatter, vnnd mein Seel vnd geist sey mit euch, durch Jesum Christum Jmer vnd ewigklichen. Amen, Amen, Jn ewigkait. Amen.

Von Mir Jacob ewren mit Brueder In Christo.

Die Ander Epistel Jacobe Huetter. An die Gemain Gottes, In Marhern.

Jnnhalt.

Hie zaigt er Mit Danckhsagung Gottes, Sein verlangen nach inen an. Auch die Freidt so er vnd die bey im sein, durch ir pottschafft empfangen haben, Mit sambt dem Trauren, derenthalben, die di warhait verlassen haben. Vnnd erbeut sein mitleiden, Mit einer kurtz Vermanung

An die Gm: Gott:

Vermanung, Dem Herren treu zu sein, Auch sein vnd anderer Wolstandt. Vnnd wie sie in gefärligkait der Schergen warten: In welchem das volckh täglich gemartert wirt. Meldet den aufschluss der zwayer, Sambt dem grueß.

Die Vnauß-sprechlich gnad vnnd Barmhertzigkait, der Ewige frid vnd Segen, die Huldtschafft vnd Hilff Gottes, vnsers himlischen Vatters, Sambt der Salbung vnd Trosst des heiligen geists, von oben herab, sey mit euch, Jr geliebten, vnd auserwelten brüeder, Mit sambt allen betrüebten frommen Christlichen hertzen. Ja Gott vom himel, tröst vnd sterckh, erhalt euch hilff vnd beystandt, In eurer grossen not vnd anligen, In eurem ellendt vnd grossem trüebsal. Ja Gott vom himel geb euch wein zu trinckhen vom himel herab, der euch sterckhe, tröste, vnd frölich mache in eurem trüebsal: Das ist der trosst seines heiligen geists. O Gott vom himel sey euer haubtman, Euer Schutzer vnd schirmer, Euer Schloss vnd Burckh. Für eure feindt vnd widersacher. Ja Gott vom himelreich, der wölle sich über euch erbarmen, Er wölle euch ansehen mit den Augen seiner grossen Barm-

Letter 7 (Codex 1)

compassionate eyes! May God in heaven, the father of all mercy, show his omnipotence in miraculous deeds and great signs and also demonstrate and prove his superabundant mercy toward you in all things.

O God in heaven, shorten the days of this great tribulation for the sake of your elect![a] Guard, protect, and sustain your holy people! Dispatch, release, rescue them from the enemies and adversaries, who stalk their souls night and day! God in heaven, have pity on the anguish, pain, and suffering, and have mercy in your heaven above upon the great tribulation of your suffering children! Just come, you merciful God, hurry and come soon, come quickly! Do not delay your assistance and compassion, for the sake of your son, Jesus Christ, and your holy name! Have mercy on your people and let them be commended to you, and give both them and us all your divine counsel, indeed the knowledge, discernment, and wisdom of your Holy Spirit from up above, so we know what we should do or leave undone, and what will please you, God in heaven, in how we live and behave and carry forward. May we order and rule every part of our lives in fear of you and to your glory and praise! Lead and guide us [through your eternal light,][132] by your holy angels and gracious Holy Spirit into all truth, wherever you will. Thus may we be able to bring you glory and praise and much fruit, serving you and your people with utmost diligence. O God in heaven, come down; stand by your people and let them be commended to you in all things through Jesus Christ and his great mercy! Amen. With all our heart we wish this for you, who are beloved and chosen by the Lord, and we pray to God earnestly, day and night without ceasing. [May the Lord God be praised in the heavens above through his son, Jesus Christ, for ever and ever. Amen.][133]

[Dear brothers and sisters, we received your message and letter. God guided your and our brothers safely to us, and we welcomed them with great joy and holy, divine love. We received and accepted all your messages eagerly and with great thankfulness in the fear of God – yes in divine, holy love. We read your letter and took it in. We read it aloud with all the children of God here and proclaimed your faith and the great love you have for God and the saints, as well as the persecution you are so patiently suffering. We took it in and proclaimed it diligently; yes, we pondered

a. Matt. 24:22.

it in our hearts. Through this our hearts have been strengthened and comforted. We praise, honor, and thank the almighty God now even more for you and for us unceasingly. Glory to God the Lord above in heaven, through Jesus Christ, for ever and ever. Amen.][134]

Furthermore, you chosen and beloved children of the eternal God, soon after we received another message through Brother Hänsel, who is dear to us and also to you, I, Jakob, heard and read this message and letter and also diligently made it known to all the children of God. Straight away we assembled the children of God and by the grace and mercy of God we were together two or three days, proclaiming the word of God. God guarded, protected, and watched over us so that we could faithfully carry out his commands, as we longed to do. We also held the Lord's Supper, celebrating it in power and truth. May this bring praise, honor, and blessing to the Father in heaven above, and may thanksgiving be given to him from the heart, through Jesus Christ forever. Amen.

We are telling you all this, beloved brothers and sisters and children of God, so that your hearts may be comforted and rejoice and that you may glorify and praise God with us and gain confidence in the Lord in the midst of your distress and tribulation. Yes, it was a wonderful, holy gathering and God granted and achieved it favorably, although the danger is great. Yet he is quite able to guard and protect. Where he shelters and watches over, guards and protects, everything is provided, and no one can prevent it. Such a house is well protected! But when God imposes and permits or stands aside for the godless to have their way, and when he himself does not shelter, watch, guard, and protect, all our wisdom, caution, and skill, and all our pleading, watchfulness, and attentiveness is for naught and in vain, as David says[b] and as we have often experienced and seen [with our eyes].[135]

Most dearly beloved children of the living God, our dear brothers and sisters, when we received your message and letter concerning the horrible persecution, tribulation, great suffering, pain, misery, and poverty, immediately a two-edged sword went right through our hearts. Yes, we tore not our garments but our hearts.[c] We are grieved to the point of death.[d] Beloved brothers and sisters, your pain and misery have touched us; we

b. E.g., Ps. 127:1–2.
c. Joel 2:13.
d. Matt. 26:38.

suffer with you and bear anguish in our hearts. The news shocked and saddened us so much that we fell in pain onto our knees and upon our faces before God with bitter tears and poured out all our distress to him. We pleaded with God in heaven, entrusting it to him, and we continue to pray unceasingly.

Most dearly beloved brothers and sisters, children of the living God, how sincerely I wish I could be with you in your tribulation! But there is great distress here too, and there is so much to be done for the Lord's sake; there are many tender vines, the children of God, who are scattered asunder, quite far from each other. Many are also asking about the truth. We have more and more to do all the time. Praise and glory to God in heaven for it all! Still, I think that if you had written or sent a message asking me to come, it would have been hard for me to refrain in this time of need. I wish to God in heaven that I could bear it all for you, even going into the grave for you, for his name's sake, if it were God's will. But with things as they are, as you know and have heard, I cannot undertake or risk this out of a great fear of God [and because of the present need][136] here, such that it would be irresponsible for me to leave them here. Moreover, I am not even sure I would be able to help you, as matters now stand. However, if it were God's will and the will of all brothers and sisters, and if there were hope that I might be of help to you, I would spare no effort. Indeed, if God, you, and all the saints wish it, I would gladly offer my life for that sake if it were pleasing to God, in order to come and serve you.

Here we are in great distress too; persecution has begun, and there is a great outcry against us, although God has shown us a way out each day. In many places we expect the henchmen and judges at any moment, day and night. They have been threatening us, and in several villages they know quite well who the brothers and sisters are. God has still been blocking their way so that they have not yet come, but when viewed from a human perspective, there would be no time left – not a day or a moment – if things were to go their way, given all their threats and menacing.

The godless judge at Vintl, Peter Mayr [Troyer],[137] has already imprisoned his own daughter, his son-in-law, and their maid – three of our dear brothers and sisters. The cruel whale and sea-dragon[a] has opened wide his

a. Rev. 13:1–10.

jaws and dragged them off to prison. The maid, our dear sister, managed to escape from the castle in Schöneck with her soul untarnished, by God's will. She confessed the Lord faithfully and gave away no information.[138] Although all three are young and lack training, as youth they have been completely devout and faithful, a blessing and pleasing to God the Lord and to his people. All of us can bear them witness. Prior to being arrested they witnessed bravely to the Lord in word and deed, with their lives and lifestyle. Also the daughter of Peter Mayr said that before she would be willing to deny the truth, she would rather suffer death ten times over, if that were possible, with God's help. Yet I cannot thereby be absolutely certain or prove that they will therefore be steadfast or persevere to the end, nor can I call them blessed before they die; for only those who endure to the end will be blessed.[b] They are especially exposed to the devil's temptation and challenges. He is still held at Schöneck while she was taken down to Greifenburg[139] in Carinthia, by her own blood brother, that villain Paul, whom the devil has made her warden.[140] So I am worried because of the great temptation or challenges she, but others too, face, of which there are many for her especially, and she may falter somewhat, also due to her young age and weakness.[141] And yet I hope and trust in the almighty God that he will not let them fall into eternal perdition, but will graciously stretch out his hand and rescue or lead them forth in his great compassion, as David said.[c] In this way, God helped Saint Peter and many of the devout, offering his merciful hand when they stumbled and fell through weakness or ignorance or misunderstanding or through martyrdom and torture and much temptation, as scripture tells.[d] Indeed, I often see and experience it this way myself, and with great pain.

Let each of you reflect and take care that you don't perceive what I write the wrong way, to your own condemnation or judgment, and that someone would therefore treat matters frivolously and simply resign themselves and be comforted [by the promise of God's grace]. This is all to be feared and I am afraid God might never offer his grace and mercy to such a person. Those who are devout and fear God do not fall into this trap. Those who are frivolous, [godless, and damned put God

b. Matt. 10:22.
c. Ps. 144:7.
d. E.g., Matt. 14:22–33; John 18:15–27.

to the test.[a] Holy scripture and the holy words are spears and nails. The frivolous][142] and blind do not understand these things; rather, they poke and stab themselves, thereby wounding, damaging, and defiling their souls and hearts by reading and understanding everything in a distorted way, leading to their own condemnation. As Saint Paul, Job, and Peter said and wrote, the godless and ignorant would falsify scripture and the truth.[b] With these words I warn each one of you, for such people will face a harsh judgment and sentence, and to them will be meted out a horrifying condemnation.

Furthermore, I want you to know, beloved in the Lord, that God the Lord has heard our prayer. He liberated our dear sister Nändl through our brother Walser and led her to us. She had been in prison a long time for the Lord's sake. She remained devout and faithful to the Lord, confessing him loyally at all times and witnessing to the divine truth in her words and holy lifestyle. Her soul remained pure and without stain. She came to us, as we hoped to God she would – and now you know everything about our present situation.

We would gladly have sent brother Hänsel back to you right away as you asked and desired; we too thought it was necessary. Yet we did not send him because, as I already wrote, we called a meeting with the whole fellowship [and there was much to do][143] day and night. Brother Hänsel came a day or two before the meeting, but not all the brothers were present; some were out visiting other brothers and sisters. I was simply not able to write because there was so much that needed to be done. Besides, Hänsel was quite exhausted from his arduous journey; [he made it in nine days, sometimes traveling day and night.][144] He was here barely a day when he fell ill with fever. So we did not dare send him this time for fear he would collapse along the way. However, we hope he will soon be well again. Apart from that, God brought him swiftly and safely to us, and he found us right away, because we were right there.

For these reasons, beloved brothers and sisters, as quickly as possible I am now sending you another brother, namely, brother Christel. And if God determines and allows, and it is his fatherly will, it is my thought

a. Deut. 6:16; Luke 4:12.

b. Job 11:7–12; 1 Cor. 15:15; 2 Cor. 11:13–26; 2 Pet. 2:1.

and intention to immediately send Hänsel or another brother after him to bring you further news, whatever God gives me to write.

Therefore, most dearly beloved brothers and sisters, be comforted; be well and put your trust and hope completely in God the Almighty. For he will not forsake you or any who fear and trust and believe in him. He will show you his mercy and power and will prove his assistance to you in this time of distress. Of this I am certain, with full confidence in God my Lord.

Lift up your heads to God in heaven, you devout and Christian hearts, for your redemption is drawing near with great power.[c] The desolation and ruin of all the godless is also approaching. So flee and seek shelter completely from the entire world, indeed from its evil words and deeds. Do not lust after its lifestyle and the sort of peace it gives so that you will not be condemned, persecuted, horribly accused, tortured, and martyred and cast out by God the Lord, out of here and into the abyss of hell. For the wickedness, sin, and arrogance of the godless is heaped as high as the heavens.[d] It has reached God's very countenance, as Saint John says, which God can no longer endure or look upon.

Therefore, the Holy Spirit says, "Flee away, come out of her, my people, lest you share in her plagues."[e] Oh, do not allow yourselves to be deceived or frightened, neither being misled or driven away from the divine truth! "Whoever endures to the end shall be saved."[f] Whoever fights virtuously and battles throughout all torture and pain, in tribulation and temptation with patience and confessing the Lord and giving him glory and praise before all people, serving God and his people obediently till death, indeed overcoming the whole world, the devil, and his own flesh,[145] fighting through this temporal death to eternal life: God will place on his head a glorious crown that never withers.[g] He will resurrect them with an immortal body like the glorified body of our Lord Jesus Christ, as Saint Paul and John tell us.[h] Yes, God will clothe them with a beautiful, gleaming robe, and the elect will become illuminated and shine like

c. Luke 21:28.
d. Rev. 18:5
e. Rev. 18:4.
f. Matt. 10:22.
g. Cf. 1 Pet. 5:4; Rev. 2:10.
h. 1 Cor. 15:53–54; Rev. 20:6.

the sun in their Father's kingdom,[a] in the new, eternal Jerusalem, in the throne of divine majesty, as the prophets and Christ himself have said. And God will wipe all tears from their faces and will take away all their pain.[b] He will give them great, glorious, and unspeakable joy that shall never be taken away from them, as the scriptures say in many places.[c] Attending to their great sorrow and the suffering they have endured, God will give them a thousand times greater comfort. Indeed, all who have suffered grief and pain with Jerusalem (that is, with God's children), will be given and receive eternal rest, peace, joy, and inexpressible glory. The chosen ones will eat and drink and rejoice and have their fill. They will completely forget their tribulation, so great will be the joy and jubilation of the chosen!

The godless, however, will weep and howl with great fear in their hearts; they will lament in great torture and torment, suffer from hunger and thirst and all kinds of privation; they will be tossed about and trampled upon like dust and dirt, banished from the land of the living, even from God the Lord himself, and will be thrown out, exterminated, and swept into hell, for ever and ever. The prophets and all of scripture tell us this.[d]

But you who are devout, you can rejoice and be comforted, for your king, Lord, and savior, Jesus Christ the son of God, is coming from the kingdom of heaven. He will soon appear on the clouds of heaven with hosts of angels, in great power and glory.[e] He will take vengeance on all his foes and will redeem the devout and chosen ones, taking care of them and saving them from their enemies and adversaries, and from every tribulation and calamity. Those who have been persecuted for his name's sake and have suffered much, who have served him and confessed him in the face of this evil generation, who have been obedient and faithful to him and to his people till death – all these God the Lord will resurrect from the dust of the earth where they sleep, even those who have been killed or

a. Matt. 13:43.
b. Rev. 21:4.
c. E.g., Isa. 35:10; John 16:22; 1 Pet. 1:8.
d. Cf. 2 Esd. 7:36–39; Matt. 22:13.
e. Matt. 24:30.

who have fallen asleep,[f] [146] since the world's beginning until now. He will take them into heaven with him as a company of hosts, as part of the heavenly hosts. They will all be caught up into the clouds to meet the Lord, to be with him for ever and ever in all eternity.[g] God will give them an everlasting kingdom where Christ will sit upon the throne of David, and of that kingdom there will be no end.[h] They will have rest, peace, and joy, praising and singing to God in the new and heavenly Jerusalem. And they will live, govern, and reign with God and Christ Jesus and all the heavenly hosts for ever and ever in unfathomable and inexpressible joy and glory. May God the Father help us all to reach this goal through our Lord Jesus Christ, and may he guide us to that day through his holy name and great and glorious mercy! Therefore, console each other with these words[i] and be courageous, you devout, Christian hearts, for God will give you everlasting comfort. Amen.

In closing my letter I entrust you to our merciful God and Father and to his word of grace. May he be with you, surround you, and be close to you, giving you help and support in your distress and give you from heaven the grace, strength, love, and faith, with great patience and the comfort of his Holy Spirit, and may he fill your hearts from his vast and divine treasury. May God himself from the kingdom of heaven be your captain, guard, and shield, your castle and mighty fortress. May he bless and provide for you in body and soul with all his heavenly riches, as well as earthly ones, giving you what is useful, good, and necessary according to the desire and longing of our hearts, according to his omnipotence, knowledge, and fatherly will, indeed, according to his great mercy through Jesus Christ. We desire and yearn for that for your sake, with our whole hearts. Amen.

I also ask you, beloved and chosen ones, to pray to the Lord God for us altogether, with utmost diligence night and day without ceasing,[j] and we will do the same for you and want to do this diligently. We know and recognize that you are doing this, for we can perceive, see, feel, and sense it in all different ways. Still we want to encourage you not to weaken,

f. Cf. 1 Cor. 15:51; 1 Thess. 4:13.
g. 1 Thess. 4:17.
h. Luke 1:32–33.
i. 1 Thess. 4:18.
j. 1 Thess. 5:17.

but instead to make your prayers longer, and fuller and more persistent. As devout and divinely blessed ministers and servants of the holy fellowship of God, guardians, watchmen, and overseers, together with all the saints and every one of God's children in Moravia, wherever you may be, scattered about and hunted and ruined, in misery, poverty, agony, and anguish, in great fear, distress, and pain, all the holy children of God, all dear brothers and sisters of the whole fellowship here with us, including everyone, we greet all of you from the depths of our hearts in faithfulness and constancy, with the warmest greetings in holy, divine, brotherly, and incorruptible love, with the holy, pure kiss of our Lord Jesus Christ, especially from the dear brothers Kaspar Kränzler, Walser, Stoffel, and Hänsel and myself, and our dear brother Jeronimus, as well as the sisters Nändl, Klärle, and my wife Traindel.[147] Greetings are also sent by the devout, divinely blessed members of this household where we have lodging, with whom we have the greatest and longest sanctuary, whose names we will not write down for obvious reasons.

And I, Jakob, your apostle and minister, your faithful brother and close friend through God's grace and mercy, greet you, all you dear brothers and those who serve the Lord and his holy people, you devout shepherds altogether with all devout brothers and sisters, wherever you may be. I greet every single one of you without exception in divine, holy, Christian, brotherly, incorruptible, and burning love, a thousand times over, as much as humanly possible from my whole heart, in faithfulness and constancy. I embrace you with the arms of my heart and greet you with the proper holy kiss of my mouth (and with my own hand), indeed with the kiss and holy peace of our Lord Jesus Christ. May my heart, soul, and spirit be with you always; may you be with me, and we with God, and God with us all through Jesus Christ and through his great mercy, for ever and ever. Amen.

O, most dearly beloved children of God, and you, our dearest brothers and sisters, members of the body of Jesus Christ, if only it were the will of God in heaven that we could serve and help you in all matters during this time of distress, to show and prove to you love and fidelity, discipline and honor, giving you shelter, accommodation, taking care of you in the Lord, even providing meals and drinks, to comfort and strengthen you! Oh, may God grant us this privilege from the kingdom of heaven! What great, sincere rejoicing and a huge celebration there would be in our hearts! How eagerly, willingly, and with such great joy we would do this in love, putting at your service our bodies, lives, and belongings, all the heavenly and temporal gifts we have received from God. We would be willing to endure much suffering to make this possible. Regardless if martyrdom or torture and any sort of tribulation were to come or result from this – whatever one might imagine – nevertheless, we would not desist. Therefore, may everything happen according to God's counsel and to his eternal praise and glory! May your hearts be ordered in this way through Jesus Christ. Amen.

[From me, Jakob, a minister of the Lord and his holy fellowship, together with all the saints and children of God who are scattered throughout the Puster and Adige valleys, your brothers and colleagues in the Lord, united in patience, in tribulation, and in Christ's kingdom. Amen. Amen in eternity.][148]

[Sent with brother Christl Schmidt from the Adige Valley][149]
[To the chosen saints and children of God . . .
sent by Wolf Zimmermann 1535, with Brother Christl][150]

Letter 8

Written from Tyrol to the fellowship in Moravia, 1535 [151]

In his last letter to the members of his fellowship, Jakob Hutter expresses his love to them and pleads that they hold on to what he taught them when he is taken from them. The Lord will redeem his own, and those who persevere will receive a crown.

[Summary: He first speaks of his calling as well as his tribulations and the pains he has taken for them. He reminds them of what he has taught them and urges them to bear it in mind in coming trials; through such trials the devout are strengthened while the others are winnowed out. He encourages them to remain faithful. He tells of the persecution they are suffering and asks them to remember him and those with him in prayer. He greets them and wishes them God's grace.] [152]

[This letter is sent to the elect saints and children of God, his beloved guests, foreigners and pilgrims on this earth, to you our beloved brothers and sisters wherever you are in all of Moravia, scattered and hunted down, in poverty and want,] [153]

From Jakob, a slave of God and apostle of Jesus Christ,[a] and a minister of all his chosen saints, here, there, and in all territories,[154] up [in Tyrol] and down in Moravia, called[155] by God in his boundless grace and unspeakable mercy. He has chosen and fitted me for this task in his grace and boundless mercy, though I have in no way earned it, but only because of his overflowing faithfulness and goodness, which has reckoned me as righteous[156] and made me worthy to serve him in the everlasting and new covenant he established and made with Abraham and his seed for eternity.[b] He has entrusted and placed his divine, eternal word into my heart and mouth, along with the heavenly properties of his Holy Spirit, which lie hidden in the tabernacle of the eternal, invisible God in heaven above, who is the Lord there and the king over all kings. He has blessed

a. 2 Pet. 1:1.
b. Cf. Gal. 3:6–9.

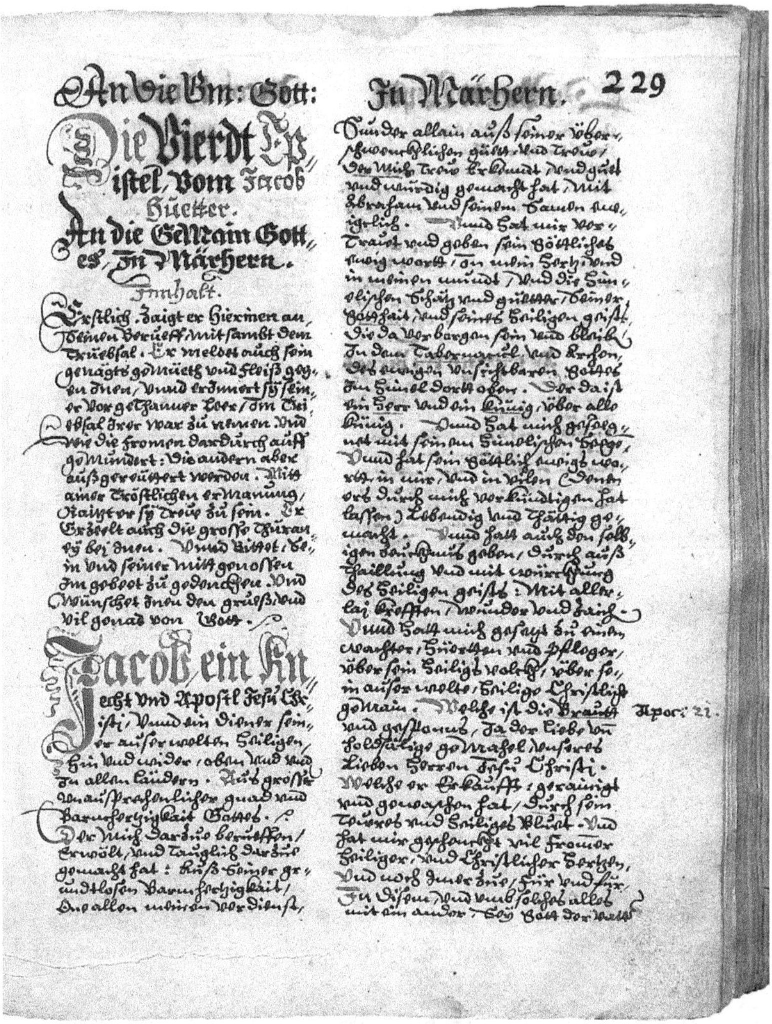
An die Gm: Gott: Zu Märhern. 229

Die Vierdt Epistel, vom Jacob Huetter. An die Gemain Gottes, In Märhern.

Inhalt.

Letter 8 (Codex 1)

me with his eternal, heavenly blessing. He has made his divine and eternal word alive and active in me, and in many to whom I proclaimed it.[157] He gave me this as a sign through the dispensation and partnership of the Holy Spirit with every sort of mighty wonder and sign. He has made me a watchman, shepherd, and tender over his holy people, over his chosen, holy, Christian fellowship. She is the bride[a] and spouse, the loving, sweet companion of our beloved Lord Jesus Christ, paid for and purified and washed with his precious and holy blood. He has given me many devout, holy, Christian hearts and is still doing this, in all things, corporately, through and through.

For all these things, may God alone, the Father in heaven, the king and creator of all things, be glorified, praised, honored, and exalted, blessed and magnified. Along with all the saints and heavenly hosts, I glorify and thank him in his kingly and eternal majesty from the depth of my heart, through Jesus Christ, forever and eternally. Amen.

To you chosen and appointed saints, the soldiers and witnesses of God and of our Lord Jesus Christ, my most dearly beloved brothers and sisters, my longed-for and chosen, dear children, whom I bore[b] and planted[c] with much labor and toil and in my great tribulation, through God's word and grace from heaven above: I write to you throughout Moravia and everywhere, who, time and again, have been hunted and scattered in misery, poverty, and tribulation, in fear and distress and in much pain and harsh persecution and amid manifold temptations, which you have suffered for the Lord's sake. I wish all of you, from the depth of my heart, grace and peace and eternal life and eternal mercy from the almighty God, and much love, faith, victory, and strength to overcome. May God in heaven comfort and strengthen you and give you food and drink; may he care for you in both body and spirit with heavenly and temporal possessions, helping and supporting you through his presence, protecting you, allowing yourselves to be commended to him through his beloved son, Jesus Christ in all eternity. Amen.

You beloved and chosen children of the living God, although we have heard about it, and to a large degree we know of the tribulation and

---

a. Eph. 5:25–27.
b. Cf. Gal. 4:19.
c. Cf. 1 Cor. 3:6.

persecution you suffer for the Lord's sake, yet we have not heard from you what has happened recently. We think of this situation constantly in our hearts, imagining what it must be like. Your suffering strikes us deeply; we suffer for you in addition to the suffering we endure here for the Lord's sake. We remember you without ceasing; we persistently bring this before God and all the saints with earnest prayer and cries. For you have been planted and grown in our hearts. You are a living letter[d] to us, written by God's love and spirit into our hearts, which is constantly being read, over and over.

Beloved and chosen ones, some time ago I sent our brother Christel to you with a letter I wrote to tell you how things are with us here and to comfort you in the way God showed me. I hope and trust you received that message. I wanted to send the dear brother Hänsel to you right away and quickly, as you asked and desired; he would gladly have come to you, urged by the divine love that he and all of us feel toward you. But this is not yet possible because he is ill. I cannot even use him here at the moment, though he and more brothers are badly needed, since the need here is great too, as you will hear. Still, because of my great love for you, I will send our dear brother Jeronimus to you in your need. We ourselves would rather suffer even greater deprivation, in order that we might fulfill your needs.

If only we could help you in the way we long to; if only we could do enough for you to satisfy our hearts! O that God in heaven might repay our love and joy in you and grant our hearts' desire to serve you and help you in your distress, to shelter and accommodate you and give you food and drink, and to show and prove to you our love and faithfulness, our discipline and honor – to serve you with both heavenly and temporal nourishment. How we would rejoice in the Holy Spirit! We could wish for no greater privilege. It is our greatest sorrow not to be able to see your faces and do all this for you. We would so gladly endure poverty and suffering, tribulation and bodily torment, even martyrdom and torture to the point of death, if only we could be united with you at this time and offer such service, love, faithfulness, and total discipline and honor to you in all ways. Our hearts and souls are wide open to you.

---

d. 2 Cor. 3:2–3.

O devout children of the living God, your misery really worries and pains me deeply. My heart is full of compassion for you in the tribulation and temptations you suffer for his sake. But be comforted, you devout Christian hearts, and remember that this happened to all the prophets, to Christ the Lord himself, and to all his apostles, in general all saints who were loved by God the Lord since the beginning of the world.[a]

You have heard this often enough, if not incessantly, and the Lord has proclaimed and shown it clearly to you and us that until the day of judgment this is and will be the lot of all the saints and the chosen ones and those who love his divine truth. This is what scripture tells us and demonstrates in all manner of passages.[b] And think of how often and how seriously I spoke to you about this while I was still with you, even before it happened. Some would not recognize God's goodness, love, and compassion, so he had to make them recognize it through tribulation and suffering. Some were not thankful to the Lord, and many of those have already been rooted out and have gone to ruin. But for us and all those who love and fear him, God wants to more fully reveal and to signify the riches of his mercy and his fatherly will through such distress and tribulation. This is so that we never forget his ways or become ungrateful to him, never growing sleepy or negligent in serving God, so that we never allow sin or our flesh to gain the upper hand and rule us. This is done so that we never allow the world with its earthly lusts to defile us. Rather, let us allow our flesh to be crucified and destroyed with its passions[c] and desires and our inner being to grow and increase. In this way God and his Holy Spirit will rule, lead, and guide us into all truth and justice, so that we will come to know God the Lord and his mercy more fully, praising, honoring, and glorifying him and serving him from our hearts with fear and trembling. That way we will grow and flourish in love and faith, in all justice and truth, into the fullness that God promises and gives to his own. Let us not become like a barren, unfruitful tree, so that we will not be burned[d] eternally in the hell fires, but like a solid, verdant, and lovely, green olive tree[e] of the Lord, yielding good fruits for the Lord. Let us not

---

a. Luke 11:50.
b. E.g., Matt. 5:12; John 15:20; 2 Tim. 3:12.
c. Gal. 5:24.
d. Matt. 7:19
e. Jer. 11:16.

waste the time we still have on earth being idle, but let us serve and obey God and all his saints as long as we live, and may we avoid doing what our flesh wants and prefers. This is why the Lord disciplines us as his dear children. In Saint Peter's words: "Whoever suffers in the flesh has ceased to sin in order that henceforth, for the time they still have to live in the flesh, they no longer serve the world and their own flesh,"[f] and "no longer doing what they want," as Paul says.[g] Rather, they consume their life and the duration of their pilgrim's sojourn to the glory and praise of God, being obedient to God and his children. Through such tribulation God liberates and cleanses us of all created things,[158] so that our hearts turn away, so that we set our whole heart solely upon the Lord. That means putting all our wants, our hope, and confidence in him, giving ourselves to him, knowing that he is our comfort. We will find our joy and delight only in the Lord and his eternal word and holy law, keeping it constantly with us. Yet we will love God the Lord in the kingdom of heaven alone, all his children, from the depths of our hearts and with all our strength and all our ability. Our treasure will be in heaven alone.[h]

Therefore, everything that is happening now comes to us from God the Almighty, from his great love and compassion, so that we may not be condemned with the world but live with him and occupy the eternal kingdom, and with him will enjoy peace and indescribable joy in the future, eternal life. Otherwise our flesh would rule us and lead us into sin.

But the wages of sin is eternal death.[i] Those who are carnal cannot please God.[j] As scripture says, fleshly and sinful people will not inherit the kingdom of God.[k] In the book of Proverbs it is written, "Wounds and blows drive evil from the body,"[l] meaning that sin and injustice is driven out by the cross of Jesus Christ, which is the Lord's rod.

So take comfort, you beloved and chosen ones, for all this is an eternal sign and real covenantal mark,[159] showing that you are dear and pleasing to God and that he will give you eternal life, eternal rest and peace, and

f. 1 Pet. 4:1–2.
g. Rom. 7:15.
h. Matt. 6:20
i. Rom. 6:23.
j. Rom. 8:8.
k. 1 Cor. 6:9.
l. Prov. 20:30.

joy and eternal glorification with all the chosen saints and all the heavenly hosts. May God help us all through his most beloved son, Jesus Christ, to whom be praise and honor, for ever and ever. Amen.

Dear and chosen children of the living God, how abundantly and powerfully and for a long time such fear and torment have been mirrored in my heart, being demonstrated through God's grace and spirit. This is why I notified and warned you day and night to prepare, correct, and resign your hearts, so that you will be ready for challenges and tribulation, and shall survive in any circumstance. Thus you shall believe and trust in God the Lord and not let fear drive you away from God and truth and his holy fellowship. Rather, remain true until the end, through all tribulation. For whoever endures to the end will be saved.[a] Fight valiantly for the divine truth, and the Lord will fight for you.[b] Be devout, righteous, and patient, trusting God and all his saints, in all things.[160]

I have also fully explained and admonished you to listen to the divine word with utmost diligence and to capture and write it into your hearts. We will not always be with you and able to speak to you if God takes us from you through imprisonment, tribulation, or death, in whatever way he may ordain. In order that in times of trouble you will have something to sustain you, you must gather together while it is summer,[c] so that in the cold and dangerous winter time you are clothed and provided for and can draw from your hearts' storage of the treasures which you had heard and collected, those which you received from God. How many times in the past and at such length I have explained and showed this to you! I hope to God you understood it deeply and fully, for you have fully heard the word of divine truth, which was quite clearly shown to you by the many powerful examples of what God has done through his many saints. Happy are those who heard it and wrote it into their hearts.

You have also heard and understood that long ago the Lord went before you in a pillar of cloud by day, that is, through his ministers and preachers.[d] But night will come, when we can or may no longer see the cloud, and the Lord no longer goes before his own in clouds, but in a pillar of fire;

a. Matt. 10:22; 24:13; Mark 13:13.
b. Cf. Exod. 14:14.
c. Cf. Prov. 6:6–8.
d. Exod. 13–14; Num. 14:14.

the light and radiance of the Holy Spirit, through God's word and spirit living in all devout Christian hearts, through which all truth is ruling, working, teaching, and guiding them, through his genuine, Christian, and well-founded faith, which is the pillar of fire in our hearts. Happy are those who are illuminated by this light; they will not stumble or be brought to shame at night. Scripture says, "The just shall live by faith"[e] and "they shall never be put to shame."[f]

Take care, then, dear brothers and sisters, and consider it well and take it to heart; assess and weigh such things fully and diligently in your hearts, for the hour is already here, and everything that was proclaimed to you in the Lord's name is happening. Happy are those who have heard God's word and recognized it in their hearts, whose hearts are filled with love and faith, great endurance, righteousness, truth, and with the fear of God, his word, and his Holy Spirit, who will remain steadfast in this time of distress and tribulation.

Beloved brothers and sisters, consider that I or other devout ministers of God may no longer be able to speak to you again in this world, nor will our eyes be able to look upon you in this world, to comfort and strengthen you with words of divine truth. Yet you must not waver, but with all your hearts firmly believe and trust in God the Lord, striving to do his will and keeping his commandments, witnessing to God in your words and deeds, in a holy, Christian way of living. Let your light illuminate and shine before others, and let your good works be seen and revealed so that God the Father is glorified through you.[g] Then Christ will also acknowledge you in the presence of his heavenly Father[h] and the holy angels in heaven as his sons and daughters, his brothers and sisters, fellow heirs of his glory, and children of the living God.[i]

If you love God and his holy people, then you will also be loved by God the Lord and his beloved Son and by all saints. If you serve God the Lord and his children faithfully and diligently with your whole heart in all things, then the angels in heaven will serve you. If you do not forget the Lord's word, his divine truth and his holy people, then God the Lord

e. Rom. 1:17; Gal. 3:11; Heb. 10:38; these all cite Hab. 2:4.
f. Rom. 10:11.
g. Matt. 5:16.
h. Matt. 10:32.
i. Cf. Rom. 8:17; 9:26.

will never forget you. And if you remain in God, in his word, his truth, and in the community of the saints with all the chosen ones, then God the Lord will abide in you forever and will never forsake or neglect you.

Keep in mind and consider what we are taught by God's grace and gifts, through God's word and his Holy Spirit. Everyone should be eager to obey it. We did not tell you fables,[a] fairy tales, or preach human ideas[b] but the divine and eternal truth, which never passes away, and the word of divine justice, which is pure and clear and well-founded, yea and Amen before God and all saints. We are sure of this, for we received it from the living God, as was fully sealed and witnessed in holy scripture and by the blood of many saints, and with God's help and strength and grace, we too desire to bear witness with our blood and with divine truth.

This is the right path and the door to the sheepfold; it is the right, uncorrupted foundation and belief, which all the prophets and apostles built upon. This is what we taught and showed you. Let no one teach or advise you otherwise, for a thief comes only to steal, rob, and kill. Thus they are all thieves and murderers before God, as Christ says.[c] Anyone who teaches you anything else is cursed, as Paul the apostle writes with his teaching,[d] for we have not lived or taught any error, nor been as a reed, which sways to and fro in the wind.[e] We are not swayed by any tribulation, temptation, or challenge, through God's help. No human, or any sort of torture or pain, violence, hunger or thirst, trouble or persecution, or any other creature, or anything that can be named, shall lead us astray or separate us or turn us away from God and his divine truth by which we live and which we preach, which is established and sealed by God and by all his saints with miracles and powerful signs, as I said before. And we are not bringing anything new to your ears; we are not fickle, or erratic, or frivolous, saying one thing today and another tomorrow, like those who are frivolous and false. We will remain firm and immovable in the divine truth through and through, whatever the cost, come what may and however it may result. What we preached from the beginning we

a. 2 Pet. 1:16.
b. Gal. 1:11.
c. Cf. John 10.
d. 1 Tim. 6:3.
e. Luke 7:24.

still preach and are not weary or ashamed. This should encourage you to be fair, certain, and bold, courageous, valiant, and confident in the Lord.

O you devout Christian hearts, how I wish that I could be with you for just one day or a single hour and let you hear my voice, my presence to give you cheer, to energize and fill you to the brim in the Lord. But this is what God has ordained, and we accept his will patiently, though with great sorrow.

Be comforted, you, the Lord's chosen ones, for the time of our deliverance is at hand. Raise your heads to God the Lord in heaven and wait meekly and with great patience, in righteousness and truth, in divine love and strong faith, for your shepherd and king from heaven is near. He that is coming will come soon on the clouds of heaven with great power and glory,[f] the king and comforter of Israel. He will redeem, save, and deliver his own, and upon their heads he will set a glorious and unfading crown.[g] But before this there will be struggle and strife. Whoever fights valiantly and is victorious and conquers through God's spirit will be crowned; he will win the victory and prize and be given peace and joy and everlasting rest and glory, along with the chosen and all the heavenly hosts. He will be with God the Father and his beloved son and will abide with the saints for ever and ever in the covenant of eternal life. May God the Father help us in this through Jesus Christ. To him be praise and honor from everlasting to everlasting. Amen.

Dear and chosen children of the living God, I rejoice and I am deeply comforted by God's pledge which he promised to us, that we shall behold[h] him in his holy and well-adorned temple, that our pain and misery shall come to an end one day and our weeping and tears shall cease,[i] and that we shall see each other again with great and unspeakable joy. And no one will hurt or abuse us any more, for all tribulation and all suffering will pass away. For the veils that were torn asunder,[j] which represent earthly power and might, will be removed through the might of the Lord. Then the devout shall reign and rule, and their lips will be full of laughter, as

f. Cf. Mark 13:26; Rev. 1:7.
g. 1 Pet. 5:4.
h. Rev. 21:9–22.
i. Rev. 21:4
j. Cf. Matt. 27:51.

the Lord says.[a] They will rejoice in the Lord and together sing praises to him forever.

May God in his mercy grant us the ability to wait for his grace and his eternal, perfect compassion; then we will receive joy a thousand times greater than all our sorrow and misery. In this world we have no rest or permanent home,[b] only tribulation, fear and pain. But be comforted, for Christ has overcome the world,[c] and he will give us grace, victory, and strength so that we too may overcome it.

For his victory was for our sake, so that the same victory may be given to us and to all who truly fear and love God with all their hearts, who believe and keep his commandments. For the true and living Christian faith is the victory that overcomes the world. May God in heaven endow and comfort you in all your tribulation. How I wish it were God's will for me to be with you and you with me! I so sincerely and solemnly long to be with you that I would rather suffer a thousand times with you in the worst tribulation, even in great torture and pain, than share in the pleasure and luxury of the ungodly. But I am comforted by the Lord, that even if this cannot happen now, still we shall be united in eternity.

Beloved and chosen children of God, my heart, soul, and spirit will be with you at all times, and you with me, God with us, and all of us with God for evermore! With this you are commended to the powerful guard and protection of the Lord God in heaven and to Jesus Christ the great shepherd. May he strengthen you and supply all your needs of both body and soul with his heavenly and temporal gifts, according to his will and the riches of his great mercy. May you entrust yourselves to him in all ways, for ever and ever. Amen.

Moreover, beloved brothers and sisters, my dear children, I want to tell you again what is happening here. We are living and carrying forth in love and faith, in peace and in the unity of the Holy Spirit. In our hearts there is great inner sorrow and tribulation for your sake, and outwardly we are suffering severe persecution. The gruesome, raging dragon has opened its jaws wide to devour the woman robed with the sun.[d] She is the fellowship and the bride of our Lord Jesus Christ.

---

a. Ps. 126:2.
b. Heb. 13:14.
c. John 16:33.
d. Rev. 12:1–4.

The first day after our fellowship gathered, a brother was captured in Taufers on his way home from the meeting. Soon afterward, the judge of Brixen rode into the village of Lüsen, summoned all the men, women, and children who were able to walk, and read out to them a cruel mandate that forbade them to house or shelter any of us. If any of them did, they would be punished more severely than ever, and their house would be burned to the ground.[161] The judge said that this thing was spreading and getting out of hand and that his devilish lord, [the prince-bishop] of Brixen, would not tolerate it but would uproot it. He has just returned home and now threatens the people with big words, forbidding what is good and right and commanding what is evil and unjust. However, the devout are still courageous [and pay no attention to his threats,][162] but serve God eagerly and do his will.

The judge would have held off for a while to see whether they would be intimidated and if they would enter their cursed, idolatrous temples, and had in mind to close one eye for a while. But the betrayers would not leave him in peace, for our dear brothers and sisters are known to everybody in the valley and in this region.

When the judge saw that his orders had no effect on the devout, he set out and captured five or six of our brothers and sisters, and took them to Brixen. God sheltered the others that time; but we have just in this last hour been informed by an unbeliever that five more have been taken from Lüsen to Brixen. We have not heard anything more, but there is good reason to worry about what is happening to them and how they are faring. At this point we do not know where they are imprisoned, but God in heaven knows. I immediately sent brothers to Lüsen and all around to visit the brothers and sisters and find out how they are. They have not returned yet, so I really do not know how matters stand. But it is very likely that all have been chased out and scattered and that they are in great danger wherever they are.

So far, everything we have heard about the prisoners and all the others points to their steadfastness and devoutness. May God comfort and strengthen them from heaven with his word and Holy Spirit. May he keep them in his name and in his divine truth to the end. May he stand by their side through Jesus Christ to help and support them in his great mercy. Amen.

Our dear brother Jeronimus will surely tell you what our situation is and whatever else there is to report. He is as well informed about everything as I am at the moment and knows what you need to be told. He is our living letter to you and will answer all your questions; you should listen to him. For the rest, let us all wait patiently for the Lord.

Finally, and in closing, we ask you for the sake of God's mercy to pray for us earnestly and persistently, without ceasing,[a] as we do for you. We know that you are doing this, only do not relent; rather, increase your efforts, for we urgently need your prayers. I know that God will provide a way out[b] for his own, as he has promised in his great compassion. May God be with us and with you; may he comfort all grieving, devout, Christian hearts with the comfort of his Holy Spirit, through Jesus Christ, here and beyond, in eternity. Amen.

All of God's children here with us, the holy Christian fellowship, greet you heartily and faithfully from the depths of their hearts in God's peace and love and with the kiss of our dear Lord Jesus Christ, each and every one of you, a thousand times over. And I, Jakob, your minister and servant, your brother and companion in the tribulation of Jesus Christ, I too greet you all together and each one personally, every devout Christian minister together with all the saints, in divine passion and brotherly love, with a peaceful heart and with the holy kiss of our Lord Jesus. May God in heaven, the father of all grace and mercy, greet, comfort, and bless you from heaven with his gracious Holy Spirit, through Jesus Christ in all eternity. Amen.

[You beloved and chosen ones in the Lord, our bodies, souls, and possessions are for the Lord and for you. Be fully assured of that and may your hearts be comforted. May God preserve us in his love and in the covenant of his peace forever. Amen.][163]

Carried from Tyrol by brother Jeronimus.

a. 1 Thess. 5:17.
b. 1 Cor. 10:13.

2

Chronicle Sources

Narrative accounts of events are an invaluable source, yet they are rarely available in translation, due to their length. Hutterites produced a wealth of chronicles, mostly anonymously. Two early chroniclers were Ambrosius Resch (d. 1592) and Kaspar Braitmichel (d. 1573), whose works were copied and recopied.[1] Resch wrote down the stories of many of the martyrs as well as important events in the Hutterian Church, including the election, confirmation, and death of the ministers and the beginnings of various "Haushaben" (communitites). His *Kleines gründliches Denckbüchel* was copied numerous times, and there are copies in libraries and archives across Europe. Josef von Beck used these codices to compile a chronological account. In this chapter, several entries from Beck's *Die Geschichts-Bücher der Wiedertäufer in Oesterreich-Ungarn* appear in English for the first time.

Hauptrecht Zapf used Braitmichel's and Resch's work to write the official church chronicle, published by Rudolf Wolkan in 1923 and by Zieglschmid in 1943, and translated into English in 1987 as *The Chronicle of the Hutterian Brethren*, vol. 1. We include here several passages from this larger chronicle that pertain to Hutter's story.

The long and detailed account of the division of 1533 (CHR-10, CHR-11, CHR-12) has never been published in German. We have translated it from several codices.

Further, a Catholic chronicler, Georg Kirchmayr, penned his observations and relayed details for decades, some of which offer insights into the state of Anabaptism in Tyrol. Therefore they are included here as chronicles, rather than among the government correspondence.

Chronicle Source 1

Early Reports on Anabaptists in Tyrol, 1526–1527, by Georg Kirchmayr, Court Judge at Bruneck [2]

Report on Wolfgang from Sarnthal

At this time, the Lutherans and Anabaptists aroused great unrest. They tried to spread their poison in Tyrol through several street preachers. One such preacher, Wolfgang by name, born in Sarnthal, once a cowherd, was captured in Brixen, and confessed in three interrogations on January 9, 16, and 18, 1527 that he had been roaming the country for a whole year, preaching in the Puster Valley, in Klausen, Bozen, Hall, and in the Upper Inn Valley. A schoolmaster in Innsbruck had said of him:

"We wanted to let him learn a skill, so that he could study the gospel and the word of God better, and so that he could resist anyone who would oppose him." This schoolmaster had always visited [Wolfgang] each time, and taught him for God's sake. Since he learned such skill at Innsbruck, he was at Vieht Peckhn on the other side of the bridge. He reported that several aristocratic, state officials, and also some clerical persons listened to his sermons, who either praised him or at least did not punish him, who allowed him to stay at their home for several days and supported him in various ways. The teaching he presented was not directly in opposition to the secular authorities, but he confessed that he preached as follows: Concerning the pope, monks, and priests, that they are the anti-Christ, and will deceive the people of Christ; that one should not believe that God is bodily present in the figure of the host; that our Lord did not institute the Mass, and that it is of no avail. He only trusts what is found in the Gospels and the epistles of Saint Paul, and he also believes in observing the Lord's Supper. He also said or preached that it is not necessary to acknowledge or confess one's sin to a priest, but to ask the priest only for advice on how to keep one's faith, and that human commands should not be obeyed. The Mother of God should be praised and honored, but not as an intercessor. He also said if he were to be drowned or killed, five others would come in his place preaching the word of God. The miners (at

Klausen) said to him that he should in no way stray from the gospel, but keep preaching the same. A majority of the miners wanted to come with him to the interrogations.[3]

Anabaptists in Tyrol (1527)

At that point, there were many dictates promulgated against Lutheran matters, and more particularly against the sect of the Anabaptists, because baptisms were held in connection with many evil articles [of faith]. At the time, many people were burned and otherwise punished because of their error. Oh, how the Lutheran way made such a riotous mess of all Christianity. . . !

The longer this matter lasted concerning heretics and particularly the Anabaptists in the empire and also here in this country, the worse it became, and I believe that in the land within the territories of Tyrol and Gorizia alone, about one thousand people were burned to death, beheaded, and drowned as a result. Yet the Anabaptists were very stubborn. Whenever a priest held Mass, and many were gathered in a church, they ran in and took the chalice from the priest, with the sacrament and paten,[4] throwing it all under his feet, saying that the baptism of children was useless, that baptism must only be done when one is capable of believing. They said holding Mass was sorcery, that it was not the venerable sacrament, that they were deceiving the people. Christ would not have died for anyone, were it not for Adam and Eve. Nobody [who is Christian] should be in government. Whoever is a ruler, pope, emperor, king – or who accepts such a role – is a pagan, the devil's child. Yet they would die for that, and say they are without sin. And all things were to be held in common. Many reasonable people were deceived, and they did not understand the *Austrunen Munich poss practica*.[5]

Both the sovereign Ferdinand and our prince-bishop considered it their highest duty to keep radicals in check who tried with fanatical fury to separate every aspect of ecclesiastical and political society. [Bishop] Georg therefore issued an emphatic circular to his officials, in which he ordered them to watch out for covert agitators, "including some who preach in corners concerning the new sect and Anabaptism," and to capture them (23 December 1527). Already on the following day Georg praised the captain at Säben, Ulrich Wittenbach, and the city judge from Klausen, Leonhard von Aichach, that they had captured a couple of such seduced persons "Ulrich Mülner and Gilg Paderinn."[6]

On December 26, Georg reported to the government at Innsbruck: "We have arrived, as the feudal lord [Mayrhofer] from Lüsen together with three others brought several men and women to the sect of Anabaptism at Sterzing. When those mentioned left Sterzing they came to a man named Ulrich Müllner in our city of Klausen, held a secret meeting in his house. There again they brought several men and women to the sect of Anabaptism, and before we were aware of it, left Klausen, and went on their way." He then goes on to say that Ulrich Müllner and Gilg Paderinn, later two others too, had become members, and promises to spare no amount of effort in the future. [7]

Chronicle Source 2

Georg Blaurock's Arrival, Ministry, and Execution in Tyrol, 1529[8]

Around this time, in the year of 1529, Brother Georg from the House of Jacob, given the name Blaurock or Blabrock,[9] was arrested in Gufidaun with his companion and condemned because of his faith. He was burned alive at the wood market[10] not far from Klausen. For the previous two or three years he had been traveling through Switzerland and especially in the region of Tyrol, where he had moved, spreading and proclaiming the teachings of truth (thereby investing his coins for profit,[11] and, as one zealous for the house of God, wanted it to provide the means of salvation for many). The crimes for which he was executed were as follows: that he had abandoned his priestly office and position that he had been serving under the pope; that he held infant baptism to be invalid, and was rebaptizing people; that he did not believe that Christ was physically in the host or the bread that was consecrated by the priest. Also that he thought nothing of confession to priests and believed that one should not pray to or worship the mother of Christ. For these reasons he was executed. He was steadfast, a knight and hero of the faith. He endured and surrendered his life and his body. He spoke powerfully to the people at the place of execution and directed them to scripture.

Chronicle Source 3

Locations of Early Anabaptist Activity in Tyrol, ca. 1529 [12]

At this time, as the love of truth was beginning to burn among the people and the fire of God had been kindled, many were killed and executed for witnessing to the truth in the region of Tyrol – ministers, both men and women, including young men and young women – particularly in the district of Gufidaun as well as in Klausen, Brixen, Sterzing, Bozen, Neumarkt, Kaltern, Terlan, Kuntersweg.[13] The same was true in the Inn Valley: Steinach, Imst, Petersburg, Stams, Innsbruck, Hall, Schwaz, Rottenburg, Kopfstein, and Kitzbühel.[14]

Chronicle Source 4

Persecution by Water, Fire, Sword and the Rise of Jakob Hutter [15]

In these towns a large number of believers, who had testified faithfully to the truth, were killed by water, fire, and the sword. Yet despite this tribulation, the people continued to increase daily.

One of the leaders and teachers in the region of Tyrol was Jakob Hutter. He and his people soon formed a union with the people gathered in Moravia. Jakob Hutter and the group from Tyrol moved to Moravia, in part forced by the great persecution. For in Tyrol the oppression was increasing tremendously day after day. The devout had nowhere to go; many of them had been arrested and executed by various means for the sake of the faith.

In addition, the priests were crying loudly and vehemently from the pulpits that everyone should watch for them, capture them, and destroy them by fire and sword. Often money was offered [as a reward] to anyone who would report them, and thus they were caught by spies. They were hunted down everywhere, in the forest and in houses where they were suspected of hiding inside of closets and locked trunks, which would need to be unlocked or broken open as a means to search.

There was a son of Judas called Praviger [Prabeiger] who used evil treachery in hopes to catch many of them. He ran to the authorities and betrayed them all, brought with him the henchmen and children of Pilate with swords, spears, and rods and went ahead of them – no different from Judas the betrayer.[a] They caught many of them and scattered and chased the others. Not long afterward, when they gathered again there was an Iscariot named Georg Frey.[16] He ran to the priests [and said] that if they would give him a reward he would be willing to go and no brother would be able to hide from him! The priests, the race of the scribes and Pharisees gave him money, a good reward, along with a letter. The scoundrel left them, disguised[b] himself in the form of an angel and hypocrisy, and went here and there to the people whom he suspected of knowing something, asking all over the Puster Valley where the brethren were and where he might find them. The scoundrel asked them to help him find them, claiming with tears that he would have no peace until he was with them. This is how he deceived them. When he finally reached them he presented himself as very sad, humble, good, as one who was seeking repentance. Then he said, “My brethren, allow me one small thing. I want to go and bring my wife and children from home.” The brethren had reservations and said to him: “If he had a false heart and was planning evil, God would find him out!” But he answered: “Oh no, may God preserve me. Come home with me to my house!” He left them and ran to the judge, the authorities, the priests. They came with violence and arrested the brothers and sisters.

There were other similar scoundrels, especially one named Peter Lantz and one called “Der Branger.”[17] Some of them traveled at night with staffs like brethren[18] as well as in the way they spoke and presented themselves. They came to the towns and houses where they thought they would be welcomed as brethren and in this way hoped to find them. But God has

a Cf. Matt. 26:47.
b Cf. 2 Cor. 11:14.

given them the reward they earned such that they would wish they had never been born.[c] [19]

Chronicle Source 5

Jakob Hutter's Union with Jakob Wiedemann in Austerlitz, 1529 [20]

Union in Austerlitz

In 1529 Jakob Hutter and other brethren came from the region of Tyrol to Austerlitz. They formed a union[21] with One-Eyed Jakob [Jakob Wiedemann] who was the shepherd and the leading minister at the time and with the other brethren in Austerlitz. Afterward Jakob Hutter returned to Tyrol.

Leadership in Austerlitz [22]

At this time a man came named Jakob, a hatmaker by trade. He was born in Moos, half a mile from Bruneck in the Puster Valley. He accepted the covenant of grace with a clear conscience in Christian baptism, fully submitting to live a godly life. Meanwhile, as God's gifts were recognized richly in him, he was elected and ordained[23] to the service of the gospel. The fellowship of God in that place understood that God the Lord had gathered a people in his name in the Margraviate of Moravia in the city of Austerlitz, to be of one heart, mind, and purpose,[d] that each should faithfully accept one another.[e] So they determined Jakob Hutter and Sigmund Schützinger and some companions be sent to the fellowship in Austerlitz to inquire as to how they operated in all respects.[24] When they had discussed these matters with the elders of the fellowship in Austerlitz, and both sides were in agreement to fear God, they formed a union with the fellowship in Austerlitz on behalf of the fellowship in the region of Tyrol. Not long afterward Jakob Hutter and his companions

c Cf. Matt. 26:24.
d Acts 4:32.
e Rom. 15:7.

left with peaceful hearts, having achieved a union of the spirit, and being commended by God's grace, returned once again to the place from which they had been sent.

The foremost teacher in Austerlitz was Jakob Wiedemann, otherwise known as One-Eyed Jakob. His assistants were Franz Intzinger, Jakob Mändel, and Kilian, plus others who had been ordained in the service of the Word.

When Jakob Hutter had been sent off to Tyrol and arrived among the believers there, he told them with joy how he had seen and experienced the fellowship of saints in Austerlitz, that he had united with them on their behalf, and that he had departed from them in peace and a unity of mind and spirit in order to return to the region of Tyrol. They had thus departed in peace. All the devout rejoiced greatly and gave heartfelt praise to God because of this. Afterward, if anyone in Tyrol was without a place to live, Jakob Hutter and Sigmund Schützinger would send them to the fellowship in Austerlitz.

He also sent a minister of the Word, Jörg Zaunring, along with them. Afterwards he sent one group after another with all their property, to form a community with the believers.

At this time a man came to Austerlitz named Wilhelm Reublin. He presented himself as a minister, but because they did not know him they did not allow him to teach.[25]

Chronicle Source 6

Emergence of Jakob Hutter, by Kaspar Braitmichel, The Chronicle of the Hutterian Brethren, *vol. 1*

The story of the beginning of the Hutterian Church was written down in their chronicle, begun by Kaspar Braitmichel in the 1560s – that is, thirty years after Jakob Hutter's death. Braitmichel was living in one of the many communities in Moravia, and he used letters, songs, and oral accounts as his sources. While the records extant in archives in Tyrol give a vivid picture of Hutter's missionary activity, the chronicle account describes his work to establish the communities in Moravia.[26]

After [Georg Blaurock's death], as the love of truth was kindled, many were killed in Tyrol for having witnessed to it, especially in the following places: in the district of Gufidaun and in Klausen, Brixen, Sterzing, Bozen, Neumarkt, Kaltern, Terlan, on the Kuntersweg; similarly in the Inn Valley, at Steinach, Imst, Petersberg, Stams, Innsbruck, Hall, Schwaz, Rattenberg, Kufstein, and Kitzbühel. In these places a great number of believers witnessed steadfastly to the truth with their blood and were killed by fire, water, or the sword. In spite of all this suffering, the people of God increased from day to day.

Around that time a man named Jakob appeared, a hatmaker by trade, born at Moos in the Puster Valley, half a mile from Bruneck. He accepted the covenant of grace, the covenant of a good conscience in Christian baptism, in true surrender, promising to live and to go the way of Jesus. When after a time it was felt that he had abundant gifts from God, he was chosen and commissioned in the ministry of the gospel. Now the fellowship in Tyrol learned that in Austerlitz, in the Margraviate of Moravia, the Lord God had gathered a people in his name to live as one heart, mind, and soul,[a] each caring faithfully for the other. So they determined they would send Jakob Hutter with Simon Schützinger and some companions to the fellowship in Austerlitz to make inquiries about all that had taken place.

After the fellowship in Tyrol had taken leave of them and commended them to the care of God, they went to Austerlitz. There they discussed everything thoroughly with the elders of the fellowship, as the fellowship in Tyrol had said they should. They found that both groups were of one heart and soul in serving and fearing God. Jakob and Simon and their companions, in the name of the whole fellowship, united in peace with the fellowship in Austerlitz.

As they had now accomplished their mission and brought to a happy conclusion all that had been entrusted to them, they wished to report all this to their own people, so Jakob and Simon with their companions prepared for the road again. They were sent off with dignity by the

---

a Acts 4:32.

community in Austerlitz, with peaceful hearts and in unity of spirit, commended to God and his grace for their return home.

In this year of 1529 many members were arrested in Upper Austria, and some were executed. Among those arrested was Peter Riedemann, born at Hirschberg in Silesia, a cobbler by trade, who was taken prisoner at Gmunden on Saint Andrew's Eve [November 29] in 1529. Although he was tortured through many and various means almost to the point of death, he remained faithful. Finally, after having lain in prison for over three years, he was freed by the providence of God.

The most prominent teacher in the fellowship at Austerlitz was Jakob Wiedemann, also known as One-Eyed Jakob. His assistants were Franz Intzinger, Jakob Mändel, Kilian [Volckamer], and others, all appointed to the ministry of the Word at Austerlitz.

When Jakob Hutter was sent back to the believers in the mountains of Tyrol, as just described, he joyfully told them about the community of saints he had seen and experienced in Austerlitz. He told how, in the name of them all, he had united with those at Austerlitz in peace and unity of soul and spirit and how they had sent him on his way home to Tyrol in peace. God had opened the way for them with his blessing and care. The whole community was full of joy, giving praise and thanks to God with all their hearts.

At this time quite a few members were living at Böhmisch Krumau,[27] with Hans Fasser as their minister or leader. These had congregated to express their unity in the spirit. Their hearts were moved when they heard of the uniting between Jakob Hutter and the fellowship in Austerlitz. All created beings demonstrate that like cleaves to like,[a] so they too enthusiastically sought out those who shared their beliefs and wanted to become one with them in Christ. They united with them in seeking a more perfect life. They were about eighty or ninety persons, among them Hans Amon, Leonhard Lanzenstiel, and Christoph Gschäl. All of them remained in the fellowship at Austerlitz except their minister, Hans Fasser, who returned to Bohemia, making it appear that he had reason to do so. But he was caught in shameful fornication and was later severely disciplined by the fellowship, then excluded, and delivered up to Satan.[b]

---

a Eccles. 13:15–16.

b 1 Cor. 5:5, 1 Tim. 1:20.

Later on, since there was no place available in Tyrol because of the excessive oppression, Jakob Hutter, with Simon Schützinger, sent people to the fellowship in Austerlitz. He sent a minister of the Word, Jörg Zaunring by name, along with them, and afterward he sent one small group after another with all their belongings to live in community with the believers.

At this time a man named Wilhelm Reublin came to Austerlitz, claiming to be a teacher or minister, but as nothing was known about him, he was not permitted to teach.

Meanwhile the devil – who does not rest but prowls around the house of God like a roaring lion,[c] seeking every opportunity to cause division, destroy the unity of spirit, and stamp out what God gives – made an attack at the critical place, namely, at the elders of the fellowship, who were responsible for the whole life of the people, as the devout Judith testifies in her book.[d]

At that time they had no place where everyone could meet to hear the teachings, because it was winter and extremely cold. Therefore they decided to hold their meetings in three places, and for each place a particular minister was appointed to teach, exhort, and comfort his little flock.

Their teachings differed, however. One taught this and another taught something different. One of them declared among other things that Christ had been a citizen of Capernaum and that therefore as citizens it was permissible to do civilian duties and swear oaths. Besides this, Jakob Wiedemann told several young sisters that if they would not follow his suggestions about marriage, he would have to give heathen wives to the brothers. He and some of his assistants alarmed the sisters with strange questions and gave them texts to learn. Those who could remember the texts and answer the questions clearly were highly praised, but the simple, unassuming sisters, although faithful and devout, were ridiculed and put to shame.

As there were so many people and their number increased daily, they were not all able to live in one house. Some of the ministers who had learned more than one language – Franz Intzinger, Jakob Mändel, among others – came to think highly of themselves and supplied food and drink

---

c 1 Pet. 5:8.

d Possibly a reference to Jth. 8:24.

to one another, which was inappropriate. As is generally known, arrogance goes before destruction and pride goes before a fall.[a] Some of them and also some self-seeking members who had kept money in their pockets went to market to buy what they liked for themselves. All these examples of impropriety, and more, were noticed by those who fought against avarice, and this caused a great deal of complaint among the people. Especially those from Tyrol complained about the teachings and said they were not as comforting and instructive as they had been at home. Similarly, many were troubled and complained about the children's education, saying that in these and related matters not nearly enough was done.

They reported these things to their particular minister, Jörg Zaunring, who also became very disturbed about it and began discussing it with some of his assistants and ministers, who all agreed with him, especially Burkhard [Braun] of Ofen, Bohemian David [Burda] von Schweinitz, and Adam Schlegel.

Early in 1530 Wilhelm Reublin began reading out loud one evening in one of the rooms. When people gathered around him to listen, he also expounded the Scriptures to them, although he had not been given the authority to teach. God cannot bear disorder in his fellowship, so he seeks ways to change it even through unredeemed men, as we can see in this and other cases.

Wilhelm Reublin began to speak openly in the fellowship against all the offenses committed by the ministers. As Jakob Wiedemann, who was entrusted with the care of the whole fellowship, was not at home, his assistants sent messengers to him to come without delay. As soon as he came, he summoned all the elders, from wherever they lived, and placed the whole matter before them in the presence of Jörg Zaunring and the other ministers who supported him. This took place in private at first. Reublin, however, persisted in what he had said and using scriptural proof tried to convince Jakob Wiedemann and all his followers that they were neither teaching nor positioned correctly. Jakob Wiedemann and his supporters did not accept this but called the fellowship as a congregation. He told the people how, in his absence, Reublin had

a Prov. 16:18.

intruded, teaching things that were opposed to what Jakob and his assistants taught, which could not be tolerated. At the end of a long speech that Jakob made before the fellowship, he said that whoever acknowledged his teaching to be right and had changed his life through it should come and stand next to him.

Wilhelm Reublin then asked them, for the sake of God, to give him a chance to answer. Likewise, Jörg Zaunring, Bohemian David [Burda], Burkhard of Ofen, and Adam Schlegel unanimously requested all the people to hear Reublin's reply, since they had heard Jakob Wiedemann's charges. The fellowship could then decide which side was right and which was wrong, as would only be fair before God and humanity. But their request was rejected outright.

Now most of the people went over to Jakob Wiedemann's side, many of them without knowing why, since not all of them had heard Jakob's accusations. About forty or fifty persons remained on the side of Zaunring and Reublin, eager to hear Reublin's reply in order to be fair. But the others would not allow it.

Thereupon Jakob Wiedemann called several of his followers and sent them to Jörg Zaunring to inquire why they had gone over to the other side. They replied that, having heard Jakob Wiedemann's accusation against Reublin, their request now as before was for God's sake to let Reublin's answer be heard as well. This would enable the fellowship to decide what was right before God, for no one should judge a matter that had not been given a hearing. But, as before, their request was unjustly refused. In other words, they attacked the flock with their horns.

Jakob Wiedemann warned his people that they should have nothing to do with the others. As a result, many who had previously followed Wiedemann now felt compelled to join with Zaunring and Reublin. When the time came for Jakob Wiedemann's people to be called to a meal, the others were treated as though they were excluded and shunned. They had contributed what little they had, and if they had been dealt with fairly, they would have remained; instead they had to leave empty handed.

Zaunring and Reublin and their people gathered outside the house, with total sorrow and afflicted hearts and minds. Reublin shook the dust from his shoes[a] as a testimony against the false and unjust judgment of Jakob Wiedemann and all who stayed with him. Then they set out, first finding lodging for their children and sick people in the town and leaving a minister, Burkhard of Ofen, to care for them and comfort them.

Zaunring and his assistants, with about 150 other people, prepared to move to Auspitz. Once outside the city of Austerlitz, the ministers named above spoke earnestly to the people, saying that whoever wanted to go with them should be ready, with them, to face the poverty of Christ and ultimately even death and destruction. All the money they had between them amounted to only a farthing per person. Therefore anyone who did not feel the courage to suffer hunger, great deprivation, misery, and poverty for the sake of truth should rather return to the city or to his home. But all of them wanted to face the consequences, trusting in God. Not one turned back.

It was in this way that God again brought about a purification, separating the devout from the non-devout. Those who remained with Jakob Wiedemann are therefore still known today as the Austerlitz Brethren.

All those who set out with Zaunring succeeded in reaching Auspitz as planned, although they traveled in great dread of thieves. They were housed and given refuge by the people there but had to suffer great deprivation and hunger, for they were quite ignorant of the work on the land and in the vineyards. Besides this, they had no provisions and often had to be content with water and a small piece of bread for a whole day, while doing hard labor. Yet they still cared for the sick and the children so far as they were able with their humble means. They brought their people from Austerlitz and lodged them at Steurowitz, half a mile away from Auspitz, hoping they would be safe there. But soon robbers came by night, took all they had, and beat some brothers so severely that one of them died. "Deep called to deep,"[b] which demanded great endurance on the part of the saints.

There was a man named Kaspar who had a house in Auspitz. Some time previously he had come from the fellowship in Austerlitz. He pretended to have a repentant heart and a wish to reunite with Zaunring and his people; but he went about with a false and deceitful appearance. He took

---

a Cf. Matt. 10:14.

b Ps. 42:5–7.

the members into his home, pretending to be happy to give them lodging. He let them work in his vineyard with scarcely any food, until the time the harvest was gathered in. Then he revealed his treachery, gave up the idea of brotherhood, and ordered them out of his house empty handed.

Throughout these hardships the believers cared faithfully for the weak and needy, supplying their needs. They brought them to Auspitz, where they had purchased a house near the horse market in an agreement with the nuns at Brünn, who also lent them money as an advance. They began to congregate in this house and to care for their children, with a God-fearing brother and several sisters to educate them in the discipline and ways of the Lord; but at night the children slept with their parents.

At this time the fellowship in Auspitz sent two brothers, Hans Tuchmacher [Amon] and a companion, to Tyrol. Austerlitz also sent two, to report to the fellowship about the division that had taken place and ask the fellowship in Tyrol to send brothers to look into the matter.

At that time, because God wished to purify his people and because sinners cannot remain in the fellowship of the righteous,[c] it happened that a minister of a little group in Swabia arrived in Auspitz to inquire about the faith, ordinances, and teaching of the fellowship of God. He spoke with Wilhelm Reublin about various articles of faith, but as they could not agree on one point, this minister from Swabia did not want to stay. The other brothers and elders asked him why he was leaving. When he told them how Reublin had explained one of the articles, the elders said, "But that is not the position of the fellowship," and suggested that perhaps he had misunderstood. But the man insisted that that was how he had heard it from Reublin, their teacher. The elders asked Reublin, but he repudiated him and denied it. The man from Swabia, however, still insisted on what he had said before and called upon God as witness. Reublin was severely admonished, but he, too, called on God as his witness. Finally others who had also heard him proved Reublin wrong, and he had to admit his guilt and confess that he had spoken as the man had testified. The elders told Reublin that the matter was too serious for them to close.

---

c Ps. 1:5.

Soon after, Reublin became extremely ill. Without the knowledge of the elders and the fellowship and regardless of the great hunger among the people, he had hidden twenty-four gulden that he had brought with him from his home. In his illness he entrusted this money to a married sister named Katharina Loy, who immediately reported it. This made it even harder for the elders to close the matter.

Around this time Jakob Hutter and Simon Schützinger arrived from Tyrol. They examined Reublin's situation carefully and summoned him before the fellowship. He was excluded as a lying, unfaithful, malicious Ananias.[a] He himself admitted and confessed that such a judgment was right.[28]

Jakob Hutter and Simon Schützinger had been asked by the communities in Austerlitz and Auspitz to go into the matter of the division and to administer discipline. They examined the matter thoroughly and considered it in the fear of God. They found those in Austerlitz most guilty, but when Jakob admonished them, they would not listen to him. But he insisted in pointing out their error and rebuking them for their lack of discernment: In the first place they had acted falsely and ignorantly in expelling the innocent; second, they had allowed freedom of the flesh in numerous ways, resulting in a return to private property in which people could do as they pleased; third, there had been marriages with unbelievers; and there were many similar points.

No warning or punishment helped, however. One freedom of the flesh led to another, as the false teaching in their printed statement of faith still proves. It was impossible to distinguish them from worldly people. Although they still claimed to hold to their first calling, their lives showed next to nothing of it. But in a wonderful way the Lord gradually brought back to the fellowship those in Austerlitz who were still devout, as will be reported later.

When Jakob Hutter and Simon Schützinger had brought this matter to a satisfactory conclusion, as they had been asked to do, they entrusted the fellowship to Jörg Zaunring. Both of them were commended to the grace of God, and they set out for the fellowship in Tyrol, where God had been powerfully at work.

---

a Cf. Acts 5:1–11.

Around the middle of 1531 other issues arose. Since God always seeks to advance the work he has begun, he resolved to build up and purify his fellowship. It will be told below how he gave his people, whom he called the salt of the earth,[b] such zeal that they would not spare the eyes, hands, or feet that were hurting the body of Christ.[c] Their minister Adam Schlegel misled some members into licentiousness and behaved in a scandalous manner. As soon as this was revealed, he was punished, dismissed from his office, and forbidden to teach. Others sided with him, including another minister, Burkhard of Ofen. These two looked for every excuse to find fault with the fellowship (as people do who want to abandon their friends), but there was nothing they could truthfully bring forward. So both of them were excluded from the fellowship as opponents of the truth.

It also became clear that Bohemian David [Burda] was not being honest. Without the advice or knowledge of the Brethren, he had paid the judge at Nikoltschitz for an armed escort to protect them from robbers on the way from Austerlitz to Auspitz. He was admonished for his faults in a brotherly way but was unable to honor God humbly, persisting in his own opinion. So he was punished before the whole fellowship because of his stubbornness.

Yet God wanted to put his people to the most challenging test to find out whether they relied on him or on humans, and therefore caused a great deal of talk and complaining to break out in the fellowship. It came to light that Bohemian David and Jörg Zaunring had agreed to settle in secret a severe affliction which should have come before the whole fellowship: A brother named Thomas Lindl had committed adultery with Jörg Zaunring's wife, so David and Jörg excluded them. Jörg did separate himself from his wife during her exclusion, but as soon as David and Jörg proclaimed the forgiveness of sin, Jörg took back his wife. When it became known, the fellowship could not accept such light punishment for adultery and fornication. For according to the word of the Lord it is better to enter the kingdom of God with one eye or as a cripple than to go to hell with pernicious, corrupt members.[d]

---

b Matt. 5:13.
c Matt. 5:29–30.
d Mark 9:43–47.

It was Leonhard Schmerbacher, a minister for temporal affairs, who brought the matter before the fellowship and told what Jörg Zaunring had done. The whole fellowship agreed unanimously that members of Christ should not be members of a harlot[a] and therefore Zaunring and his wife should be excluded and separated from the fellowship. Now the fellowship was without a shepherd, teacher, or minister of the Word, but they were zealous for the truth, punishing wrong without regard of a person's status.

The ministers for temporal affairs, with the whole fellowship, immediately let those in Tyrol know of their need by letter and word of mouth. They made a heartfelt plea for a minister to be sent to care for them with the word of the Lord.

Jakob Hutter and Simon Schützinger were sent off immediately, arriving in Auspitz around Easter [1532]. They consoled the fellowship and praised them for acting so zealously against wrongful actions, which pleased Jakob, although he said he wished there had been another means for it to be resolved; yet he was satisfied that everything had been handled in the right way. Simon Schützinger was appointed shepherd of the fellowship in place of Jörg Zaunring.

Jakob and Simon soon united with Gabriel Ascherham and Philip Blauärmel [Plener] and their people in Rossitz and Auspitz. From now on the three groups were no longer to act separately in difficult matters but to seek each other's counsel as befits a united people.

Since all the needs of the fellowship had been seen to and all disorder put right, Jakob Hutter returned once more to his place, the fellowship in Tyrol. Simon, Gabriel, and Philip looked after the three fellowships, Austerlitz, Auspitz, and Rossitz, jointly, yet each remained at his own place with his group.

However, Zaunring admitted his impropriety and said many times that his heartfelt wish was to change. He was taken back into the fellowship with intercession to the Lord on his behalf. As his whole life continued upright, he was again entrusted with the ministry of the gospel and later sent to Franconia. Not far from Bamberg, he was executed with the sword for the sake of divine truth.

---

a 1 Cor. 6:15.

During this time the number of people in the fellowship increased daily at all three places. From Silesia they came to Rossitz, from Swabia and the Palatinate they joined Philip's group, and Jakob Hutter sent many from Tyrol to Schützinger. Thus the work of the Lord spread more and more.

In 1532 a profane mob of godless, wicked soldiers on their way from Prague in Bohemia to Hungary attacked the devout. At Rossitz they plundered Gabriel's people, using violence and clamor. Then they came to Auspitz, where they attacked Schützinger's people and carried off all they could. The brothers and sisters had to remain and were seated in one place as they watched helplessly. The wanton rabble treated the elders of the fellowship outrageously. They wanted money, but as there was very little, they beat the brothers and tore off their clothes. Then they turned on the sisters and neither respected nor spared their womanhood. In the middle of their attack, they found a little money in a small earthenware pot. But God, who hates robbery, caused them to fight over this small sum, each one hoping to get a large amount. During the struggle one of them shot and killed a fellow soldier. As Job says, robbery became "the poison of cobras within his belly."[b] The soldiers were so shocked that they ran away and ceased their violence. Although they attacked Philip's people too, they did not do as much harm there compared to the other two fellowships. The devout left all vengeance to God, the just Judge, who rewards each one according to his deeds.

Chronicle Source 7

Excommunication of Reublin and the 1531 Division at Austerlitz[29]

After Jakob Hutter had returned to Tyrol, a disagreement arose among the ministers[30] in Austerlitz. At this time Jörg Zaunring and several ministers had been sent out of the region [of Tyrol to Moravia], followed by more people. Brother Jörg, who was a minister of God, and some of the others, took issue with how matters of conduct had been dealt with, as well as what was being taught. During the absence of One-Eyed Jakob,

b Job 20:14.

and against the wishes of the brethren at Austerlitz, Wilhelm Reublin had dared to create controversy and point out the shortcomings of the people. When One-Eyed Jakob returned home, he and other ministers admonished Wilhelm and asked him why he was contradicting them. Then Wilhelm declared to them his grievances and those of others, that they were neither teaching correctly nor judging matters appropriately. He pointed some articles [of faith] out to them, wanting to prove to them by scripture. Zaunring and the brothers who stood with him, namely, Burkhart of Ofen, Adam Schlegel, and Bohemian David,[31] had previously also found issue with these matters. Thus the ministers held a discussion in secret, apart from the fellowship, but they could not come to an agreement. For this reason, the eldest brethren of the fellowship were summoned as well as all the people. One-Eyed Jakob, as the leading minister, spoke against Wilhelm and denounced him. Wilhelm then wanted to respond. But One-Eyed Jakob and his assistants would not let him respond but told the gathered people: Whoever considers his teaching to be of God should go with him to another place. Wilhelm, Jörg Zaunring, and a small number of others stood up. Wilhelm spoke and wished that he should be allowed to respond. Zaunring and other brothers said he should be given a chance to respond.

Afterward One-Eyed Jakob sent some men to Wilhelm and those who stood with him, telling them to state their reasons for remaining [on Reublin's side]. Zaunring and the other brothers answered: "We heard Jakob's accusation of Wilhelm. Now we would like to hear Wilhelm's response and then the fellowship should judge." Zaunring and those with him pleaded: "Come to our side and hear our response, or let us go over to you and let the fellowship decide."

But they did not choose this, but instead warned the people of us and shunned those of us who were with Zaunring. Because of this, the brethren, that is Zaunring and Wilhelm and the small group that stood with them, had to leave them. As they were leaving the house, Wilhelm shook the dust over the ministers of the Word in Austerlitz,[a] calling out their names. As they left, they admonished one another that whoever went with them would have to be prepared for poverty, for they had few

a Matt. 10:14.

provisions. They moved away as far as Auspitz where they lived in great need and poverty.

Meanwhile it was discovered that Wilhelm Reublin had secretly withheld money, without regard for the fact that they were suffering.

At the same time, the brethren [in Austerlitz] wrote to Jakob Hutter and Simon Schützinger in Tyrol, asking them to come immediately. The brethren in Auspitz also wrote to them concerning what was happening. Jakob Hutter and Schützinger arrived and investigated the dispute from both sides and then deliberated.

They concluded that those in Austerlitz had not done right. But when it became known that Reublin had withheld money, and for other reasons as well, he was excommunicated[32] from the fellowship in Auspitz by Jakob Hutter and Simon Schützinger. The fellowship was commended to the care of Jörg Zaunring; this was the reason he had been sent with them from Tyrol.

Then Bohemian David, Burkhart von Ofen, and Adam Schlegel, who had moved with him from Austerlitz, became his assistants, although they were subsequently excommunicated from the fellowship because of their heedlessness.

Chronicle Source 8

Mandates against Anabaptism, 1533, by Georg Kirchmayr [33]

In August 1532, a comet appeared. In July 1533, a huge comet appeared. The Roman Royal Majesty King Ferdinand remained quiet after the departure of the emperor, and dealt with the Turks in an effort to obtain a truce. But there were financial constraints at the court. His Royal Majesty issued many ordinances against the Anabaptists. July 14, 1533, a rebellious woman and man were executed by the sword at Brixen. O such outpouring of blood at that time!

Chronicle Source 9

Hutter's Arrival in Auspitz; Separation from Gabriel and Philip[34]

In 1533, on the 12th [*or* 11th][35] of August, brother Jakob Hutter, an outstanding minister of the word of the gospel, came from the region of Tyrol to Auspitz in Moravia. He excommunicated Simon Schützinger and many others from the fellowship because they held private property, something Schützinger also admitted he believed to be appropriate. Yet Gabriel at Rossitz and Philip at Auspitz and their followers interjected and wanted to accept Schützinger back, after he had been excommunicated. They called Jakob an idol and false god. The fellowship of the Lord, after intense prayer to God, did accept him as a shepherd and teacher. He carried out his service in the evangelical office faithfully according to the truth.

At this time there arose a great discord between Jakob Hutter, Philip, and Gabriel. Jakob tried by numerous ways and means to resolve it, but they would not accept it, even after much debate. Instead, the longer it carried on, the further they fell into lies and horrific slander, so that Jakob was obliged to refuse to recognize them as brethren. He warned other brothers and sisters about them, relaying the reasons, and discussions proceeded and took place, which is described elsewhere.[36]

Afterward, brother Jakob Hutter, through the help and grace of God, brought the true community into order. For this reason we are still called Hutterites.

Chronicle Source 10

The Division of 1533[37]

This text has been pieced together from several codices. Triangular brackets mark the beginning and end of the various sections.

True divine zeal has urged me to briefly describe what transpired.[38]

On August 11, 1533[39] our dear brother and minister of the Lord Jesus Christ, Jakob Hutter, came to us through the grace and mercy and leading of God our heavenly Father. The entire holy fellowship of God received him and welcomed him as they would the Lord himself.[a] All devout hearts rejoiced in his arrival, and he too rejoiced that he had arrived safely among us. He said to Sigmund Schützinger <who was our minister at the time>[40] and to other ministers and brothers and sisters that he came to us not as strangers but as to his dear brothers, friends, and children. Sigmund and the elders acknowledged that this was right and true, and they asked and admonished him to help them care for the people with the greatest diligence. He agreed to do so.

The following Sunday he brought us the holy message from our dear brothers and sisters who had sent him to us. He also proclaimed the great wonders that God had worked through him and other saints. Then he said openly that it had come to his attention that there were some who hoped that when he arrived he would move with them to another location. He openly admonished them <their superficiality for accusing him of saying so>[41] and declared that he had never taught or said that. With all his strength he would call upon and chastise, in the strength of God, any superficial hearts who wanted to move to a different location. Nobody came forward who wanted that. He said further that since God had sent him to us, he would exert all his energy to improve anything in the house of God that needed to be improved.

After a few days he began addressing some things that needed improvement; however, Sigmund resisted him. So Jakob had cause to ask the people whether they wanted him as a shepherd and minister or not, whether they needed him or not, for he was not at liberty before the Lord to remain silent and not exercise his service. <If they did not need him, he would move on and serve the Lord wherever the Lord sent him.>[42]

He told Gabriel about it and complained to him that he did not know whether the people wanted him or not. He was willing to say this to the people, and whatever the people of God wanted of him after that,[43] <in the name of God, he would do. Gabriel did not disagree, but told him to do it humbly.

But while Jakob was in Rossitz [Gabriel's community] Sigmund said to Leonard [Schmerbacher] and Wilhelm [Griesbacher] that he wanted

a Gal. 4:14.

to continue in his office and would not give Jakob much chance to speak. The two brothers opposed him and said he should remain in his office but that Jakob should serve with him. Yet Sigmund did not want this.

When Jakob returned from Rossitz he wanted to pass on to the brothers and sisters greetings from Gabriel and the brothers and sisters there. Sigmund addressed him and asked him what he wanted to do. What Sigmund had in mind became clear later, as described briefly below.

Soon after this Jakob told Sigmund and the elders (Caspar, a minister from Rossitz was there too) what his opinion and desire was, namely, that he wanted to know from the people whether they needed him or not. For he was not free before the Lord to walk around without practicing his office, and he could not answer for it before God. Then Sigmund began, saying that God had entrusted the people to him and set him over them as their shepherd by lot. He wanted to continue in this office. If Jakob had something to say he could do so with a few words, but he could not allow him to speak long. Although the other ministers disagreed, [Sigmund] wanted to remain the shepherd, to teach and pasture the people. The elders, including Caspar from Rossitz, said that both should care for the people, but he wanted to be the only shepherd.

The ministers wanted to meet with the people immediately the next day, but it was delayed until Sunday because many of the brethren were working. In the meantime, Sigmund>[44] secretly sent for Gabriel, who came to the Philippites.[45] Sigmund met with them and told them that Jakob wanted to push in before him. So they sent for Jakob, who went to them ignorant of what they wanted of him. Some time later, in the night, Leonard, Caspar, and Wilhelm were also called over.[46] <Gabriel began and said to Jakob that he understood that he wanted to intrude upon Sigmund.

Jakob said, no, he could not allow himself to intrude, but he desired to serve these people because he had been sent here by God through great intercession, and this people had been committed to him just as much as to Sigmund. Therefore he desired nothing more than to carry out his office. Philip immediately retorted that if that is what he wanted, no worse devil than him had ever come to the land. But Jakob held firm as before. He also asked them how they would like it if they left, entrusting the people to someone else, and when they returned had to step down.

After much talk, which would be impossible to transcribe, Philip said that in his opinion they should both care faithfully for the people as he and Blasy [Blasius Kuhn] did, serving equally. He asked Jakob what he thought. Jakob said he wanted nothing else but to stand with Sigmund in the same role, and he thus praised God.

But Gabriel said, "No, I disagree. Instead, I would ask you, Sigmund, to continue in your role as shepherd for this people. If you would diminish your role or become timid, thinking that Jakob has more gifts than you and is a better speaker, God will punish you. The same will happen to you as happened to me with the Swiss Brethren.">[47]

Sigmund quickly answered, "Yes, yes, my brother, yes, praise the Lord. That's true, my brother Gabriel, that's true." But Leonard [Schmerbacher] said, "Philip just said you should both serve together, caring for the people, one like the other, and now Gabriel says something quite different." Philip answered that his position was exactly like Gabriel's. Even if what he said didn't sound like it, that is what his heart and his opinion had been.

There was a lot more discussion, and Jakob remained firm as before and wanted to hear what the people felt regarding him. They could not deny him this, but told him he should be flexible.

Early on Sunday Jakob began speaking to the people. He told them the reason for his coming and that he had had to lay down the work that God had entrusted him with for a while. He described his discussions with the elders and with Sigmund and briefly what had been discussed with Gabriel and Philip.

Then Sigmund spoke. He told how he had been elected and that he wanted to stand by it. Gabriel confirmed him with a long speech, telling how [Sigmund] had been chosen by lot and presented to the people, and that if they would curtail him because they preferred to hear Jakob because he could speak better, or if they would set him equal to Sigmund, he [Gabriel] would have no part in it. He would leave by the road he had come on. He also said that in Jerusalem there was only one shepherd, James.

Jakob contradicted him. But Gabriel continued in his speech and admonished the people with the shocking example of Korah.[a] He said

a Num. 16.

if they disregarded Sigmund for his simplicity and preferred to hear Jakob because of his fine speech, God would punish them with his rod as he punished Korah. He admonished the people to see that they not make an idol of Jakob, because it seemed to him that he had an arrogant, proud spirit. After a lengthy discussion he also said that Jakob did not have the gifts to serve such a people as shepherd; he only had the gifts of an apostle.

At this, the congregation was asked for their judgment regarding Sigmund and Jakob. Two or three brothers said Sigmund should continue in his office and Jakob should assist him. Then Peter Hueter spoke, saying in his opinion neither should be considered higher or lower, greater or smaller; to him one was as good as the other. He also quoted scripture. But Sigmund cut him short, saying how stupid he was and that he had thought him a lot wiser. He was contradicted by Sigmund as well as by Gabriel, without any reason or any truth.

Then Leonard said he also couldn't say that one was better than the other. The people had been entrusted to each of them equally, and for the sake of peace, love, and unity Jakob should give honor and precedence to Sigmund. At this all the people said, Yes, yes. Yet one member of the fellowship said he had nothing against this decision, but if Jakob weren't there, Sigmund would suffice for us.

After all this Gabriel spoke to Jakob and asked him whether he would accept this decision of the fellowship and give Sigmund precedence. Jakob answered that he wished to consider it before God and with the elders and ministers; he couldn't <give an answer>[48] at this point. Gabriel said he had nothing to discuss with him and would be on his way.

The people separated, but there was great pain and anguish of heart among the brothers and sisters.[49] <Jakob too was deeply distressed. Some brothers went to him to comfort him. Others, when they saw this, thought he wanted to lead some to a separate location. One said this, and another that. In essence, the whole congregation was mortally troubled.

On the following Tuesday morning the people were called together again. Jakob said that he had spoken with the brethren and taken counsel with God the Lord. He could only say that God in his providence had ordained him and sent him to this people, but the brethren did not understand him correctly. However, they admittedly were prepared to drop the issue, and for the sake of love, peace, and unity he wanted to accept this decision, though it was not an equitable decision. Gabriel said to Jakob, You said we didn't understand you, but we are German. There was no need for you to speak. Although the people were distressed about this exchange,>[50] they were happy and hoped that God would lead everything for the best.

Fourteen days later the Lord struck Sigmund with illness so that he was bedridden. Jakob spoke the word of the Lord. The elders asked him to hold a sermon on the topic of community, which he did the next Sunday, September 28. Jakob spoke in the power of God about the true community of Jesus Christ. At this there was renewed murmuring among some and muttering against him.

Around this time Jörg Fasser wanted to bring his temporal possessions to the fellowship of God.[51] He announced this and (as their head) asked his wife and children to do the same and willingly present themselves to the Lord and his people that they were in agreement. He immediately brought beds and chests to the communal storage. But when the ministers examined it all, they found that his wife had held back and hidden money away for herself and the children. At this, she was soundly admonished and chastised by the ministers, her husband, <and Sigmund>.[52]

Since this woman had deceived her husband and hidden so much money, it occurred to Jakob (as the spirit of God in many other ways too had previously been reflected in him) that Sigmund's wife was also such a Sapphira.[a] [53] <He said to the elders that if they would stand behind him in the strength of God, he would like to investigate and explore it further. The elders agreed that he should go ahead; he should begin in his own room, then the trunks and beds of all the elders, and then look in Sigmund's room as well.

This took place, and when they got to Sigmund's room and asked him to let them look in his trunks and elsewhere, so that their hearts would rest easy, he agreed. They looked into a trunk and found an overabundance of linen and shirts as well as four Bernese pounds. Jakob asked him in the name and power of God, whether he knew about the money. He

a Cf. Acts 5:1–11.

answered yes, and pulled forty florins out from under the eaves. Jakob and the other ministers were shocked; they had not imagined he would knowingly do such a thing. Jakob denounced his cunning behavior and sent immediately for Philip, but he was not home.

Since this sly deceiver had been found out, they could not wait. Early the next morning, October 5, they brought him before the fellowship. Jakob denounced his duplicity and deception. All the children of God were shocked, and there was great pain. Brothers and sisters wept loudly. He was excommunicated according to the word of God (as is right and just), and delivered over to the devil.[a] He himself admitted that this was just, and he desired grace and mercy. Jakob faithfully admonished and exhorted him to repent. The same day Fasser's wife and other corrupt members were excluded from the fellowship.

Since this deceiver had been revealed (whom the whole fellowship had exalted above Jakob), Jakob urged us all to consider the decision we had made, what we had said and decided. He reminded us that it had been said that he didn't have the gifts to lead such a congregation or to be their shepherd.>[54] Since we had chosen Sigmund as our shepherd, and he was now revealed to be a scoundrel, we now had no shepherd. Since we had so little respect for the Lord's word and message, Jakob was now not certain that he should serve us. He admonished us to call earnestly to God and pray that he raise up a devout shepherd and minister.

We began to pray for eight full days and nights, pleading to God. We sent two men to Rossitz to tell Gabriel of our need. He suggested[55] <Jakob, [it was due to our praying so earnestly to God, that the Lord gave us Jakob][56] and bound him and us deeply together in love. On October 12, we, the entire fellowship, rejoiced in spite of all our troubles. We acknowledged and confessed before God and before him that we had done wrong in giving precedence and honor to the scoundrel Sigmund, that we realized that Sigmund was not a minister of God as we had thought, but the Lord knew him.

We prayed in a spirit of unity and earnestly, asking for forgiveness for our ignorance. God forgave us and saw that we had acted in blindness.

---

a 1 Cor. 5:5.

God the Lord blessed us too, and the word of God grew; peace, love, and the fear of God increased. The evil were put out of the fellowship and the devout were welcomed in.

But as love and godliness and the true judgment of God grew and increased among us, and the entire holy fellowship lived at peace, yet the devil never goes on furlough. He strives day and night to find a way with his cunning, to destroy the love among us.

We were together on October 26 to hear the word of God. Before daybreak Philip and Blasy as well as Gabriel and Peter Hueter slipped in, in sheep's clothing,[b] groomed in hypocrisy.>[57] We were all shocked, and many of us worried that the devil planned to bring disaster. But Jakob and the ministers and elders received them. At the beginning they were friendly, and we trusted them. They were asked to tell why they had come.

Philip began and asked first why we hadn't accepted David von Schweinitz[58] even though we had given him a good testimony on account of his rectitude, and why we would ask him to leave. Second, why we excommunicated Bernhard Glaser. Third, he understood our claim that the election and instatement of Sigmund was not of God, but he said it was and is of God and is eternally valid before God the Lord.

There was so much discussion and argument that the fellowship could not come to clarity. One called the other a liar and so much was said that we were very heavy-hearted. There were many deep sighs and dismayed hearts. We didn't know what would come of it or who else was guilty until Philip and Gabriel came out with their roguery (which can never remain hidden).

Jakob spoke to them in the power of God saying, You have accused the fellowship. If what you say is true, we must be the most wicked scoundrels. Philip denied it and said Jakob was lying. But Jakob said, The lie will fall on your head.

Philip continued, Yes, I said that you are an idol. They worship you. This is the truth. At this, there was a great commotion and the brothers and sisters said, You are lying.

---

b Matt. 7:15.

As soon as Philip was called a liar by the whole fellowship because of this abuse, he tried to cover it and take it back, denying it. But after much abuse they stood up and said, Dear fellowship, we have nothing against you, only against your ministers. We desire and advise you to send some of your men out. We will do the same, and they will judge between us. But nobody answered them, and they left.

However, on Monday the fellowship sent eight men out[59] <to the other two fellowships to give an account on their behalf of what we had done, saying also that the whole fellowship stood behind them and behind their ministers. Of these eight men, four were sent to Philip to tell him that tomorrow (or when it suited them) we would come and give an account of all we had done. But Philip received them not as children of God but as children of wickedness and of the devil. He reprimanded them for making an idol of Jakob because of money and for worshiping him. Also that we had excommunicated Sigmund Schützinger out of envy and hatred and accepted Jörg Fasser for the sake of money. The four men contradicted him. There was more ungodly abusive speech that I will omit for the sake of brevity, but when the four brothers told us about it the whole fellowship was greatly shocked; he had recently recognized us as children of peace and so quickly changed his heart.

The next day eight men came to us from Rossitz and told us how Gabriel and Peter Hueter had brought them a message that did not cheer them but greatly distressed them. So they had been quickly dispatched from their whole fellowship to investigate what we had done. The Rossitz fellowship desired that all three groups would come together without the ministers Jakob, Philip, and Gabriel.>[60] We were to give an account and the other two fellowships would make a judgment (although initially they wanted us to decide with them).

But that same night the devil gave them another idea. In the morning, when we sent our agreement with their eight brothers, they denied it. They thought we would not realize the source of this.[61] <But we answered that we wanted to discuss with each other in the Lord what we should do and we would let them know. They left peacefully.

We decided in great fear of God that we would like the other two fellowships to come to us, with Philip and Gabriel, and if they wished we would give account of all we had done. We let them know through our brothers, but they would not accept it. They wanted to know if we would meet without our ministers. The eight brothers went around again and spoke with brother Jakob and the other ministers. They agreed that they were willing, if they were convinced through God's word and true testimony, to wait in another location. They told this to the eight men, but they wouldn't accept it. They wanted assurance from the whole fellowship. To avoid more trouble, we let them come before the congregation. We told them right away what we had said to the eight men. But we said to them they should let us know in the morning when the congregation gathered. But they came that night when we were together, sneaking in secretly and listening to what we said. But our minister Jakob was aware of them and spoke to them directly, and they went out. But we told them of our decision, which they still would not accept. They spoke to us: Dear fellowship, dear children of God, we have no authority to accept this. We can do nothing without our fellowship. We will take leave of you now in peace, as our brothers and sisters. We will tell our people of your decision and will let you know what our fellowship wants to do.

With this, they took leave of Jakob, embracing and kissing him as well as Leonard and others, kissing one another. They spoke peace to the whole congregation and everyone said, Amen, amen. We were happy, hoping that the Lord would provide a solution. But then one of them asked if we had excommunicated Gabriel. Jakob answered, We do not consider him a brother or a minister of God.

As the wolf never likes to remain in sheepskin for long, one of them named Hans of Strassburg jumped forward, speaking abusively and calling Jakob a liar and false prophet. He shook out his sack with terrible verbal abuse, which they had suppressed with hypocrisy, one after the next, before taking leave in peace, so that we could now see what the devil had in mind.

But God no longer wished to tolerate their continued mockery of us. There was such pain in the congregation that I know it moved God in heaven to pity. Then Jakob, our minister, wanted to hear from the fellowship whether these men had come seeking peace or not, and who they were. One brother [62] began speaking in great fervor (as God knows), saying that they had come with the appearance of peace. They said in front of us all that they could do nothing in terms of coming to an accord without their fellowship, and yet they had reviled and were abusive toward us, lying and deceiving us without their fellowship. They had made their words and kiss of peace into a lie. Since they had illustrated such wickedness that a blind person could perceive it, he would consider them the same as Gabriel and Philip.

Then they began to revile that brother and then ran out the door. The brother, however, continued speaking, comforting the congregation, which was greatly pained, some of them trembling but comforted in the Lord. Only a few reckless souls banded together and wanted to cause an uproar among the people, but the Lord did not allow it.

There was also a minister of the word there who had brought a group from Hessen to us.[63] He also had in mind to steal something from the Lord's hand, but he was unable to because the people looked to the Lord and not to him. We excommunicated him later according to the word of the Lord. Although he had testified before us all not once but often that he recognized clearly that Philip and Gabriel had acted wrongly, that they were not his brothers and we had done right – yet after we excommunicated him, he went to Philip and treated him as a dear brother. From this we could see his wicked heart still more clearly. If he could have caused a rift in the fellowship, he would have liked to do so. He never said plainly that he wanted to leave but repeated before the fellowship and before the brothers that he knew them well and would not go to them. But God protected us from this wolf.

The following Sunday we sent eight men to Philip to tell his fellowship what had taken place and also to warn them regarding Philip. But they were not allowed to speak to the congregation. They were reviled and treated badly.

After this, on the following Thursday, we sent six men to Rossitz to advise the fellowship there to separate from Gabriel and other wicked people because they had been excommunicated by us and delivered to the devil. But they too were not allowed to speak to the congregation, for Gabriel>[64] had bewitched the people and not one of them said they should be heard. But we told them to flee from evil, otherwise we would consider them as we did Gabriel. The brothers who were up there told us that they had little hope, as they all agreed with Gabriel. May God save the simple and innocent from among them, through Jesus Christ our Lord. Amen.

This is a short but truthful account of what took place in the house of God in Auspitz in Moravia through an attack of Satan. Anyone who reads this should take care that it does not become a stumbling block for him to read of the rebellion of false spirits. These things must happen so that the chosen[a] are purified like gold. But rejoice, you honest reader of the Lord. Amen.[65]

Chronicle Source 11

Summary of the Articles and Accusations against Gabriel and Philip[66]

This text has been pieced together from several codices; see note 37. Triangular brackets mark the beginning and end of the various sections.

These are the articles and accusations we have against Gabriel and Philip:

First: Gabriel said before the entire congregation that Jakob wanted to intrude on Sigmund. They also called Jakob a liar without giving any testimony. They also said Jakob was our idol and the whole fellowship worships him. Even though they later denied it, we all heard it. They also said that Jakob accused Sigmund and Gabriel because of envy and hatred and then excommunicated them, and that he admitted Jörg Fasser out of favoritism and because of his money and had accepted a scoundrel and excluded the other.

Also: as they were leaving they said they parted from us not as from impure people, and they had no desire to be disunited with us, but that we should die with and for one another and live amicably together. But the next day when we sent four brothers to Philip, he denied everything he had said and he reviled and berated us, calling us children of the devil and

a 2 Esd. 16:73.

of wickedness. He said Jakob had bought us with the money he brought, and therefore we had made him an idol and nobody more wicked had come to the land. Philip also said that Bernhard <Glaser>,[67] who was excommunicated and put out from us because of his <lies and untruthfulness and>[68] sin, was more devout and he would believe him before the whole pile of us.

He had reviled and slandered Jakob and us in front of the fellowship and behind our backs without cause. It would be too much and take too long to write down everything we saw, heard, and perceived from him. They have never repented. Each one can consider how they quoted scripture with all their machinations, saying the Lord had said such and such, although the Lord never did. In this they condemned us wrongly, as we have faithfully confessed before the Lord. But they, the liars, still say today that this stands in eternity – although it didn't stand for four weeks.

<*Concluded November 22, 1533*>[69]

Further, Gabriel said we should have found another solution with Sigmund and not made such a fuss, and so on – although he had done wrong deliberately and deceived [the fellowship] for a long time, which has now been revealed as the truth before God. Regarding Jörg Zaunring, they were unable to find a different solution, for the name of God had been seriously reviled, since he had always been faithful of heart. We say before God and in truth that this is true and remains true in eternity. Jörg Zaunring was punished faithfully and adequately before the whole fellowship for what he did in ignorance on account of his wife and everything he had done. The fellowship forgave and pardoned him and recognized him as a dear brother. No wrong was found in him, neither small nor big, yet [they said he should have been] excommunicated and delivered to the devil, regarded as a whore and rogue, regardless of how the fellowship had handled his situation. That would have pleased Gabriel and Philip and they still say the same today. Jörg Zaunring never said or confessed that he was such, but Gabriel refused to listen to him or accept him without such a confession.

Regarding David they say it was not right that we wanted to make him confess that he dealt with Jörg Zaunring out of envy and hatred – although this is now clearly revealed before God and he also admitted it once.

For all these reasons we can recognize and conclude nothing else (for they accuse us of dealing with one person out of envy and hatred and the other with favoritism) but that they are the ones who have higher regard for human considerations than the will of God. <This great foolishness is clear and obvious, and everyone should and must recognize it.>[70] Such is not found among us and never will be, by God's grace. Nobody can truthfully accuse us, and we have no regard for false testimony. Whoever has eyes will see it; it is clear as day.[71]

Chronicle Source 12

Account of the Discernment Process[72]

This text has been pieced together from several codices; see note 37. Triangular brackets mark the beginning and end of the various sections.

<How[73] the final decision took place must also be told in brief.

To begin with, the whole fellowship recognized that our dear, devout brother Jakob was a gift from God, ordained as a minister and shepherd. They never said anything else of him; he always had a good testimony everywhere as befits a devout minister and shepherd, commissioned by God, as attested in his work. Philip and the others openly said that at this time nobody cared for the people as faithfully as Jakob, concerning both temporal and spiritual gifts.

We never found any deceit in him, but he served the Lord and us faithfully, bearing quite a lot of fruit for the Lord, as his work testifies. The Lord brought this people here and gathered them, cared for and preserved them, using [Jakob] as his instrument. Although we had thought that Sigmund too was faithful in his office and did not consider one better than the other, all of us including Sigmund welcomed him not as a stranger but as one who had always served us and should continue to serve us with full status and authority (as described above). [We thought] each of them would serve to the best of his ability, with all the gifts they had received from God. Philip recognized this too, with his own lips before the whole fellowship.

But then Sigmund asserted himself, saying the congregation had been entrusted to him by lot, and not to Jakob, with Gabriel supporting him in this by using a deceptive approach and testimony. From that moment on, Philip reneged on everything he had said and denied it. Everyone who loves the truth can consider for himself if our decision was of God. At that point God could no longer tolerate the unfair decision but uprooted the unjust plant.[a] And with great and wonderful strength, God put to shame the false praise and honor that had been given to Sigmund, bringing it to nothing, for the elevated status, honor, and praise that had been given to him was contrary to God's word. This is the truth and>[74] not empty words, such as that which Gabriel speaks and testifies.

Gabriel said before us all (as has already been described but as further proof I have to say again that he used a deceptive approach) that the church in Jerusalem only had one shepherd, James. With this he wanted to prove that Sigmund alone should be our shepherd, and he was heard saying that if we did not do this, he would leave the way he had come and have no part in it. With these words he shocked and dismayed us simple sheep. Jakob, our minister, also contradicted him, but he stuck to his words that James alone was the shepherd in Jerusalem. He cannot prove this, for in holy scripture we find others who served the people and preached, namely in the Acts of the Apostles chapters 1, 2, 3, 4, 5, 6, 7, 11, 12, 15, 21; and Colossians 1 and 2. And even if there was only one in Jerusalem, that does not prove that there should only be one minister or shepherd. That is an unhealthy and false teaching, and many devout people have been deceived and betrayed by it. We can simply lay this before God.

Gabriel also introduced the terrible example of Korah[b] – that if we contradicted Sigmund the same would happen to us. In this he deceived us who believed him, thinking he spoke God's word. But if one looks at it properly, Philip, Gabriel, and Sigmund have been Korah, Dathan, and Abiram who spoke against the devout Jakob who, in all fairness, was our minister. They reviled and dishonored him with unchristian, unbrotherly words. For this reason, the fire of heaven[c] has fallen on them and will fall on all those who give credence to their lies and untruthfulness; moreover,

a Matt. 15:13.
b Cf. Num. 16.
c Cf. Num. 16:35; Rev. 20:9.

we should not honor anybody above another or consider one higher than another, as Christ clearly says.[d]

With such words, examples, and threats we let our hearts be persuaded for the sake of peace and unity. We are deeply sorry whenever we think of it. We have also reconciled with our beloved Father and repented with weeping hearts that we followed a false teaching and regarded Sigmund above Jakob (even though we did it with our best intentions, to preserve peace and unity). We were ignorant of God's will and saw the matter naively, and God has forgiven us and pardoned us, and we owe him great praise and thanks forever.

But woe to those who misled us with crafty displays, false testimony, and terrible threats. At the beginning, when Sigmund was exposed, we thought they would renounce before the Lord everything for which they had inappropriately praised Sigmund, without us having to point it out to them. But their proud spirit would not be humbled or put to shame. We would gladly have stayed if they had asked for an explanation, for such reasons as we are compelled by God's love to point out to them, but they did not want to give us a hearing.

Since they also want to count as just[e] what is unjust and call us children of the devil, we desire, as God teaches us, to give our reasons to you brothers and sisters and to all people. They have not taught us one word that God spoke, for they have said nothing but evil. Among them is nothing but sin, deception, and injustice. We recognize and conclude in the fear of God and the name of the Lord, with carefully considered thought and courage, in the strength and grace of the Holy Spirit that these men, who contrived such abuse and shame, are not ministers of God, nor children of God, but children of the abuse of the devil. They are excommunicated and separated from us, and we will neither take part nor have community with them as they are. This is our resolve in the name and strength of the Holy Spirit.

But we still accept the common brothers and sisters, until we see how they respond to what transpired, which we are doing in the Lord. If they despise it and count it for nothing, God will also despise them. And it

d E.g., Matt. 18:1–5; 20:20–28; 23:1–12.
e Cf. Isa 5:20.

was and is greater and more significant for us that they don't have one spark of true, godly love. They are not merely godless, but they spend all their energy to influence others. Those whom we have excommunicated because of their sin and wickedness, separated from us and delivered to the devil, are welcome among them and are their dear brothers and sisters.

As such they are a shelter for all wild and impure spirits. They derail anyone who wants to come to us in repentance, as they did with Sigmund, who wanted to repent before the whole fellowship at the beginning, saying we judged him rightly and recognizing Jakob's and our decisions as just.

<But the godless rogues turned him around so that now he reviles and verbally abuses more than anyone else. They also set him up so that he now causes us great pain for the sake of his children, whom he had given to us and the Lord and now he wants to take them back – although the children run away from him like a scorpion. It is a great wonder and sign to us that his little children have such grace from God. May the Lord be with us. Amen.>[75]

But corrupt people constantly try to bring confusion. Let all devout believers be warned. Through Jesus Christ. Amen.

[Written and completed in November, the 22nd day, 1533.] [76]

<How the fellowship of Christ has henceforth been gathered and increased, and also the persecution within and outside of the country of the Hutterian Brethren and fellowship, and other individuals who left other fellowships and returned to the world has been described extensively (as reported to me) by Kaspar Braitmichel, minister of the fellowship, namely, what took place in the forty-five years from 1525 to 1570. I direct you to that account; for now, be satisfied with this short report.>[77]

Chronicle Source 13

First Great Persecution in Moravia [78]

In 1535, a great persecution of the devout and true Christian believers began in Moravia. In Schakwitz they had built homes and houses on the land of the noblemen of Mährisch Kromau and had lived there for a few weeks. They were forcefully driven out of their homes and houses to live in the fields and meadows under the open sky, with those who were sick and weak, and their small children.

At the same time the Moravian nobles, on the command of King Ferdinand, sternly ordered them to leave the territory. They could not and would not obey this order, without the promise and command from God. Because of this Jakob Hutter was obliged to write to the governor of Moravia, for himself and in the name of all brethren, stating his and the whole fellowship's opinion, in a manner that was stern, yet humble and submissive [L-4]. After this had taken place, the tribulation of the devout intensified, and the authorities hunted brother Jakob with rigor. They were heard to say often, "If they only had Jakob Hutter," as if to say that then everything would return to the former silence.

Therefore the brethren and the entire fellowship were obliged to let Brother Jakob return to the region of Tyrol (due to the great danger, he could not serve the fellowship openly in Moravia). He went to gather the saints of the Lord and carry out the Lord's work there for a while, for which he had always had great zeal and courage.

He commended the fellowship of God to the care of Hans Amon or Tuchmacher. He left in peace, while the fellowship commended him to God's grace with much shedding of tears and great heartache, taking leave of him with dignity and the earnest prayers of the saints. He served the Lord and the fellowship of God with the word of God and testified with the word of God to many who adhered to God.

Chronicle Source 14

Controversies in the Fellowship, 1535, by Kaspar Braitmichel, The Chronicle of the Hutterian Brethren, *vol. 1* [79]

In the middle of the affair described above, a minister named Gilg Schneider arrived and soon after him Hans Both, his fellow worker, with a group from Hesse. They acted as if they sought nothing but peace and unity, and for a time they proved peaceable, but in reality it was hypocrisy. The fellowship accepted them in good faith, trusting in the good impression they made. But Hans Both was not honest at heart. It was soon clear that he wanted to increase his own little flock by snatching some of the faithful out of the Lord's hands. But he did not succeed, because the fellowship looked to the Lord and not to Hans Both and his followers or to any other human being.

Hans Both and his adherents held the false opinion that there were no longer such things as angels or demons. They refused to be corrected, despising all sound teaching, so they and all who persisted in this error were excluded from the fellowship of God in accordance with the Lord's word. They talked a great deal. It was especially Hans Both who admitted that Philip and Gabriel had acted wrongly and were therefore no longer his brothers; the treatment they had received was right. Yet as soon as those two received the fellowship's judgment, Hans Both went to Philip who was clearly his dear friend. This revealed his deceitful heart even more plainly. If he could have split the fellowship with his hypocrisy, it would have delighted him greatly. He never wanted to come out clearly with what he was thinking. He said he knew the fellowship and the members and the other communities very well, and he didn't want to go to them. But his actions clearly belied his words. In this way God once more protected and rescued his own from these erring people.

After all this, the fellowship suffered a great deal of abuse and slander from the renegades, especially from Philip and his people. Whenever a lord, citizen, or farmer needed help and employed brothers and sisters from both fellowships, the Philippites refused to work, sit, eat, or drink with those who sided with Jakob Hutter, despite the fact that their employers made the arrangement. This brought abuse and disgrace to God's name. Although Jakob Hutter's people would much rather have worked quietly by themselves, they accepted and enjoyed the food and drink of their employers and gave thanks to God for it, regardless of who worked with them.

In addition, Philip's people refused to greet anyone on the street. They neither gave nor returned any good wishes, nor expressed thanks, and those who were devout and innocent often had to suffer for this.

To make matters worse, a minister named Jörg Scherer came to Auspitz and brought a group with him. They inquired about everything that was done in the fellowship and then united with Jakob Hutter and the entire holy congregation. But meanwhile they began to criticize many things in the fellowship. As people always do when they want to break with their friends, they find fault even with the best things.[a] They said it was not right that some wore gold or silken trim on their head coverings and that the thread for their cotton material and head coverings was spun much too fine.

In his compassion, Jakob Hutter offered to make changes and give up anything that was not good, for he desired greater perfection. He did not want to permit anything that was against the Lord. When they complained about the food because they were not used to it, Jakob said that he would arrange for their cooks in the kitchen to cook according to their custom and that the community should eat what their cooks prepared. He was even willing to let them move to Schakwitz to live under the lord marshal of Mährisch Kromau, where they had bought a house half a mile from Auspitz, if only they would remain in the Lord and in the fellowship. But nothing helped. They only laughed and mocked us. When the fellowship was informed of their contempt for every kindness, Jörg Scherer was excluded and separated from the fellowship, and all his people were sent away with him.

In Tyrol, tyranny increased day by day, and there was no place for the devout to go. Many were captured and killed for the sake of truth in all sorts of ways. The priests, too, violently thundered from their pulpits that people should be on the lookout for them, seize them, and destroy them by fire and the sword. Again and again, large sums of money were promised to anyone who would inform on them. They were often spied on. The woods were searched and any house suspected of harboring them; every room was ransacked. Locked chests had to be opened, or else they were broken open and searched.

There was a son of Judas named Prabeiger.[80] He set cunning traps to catch believers, then hurried to the magistrates and informed on them, bringing back constables and the children of Pilate with swords, spears,

a Ecclus. 11:7

and clubs, going in front of them just like the traitor Judas.[a] In this way they caught many and scattered and drove away the rest.

Not long after, when they gathered again, another child of Judas, Jörg Früe, ran to the priests. If they would reward him, he was willing to pursue the members and not one would be able to hide from him. That lineage of scribes and Pharisees, the priests, soon provided him with a substantial reward as well as a wage and a letter. This deceiver hid his hypocrisy under an angel's likeness[b] and visited people, especially those he suspected of knowing something about the members, inquiring up and down the Puster Valley where they might be. The scoundrel begged for help, pleading with palpable tears and declaring that he could have no peace until he found them. In this way he deceived them and gained entry among them. He pretended to be sorrowful, humble, and virtuous, like someone seeking to repent and change his life.

A little later he said, "My brothers, be so good as to let me return home to fetch my wife and child and bring them here too." The minister did have misgivings and told him that if he was falsehearted and was planning evil, God would certainly know it, and he would have to bear hard punishment. But he answered, "Oh, no! May God protect me from any such thing. Come home with me to my house!" He left and hurried to the judge, priests, and magistrates, who came with swords and cudgels and took the brothers and sisters by force.

There were other such deceivers, in particular one named Peter Lantz and another named Christel Pranger. Some went about at night, carrying a staff and talking and acting like brethren. In order to find believers, they visited places and houses where they thought people would open their doors to them as brethren. But God has given them their recompense, striking some with great terror and a horrible death to make them realize what they have done, like Judas[c] the betrayer of Christ. On God's judgment day their hair will stand on end. These deceivers will sweat blood and wish they had never been born.

Because the members there were so hard pressed that they were unable to stay in Tyrol, Jakob Hutter and the fellowship with him were moved to send messages by letter and word of mouth, telling them to leave Tyrol

a Cf. Matt. 26:47.
b 2 Cor. 11:14.
c Matt. 27:3–5; Acts 1:18.

as soon as possible and come to the fellowship in Moravia. In response, Hans Tuchmacher and several brothers and sisters set out and with God's help reached the fellowship at Auspitz.

Meanwhile one of the brethren named Bastel Glaser and his people in Tyrol were on their way to join the fellowship, but on arriving at Hohenwart, a village in Austria, they were arrested. Jakob Hutter wrote them a letter of comfort, which is still in existence.[81]

They were then taken to Eggenburg, where their cheeks were burned through, and they were released. This is the Bastel Glaser who wrote several songs, which we still have.

Another brother, named Peter Voit, was imprisoned at Eggenburg. Both his legs were so tightly clamped in stocks that gangrene set in and they rotted away; then the mice took the toes from his feet right before his eyes. After they totally destroyed his body, they released him from prison. He returned to the fellowship and found the people had been driven from their homes and were living in open fields; then he had both legs amputated. He lived for many years after this and fell asleep in the Lord at the age of seventy.

Around that time Onophrius Griesinger, a minister of the fellowship, traveled from Tyrol with other devout brothers and sisters and under God's protection reached the fellowship of God at Auspitz. Somewhat later he was involved in sin on his wife's account, and because of this his role and status were taken away from him. His wife also received the punishment she deserved.

About that time the abbess at Brünn, who was landowner of Auspitz, asked the elders of the fellowship to lend her some money. When they refused because the fellowship itself was in great need of the money, she had Jakob Hutter, Hans Amon, and other elders put in prison, also Jeronimus Käls, who was schoolmaster for the fellowship's children at the time. She tried in this way to force them to lend her the money, but when she did not succeed, she released them and ordered them off her property. She let them stay for a time, however, as will be described later.

Since Jakob Hutter himself was under attack as the cause of every evil and conflict, he asked Hans Tuchmacher whether he felt any particular urgency to travel to Tyrol. Hans replied that he felt no special urge but was ready to follow whatever the Lord showed to his people. But Jakob said, "I feel great courage and zeal for it, and I hope God will still grant it." Jakob announced this with many brethren present, and to a large extent they agreed to his acting on this urge, but they waited for the right time.

God wanted it to be clear who were his elect. They are revealed by great afflictions, as gold is proved in the fire.[a] So he tested the faithful but hardened the hearts of sinners and hypocrites. In any case, the devil begins all his work in the name of God and under the appearance of truth. Wherever God builds his church, the devil often builds a new chapel alongside to confuse and blind people.

[Summary of the Anabaptist rebellion in the northern German city of Münster]

The actions of these corrupt and ungodly people brought intense suffering to the fellowship of God in many places. A great number of the devout were imprisoned, tortured, and accused of belonging to this sect. But the whole fellowship and all devout hearts testified steadfastly, yes, some even with their death, against all this cruel abomination, this invention of the devil. The fellowship or congregation of true believers will never have outward weapons of vengeance, whether few or many, with which to fight their misguided enemies. Vengeance is the Lord's[b] – believers do not thirst for it. The Lord knows how to repay each person according to their deeds.

In 1535 the whole fellowship, wanting from the beginning to follow the best and perfect way and to abstain from the world and all ungodliness, unanimously decided in the fear of God to be on their guard against the leaven of the scribes and Pharisees, in accordance with Christ's teaching.[c] Because the pope, priests, monks, nuns, and all who preach for their belly's[d] sake are the greatest cause of idolatry and of hypocritical, sinful, and corrupt living, they decided that from then on, the fellowship would have nothing to do with them. They would not work for them, trade with them, eat or drink with them without a very specific and godly reason, because all their profits come from and are used in the service of

---

a 2 Esd. 16:74.
b Rom. 12:19.
c Matt. 16:6.
d Phil. 3:19.

idolatry – they proclaim themselves as preachers of the gospel, yet they neither practice Christ's teaching nor bring it to others.

After this decision the fellowship gave notice to the abbess of the Queen's Cloister at Brünn, the landowner of Auspitz, that they could no longer work in the vineyards or other places for her or for other people in the same position. This was not because of pride but because, in the fear of God, they were troubled that they might take part in serving idolatry, which would surely be against God.

This declaration made the abbess furious, and she ordered the fellowship off her lands. Since no other way was found, they moved out of Auspitz on Ascension Day 1535, leaving their houses and going to Schakwitz on the lands of the lord marshal. There they made every effort to start building for themselves and their children, but this did not last.

The events at Münster already reported were now running their course and furthering the God-ordained work of testing the devout. They caused the emperor, king, princes, and all the worldly leaders to oppose the congregation of the faithful. There soon came a stern command from the king that no one belonging to the congregation of true believers should be tolerated in the land.

In particular a strict order was sent to the lord marshal at Mährisch Kromau to expel the Brethren without delay on pain of great disgrace and punishment. So he had to do it, however reluctantly. (He had a great love for the Lord's people and instructed Jakob Hutter, that heroic Christian, to gather his people together again when these troubles were over.) He sent his officers to summon all the neighbors from the villages in that vicinity. They soon came with drums beating, flags flying, and weapons in hand to the fellowship's house at Schakwitz. Then the officers began by expressing the earnest request of their master that the members should spare him and not bring disgrace on him, for he, too, could not oppose the higher authorities but had to be obedient to them. They talked for a long time, taking counsel together, but there was no other way. The faithful had to leave their home, as it is written: They had to leave city or village and camp out in the open fields.[e]

e Mic. 4:10

So Jakob Hutter took his bundle on his back. His assistants did the same, and the brothers and sisters and all their children went in pairs, following their shepherd Jakob Hutter through the crowd of godless, villainous robbers, who ground their teeth in rage, full of lust to rob and attack. They were unable to do so, however, because of the presence of the officers, which was in accordance with God's will.

Thus the little band of the righteous was driven into the open like a herd of sheep. They were not permitted to camp anywhere until they had left their lord's lands. Although they had only just moved to Schakwitz a few days earlier, they were driven out again. A very few of the sick people remained in the house, but not for long. This persecution took place in 1535.

After their move into the open fields, while they were encamped on Lord von Liechtenstein's land at Nikolsburg, the Philippites, too, were driven out of Auspitz into the open fields. They reached the hill near Lassling, singing joyfully, and set up camp there. Their leading ministers, Philip [Blauärmel] and Blasius [Kuhn], mounted horses and set off from there, pretending to search for a place of shelter for their people. But after a long time, a message came back that everyone should look after himself and find a place to live as best he could. They are still searching to this day and have found no place. So they were like false shepherds and day laborers, who allowed the flock to be scattered among the wolves.[a] Their judgment on Jakob Hutter, recorded earlier, now proved to be true for themselves. Their flock has indeed been scattered, and many have come to ruin. Some cannot return even today. In the beginning they surely followed God's command to leave their country of origin and their family,[b] but they looked back and fell in love with the world once again.[c]

They separated into small groups, some going to Württemberg and others to the Palatinate, but a large group was captured at Wegscheid and at Ilzstadt near Passau. About sixty people in all were taken to Passau, and some were in prison there for up to five years, suffering acute hunger and severe treatment as well. Many of them fell asleep in the Lord while in

---

a John 10:12–13.
b Gen. 12:1.
c Luke 9:61–62.

prison. A few returned to the fellowship of God after their release, but the rest went to utter ruin, their hearts perverted and bent on doing wrong.

While the fellowship of the Lord camped on Liechtenstein's land near Tracht in Starnitz under Lassling, as told above, they were betrayed to the authorities and falsely accused of carrying guns. The governor sent his couriers to the camp to find out if it was true, but instead of muskets and spears they found many children and sick people.

When Jakob Hutter earnestly pleaded with the governor's ministers and told them the whole truth, they requested that the fellowship's ideas and intentions be conveyed to their lord in writing. Therefore Jakob Hutter, who at that time was the leading minister and shepherd of the believers, wrote a letter to the governor and sent it by his messengers. This letter was attacked and evilly misrepresented by Philip's and Gabriel's people and others, as if Jakob Hutter had called King Ferdinand a bloodhound and was put to death on this account and not for the sake of God's truth. For this reason the letter is included here, taken from the first copy, and each should judge for himself [L-4].

Chronicle Source 15

Anabaptism in the Holy Roman Empire, 1536, by Georg Kirchmayr [82]

In the year 1536, because of Anabaptism and the Lutherans, Zwinglians, and various heretical sects, many wounds were suffered in the Holy Empire. All the surrounding lands experienced departures from the priesthood. Reading of Mass and all worship services were even ceased in many locales. O how many devout hearts have been lost! Not only in the country, or in one city, or in the village, but practically in all houses there was a division of faith and unity. The darkness of the moon and the sun have made the year so dark that it is hardly possible for one to know that someone is a good, just, and loyal friend.

Chronicle Source 16

Persecution in Tyrol: Jakob Hutter's Arrest and Execution [83]

Not long afterward, in 1535, dear Brother Jakob Hutter was arrested in Klausen on the Eisack River in Adige, in the home of an old man. He was betrayed by treachery, an act of divine calamity, during the night of the feast of Saint Andrew, and he was taken to Branzoll Castle.

They put a gag in his mouth so that he couldn't speak and led him on a horse to Innsbruck, [the seat of] King Ferdinand's government. They tortured him and made him suffer greatly, using all sorts of means. But they could not break his spirit or make him abandon his faith and the divine truth. They also tried to convince him by scripture but they were unable to prevail over him and were put to shame. They decided to attempt to drive the devil from him by setting him in ice water and then bringing him into a hot room to beat him with rods. They also lacerated his body, poured brandy into the wounds, ignited it, and let it burn. Then they bound him hand and foot, gagged him again so that he would not be able to speak to the crowd and denounce their malice. They put a hat with a tuft of feathers on his head and led him through their house of idols because they knew this was an abomination to him. In numerous ways they made a fool and a mockery of him. But he remained faithful and true in his faith, like a Christian hero.

After bearing great cruelty, he was condemned to death by the children of Pilate. As he was led to the fire he said: "Come closer, those of you who would contradict me! Let us test our faith in the fire. This fire will harm my soul as little as the fiery furnace harmed Shadrach, Meshach, and Abednego."[a] Thus he was placed onto the pyre[84] while still living and burned [at the stake]. A huge crowd was present and saw his integrity, patience, and steadfastness. This took place about the time of Candlemas, on the Friday before the first week of Lent, 1536.

This Jakob Hutter, a man with a glorious disposition toward God, a man tested by fire, a faithful minister of Jesus Christ, had led the

a Cf. Dan. 3:19–25.

fellowship of God into its third year,[85] nurturing them with the word of God in this land of Moravia. He left behind him a people gathered and built up for the Lord. From him the fellowship inherited the name Hutterian Brethren, because of his courage and the steadfastness of his faith, to which he testified in all pain and torture. To this day the fellowship is not ashamed of this name, for, just as the writings and letters he left behind demonstrate, he persisted as a man of God who was zealous, sincere, and encouraging, yes, a true lover of God, of the truth, in complete joyfulness unto death. He witnessed to his faith and teaching with his blood, as it has been for all slaves of God on earth and for Christ's apostles.

Chronicle Source 17

Hutter's Arrest and Execution, 1535–1536, by Kaspar Braitmichel, The Chronicle of the Hutterian Brethren, *vol. 1* [86]

After the governor read this letter [L-4] addressed to him from the fellowship, which was brought to him by his couriers, he immediately sent his couriers back with strict orders to arrest Jakob Hutter. Thanks to the foresight and presence of mind of the faithful, they did not find him in the house at Schakwitz or among the people in the camp. So they arrested Wilhelm Griesbacher of Kitzbühel, a minister in charge of public affairs, and Loy Salztrager of Hall in the Inn Valley and took these two to Brünn, where they racked and burned them, questioning them under torture about money or goods that were supposed to be in the possession of the poor fugitives. The brothers simply told them that they and their fellow believers had not been driven out of their fatherland and inheritance for the sake of money or earthly treasure but had come to this country for the sake of God's truth. On the basis of this confession, Wilhelm was sent, innocently, to be burned alive. Loy gave way under the great agony of torture. Later, however, he repented deeply and in the end fell asleep in the Lord.

Since Jakob Hutter was in such great danger that he could no longer serve the fellowship by teaching in public and could never let himself be seen, it was unanimously decided by the fellowship of God that he should move for a time to Tyrol, to gather the saints of the Lord there.

Jakob Hutter entrusted the fellowship to Hans Tuchmacher (Amon) and advised them how to proceed in case they needed another minister. The fellowship accepted this from God in great thankfulness. They commended Jakob to the grace of God with many tears and sorrowful hearts, and after a solemn commissioning, they sent him on his way with the prayers of the fellowship.

The people out on the open fields moved from place to place, unwilling to part from one another. But when they were refused all provisions and even water, they finally had to separate into groups of eight or ten. Each brother with the little group entrusted to him had it laid on his heart very earnestly that they should care for one another as God gave them grace and that no one should hold back from helping another. It was said in particular that nobody should leave Moravia without asking advice. This separation was quite pitiful; with many tears they set off like Abraham, not knowing where God would grant them a place to live.[a]

Subsequently, Hans Tuchmacher and his assistants carried out their ministry as well as they could, making every effort to visit the people wherever they were, throughout the land, faithfully providing for all their needs to the degree possible. The people wandered about the land in misery and suffering for almost an entire year.

As there was little hope then of finding a place in Moravia where they could settle, Leonhard Seiler,[87] with those entrusted to him, did harvesting and eventually other labor for Lord Hans Fünfkirchen at Steinebrunn in Austria, not far from the Moravian border. They remained there for some time.

In Tyrol, Jakob Hutter traveled about in great distress and anguish in his soul, called to use his utmost effort as an instrument of blessedness. He visited and gathered the people with the word of God and gathered them in a state of affliction, for throughout the country strict mandates were issued against them. For example, the judge of Brixen rode into Lüsen, summoned all the men, women, and children who were able to walk, and read out a brutal mandate forbidding anyone to lodge or shelter us. If

a Heb. 11:8.

anyone did, he would be punished more severely than ever before and his house would be burned to the ground, for his lord at Brixen would not tolerate such people but would root them out. Soon after this he captured several brothers and sisters and took them to Brixen.[88]

Soon after these events, on the night of Saint Andrew's Eve [November 29] 1535, God allowed it to happen that Jakob Hutter was arrested. He was deceived and betrayed in Klausen on the Eisack River in the Adige region. They bound and gagged his mouth and brought him to Innsbruck, the seat of King Ferdinand's government. They tortured him and caused him great torment through all their efforts, yet they were not able to change his heart or make him deny the truth. Even when they tried to prove him wrong with scripture, they could not stand up to him. Full of hatred and revenge, the priests imagined they would drive the devil out of him. They put him in ice cold water and then took him into a warm room and had him beaten with rods. They lacerated his body, poured brandy into the wounds, and set it on fire. They tied his hands and once again gagged him to prevent him from denouncing their wickedness. Putting a hat with a tuft of feathers on his head, they led him into the house of their idols and in every way made a laughingstock of him. After he had suffered all their cruelty and yet remained firm and upright, a Christian hero, steadfast in faith, these wicked sons of Caiaphas and Pilate condemned him and burned him alive at the stake. A huge crowd was present and saw his steadfast witness. This took place about the time of Candlemas, on the Friday before the first week of Lent [February 25], 1536.

Jakob Hutter had led the fellowship for nearly three years and left behind him a people gathered and built up for the Lord. It is from this Jakob Hutter that the fellowship inherited the name Hutterite, or Hutterian Brethren. To this day the fellowship is not ashamed of this name. He stood joyfully for the truth unto death and gave his life for it. This has been the fate of all Christ's apostles.

When Jakob Hutter was captured, the brothers in Tyrol immediately sent word to Hans Tuchmacher and the whole fellowship at Auspitz in Moravia.

Chronicle Source 18

Summary of Jakob Hutter's Arrest and Execution, 1535–1536 [89]

That same year 1535, it was a divine calamity that Brother Jakob was arrested while at the former sexton's home in Klausen in the Adige. He was put on a horse and taken to Innsbruck, being severely ridiculed by his enemies. They put a hat with a tuft of feathers on his head and a gag in his mouth, and led him as a laughingstock through the villages until they got to Innsbruck. They put him in ice cold water and then took him into a warm room. They lacerated his body, poured brandy into the wounds, and set it on fire. After he had suffered all their cruelty and horrific torture, for the sake of his witness to our Lord Jesus Christ, he was executed by fire and burned in 1536 on the Friday before the first week of Lent. He testified to God and his holy truth through all pain and torture until his death, valiantly and without wavering, as can be seen from his teaching and writings. He had led the fellowship of God into its third year.

3

Witnesses

Testimonies from Other Anabaptists

Documents in the source collections, "Witnesses" (WIT) and "Governmental Correspondence" (GOV) are, for the most part, taken from the published series of government records concerning Anabaptists, most of which bear the title, *Quellen zur Geschichte der Täufer* (*QGT*). These volumes were edited by scholars and vetted by review committees, and aimed to present the fullest and most balanced accounts available in extant sources. In many cases, these volumes are the results of research teams spending years combing through government and church archives to locate any significant references to Anabaptist activity throughout Europe. Documents edited in the *QGT* volumes appear in the original language either quoted verbatim or summarized, with editorial annotations. For researchers seeking details about the context or the persons mentioned in the documents translated below, the *QGT* volumes will provide further information, which was not deemed essential for the purposes of the present edition. In addition, some of the translations below are based on original documents, which were not included, or are only summarized, in the *QGT* volumes.

Accounts of Hutter's activity collected below in Chapter 5, "Governmental Correspondence," will offer an entirely different perspective than the sources here in "Witnesses." However, these witnesses and testimonies were typically written down by a state official during an interrogation process, which could take place over hours or days, often involving torture, and the bias of the interrogator should be considered when reading these documents. The information found here sheds light on Hutter's activities and teachings, including the diversity of belief and practice through the Tyrolean Anabaptist communities, and the degree to which Hutter appears as a central leader, alongside others in the regions of Austria. Captives were generally asked who had baptized them and the names of other converts. It is apparent that the names they gave were usually of people who had fled or had been executed, in lieu of betraying their fellow believers.

Witness 1

February 11, 1532, Michelsburg, testimony of Sigmund of Kiens, Part 1 [1]

Sigmund, born in Kiens, now a servant of Ebner at Hörschwang, testified, saying: Around last Easter, Mair of Hörschwang sent him with a half measure of wheat to the miller in Au, . . . where he met a leader, Georg Vasser on Wednesday. Vasser explained that he was sinning, and why. Then he went home again. Vasser had also told him to turn away from sin and unrighteousness and follow the Lord.

The following Saturday he was baptized by this Georg Vasser in the bath house of Pirchner zu Saalen. Hans Mair Paulle, Jörg Schräffl, and Joseph Schuester zu Stegen were there. Vasser poured water over his head and baptized him in the name of the Father, the Son, and the Holy Spirit.

After they came out of the bath house into Schräffl's house, Schräffl gave them soup.

Vasser also warned him to get control of his sin, and not to go into any church because everything there is against God and it is idolatry.

Sigmund Kropf's wife was also at Schräffl's. His master, the farmer Mair, knew of this but did not forbid him, although he didn't like it. He said he should not put himself in danger.

Again he was at a fellowship meeting in the Aichhornin Voglhuttn on Zisers around the time of the solstice festival. Michel, son of Ebner at Hörschwang, Jakob Hutter the leader, Hans Mair Paulle, and others whom he did not know were there. Hutter preached the word of God to all who were present. After that he went home, taking the path back to Mair, his master, as shown to him. . . .

Vasser also forbade him to let it be known who the brothers and sisters are. . . .

Sixty or seventy people were present. Hutter held the Remembrance of our Lord, breaking the bread and passing it to all of them; but those who were not baptized were treated as heathen. After that the leaders went to Ober's again. . . .

The leaders forbid them to carry any weapon other than a stick. If anyone should attack or fight them, they should not defend themselves.

They were also warned that they should be more cautious when the authorities come to Hörschwang in the next three days; however, he doesn't know who is responsible.

Since Candlemass 1531 he [Sigmund of Kiens] has not entered a church or received the sacrament. He thinks nothing of the sacrament that the priests offer but believes as Hutter taught him. The images in the churches are also idolatry. The sacrament of the altar is a devil.

The dear saints are not able to intercede for us, because one should call out to God alone. He will leave Our Lady in honor, as God created her.[2]

Luther, Zwingli, and the pope are all the same; what they teach is mere human statements and they are all from the devil. This is what their [Anabaptist] leaders have taught them.

Hans Mair Paulle is their treasurer.

Anyone who is not in their brotherhood and has not repented is truly a heathen.

Christ died only because Adam and Eve disobeyed the Lord's command, and not for our sake. Also, since priests are not pure, they cannot preach anything true.

His flesh is from the devil and worth nothing.

Witness 2

February 11, 1532, Michelsburg, testimony of Michael Ebner, son of Jörg Ebner of Hörschwang, confessed without torture [3]

To begin with he prayed devoutly to God, for removing his burden with his grace. Hans Mair Paulle first admonished him and led him to the Aichhornin Voglhuttn on Zisers. Jakob Hutter was there and others whom he didn't know. Hutter preached the word of God to all who were there, which happened around Saint Laurence Day [August 10]. . . .

Hutter forbade him to enter any church, and he gladly agreed. Although it is a command of the pope, when Christ says we should make temples he is speaking about a pure heart.[a]

Since then he has not gone into a church, because if he did, it would be hypocrisy.

The teachings of Saint Paul, the twelve apostles, and Jakob Hutter are one and the same.[4]

He thinks nothing of the sacrament of the altar; it is nothing but bread, and what the priests make of it is all for nothing. But the words of Jakob Hutter are powerful, for God speaks through him – he does not speak from his own flesh. The Mass and the liturgy held by the priests are idolatry. He did in fact take Mass this past Lent, but it is nothing but bread. He didn't eat anything but a wafer. At the time he had not yet received God's grace.

Jakob Huter, Hans Tuchmacher, and Christan Gschäl stayed overnight at his father's. . . .

He does not believe that Our Lady, nor the dear saints, intercede to God for us, for God alone is the true intercessor.

Baptism of children should also not be performed for youth, for faith should precede baptism.

Luther's, Zwingli's, and the pope's teaching and writing are worthless.

Also, the emperor, king, and anyone who has not repented and joined their brotherhood are heathens.

Also he is now pure and no longer a sinner.

---

a Reference unclear. Cf. John 2:19–21.

Witness 3

February 16, 1532, Michelsburg, selections from the testimony of Sigmund of Kiens, Part II, confessed under torture [5]

Anyone in their brotherhood who has money or anything else must give it to the treasurer,[6] who pays for everything and all is to be used by all, in common.

He was invited to other fellowship meetings but he was unable to attend due to his need to be at work.

The wives of the leaders read just as much as the men do. . . . When one of them greets another he says "Peace be with you," and they answer, "God be praised" or "honored." . . .

Sigmund wants to persevere in this testimony and endure death.

Witness 4

July 26, 1532, Sarnthein,
testimony of Valtein Fell and Oswald Spies (summarized) [7]

Valtein Fell from Flass and the shoemaker's assistant Oswald Spies were arrested because of their connection to the Anabaptist sect on the basis of the royal mandates. They were interrogated with and without torture.

Valtein admitted that he was unfortunately misled by Ull Müllerin from Klausen who had been involved with the sect and had stayed in his house for a while. She often told him that her faith was the true way to eternal blessedness and that he should turn away from his former, false faith and follow her teaching. When she left his house she was arrested and then, because of her, he was imprisoned too. But he escaped secretly and was heading to Klausen. On his way he met Paul from Villnöß. Paul asked him where he was going and he told him what had happèned. The Anabaptist told him he was going to a fellowship meeting on the Brenner. Since Valtein couldn't go home he should come too, with the two servants he would send. He agreed. When the two servants came he took two oxen from his stall at home and drove them up to the woods on the Brenner.

There were more than ninety people there, men and women. He recognized their leader Jakob Hutter from the Puster Valley and Paul from Villnöß among them. He didn't know any of the others; there were some from Moravia.

Hutter read out of a book of Gospels and said among other things:

The Mass is nothing but a devilish ghost; they should not worship it or believe in it.

They should not enter any church but only pray to God the Almighty who lives in heaven.

They should not worship saints.

They should think nothing of the old baptism or of the sacraments and Mass.

They should not be subject to or obey any authorities except their leaders, who will show them the right way.

He was moved to have himself baptized by the leader in the name of the Father, the Son, and the Holy Spirit.

Then the leader spoke further:

Wherever they are needed for work they should work faithfully and diligently, whether they are paid or not.

They should move to wherever one knows they ought to go.

Otherwise he didn't notice anything wrong as long as he was there. After that he and Oswald came over the Penser Joch to Urscher's in Sarnthein and asked him for lodging. They told him where they had come from. He said they could sleep in his barn in the hay. This they did. In the meantime, the authorities came and arrested them. He swears by his oath that he has nothing more to confess.

Oswald Spies, the shoemaker's assistant confessed: Last Saint George's Day he was on his way to Bozen and met Lienhart Praitenberger, who was traveling to Terlan. Praitenberger asked him if he was also a Christian. He said yes. Praitenberger asked him what Christian works he had done? He said he did what his parents taught him. Praitenberger asked him what he thought of the sacraments and if he really believed in them. He answered that regarding the sacraments and baptism he believes what all Christians believe.

Praitenberger said he neither believes in any of it, nor in the Mass.... There is one God in heaven and we should follow him; Praitenberger told him he would show him the way to blessedness. He led him up the Brenner where he found food and the people Fell mentioned....

Hutter lived in a small hut apart from others.

He preached the gospel and spoke against the Mass, which is false and does not justify, and against the old baptism and the sacrament. They should not believe in them.

They should not enter any church.

Whoever believes and is baptized will be saved and will become a child of God.

So he was baptized in the name of the Father, the Son, and the Holy Spirit. When the crowd was about to disperse the leader said they should all be equal; they should not obey any church or government authority but only the leader, who will show them the way to salvation and they should follow him.

Witness 5

January 8, 1533, Sarnthein, interrogation of Erhard Urscher (summarized) [8]

On the command of the government in Innsbruck, Urscher should be asked:

1. Where did he, his wife, and children go after they had left their home? Who gave them lodging?

Urscher testified: When the authorities found Valtein Fell and Oswald Spiess from Bozen in his barn and arrested them, his pregnant wife was very shocked. They didn't know that the two of them were such people. He regretted very much that he had given them a place to stay. His wife feared the worst and told him to flee. She would have gone with him but was afraid she would lose her baby. He said he didn't know where they should go, that anywhere would be less safe than at home. She pleaded again that he leave, so they both left the house. He sent a message to the authorities but received no answer. When his wife got weak, he sent for Valtein the shoemaker, who advised them to go to an inn that would take in such people. The inn is called "Pögglhaube." The shoemaker directed them there; they went through the Schalderer Valley to the house, which is about a mile from Brixen. There his wife gave birth. They stayed eight days. They will only baptize the child when it reaches the age of accountability.[9]

Urscher camped in the woods and sheds for nine days; he made a fire when he got cold. He went to his oldest son Valtein who was guarding the cows in that locale. Then he returned to the Pögglhaube and brought his wife and children to an alpine hut belonging to Rabenstein. They stayed there for a while.

Then they went to the Prunnleiten, where he left his wife and children and went back to court, and with him were two Anabaptists, one named Thomas, the other Klainstoffl. They helped him bring his children to him because he so longed to be with them. He was willing to move with his wife and children to his cousin in Meyxn, whom he still knew was there. Then he came back to the Pögglhaube and stayed that day and one night. Then he brought his wife and children back to the alpine hut. They were there for twelve weeks. During this time he had worked in the Pögglhaube about thirty-five days, to receive support for his wife and children. Then he wanted to move back to his father's, because he had promised to help him. But because autumn was so close, he postponed it. People would have advised him not to do it; he was nowhere safe from the soldiers. Then the prince passed by, and he wanted to fall at his feet. Then one of the nobles told him that the prince had ordered that the Anabaptists should no longer be harmed, but that they be referred to the [General] Council.[10] It was a relief because he no longer wanted to move back and forth in misery, and he then moved with his wife and children from the Pögglhaube to Saupach; there he left his wife and children; he wanted to go back to court and to seek mercy from respectable people in the government. She was supposed to stay with the children until he had sorted out matters. Then he had a fever while he stayed with his eldest son Valtein; then Urscher went to Mair at Eggen bringing with him two oxen and asked him to pay [Urscher] his debt. But he had no money and postponed the payment until later. Otherwise he hadn't spoken to Mair or seen anyone. Then they moved into the valley and went to Fronbote[11] and asked for advice. He said that he should go wherever he wanted; he couldn't advise him. Then he went toward Winkler to visit Fuesperg and asked him for advice. He also asked him to choose two neighbors, Mr. Leitter and Mr. Oberdimpfler, whom he wanted to send to the landlord[12] with others, and that he himself did not want to go to them. He had also asked him about how to travel from Hueber to Norital. He also wanted them to send two neighbors, Mr. Möstetter and Mr. Unternhambler; they should all go to the landlord and obtain mercy for him so that he and his wife could return to their home – all based on the alleged orders from the prince. Then he went to Hanns Madlegger whom he wanted to care for his children. However, Hansl Madlegger said that without an order from the government he would not take in the children. Afterward he went with his son to Reichart, who took them in. Reichart's son bought provisions for them. He remained there three days, until they were found and captured.

2. Secondly, Urscher was questioned as to whether he met with the Anabaptists. Where are their meetings or conferences held, and whether he knows who are the members of the Anabaptist sect? He answered:

When he was in Pögglhaube, Jakob Hutter came with someone called Hans [Amon], two of their leaders, including one named Valtein [Luckner][13] the treasurer, and one called Augustin who served in an inn at Jaufenpass.

They spoke about their faith and how the manner they live together is justified; this is the correct path to salvation, the path to reach the Father in heaven. But the path the world is taking will lead no one to heaven.

They also spoke about all things being equal among them.

If one has one thousand gulden he should share it with his brothers. Anyone who doesn't do that should not be tolerated among them. Even if he only has a farthing but hides it, he will be condemned. In conclusion, whoever has more should share with his brethren.

They are not allowed to enter a church or accept teachings from others.

[Churches] put up our Lord for sale; one should not make him their sacrifice, yet this is how they operate, like a brothel.

They should not believe in the sacrament; it is just a piece of bread.

Concerning Our Lady, they teach that she was the Mother of God and no one born is holier than she. But she should not be given more honor than our Father in heaven.

The government and nobility should be paid taxes, but they should not be given reverence or considered worthier than simple folk.

If someone dies and is buried by a scree[14] or fence, they will rest just as well as in the cemetery.

Such teachings convinced Urscher to join them. He asserts that he did not receive any other teachings from them. He also went to them alone because of two hundred gulden which he had given one of their leaders named Blasi during the previous Lenten season, when he joined the sect. In the meantime, this Blasi may have been executed at Oberrasen in the Puster Valley. But they didn't give him anything.

3. Urscher was asked whether he and his wife and children have been baptized. He said he had not been at this point, but when he came to the new faith he and his wife were baptized in Leifers by Blasius, whom he had given the money. He will not have his children baptized.

Witness 6

March 3, 1533, Sarnthein, testimony of Erhard Urscher (summarized) [15]

Erhard Urscher and his wife joined the Anabaptist sect some time ago and were arrested in Bozen, but were pardoned by the king. They swore an oath that they would not join the sect again. A copy of this oath was read out. They performed their recantation in the church during holy Mass and promised no longer to adhere to the sect; their goods were returned to them. However, Urscher took in two Anabaptists, who were arrested by the authorities [Valtein Fell and Oswald Spiess]. Urscher and his wife left their small children and joined the Anabaptist sect again. Urscher was recently arrested once more and, according to royal command, was interrogated with and without torture.

When Urscher was offered the sacrament in the presence of the judge and jurors … he refused. He said it is only natural bread that one is offered, and nowhere is it written that it is the true sacrament; he does not believe that our Lord allows himself to come down into the priest's hand and transforms himself, so he doesn't think it is anything special. The same is true of baptism. He has a true faith and has already received the Lord in his holy word as God his heavenly Father has ordained. He will abide by this. Before he denies his faith, he would die eight times; he thanks and praises the Father for calling him to the correct path of salvation.

Regarding the money that he gave to his fellow brethren some time ago, it was a good investment; he is glad they have it and does not regret it.

Urscher confirmed this statement and testimony with an oath before the court. On the basis of this hearing, he is brought to the criminal court. Although he should have been punished severely for his unbelief and rebaptism, he was given mitigation and mercy because of the petition of his honorable relatives. It is recognized that Urscher deserves death. He is handed over to the judge in Meran, who will bring him to the judgment seat in Öttnbach; he will be executed with the sword and afterward his body will be branded and then buried at the place of execution.[16]

Witness 7

April 2, 1533, Innsbruck, testimony of Friedrich Brandenberger[17]

Jakob Hutter, the leader, is staying in the Michelsburg region at a farmer's named Pirkher near Michelsburg Castle. Pirkher is not a member of the sect, although his wife is; Friedrich also once spent the night in their house a year ago. At that time the wife and her daughter belonged to the sect – not the man; he knew nothing about it.

Jakob Hutter sometimes stays at a farmer's above Ehrenburg Castle (he doesn't know the farmer's name); a shoemaker also stays there. The house is above the castle, up a steep path on the left. It is the first house when you come through the wood; only a trail leads to it. Both the farmer and his wife are Anabaptists.

Koffler and his wife of Götzenberg above Ehrenburg were both baptized by Jakob Hutter. Friedrich stayed there a year ago. They ate meat on Friday and Saturday.

Witness 8

September 19, 1533, Michelsburg, testimony of Paul and Leonhard Rumer, sons of Jörg Rumer in St. Georgen [18]

Paul Rumer confessed, with and without torture: To begin with, Balthasar Mairhofer's wife talked to him, while she and her daughter were in Mülbach washing clothes. She asked him if he didn't want to become devout and put away his pride.

After that he wanted to lease land in Mülbach and stayed some weeks at home with his father. The brethren gathered in a house, and his younger sister also joined them. He punished her for it, but afterwards asked them about it out of curiosity, but they didn't want to trust him. Afterwards he followed them to Klausen, and from Klausen to Mauls, from Mauls to the meeting in the Jaufen Valley near Sterzing. He was baptized there about two years ago by Jakob Hutter. Three girls were baptized with him; one was the daughter of Steger in Sterzing. Three leaders were at that meeting in the Jaufen Valley: Jakob Hutter, Hans Tuchmacher, and Christoph Gschäl, besides many brothers and sisters.

When he planned to take out the lease in Mülbach, his father Jörg Rumer gave him his inheritance through his mother, forty-three gulden; since he was now part of the brotherhood he gave this money to the church, except for twelve gulden. Then he moved to Moravia and gave the rest of his money to the brotherhood. In Moravia he worked for a while in the mill and bakery.

He has no regard for our [Catholic] churches, but only for the fellowship of God, those who lead a Christian life, since Christ himself also went to the wilderness when he preached.

Christ also commanded people to flee from the assembly of the godless.[a] And since our churches contain adulterers, fornicators, murderers, and godless people, they are of no value.

The false preachers also murder and strangle in the churches. He has no hope of [hearing] the gospel from the papists, for it is written: a bad tree can bear no good fruit.[b]

The Mass is also of no value, for it is not of God, yet God is forbearing and watches over it.

He has no regard for our sacraments, but only as God commanded it: that when they break bread, as Christ broke it, they agree to die for the sake of God's word, as Christ gave up his own body for them on the cross; for such bread is composed of many little grains altogether, and thus many of them are unified as one into a Christian community. The sacrament of the altar saves no one, for the priests eat it day in and out, and they don't show any improvement from it; rather, they are the worst of fornicators and adulterers.

Also God is merciful, having pardoned him from his sin, and he no longer sins, for whoever is of God sins no longer,[c] but whoever is of the flesh, is flesh and is sinful.

Just now when he came from the Inn Valley, Kräntzer from Trenns near Sterzing met him. He led him over Rodeneck to this fellowship in Götzenberg. At the fellowship meeting in Gufidaun they decided that there are not enough leaders in Moravia and there is no one here who desires repentance, but there are many other regions such as Thuringia and Hessen where people do desire repentance. So leaders were sent to these districts and now there are not enough in Moravia. Therefore, Jakob Hutter went down [to Moravia] and ordered them to send the people down immediately and depart from the rampage and rioting here.

He wants only to speak the truth, for he knows that no liar will inherit the Kingdom of God,[d] and therefore, he doesn't want to lie.

He had previously had a discussion with Schäffer at Sterzing.

a Rev. 18:4.
b Matt. 7:18.
c 1 John 3:6, 9.
d 1 Cor. 6:9.

The fellowship of brethren that moved out of this region is in Moravia, in a small marketplace settlement, belonging to the abess at Brno, and from this region there are about 600, who live together. . . .

Often there are also those who go to them who don't want to be baptized, and also some whom they don't want to accept. . . .

The little book of epistles [found on him] he copied out himself. He collected the epistles from brothers and sisters everywhere, who escaped from prison. The last epistle is written by Hans Beck from Brixen who was executed in Gufidaun. Concerning the words, "the squirrel that ran out through the window," this means: In Rattenberg there were some brothers and sisters in a house with Simon Päntzel. This Päntzel had a squirrel, and when they opened the window it ran out. Beck wanted to send a greeting to the brothers and sisters but he didn't want to mention Päntzel by name so he greeted him with a drawing of the squirrel.[19] . . .

Leonhard Rumer confessed, with and without torture, saying: Initially, he was disturbed by this sect. Then on this past New Year's Day his brother Paul Rumer came to Tallaker in Meran where he was a waiter, and pointed out the divine truth to him. He prayed to God for grace, and God enlightened him, and he found the divine truth, praise God. Then about three weeks after Candlemas he went with his brother to Klausen. There, in the house of old Peter Pinter next to the bridge, he was baptized according to the customs of their sect, by Hans Tuchmacher, their leader. Others present were his brother Paul Rumer and Christoph Schuster, son of Andrew Zimmermann, nobody else. . . .

He regards churches as no more than cursed temples of idols, as an assembly of all godless people.

The Mass means nothing to him, for Christ did not command it, and it's also an abomination before God.

The sacrament he considers a work of idols and this accursed idol is something putrid and horrid before God. For Paul says in Acts 7[:48] and 17[:24] that Christ does not want to dwell in temples made by humans hands.

He also holds no hope for an impure gospel, for our monks and priests are full of the devil and speak no truth.

The celebration and feast days are mere human laws.

He considers Our Lady as a pure virgin, both before and after the birth. Yet he doesn't revere Our Lady, although she is holy and pure before God, and that [Christ] was born of God and not of Our Lady.

The saints in heaven are equal to the Anabaptists and have also suffered for the sake of the word of the Lord.

Fasting was begun by the papists in order to fill their purses, and for that reason they will be punished eternally.

He does not know who gave meat, wheat, flour, bread, etc. for the conference in Götzenberg, because he just arrived from the Inn Valley. He never heard where the brethren, who are commissioned to carry this food, obtained it. He doesn't know any brothers and sisters in Klausen who are not already known.

At Candlemas he was at his father's house for fourteen days. He told him what he should do to become a Christian. His father said he should leave the sect alone and threw him out of the house. Since then he hasn't let him into the house.

The brethren who carry the food are called: Ruprecht Huber from Götzenberg; Hans Maurer, son of Niclas im Garten of St. Georgen; Hansel Decker from the Ritten; and Bastel from Villnöß. These four do not tell anyone what they are carrying. Since he came from the Inn Valley he has not been in any house.

Sebastian Knapp was imprisoned in Schwaz; he recanted and then ran away.

The two Rumer brothers want to remain true to their faith, with strength from God; they do not want to recant because they know this is the divine truth.

Witness 9

October 6, 1533, Brixen, testimony of Valentin Luckner [20]

Valtein Luckner from Taufers, testimony given with and without torture, before Leonhard Mair am Creutz and jurors. . . .

First he confessed that a shoemaker's apprentice named Mathes, brother of the sexton of the parish of Taufers, who had worked for Peter Schuster, worked for him for four years (he has died in the meantime in Bavaria). Valtein had a New Testament which he often read. This Mathes the shoemaker asked him if he lived according to what he read, saying that one must believe in the one God, as revealed by faith. Valtein said, yes, he did believe in that way. Mathes then answered, however, that more was required [than faith alone]; one must live according to God's will and be baptized according to one's faith. He said infant baptism was commanded by the pope but this baptism [according to one's faith] was commanded by God. Valtein must be baptized and follow God's command. Valtein then asked Mathes where he could find someone to baptize him. Mathes answered: in Augsburg, and he explained much about God's word to him. After that, Valtein had no peace but kept thinking about it.

Sometime later Peter Gerber, his brother, together with [Hans] Krumschuster who had also received this faith came to Valtein, and talked to him in the same way as Mathes had. He asked them where he could find someone to baptize him. They said they would send a servant of God to him. After this, the authorities learned of it. Valtein was called before Leonard am Creutz, judge of Taufers, who forbade him to go to Peter Gerber, or he would be exiled.

After this his brother according to the flesh Peter Gerber and Hans Krumschuester left. They recanted and gave themselves over to the devil.

The month before Ascension Day three years ago, Jakob Hutter and a cabinet maker who has since then been executed in Kufstein or Rattenberg came to Valtein in his house and asked for food and drink, which he gave them. Among other things Hutter asked him if he wanted to know the divine truth. He said yes, if only there were someone who could teach him. They talked for a long time. Then they went outside to the meadow; Hutter explained the divine truth and baptism to him again and how he should live accordingly.

Then Valtein kneeled down and prayed God to forgive his sins. Then Hutter asked him if he believed in God, in Jesus Christ, and in the Holy Christian church. He answered, Yes. Hutter said, "Now God has forgiven your sins," and told him he had to renounce his flesh and blood, his wife and child. Then he took water and baptized him in the name of the Father, the Son, and the Holy Spirit. Afterward Valtein left his family and has not seen them for a long time.

On Saint Martin's Day [November 11], when his maid was arrested in Taufers also because she belonged to the sect, the judge visited him at home. But he hid in the bathhouse so that the judge didn't find him. That same night Jakob Hutter and Hansl Maier came to his house and the same night led him, Valtein Luckner, to his brother, Peter Gerber, who was in the village above Bruneck in a separate house. He stayed there until his brother moved to Moravia.

After that Valtein and his brethren including Jörg Fasser, Jeronimus, the clerk from Kufstein and their wives, Lamprecht who since then was executed in Sterzing, and others who have moved to Moravia in the meantime, lived together in the woods and held fellowship meetings.

When they held a meeting, everything was already prepared ahead of time by Hansl Mair and other brothers who were commissioned to do this. At the home of Schraffl at Michelsburg, who was one of the brethren, and who was later executed, they held discussions. Jakob Hutter, Hans Tuchmacher, Hans Mair were also at Schraffl's with them.

[Luckner went on to name several Anabaptists and places where they stayed.]

They went to Villnöß below a hill where they held a meeting of about eighty brothers and sisters. They were together for three days. After that many of them moved to Moravia and many were executed. On the third day about forty heathen came and mocked them.

When the fellowship meeting was finished they parted and went to their brothers and sisters in the Puster Valley and dispersed everywhere.

Platzer at Gufidaun was also baptized into this sect and moved to Moravia.

Afterward, Valtein, together with Jakob Hutter, traveled toward Sterzing up to the valley at Tulfer, to share with them about the truth. Later they, the young women, up to ten people in total, were baptized. . . .

In the Puster Valley, in a woods behind Michelsburg, Jörg Fasser of Kitzbühel held a meeting. He only entered Schraffl's house, where twenty to thirty people were gathered, among them Tuchmacher, Onophrius, Lamprecht, Hansl Mair, Schraffl, and Stoffl his servant, both of whom were executed. Luckner didn't know the others.

Over the winter they stayed with their sisters and brothers who had not been driven out, like Schaffer in Sterzing and Martin Rädler. Both of these men and their wives belonged to their faith but recanted. But they stayed there a long time and held meetings twice at Schaffer's. Paul Gall and his wife and others, who have been executed or else gone to Moravia, were there. . . .

Afterward, they stayed in a forest near Gufidaun for eight days holding meetings, where there were about eighty people until the henchmen came, captured several, and drove away the others.

Jakob Hutter had remained there for fourteen days before they held the meetings, and stayed with Luckner's sister and brother-in-law, Hainrich and Frondl. . . .

They had a conference including about thirty people at Paul Gall's, before he was arrested in Sterzing. Some of those mentioned above were present. Paul Gall gave them food and drink. They came and went at nighttime so that the neighborhood didn't notice anything.

They were in Freyenberg eight or nine weeks. They held meetings and got their food from Flass by Serntal in the district of Genesy. There they emptied out five "Haushaben": the homes of Epp, Wegman, old Piganer, the bricklayer's wife, and another whose name he doesn't know. They took their meals outdoors. They took two oxen to Epp and drove them through Dürnholz and slaughtered them.

They held a meeting in the barns of Peckelhaub. There were seventy people. Peckelhaub himself did not know about this, but his wife did. Valtein often went to Peckelhaub for food, which he paid for. But since

Peckelhaub had been arrested and, as he heard, had to pay a fine of one hundred gulden, Peckelhaub didn't want to help them any more.

For a while they went in and out of Lower Saller in the Neustift district. Here they got their sugar and provisions. They only went to Upper Saller once, for food and drink that they paid for. In both places it was known that they belonged to the faith and were brothers. There was a boy who belonged to the farmstead at Lower Saller. He was baptized in Jauffental and moved to Moravia; he is the one who led them to the Sallers. But in the meantime the provost at Neustift punished the Sallers and threatened to burn their houses down, so they no longer want to help. . . .

Valtein was at the meeting in Götzenberg where he heard Hutter and Tuchmacher preach. Hutter himself took leave of them all as he was planning to go to Moravia. Afterward Valtein went to Freiberg with Hansel Decker; the others went to Moravia. . . .

He testified further: Tuchmacher and Valtein came into Nidervintl around midnight. Tuchmacher went to the new house, while Valtein stayed at the temple of idols; then Tuchmacher came again and took him with him over the wood pile in order to climb into the house and into the room of Mrs. Mair and her daughter. In the meantime, Balthasar Mairhofer came and said there was danger, but Peter Lantz[21] didn't recognize them. As they were sitting together, old Mrs. Mair looked out the window and said, "The police are walking around in the garden; they want to catch you." They wanted to flee, but Valtein saw the captain outside the room and they couldn't get away.

He testified further: His brothers sent him to the Adige Valley and commissioned him to visit wherever he knew there were brothers. What the others did in the meantime when he was gone, or where they got provisions, he does not know.

Valtein was sick for a while and was unable to bring the brothers and sisters food.

About a year ago Jakob Hutter gave him one hundred gulden. He distributed it among the brothers and sisters who were going to Moravia.

When someone becomes a brother or sister they sometimes give him one or two gulden from time to time; he distributed it among them again. . . .

Valtein was at the meeting that was just held in Götzenberg, but he was sick. Tuchmacher preached. The oxen and everything were prepared ahead of time by Hannsl Mair who had been commissioned for this; he does not know where the oxen came from.

Brother Conntzen [Kuntz Fichter] was given money to take to Moravia; he doesn't really know whose money it was, but it was probably Balthasar Mairhofer's.

When Christ our Lord was on earth there were no churches, only the temple that Solomon had had built in Jerusalem.

The priest is the first fornicator; they are not allowed to marry but they are allowed to commit fornication.

Mass is worth nothing.

He considers the sacrament to be worth nothing; it is flour and bread and a trick of the devil, invented by the pope, who is a servant of the devil.

The preaching of the priests is worth nothing; they do not preach the gospel and have not been commissioned for it; but Hutter was commissioned by the church of God.

Infant baptism is worth nothing. Christ did not command children, but the faithful, to be baptized. Children are baptized by the Holy Spirit.

Confession to the priest is worth nothing. Christ said to the leper who had been cleansed that he should show the priest that he was clean.[a]

About the Virgin Mary he believes that she bore Jesus Christ and before and also after the birth she was a pure virgin.

He considers the priests to be false prophets.

The brethren who were in Götzenberg have gone to Moravia, but Hansel Decker and Hannsl Maurer might still be in the Puster Valley.

Valtein will not turn away from this faith; may God's grace protect him. With the help and strength of God he wants to endure, suffer death, and witness with his blood that this is the divine truth, may God help him.

Even if they sin against him by forcing more out of him, he will not recant.

---

a Matt. 8:1–4.

Witness 10

October 15, 1533, Michelsburg, testimony of Christoph Schueknecht[22]

Christoph Schueknecht, son of Andrew Zimmermann of St. Georgen, who was executed here, confessed with and without torture:

A while ago he was in a foreign country and he heard that everyone here was a heretic and people said all kinds of terrible things about them. He wondered what kind of people these could be. When he came home to St. Georgen he heard that the brethren were moving from place to place. After a while, he came to Mrs. Mairhofer and noticed that she was one of them. He asked her if this was the divine truth. She said, "Yes, if only you live accordingly." Afterward he went to Steffl Zimmerman, who used to live in St. Georgen but has now moved, and asked him to read out of the Testament to him. He did that. One night when he was at Zimmerman's, Valtein Luckner came in and wished them the peace of God. Schueknecht wondered at this greeting and asked Zimmerman who it was. He told him it was a Christian. He said, "I think I am also a Christian." Luckner said to him, "You are not a Christian; you don't look like a Christian." Christoph answered that if knew the real divine truth, he would want to live according to it. Luckner told him he needed to repent of his sins, but he, Luckner, was not commissioned to speak with him further. Later, Valtein Luckner came to him and led him to a fellowship meeting in Villnöß. There he heard the word of God from Jakob Hutter, one of the leaders, and he was baptized by him. This was about two years ago.

He considers their churches and temples as worthless places for fornicators and crooks, and if he were to enter, he would also become a sinner.

He considers the Mass to be nothing but an abomination and stench before God.

They share everything in common that God gives them, both heavenly and earthly goods. Each has as much as the other. With us, the community we have is that one is rich, the other is poor and has to beg, and we chop off one another's hands and feet, and such is our Christian life.

Infant baptism is nothing but an accursed dirt-bath and stench before God.

Our Lady was a pure virgin before, during and after the birth [of Jesus].
He is without sin, by God's grace and mercy. . . .
Also, our government is strictly from the devil and not from God.

Witness 11

October 15, 1533, Michelsburg, testimony of Ruprecht Huber [23]

Ruprecht Huber from Götzenberg, the smith's apprentice, testified saying: He worked for a while for Sigmund, the smith in Bozen. At Easter 1531 he came home to Götzenberg. His father and siblings asked him if he would want to repent, as he was living in sin and unrighteousness. Afterward he moved to Brixen and again came home for a week. Hans Mair Paulle and Valtein Luckner came to Huber's house and pointed out the divine truth to him. On Saint Michael's Day that same year, 1531, Jakob Hutter, a devout preacher, came to their house and held a fellowship meeting there. Hutter baptized him there according to God's command.

He doesn't hold to infant baptism, for it is an accursed dirt-bath – may God condemn it – as it was established solely by the pope and not by God.

He doesn't believe in the sacrament of the altar and the Mass, as it is a condemned thing before God; he believes in God alone, the God who created heaven and earth and not in our sacrament.

Our churches are an accursed temple of whoring and idolatry, in which all manner of unrighteousness occurs. They are frequented by all sorts of fornicators, arrogant and proud hearts, and he laments to God that he visited churches for so long.

He is without sin, through the grace and mercy of God, and also for two years he has not sinned at all.

Our Lady is the Mother of God and he has more regard for her than for us.

He had been on a hill above Varn and then walked to the Puster Valley. Hansl Mair Paulle and Tuchmacher were on the hill by Geiss. They said they wanted to hold a fellowship meeting but didn't know where. Then Hansl Mair Paulle said, Let's go to the huts in Götzenberg and take the chance of holding it there. After that Huber went back to Varn and brought the brothers and sisters to the meeting. . . .

More than once he brought children over the Brenner Pass and sent them further, to Schwaz and Moravia.

Twice he brought bread to the meeting in Götzenberg, each time fifty loaves. He got it from Liendl Schneider at the mills near Schöneck. This took place Saturday night and Schneider gave it to him for nothing. He does not know who gave them the meat because when he arrived he saw the meat hanging in pieces. The following people brought food to this conference: Hannsl Maurer, Hansel Decker, Bastel from Villnöß. He brought the people to the conference, leading them to Runndl by Rodeneck, over the bridge, and through the woods to Götzenberg. . . .

The leader didn't want him to stay here in the Puster Valley because he was known; instead they sent him again and again to take people over the Brenner to Schwaz.

When he took groups, they always stopped at inns; one innkeeper knew them, the next didn't. At Steltzer in Brenner, he and Stoffl Schuster were beaten up by a drunkard who knew them.

He had just come from Kniepass to St. Georgen and then to Mrs. Zimmerman. Then he was arrested. At Kniepass they only gave him dry polenta.

Witness 12

October 21, St. Lorenzen,
second hearing of Christoph Schueknecht and Ruprecht Huber [24]

They were condemned on October 20. They will be executed by sword as soon as the bishop has sent word.

Christoph Schueknecht, [confessed] without torture: . . . From the time of the first meeting in Götzenberg until the next meeting there he worked in Neuhaus Castle and made shoes for the brothers and sisters. Hansl Mair Paulle, the steward, paid the administrator for housing him. He doesn't know how much. The administrator knew that Christoph had been rebaptized. But the administrator and his wife and children are not baptized and are not even Christians. The administrator walked around and told him that the brothers and sisters were on the knoll behind Neuhaus. That was where they were ambushed by three men.

As far as he knows, the administrator didn't give them anything. But with his knowledge and agreement the brothers and sisters went in and out of the castle at night, and from time to time slept at night in the castle.

Ruprecht Huber from Götzenberg took the following over the Brenner: the three children of Ulrich Weber from the Schöneck district. Weber recanted in Gufidaun and then returned to Moravia. Also several children from Flass such as Peter Maurer's, Vell's, and Alpiganer's, all three of whom were executed.

Hans Tuchmacher and Valtein Luckner gave Ulrich Weber's children to him, Christoph, and Ruprecht Huber, in a wood above Varn. They carried them into the Zillertal. There they met brothers from Schwaz. In Zillertal they stayed at an inn belonging to a small man and a wagoner, but he doesn't know his name. The innkeeper did not ask them who they were and they did not make themselves known. Christoph has been back and forth over the Brenner and stopped at various inns. He does not know if the innkeepers knew him or not. No one asked them who they were, except at Stelzer in Brenner where they were beaten up by a godless drunkard.

His two children were brought by Hans Maller of Bozen to the administrator at Neuhaus.

Witness 13

February 15, 1534, interrogation of Erhard Zimmerman, administrator of Neuhaus Castle[25]

First he stated that he has not been baptized; he has never attended their meetings or conferences and never seen a rebaptism.

Then he confessed: On Saint James' Day [July 25] last year 1533, his two children, a son and daughter about fourteen years old, were herding the goats at Pfaffenbach, the stream above the Neuhaus Castle. When they came home at night they told him that there were strange people up there under the cliff and they had built a hut.

The next day he went up to the stream to see what kind of people they were. He saw only a man and three women whom he did not know. They had built a fire. He asked them what their business there was. They pleaded with him, for God's sake, to allow them to stay; they would not disturb him. He didn't answer but left them and told his wife about it. Three days later his children came home again and told him that now there were more than eight people there. A week later he went to Brixen, wanting to see his lord Michel Teutenhofer.[26] He was unable to see Teutenhofer as he was out, so he told his wife. She said her husband was not home but she would let him know about it when he returned, and he would travel to the St. Lorenz market [festival, August 10], so that he could explain it to him.

Teutenhofer came to the St. Lorenz festival at the Neuhaus Castle, where [Zimmermann] told him that people, who appeared to be Anabaptists, had been near Pfaffenbach. He tried to show that they were still there and that they were coming into the castle at night. He asked [Teutenhofen], what should he do so as not to get into trouble? Teutenhofer told him to leave them alone and not say anything. But Zimmermann told him that his children knew about it and they might talk to others about it. Teutenhofer told him to convince them just to be quiet about it. He said, Yes, as long as I don't get into trouble; he answered that he should just keep quiet. . . .

Around that time, when he wasn't home, one of them called Hans Mair, the treasurer, came to his wife in the castle and said that one of the sisters was going to have a baby. He asked if she could be taken into the castle and he would pay for everything she needed. His wife answered that she didn't think her husband would agree but she would ask him. When he came home, she asked him about it. He did not want to permit it or allow it at all. The woman did not stay in the castle for her confinement but stayed up by the Pfaffenbach stream. Six days later he drove them off.

Witness 14

November 22, 1535, Michelsburg, testimony of Katharina Tagwericher [27]

Among those Jakob Hutter baptized in his last weeks was a seventeen-year-old girl. She was arrested and imprisoned in Michelsburg; a transcript of her interrogation was sent to the bishop in Brixen. Her name was Katharina, daughter of Hans Tagwericher in Schöneck, and she had worked as a maid for magistrate Peter Troyer's daughter. She escaped but was arrested again. Christoph Ochs, the magistrate, asked Brixen for advice as to how to deal with this ignorant young woman.[28] *Her testimony is summarized as follows.*

She worked as a maid for Niderhofer in Terenten.[29] The heavenly Father sent his people to her, so that she could learn the divine truth. It was about three years ago this coming spring[30] that Hans Mair Paulle, the treasurer, came to Niderhofer's house in Terenten. He taught the people in the house, telling them to repent. He did not stay more than two hours in the house.

About two days later somebody came to the house. They called him Sigl, who was from Kiens.[31] He spoke with Niderhofer, but she doesn't know what they talked about.

Further: About three weeks prior to Saint Bartholomew's Day [August 24] she went with Niderhofer's wife to the woods above Ehrenburg where the Anabaptists used to meet. Jakob Hutter, the leader, was there, as well as some from Lüsen, including two girls, an old woman, and several men. She did not know them. She was baptized at that time by Jakob Hutter, along with the two girls and the old woman from Lüsen, a girl from Kiens who served as a maid to Velser in Kiens, and Mrs. Rasstainer. Ober from Hörschwang[32] and his wife have also been baptized, but she doesn't know where they were baptized.

Ober was also at this fellowship meeting. They also met in the woods on Saturday night and left on Sunday evening. Further: By the pond in Vintl, Huber was also present at the meeting, but she doesn't know if he is also a Christian.

About a week before Saint Bartholomew's Day of this year,[33] Jakob Hutter, the leader, came again to Niderhof and stayed about three days. He did not preach. He only spoke with Niderhofer and his wife. She doesn't know what they talked about, but he himself baptized Niderhofer's wife.

Further: On this past Saint Bartholomew's Day a conference was held right in this place. Jakob Hutter, the leader, was present as well as Niderhofer and his wife, along with Ober of Hörschwang, the girl from Kiens, Mrs. Rasstainer, and herself Katharina, and also someone from Mühlwald called Balthasar. He is a big man and wore a black loden coat.[34] There were others whom she did not know. She doesn't know how many people there were. Niderhofer and Balthasar from Mühlwald were baptized at this occasion.

Further: About a week or more after Saint Bartholomew's Day Jakob Hutter, the leader, came to Niederhof in Terenten and preached there. Those present were Niderhofer and his family, Mrs. Rasstainer, and the girl from Kiens.

Further: Just eight days before she was arrested, Jakob Hutter, the leader, was at Ober's at Hörschwang. He and one of the brethren whom she does not know came Thursday night and stayed until Saturday.

Further: Hutter wears a long leather-colored coat with pleats front and back, a black felt hat, white cut-off pants. He is clean shaven.

There were three other brethren at Ober's who were threshing. She didn't know them.

Further: The Saturday night when she was captured, Ober and his wife went to Lüsen. But she doesn't know what they were doing there.

Further: Wolfl Tagwericher from St. Sigmund slaughtered an ox at Ober's at Hörschwang, but she doesn't know where the meat came from.

She thinks nothing of the sacrament of the altar; it is useless. It is a damned, useless idol introduced by the priests. They know it well.

Further: Infant baptism is worthless. The priests introduced it for the sake of money.

The Mass is useless and accursed, for our Lord did not command it.

The church is a damned, idolatrous temple, a whorehouse, and murderers' den, for the priests murder souls there. Hutter pointed out in his sermon that the emperor, king, and lords let the Christians be persecuted, because they are worried that if the Christians are allowed to continue, their own glory will grow less and diminish.

Sworn witnesses to this testimony are: Hans Veuchter, Hinterhauser of Moos, Marx Undergasser of St. Stefansdorf, and Bartholomew Hechtl of Loettn.

Witness 15

November 25, 1535, Schöneck, testimony of Niclas Niderhofer (summarized) [35]

Last Lent, three Anabaptist men came to him and said they had heard that he and his wife were willing to become followers of the truth. If this was the case, one of them would go down and bring one of the leaders. Who they were, and where they had come from, he didn't know.

Then a few days before Saint James Day [July 25] two people came again and told him there were two brothers, among them a leader, and if he wished, he would come to him. He answered that if they were planning a meeting he would like to come. They informed him that he should come to the bridge at Alstern, but he didn't go.

About three weeks later, they visited him at home and taught him the way of God according to the Gospels. At that time his wife was baptized.

He and his wife attended the next meeting in the woods above Ehrenburg on Saint Bartholomew's Day [August 24], and he was baptized. There were nineteen people present, one from Mühlwald,[36] whose name he didn't know. He didn't know anyone except for Mrs. Rasstainer from Schöneck. Four weeks later the same people were in his house again; they stayed for two days. They taught and comforted him, so that he should not regret [the step he had taken], and if it should come to that, that he would endure bravely. No one else came until fourteen days before Michaelmas [September 29]. He gave about thirty florins to the brotherhood, besides what they used when they were with him.

Witness 16

December 3, 1535, Klausen, testimony of Niclas and Appolonia Praun [37]

Jakob Hutter baptized him this past Saint James' Day [July 25] in the woods, under a spruce tree behind the city wall. Also his wife, with young Fallerin, a young man name Achaci from Auer, young Obereck from Auer, Mulner and his wife in Villnößs, and Marina, Mulner's maid, were all baptized. Otherwise, no one was there except one named Michl, whom Niclas thinks is from Götzenberg, a big man wearing a black cape.[38] He led them to the spruce tree. Jakob Hutter has been in his house about six times but he always left at nighttime.

There is a little hut in the mountains of Niederwies.[39] He brought bread, sausage, flour, cheese, two pounds of lard. Obereck helped him. Melchior, Prader's boy, was also with him. Ortl was also baptized and two people came into his house.

He will renounce this superstition and as before will believe in Mass and the holy sacrament. He will renounce the Anabaptist sect, go to confession, and receive communion.

When did Hutter stay overnight at his place? He thinks he went either to Hörschwang or Auer or Villnöß.

Ortl came to him once and told him Hutter was coming and they should meet in the bathhouse.

They were also together once at the mill in Laseider.

Hutter and his wife stayed with him two or three nights.

Prader's girl, Magidlin, who was imprisoned, was the cause of his rebaptism.

On Saint Martin's Day someone called Jeronimus [Käls] stayed with him. He is a baptizer, wears a black surcoat, has a big black beard, and black cap. He is a big man. He heard it said that Jeronimus had been a priest. The sister of young Oberecker from Auer has also been baptized.

Jakob Hutter also stayed at Prader's, but Prader was not baptized, although his wife and Melchior were.

He, Praun, had three bags of money, thirty gulden, which he gave to Jakob Hutter. Hutter said he would share it among the sisters, and he gave four of the gulden back to him.

The money and food that he gave Hutter and the sisters is worth more than fifty gulden. . . .

Appolonia Praun confessed that on Saint James' Day, Hutter baptized her in the woods, and Melchior was also baptized there.

She doesn't believe in the Mass, the sacrament, or Christian churches.

Witness 17

December 3, 1535, Klausen,
testimony of Anna, daughter of Hans Stainer[40] *(Nändl)*

Anna, daughter of Hans Stainer of St. Georgen, administrator of Michelsburg, and his wife Margaret, admitted after being interrogated without torture:

Verena, the daughter of Grembs, who is now in Moravia, convinced her to join this sect about four years ago. After she was at Huber's place on Götzenberg for a while – Huber and his wife are now in Moravia – she received baptism there by Jakob Hutter.

Soon after she joined the sect, Onophrius [Griesinger], Hans Meier, and Jörg Fasser came to her at the Grembs's in St. Georgen. All three of them are leaders and as far as she knows all are currently in Moravia.

From Götzenberg she first went to the tailor's hut in Varn, where she stayed about three weeks. There was also a woman called Jaindl from Villnöß, who is a smith's wife. Since then they have all moved to Moravia.

After that she went to Gaismair's in Sterzing to work as a maid for a while and from there to Chonz's on the cliff near Stilfes. Soon after that a fellowship meeting was held in the woods at Grasstain. More than one hundred people were there. Stoffle Schuster from St. Lorenz and Hans Mair brought them food in the woods. She didn't know all the people, only Hutter and his wife.

After that there was a fellowship meeting in a shed at Grasstain. From there she went to Grenken at Vonhoch and from there to Vilgraten, from there to Tobloch. There she was arrested. She was imprisoned for a long time but was allowed to walk around freely and then, since no one was watching, she walked out. She went to Ober's at Hörschwang, where she stayed for three weeks. She worked and slept there until a fellowship meeting was held there.

After that she took Hutter and his wife and one of the brethren called Jeronimus, who has since then gone to Moravia, to a place near Sterzing called Trens, to the house of a wagoner called Schachner or Schupfer. Hutter baptized seven or eight people there. She doesn't know their names but thinks some of them were miners. There were also other people who had been baptized earlier there, about fifteen people. But the wagoner was out at the time and didn't know anything about it.

After that they stayed in the woods during the day. On Saint Andrew's Day [November 30], they traveled secretly at night through the woods to the Eisack River, past the watchman's hut, over the bridge, through the city of Klausen and back over the bridge to the sexton's house. They were arrested there. She did not know that Hutter was planning to leave.

She doesn't think anything of the church, infant baptism, the sacrament of the altar; they are useless, and an abomination before God.[41]

Witness 18

December 3, 1535, Klausen, testimony of Katharina Hutter [42]

Katharina, daughter of Laurence Prast, confessed:

It was about three years ago when she was serving as a maid in Paul Gall's house in Trens that she was convinced to join the Anabaptist sect through Paul Gall and also Paul Rumer and others, some of whom have been executed and some who have moved to Moravia. Jakob Hutter, the leader, who is now her brother in marriage and her husband,[43] baptized her there. After that she moved down to Moravia. Around this past Pentecost she married Jakob Hutter in Moravia. Hans Tuchmacher [Amon], who is also one of their brethren and a leader, married them.

Around Saint James' Day [July 25] she and her brother in marriage or husband and another brother named Jeronimus, the schoolmaster, who was also baptized by Jakob Hutter, came up from Moravia over the Tauern to Taufers. They camped out in the woods in Taufers for a while. Then they went to Waldner's in Ellen,[44] but he had recanted and became a destructive person.

From there they went to Ober's in Hörschwang. He is a dear brother, as is his wife, their daughter Dorothy, also two servants (both called Martin), a young man Hans Wolf, and his wife, Else. Her husband Jakob Hutter baptized and converted all of them. Hutter also baptized Waldner in Ellen, mentioned earlier, but he has recanted and become a destructive Christian.

From there they went several times to Prader and Praun in Lüsen. Prader is not of their opinion or faith, but his wife and son, Melchior are. They often found accommodation and food there, with Jeronimus (mentioned above) who was with them. Those whom her husband Hutter baptized in Lüsen were baptized in the woods.

About fourteen days ago in the house of a wagoner named Schaffer or Schacher in Trens by Sterzing (the man was not home, and he is not an Anabaptist), Hutter baptized seven or eight people in a cellar; she doesn't know exactly how many but she thinks they were miners.

From there she and Hutter and Stainer's daughter Anna went back to Ober's in Hörschwang. They stayed there for a while but then realized that they were being hunted and left. They went through the woods and on the roads at night, until they got to Klausen. They passed the watchman's hut, crossed the bridge, and walked through the town. Then they crossed back over the bridge and came to the sexton's house around midnight. They wanted to leave immediately, but didn't know where to go. Her husband and brother Jakob Hutter said they should go to Niclau or Jörg Müller in Villnöß or wherever God would lead them.

Niclau's wife is her dear sister, but he is not dear to her; likewise with Jörg Müller and his wife in Villnöß. They were baptized by Hutter last fall, but Müller is good for nothing.

Further: She thinks nothing of Mass or the sacrament of the altar, which monks and priests raise above their heads;

nor does she have regard for the piled up walls of stone [churches];

nor of infant baptism, which is nothing but a dirt-bath.

Mass is an abomination and a stench before God.

All of this is from the devil.

Niclas Niderhofer in the Schöneck district and a girl named Ulian, who was a maid in Kiens, and another person whom she doesn't know, were baptized by Hutter on Saint James' Day. They also took lodging with them a few times.

Regarding her husband Jakob Hutter's assets, or what money he has, he shares it with poor widows, poor little children, and other poor brothers and sisters who need it.

As far as she knows, there are no leaders or brethren in this land. They are all in Moravia.

Witness 19

December 3, 1535, Klausen,
testimony of Anna, wife of Jacob Stainer [45]

Anna, wife of Jacob Stainer, who used to be the sexton in Klausen, living on the far side of the bridge over the Eisack, in Gufidaun district, confessed:

About two years ago she was in prison at Michelsburg because of Anabaptism. She recanted publicly there, and she stays true to the recantation oath that she made then, and wants to live like other pious Christians. She believes in Mass and the holy sacrament, in infant baptism and all Christian orders held by the Christian church, as all other Christians confess and maintain.

Since she recanted she has never taken in an Anabaptist or given them lodging except just now on Saint Andrew's Day. Around twelve midnight there was a knock on her door and someone wanted to come in. But since there was a drunken crowd in the alley earlier she didn't want to let anyone in. But a woman knocked again, and she opened the door. There were two women and a man who wanted to come in and get warm. As soon as she saw them properly she realized that they were people stained with Anabaptism. Out of mercy and for God's sake she allowed them to come in for a short time and get warm, but then wanted to send them out again immediately. She did not give them anything to eat or drink or accommodate them at all. As the three of them, Hutter and the two women, were about to leave, the Klausen authorities came and arrested all three of them. She does not know what they were planning or where they were going to go. . . .

Witness 20

ca. March 1536, Vienna, Jeronimus Käls's confession of faith [46]

Jeronimus Käls, the fellowship's schoolmaster, accompanied Hutter on his final trip to Tyrol and then carried his last letter back to the fellowship in Moravia. He and two others were arrested early in 1536 and executed two weeks before Easter.[47] *While in prison, Käls wrote a statement of their faith (Cf. the Apostles' Creed), which he submitted to the judge. It is included here because it can be assumed that it significantly reflects Hutter's teaching.*

Dear friend judge and all of you who have taken time for us and imagine that you can turn us from our holy Christian faith to return to the old shoes of our heathen life: We, bound and imprisoned for the sake of truth, wish you all the best, grace and eternal mercy from the almighty God, and the true sight of your life, through Jesus Christ our dear Lord. Amen.

We have appeared before you four times and answered your questions truthfully (as we must answer to God); we still stand to what we said, and we will also endure to the end through God's help and grace. Therefore we plead with you, for God's sake, do not try further to change our minds, because we ourselves will stand, as all men must, each for himself, before the just judge Christ Jesus on that day.[a] Each will have to bear his burden. Just as you refuse to turn away from the Babylonian whore,[b] that is, the pope and his train, so do we refuse to be turned away from Christ. But so that you do not sin more deeply against the innocent blood of the saints, we want to make a written account to you in short, truthful words. If you will see the truth differently, test and consider our innocence and your miserable life, whether you will also turn away from the world, to a Christian, God-fearing life, and be saved. May God the almighty give you the humility to hear us who are small and despised by this world and accept you in grace, through Jesus his beloved Son. Amen.

First, we believe in the one God, creator of heaven and earth, and all that is in and on it. Therefore we despise all idolatry, wooden, stone, silver, gold – in short, all painted or sculpted images, according to the word of

---

a 2 Cor. 5:10.
b Rev. 17.

God,[a] of Christ,[b] of the apostles.[c] We read it in the Old and New Testaments, and through God's grace we will endure constantly.

We also believe in Jesus the Christ of God, that he was sent from the bosom of the heavenly Father from heaven to redeem all mankind. He took human form in the virginal pure vessel Mary. She conceived him through the Holy Spirit, without man's seed; she bore him and on the eighth day had him circumcised to fulfill the promise of the Father.

We testify in word and deed that what Christ demanded, taught, and promised is the divine, eternal truth. We consider all those who believe him and his word and follow him obediently to be worthy of his name as Christians. But all others, who say they believe in Christ but do not obey his words nor do what he taught and commanded, we say that they are anti-Christians, not Christians. By this we mean the papal church in which all things against Christ are done, yet they falsely claim to belong to Christ. They want to make Christ a cover for their prostitution. In witness: Matthew 12:2, 10:24; John 15:21–22; Romans 8:3–4. All truth is testified by two or three witnesses.

In this is included Christian and truthful baptism of water. Matthew 3: Christ himself was baptized and afterward baptized others.[d] It is also written clearly in his last farewell command.[e] We practice it as the dear apostle did.[f] Here the pope's infant baptism is negated, the first and greatest abomination in the eyes of the Lord, for by this every man beautifies his gruesome burdens and takes to himself, through this supposed baptism, the precious name of Christ – whether he is a whoremonger, thief, or murderer. A Christian should have the name of Christ, not of baptism. We want to hold to this through God's help, for we have already been buried with Christ through baptism.[g]

We confess to this Jesus Christ, our beloved Lord, and we testify that as soon as he gave the command of the Father, of true righteousness, and instituted baptism he was persecuted, despised, betrayed by Judas, and

---

a Exod. 20:4–6.
b E.g., Matt. 4:10.
c E.g., Rom. 1:18–25; 1 John 5:21.
d Matt. 3:13–17.
e Matt. 28:19; Mark 16:16.
f Acts 2:41; 8:12; 19:4–5.
g Rom. 6:4; Col. 2:12.

cruelly tortured under the authority of Pontius Pilate, who condemned him to death (although unwillingly), and crucified. With his bitter death and red blood he won salvation for all those who believe in him and follow him faithfully; to the others his suffering becomes a testimony to eternal death. For whoever does not suffer with Christ will not inherit with him, as holy scripture testifies.[h] All scripture tells us that Christ and all the prophets [promise] nothing but persecution, cross, suffering, distress, abandonment, denying oneself.[i]

After he preached his comforting word to the imprisoned spirits,[j] he rose from the dead undecayed in a clarified body. He showed himself to his beloved disciples and commanded them, as mentioned above. Then he ascended to heaven in his body; and as he ascended,[k] in the same way will he return. He sits at the Father's right hand. From there we await him, according to scripture, that he will come in the clouds of heaven, as the lightning strikes, and thousands of angels with him.[l] Here scripture tells us that Christ is sitting in heaven with the Father and is not in temples built by human hands; neither does he want to be tended with human hands.[m] That is why we plead and admonish you not to serve the idol of bread [in Mass] but rather to root it out.

We believe in the Holy Spirit, that he is the comforter of all depressed and sad hearts, and that he is and will be sent from the Father by Christ Jesus to all believing chosen people as Christ promised.[n] Anyone who does not have this Holy Spirit is not a Christian; anyone who claims he has the Holy Spirit and Christ but does works of the flesh is a liar, as Paul tells us[o] and in many passages Christ tells us.[p]

We also believe and know that there is a holy Christian church and a godly Christian fellowship. This church is the body of Christ, of which he is the head and rules his whole body. This Christian church is holy, without stain. But if a disruptive member should be found in the body

h E.g., Matt. 16:24; Phil. 1:29.
i E.g., Matt. 10:22; John 15:20; Phil. 1:29.
j 1 Pet. 3:19.
k Acts 1:1–11.
l E.g., Matt. 24:30–31.
m Acts 7:48; 17:24.
n John 14–15.
o E.g., Rom. 8:9; Gal. 5:16–26; cf. 1 John 2:4.
p E.g., Matt. 7:15–27; John 15:1–7.

and can be improved in no other way, it is excluded from the church and treated as a heathen. Other punishment is not practiced in the Christian church, as Christ forbade it: The worldly princes and lords practice violence but you should not.[a] Neither did Christ want to rule a temporal kingdom[b] but said "My kingdom is not of this world."[c]

Regarding governing authorities, we stand as Christ taught us: to give taxes, tithes, rent, and labor to emperor, king, or governor as long as it does not serve war or execution.[d] Paul teaches the same in Romans 13, and Saint Peter in 1 Peter 2. Here Peter says one should submit to human institutions; by this we understand how he acted himself.[e] But laws that are against God he forbids us to obey, just like Daniel; Shadrach, Meshach and Abednego; and others in the Old and New Testaments.[f]

We believe immovably, through God's help, that the Christian church has the key to loose and to bind sin, as Christ himself gave her this authority.[g] In 1 Corinthians 5 Paul also used this authority. It is given to the Christian church, not the papal church.

We also believe the truth that all flesh will be awakened on the great day of the Lord God, and will be brought to judgment.[h] There the Lord will separate the sheep to his right and the goats to his left.[i] There will be one shepherd and one fold, but hell will be the fold of the goats.

We believe that after this temporal life and death there will be an eternal life in the kingdom of God, and also an eternal life in the fiery pool.[j]

Here you have a short account of the basis of our Christian faith. May God grant that it is a testimony to eternal joy and not to the destruction of your souls. The other points, such as the salvation of children, mission, swearing of oaths we will not discuss; because, for the sake of brevity, we do not consider it necessary and because we have already said enough to you previously.

---

a Matt. 20:25–28; 26:52.
b John 6:15.
c John 18:36.
d E.g., Matt. 17:24–27; 22:15–22.
e Acts 4:1–22.
f E.g., Dan. 1:8; 4; 6.
g Matt. 16:19; 18:18; John 20:23.
h Dan. 12:2; John 5:28–29.
i Matt. 25:31–46.
j Rev. 21:8.

We think we have proved the faith of our hearts sufficiently with two or three witnesses. If anyone finds it insufficient, we cannot give him faith for that comes from God alone. The reason for our writing, however, is that we are not capable of speaking to you, nor are you able to hear us. We ask you to receive it well and make your judgment without being annoyed. Consider carefully beforehand what you are doing, in the fear of God, for he is still a judge over you before whom you, as well as we, will have to appear and give account for the innocent blood that will not remain hidden. Truly, we do not wish to fall into the stream, but if you throw us in we will suffer it patiently as Christians. We commend ourselves to God. We wish and desire to hurt nobody, neither pope, bishop, monk nor priest, neither king nor Kaiser, not a single creature. Our conscience is pure and free; we have done no evil nor had revenge in our hearts. Therefore we will suffer joyfully and with great patience whatever God allows through you. We know you can do no more than that to us. If the righteous Joseph had granted the whore her treachery, he would have been protected by her; but since he remained righteous he was thrown into prison by her false testimony, but the Lord turned his bonds and suffering to great joy.[k] Thus, even if the whore has falsely accused us with her lies and brought us into prison, we have the certain hope and do not doubt that God will free us in his right time and help us out of this misery into peace, as Christ himself has promised.[l] But we feel sorry for you that you are sinning so deeply against the blood of the saints. Oh, if you are Saul, we wish you the grace to be a Paul,[48] but it is a great concern because the word of the cross[m] of Christ is despicable to you, although to us it is the strength of God. You desire to follow Christ and would gladly go with him to heaven, but you do not want to taste the eagerness to suffer with him and descend to hell. Whoever will not eat bitter salt will also not taste the Easter lamb in all eternity.

We commend ourselves to the protection of the highest. May he help us drink the cup of suffering. Amen.

Written in our miserable imprisonment under the authority of Ferdinand in 1536.

---

k Gen. 39.
l John 16:33.
m 1 Cor. 1:18.

Witness 21

ca. March 1536,[49] *Vienna, testimony of Hansel Zimmerman* [50]

Hansel Zimmerman testified that he was the son of a farmer from Affers in the district of Rodeneck, where his wife and child are staying with his father. He supported himself and his wife and child by farming for his father. When he read in [saints'] legends and in the books of the Testament and saw Christians martyred and executed for their faith and heard their testimonies, he concluded that the same thing was happening, the torture and pain against the Christians as against the saints, and that their way of life was the same as that of the earlier saints. So he was moved to accept the Christian faith and had himself baptized according to God's command. He was baptized by Jakob Hutter around last Saint Jacob's Day, as stated above, in a valley called Im Liser. He thinks about eight persons were baptized with him by Hutter by a stream.

He also confessed that about two weeks before he was baptized he listened to sermons by the stream. After he was baptized he returned home. When people noticed that he was no longer attending the unrighteous idolatry in the temple of their idols and the *Pailerey*,[51] they realized that he had been baptized. So the judge tried to catch him at his father's, but he left and within eight days was in Moravia, looking for sisters and brothers. He met Jeronimus, the carpetmaker, and Michael and came here with them, looking for work in the mines. They spent a night here and somebody sat with them at the table in the inn. He broke bread with them and dipped it in the bowl. He tried to get them to drink, but they would not. By this he recognized them to be Anabaptists, and the city judge arrested them.

Witness 22

January 1561, Innsbruck, testimony of Jörg Rack [52]

Before Jörg came to faith, he had heard about a man named Jakob Hutter, who was burned at the stake here at Innsbruck. He heard that he was gagged on the way here to prevent people from hearing the truth he proclaimed. . . . He had seen with his own eyes how they burned Mair at the stake in Steinach, who was of the same faith. Jörg had taken all this to heart to the highest degree, considering that there must have been a powerful grace and strength that enabled them to remain firm in their faith unto death.[53]

4
Hutterian Epistles

Correspondence between the Hutterian Brethren has been preserved in multiple manuscript sources. A four-volume edition of the German-language letters appeared as *Die Hutterischen Epistel: 1527 bis 1767.*[1] The following excerpts from letters present the most significant references to Hutter from the writings of fellow Hutterian Brethren, written both during his life and after his death, although this selection does not include an exhaustive listing of all minor, passing references to Hutter in the epistle collections.

Hutterian Epistle 1

Hans Amon to Leonard Schmerbacher, summer 1533 [2]

Written from Tyrol to Moravia. Hutter's colleague and successor sent this letter along with Jakob Hutter to one of the deacons in Moravia, anxious that Hutter's arrival might be resented.

Dear brother Leonard,

I thank my God, our heavenly Father from my heart when I think of your faithfulness and how you care for the dear saints in all your works. These come from the good treasure of your heart, so that you might diligently serve the dear children of God. God knows that I truly love you sincerely. You have been written into my heart by the finger of God, and I sincerely rejoice in your love and integrity. Therefore, I constantly remember you in prayer and earnestly pray, if it be God's will, that God, our heavenly Father, wants to unite us, face to face, that we may rejoice together and that our joy may be even fuller. But I leave it completely to the Lord, as other things, that he may lead and direct it according to his will.

My dear brother, I ask you sincerely to love the children of God and rejoice in suffering with them like the devout Moses, for the sake of the hope that is promised us. Take care in all things, embracing the Lord's work and fulfilling your office in earnest. I ask you especially regarding our brother Jakob, that you allow him to take charge over you,[3] receiving him with joy, and assisting him in all matters.

Dear brother, I'm writing in confidence to you as a faithful caution for the sake of the dear brothers and sisters: If brother Jakob comes down [to Moravia] to preside over God's people and serve them, as I hope he does, and were the dear children of God to have an exceptional trust to him while others are annoyed or envious, then, my dear brother, I would ask that you do your utmost, to the extent that God gives you grace and understanding, so that this not come to pass and that no bitter root[a] grows among the servants of God. This has happened before, and it is to be lamented to God. Yet I hope to God and all of you that it does not

a Heb. 12:15.

happen. However, cursed Satan, our adversary, does not [rest], and Christ especially warns his disciples, saying, "I see Satan falling from heaven like lightning."[a] Therefore, he tells us to guard against arrogance and pride, for God has hated and cast them out from the beginning, as scripture tells us.[b]

Hutterian Epistle 2

Hans Amon to Jörg Fasser and Leonard Seiler, 1536 [4]

In three letters that Bishop Hans Amon wrote to Jörg Fasser and Leonard Seiler, in prison in Vienna in 1536, he mentioned Hutter's recent death.

O, my dear brothers, our dear Father is now taking all the old, devout brethren away. . . .

O, you heroes of Israel, you who are strong in Zion, rejoice and be glad, for you have faithfully grieved and mourned with Zion. You will also sincerely rejoice with her and find great glory, joy and great adornment and beauty in the kingdom of God. Yes, in Paradise where our dear brethren are waiting for us, Abel[c] and all who are devout, our dear Jakob and Jeronimus [Käls]. O, I cannot count the great and glorious number or crowd of the elect who are praising God with great joy and hymns of praise. O, fight and struggle to the end, and you will receive the crown of glory.[d]

Hutterian Epistle 3

Hans Amon to Jörg Fasser and Leonard Seiler, 1536, second letter [5]

Remember dear Jakob [Hutter]: Didn't he remain faithful through all his suffering, and wasn't God with him? The same is true of Jeremia [Jeronimus Käls], Michl [Michael Seifensieder], Hansl [Hans Oberecker].[6]

a Luke 10:18.
b Cf. Prov. 8:13.
c Heb. 11:4.
d Cf. 1 Pet. 5:4.

Remember also Peter [Riedemann] of Gmunden and Hans von Lichtenfels. Isn't it true that they have been in prison for a long time and are true witnesses? The same can be said of many hundreds, whom I cannot name and tell about, who are examples for us in the integrity and virility of their faith, as heirs of the promise of life (in contrast to the tyrants who have persecuted the devout.)

Hutterian Epistle 4

Hans Amon to Jörg Fasser and Leonard Seiler, 1536, third letter [7]

We are proclaiming to you comfort, joy, and good news from our dear brothers and sisters from the Adige Valley, for Offrus trekked there and found Christians present. Stoffel Schneider also came to us; Kränzler has been executed. Jakob's Treindl[8] escaped with the sister and both remained devout. . . .

O my beloved friends in the Lord, take whole-hearted comfort in the Lord. What God wants to do with you, nobody can hinder. Dear Jakob held a great sermon during his death which resounded and carried forth far and wide. Thus, God knows all things and knows how each one shall or will praise him.

Hutterian Epistle 5

Jörg Fasser and Leonard Seiler to Hans Amon, 1536 [9]

Fasser and Seiler mentioned Jakob Hutter in their letters to Hans Amon, written from prison in Vienna in 1536.

O my Hans, we remember you constantly before God in our prayers, for you have a great responsibility. But the Lord has stood by his devout and faithful servants and slaves from the beginning, and he will stand by you in all things, for you fear him from your heart – of that I am certain. All honor to him, my God, the Lord. Yes, God in heaven knows that I rejoice with my whole heart that you are there with the dear children of God. For with you they are cared for.

O my Hans, our wish and sincere request is that God the Almighty allows you to stay with his people for a long time. O my God, how wretched the dear children of God are when they lose their devout shepherds. O my God, do not give power over to the godless. Do not let your dear children be robbed of your word. O my Hans, our request is that we do not have to experience the hour in our shelters [bodies],[10] when you might depart from the people of God – by any means. Yet we know that even then, the Lord will preserve[a] those who are devout. I also know that the other ministers and brethren are truly faithful and in all things are by your side. I feel so sorry for the dear children of God when I think of them and of dear Jakob [Hutter] and others who have departed – the devout shepherds who bore the children of God with much pain, and who constantly dedicated and gave their lives faithfully for them. I hope you understand what I mean.

Hutterian Epistle 6

Jörg Fasser and Leonard Seiler
to Hans Amon, 1536, second letter [11]

My Hans, as a token of my love I am sending you Jakob's wash cloth. Of such material items, we have little else. My fellow prisoners and I send you our whole heart along with it. . . . I, Leonard, am sending to dear Oswald and to his and my Martl a gift and my whole heart along with it. Keep it for the sake of my love, and accept my heartfelt greetings in divine love. Also, my Hans, tell my Michl, the small shoemaker, that I will soon send him my Testament. Give him my heartfelt greetings.

---

a Ps. 31:23.

Hutterian Epistle 7

Jörg Fasser and Leonard Seiler to the fellowship in Moravia [12]

Further, beloved brothers and sisters, a woman visited us in prison, a wealthy merchant. She had come down from Innsbruck. She told us about our dear Jakob's integrity, which was a deep joy to us. She said a huge crowd was present. We spoke with her and pointed her toward repentance. She wept; we will leave it at that.

Hutterian Epistle 8

Jeronimus Käls to Hans Amon and the fellowship in Moravia, February 1536 [13]

Jeronimus Käls, who had been with Hutter in Tyrol and carried back his last letter to the fellowship in Moravia in November 1535, was arrested in Vienna in January 1536 and executed during Lent, just weeks after Hutter himself. With him were two other brethren, Michael Seifensieder and Hans Oberecker (or Zimmermann). The latter was one of the last people Hutter had baptized in Tyrol.[14]

After about two hours, the soldiers came. They bound us and took us to the judge. When he heard that we were from Jakob Hutter's fellowship, he said we must be the right ones. We said, yes, praise God, we are the right ones, so he put us in a common jail, where we had to endure much humiliation and mockery. . . .[15]

We ask you from our hearts, dearly beloved brother Hans and all the dear brothers and sisters, to constantly pray for us to God, our beloved Father, that he might uphold us and strengthen us to struggle joyfully against the anti-Christians and that our joy in eternal gladness might be preserved. Also pray faithfully and from your whole hearts for our dear, devout brother and faithful minister, Jakob. Oh, how we would like to know how he is doing. We pray to God faithfully for him and for all prisoners, for we realize their suffering through our own. We know well that you are doing so, for we know the love that you bear toward us and all children of God, yet we do not wish to neglect reminding you. May the Lord, our God, be with you and us all. Amen.

Hutterian Epistle 9

Jeronimus Käls to Hans Amon, 1536 [16]

Dear, devout brother Hans [Oberecker] asks if you would visit his wife and child and sister in the flesh, who is married, and tell them about his zeal. It is also his heart's desire, for God's sake, that you would bring his dear sister Gredl, who is his sister in the flesh, down to the fellowship of God [in Moravia] so that she can be instructed and raised in the fear of God. It is the heartfelt desire of all of us that you would let them know of our love to them. Give them our greetings from the depths of our hearts. Faithful brother Hans wants them to know that the zeal with which he spoke to them [in Tyrol] is now being fulfilled, that is, that he wanted to be arrested with dear brother Jakob or with Jeronimus. He had to go down from the Puster Valley to be led to prison with him. . . .

Further, I ask from the depths of my heart, according to the good will of God, if you could visit my mother and brother in the flesh. Because when brother Jakob and I were with them, he said that if God grants it he wanted to send me out to them or offer to them to come down. For they had agreed that they were willing to suffer whatever God lays upon them.

Hutterian Epistle 10

Hans Amon to Matthesen in Hessen, 1538 [17]

Also the dear brother Jakob, minister of the Lord, confessed his word with complete joy.

5

Governmental Correspondence

Records of Internal Correspondence by Imperial, Regional, and Municipal Authorities

The accounts presented here are translations from government archival sources, many of them published in the QGT series. Although similar to the accounts in "Witnesses" (chapter 3), they offer an entirely different perspective – that of the officials attempting to put a stop to the Anabaptist movement.

Some of the pieces were selected because of their specific instructions on punishing Anabaptists, even though they might not speak of Jakob Hutter himself.

Governmental Correspondence 1

July 24, 1529, from Innsbruck to the warden in Toblach [1]

From your letter of June 23 to our Upper Austrian government with the enclosed testimonies, we have read what you have done with the fourteen Anabaptists and what they have confessed. You have found that ten of them were rebaptized by a Jakob Hutter from Spittal in Carinthia, who is their leader. . . .

From the testimonies of Balthasar Hutter and Andrew Planer, it is evident that they have not been baptized, but Balthasar Hutter gave lodging to Anabaptists, namely Gregori Weber who was executed in Brixen and Jakob Hutter, who is a leader and has baptized for money and escaped.[2] Hutter also held a Lord's Supper in a downstairs room in Andre Planer's house, the 'breaking of bread' as they call it. Ursel, Till's daughter (one of those arrested), the smith's apprentice, and possibly others read from a book of the Gospels. It is forbidden to house persons from this forbidden sect or to mislead others with their reading. Till's daughter fell into error through such reading. It is our command that Balthasar Hutter and Andrew Planer be questioned further under torture. Hutter in particular should be questioned as to why he took in these Anabaptists, including their leader Jakob Hutter, also why they were reading and what they read from the book of the Gospels. Ask them whether they believe that rebaptism is justified and whether infant baptism is worthless. . . .

Regarding the wives of Andrew Planer and Balthasar Hutter, who have been rebaptized but whom you let go for the sake of their nursing infants – follow them home, and if you think it is no longer necessary for them to nurse their babies, arrest them because of their error. Find out if they are ready to turn from their error, and report back to our government.

Governmental Correspondence 2

July 24, 1529, from Innsbruck to the judge in Rattenberg, instructing him on dealing with a pregnant woman [3]

He is to determine, through a knowledgeable woman, whether Anna Gasteigerin is pregnant; if so, he should take care that the child comes safely into the world and then that it receives Christian baptism. It should be nursed by a wet-nurse so that it does not die, and the mother should be executed.

Governmental Correspondence 3

December 8, 1529, from Innsbruck to the warden in Toblach [4]

With reference to his report of a female prisoner, Agnes Hutter of Moos in the Michelsburg district, who was imprisoned because of Anabaptism, and who has fallen into this error for the second time and refuses to change her mind despite his instruction and that of other religious and secular persons: we recommend that he continue to interrogate her with and without torture. She should be brought before the criminal court and dealt with according to the mandates. Before the jurors consider her case, they should swear by oath to judge and sentence her according to the mandates.

Governmental Correspondence 4

December 24, 1529, from Innsbruck to the bishop's office in Brixen [5]

Our dear cousins and princes, Duke Ludwig and Duke Wilhelm of Bavaria sent the testimony of an Anabaptist, Christoph Schauer, who was arrested in Auerburg near Kufstein, to our Upper Austrian government. Among other things, Schauer says that Jakob Hutter from Bruneck and Georg Zaunring are their leaders. . . . The brothers of this sect have a common treasury in every town in the Puster Valley and on the Ritten; everyone puts what he has into it and they care for one another from it. This Zaunring is the master of the purse [treasurer][6] on the Ritten, and he gave Christoph Schauer twelve kreuzer from it. We seriously desire that, in Bruneck and other towns in the Puster Valley under your jurisdiction, you give an order in secret to watch for these leaders and rebaptized persons. They should be imprisoned. If one or more is arrested, they should be questioned and a report sent to our Upper Austrian government.

Governmental Correspondence 5

March 10, 1532, from Innsbruck
to the mayors of several towns on the Inn River[7]

Faithful servants! We have received reliable word that some Anabaptist persons are leaving this region of Tyrol for Moravia, notably with a leader, Jakob Hutter of Welsberg, sun-tanned with a black beard, dressed in a felt cape, a blue doublet, white trousers, a black hat, and carrying a hatchet.[8] Without a doubt, these persons are traveling down the Inn River into Austria, to make their way from there to Moravia, as they did last year. Therefore, it is our earnest command to you, to watch carefully for these Anabaptist persons, and especially for Jakob Hutter in the district of Hall and otherwise, on the paths and roads in your jurisdiction. Give orders that nobody who is unknown, who is without sponsor or guarantee[9] or cannot convincingly prove where he is going, should be allowed onto the ships. If any such suspicious persons are found, they should be stopped, arrested, and given their just punishment.

Governmental Correspondence 6

March 26, 1532, from Innsbruck to the warden in Kitzbühel [10]

Faithful servant! We received your letter of [March] 21 regarding the number of persons contaminated with Anabaptism and what they have confessed, both with and without torture, and also the other people whom they have named belonging to their brotherhood. We also received transcriptions of their confessions. We appreciate your diligent work and your obedience to our mandates.

Since Veyt Schwaigl and his wife Magdalena, Barbara, the wife of Christan in Pachs, Hans Wagner's wife, and Hans von Hallerdorf's wife have already been pardoned once of belonging to this sect and, in spite of the oath they swore, fell back into this seductive sect and are *relapsi,* it is our command that you bring them to criminal court immediately after Easter and treat them according to our mandates. But for the salvation of their souls you should not be negligent in sending educated priests and others to them in prison to instruct them to give up this sect and error before their death. If they renounce it and you pardon them and administer the holy sacrament to them, the men should be beheaded and the women drowned; the dead corpses can be given Christian burial in consecrated ground. But if anyone will not turn from his error despite all Christian admonition and instruction, he should be burned, according to our mandates. But Hans Wagner's wife should be held in prison until her baby is born; then she should be treated as stated above as one who has been pardoned and has fallen again.

Regarding Christan Pach's daughter Ursula, who was recently rebaptized, who has no regard for the sacrament of the altar: she is stubborn in her error and will not turn from it. Thus you should act according to the mandates: If she holds to her stubborn opinion, disregarding instruction of educated priests, those whom you send to her, and still will not turn around, she should also be brought before a criminal court and the law should be carried out. If she recants, however, then she and Margret Schwaiglin, Hans Rieder's wife, Christian from Niderberg, and Hans Rieder – if all five are ready to recant and have not been contaminated before – according to the mandates, they should swear and sign a statement and recant publicly in church on three consecutive Sundays, accept the penance their priest demands of them, and never join the sect again. For one year they should be forbidden to leave the district where they live and for their whole life they may not move out of Tyrol. They can be released from prison after paying the cost of their imprisonment.

Governmental Correspondence 7

December 13, 1532, from Innsbruck to the judge in Sterzing [11]

We received your letter and the testimonies you enclosed of the rebaptized persons, which were given without using torture, stating which of them are determined to persist in their error and which agreed to recant, after the preachers from Hall, Christoph Landsperger and Linhart Ottental, taught and instructed them. . . . From this we understand that of the fifteen prisoners, four, namely a pregnant woman and three elderly men, are ready to recant of their error and do penance. But the other eleven persons, including some young girls twelve or thirteen years old and a young boy of about twelve, will not turn from their error and are determined to persist unto death.

Our command, in the name of our gracious lord, his Royal Majesty, is that those who will not recant, except for the young people under fourteen years, should be questioned again under severe torture. Besides the general questions which we are sending you, they should be asked:

Who calls them to the fellowship meetings?

Where they take place one after another, and where the next one will be?

Where they have received food and lodging in the meantime?

What form do their meetings take?

Whether meetings only consist of preaching by their leader or if they hold the Supper of Christ, as they say, with breaking bread.

Also they should not withhold where the three leaders, [Hans] Tuchmacher, [Jakob] Hutter, and Onophrius [Griesinger] can be found, especially where they plan to spend the winter, since they cannot live in the woods. Assure them that if they tell the truth you will do your best to gain their pardon. When you have a clear statement from them all, each one individually after harsh interrogation, admonish them sternly to turn from their error, do penance, and recant. If they will not desist after such admonition, they should be brought before the criminal court, and the emperor's and king's edict and mandates should be carried out.

Those who recant and are willing to do penance after the two preachers have instructed them should be treated as you have done with others in the past, according to our commands: They can be released from prison, do penance, and recant. When they make their recantation, you should be personally present and make sure that they speak clearly and understandably and hold everything in good order.

But the young people under fourteen years of age should be held in separate cells in prison. For several days they should be given little food, that is, bread and water. Every day they should be given physical discipline, such as beating with rods. They should be constantly urged to turn from their error and threatened that they will be treated like this every day of their life. See if this works, and report back to us.

Because it is not good that these persons are together in prison, not only the young people, but also the older ones mentioned above should be interrogated under torture and from this moment on, they shall be separated. Also, apart from spiritual persons or people who are trying to turn them from their error, nobody should be allowed to see them.

Governmental Correspondence 8

April 20, 1532, from Innsbruck to the warden in Sterzing [12]

We received your report of the 18th of this month with the transcript of the hearing of Paul Gall and his wife. If they are still willing to recant of their error and repent, as stated at the conclusion of their confession, we command you, in the name of his Royal Majesty, our gracious lord, to take a written sworn statement from them and a guarantee of 500 gulden. . . .

When they have done this and paid the cost of their imprisonment they should both make their recantation on the chancel in the Sterzing church, using the same words as others who have recanted, and for three consecutive Sundays they should stand behind the altar during Mass to complete their penance.

Governmental Correspondence 9

January 14, 1533, from Innsbruck to the warden in Rodeneck (summarized) [13]

Response to a letter of January 6 about the arrest of five Anabaptists in the Rodeneck district on December 31, 1532: Paul Gall, a miller's boy, two adult women, and a girl from Bruneck named Sollin. Gall is a *relapsus* besides being the treasurer and a well-known leader of the Anabaptists. He should be treated according to the mandates. Attempt to learn from him who the principle leaders are, what their first and last names are, what they look like, and where they are staying.

Governmental Correspondence 10

April 4, 1533, from Innsbruck to Jakob Hupher, judge of Gries and Bozen [14]

Faithful servant! We received your report of March 25 with the testimonies of four Anabaptist persons: Clara, daughter of Balthasar Schneider of Villnöß; Katharina, daughter of Laurence Prast of Taufers; Anna, daughter of Leonard Gerber of Tisen; and Elspet, daughter of Hans Lippen, also of Villnöß. You wrote that after a small amount of adjudication and instruction, Anna, Leonard Gerber's daughter, is renouncing her error and false belief and will recant and do penance. We recommend that if her resolution is dependable, you deal with her according to the regulations as you have with other Anabaptists: She should recant publicly on the church chancel and do the penance her priest lays on her. She should sign a written oath,[15] and then you can release her.

Furthermore, you write that the other three women still persist in their wicked Anabaptist belief with a perverted persistence. It is our command that you continue to have educated and knowledgeable priests instruct all three of them to abandon their error of Anabaptism. In addition, with the exception of the woman who is supposedly pregnant, the two other women should be threatened with beatings, using rods and switches.[16] If necessary, and with the counsel of the jury, they should be beaten on the appropriate parts of their bodies to bring them to a permanent conversion and renunciation of their error. If the three of them recant as a result of such instruction and discipline of the rod, then, like Anna, Gerber's daughter, they should make a public statement and do penance if there is a sound basis for it. But if such instruction and discipline of the rod does not help, and they persist in their stubborn error, on the basis of their statements and in the presence of the jury, they should be brought before the criminal court and treated according to the emperor's edict and our published mandates.

The one named Clara, who appears to be pregnant, should be examined by a knowledgeable woman. If she is in fact found to be pregnant, she should be isolated in the prison until delivery. Then, if she does not recant, she should also be brought before the criminal court.

In addition, because these prisoners have mentioned other Anabaptists in Gufidaun, Flass, Afing, the district of Jenesien, and other towns, you should pass on the first and last names of these persons to the judges of those towns if you have not already done so, so that they can take suitable action against them.

Governmental Correspondence 11

May 11, 1533, from Innsbruck to Jakob Hupher, judge of Gries and Bozen [17]

With reference to his letter of April 29: If Anna Gerber is willing to recant, this should proceed according to protocol. But since the other three women persist in their error, and the disciplinarian sent from Meran refuses to beat them, the under-marshal Erasmus Offenhauser should write to him:

He should not hesitate to beat Katharina and Elisabeth, and if this does not have the desired effect the first time, to continue two or three more times and threaten that this discipline will continue every day that they refuse to turn from their error. If this discipline of the rod and additional instruction helps them turn around, the judge should proceed accordingly. If, however, it does not help then, as commanded earlier, they should be brought before the criminal court.

Since there is still a question whether Clara is pregnant, she should continue to be held in prison and given instruction.

Governmental Correspondence 12

June 3, 1533, from Georg, bishop of Brixen, to all towns in his jurisdiction (summarized) [18]

Jörg Frue and Hans Mall have permission to infiltrate meetings of the Anabaptists. In this way they hope to catch Jakob Hutter, Hans Tuchmacher, and the other leaders.

Governmental Correspondence 13

June 7, 1533, from Innsbruck to Jakob Hupher, judge of Gries and Bozen [19]

Faithful servant! We understand from your letter to our government, regarding the three Anabaptist women, that in spite of the discipline administered to them by the disciplinarian from Meran, who beat them with rods or switches, they will not desist. Since they say nothing malicious about the sacrament of the altar insofar as it is practiced by priests who live according to God's will and practice Christian baptism, or about the Mother of God and the saints, you are at a loss and don't know what to do.

We wrote to you on May 11 that the discipline of beating them with rods or switches should not take place only once, but if it does not have the desired effect the first time it should be repeated two or three times, or as often as seems good to you. Once again, we recommend sincerely that you continue with this punishment against these captive women and that talented, worthy, educated persons would instruct them with holy scripture and persuasion, attempting to convince them to desist from their newly accepted baptism, to recant and do penance. This is what our mandates demand and what we have written to you.

But if they will not renounce their new rebaptism and observe infant baptism then, regardless what they say about the sacrament of the altar, or the devoutness of the priests who live according to the will of God, they should be brought before the criminal court and judged according to the mandate. For our mandates concerning Anabaptists are not established in order for them to state their accordance with the sacrament of the altar, or so that they do not state anything malicious about the Mother of God or our dear saints, but rather so those who renounce and do not observe infant baptism (such as has been been established and accepted by Christian churches) shall be brought before the criminal court, as well as those who are newly rebaptized and refuse to renounce this accursed sect, even after its suppression by hereditary lords and governing authorities, but wish to remain in it. That is why you and your jurors still need to make a judgment concerning these three women and others, who do not want to recant or abstain from their error, for our mandates indicate the necessity of a guilty verdict for the *relapsi* in all cases, where they have reneged [on their recantation] or remained [in their Anabaptist convictions], and to apply a special order, measure, and statute, in which they are guilty, regardless of whether there is any further backsliding, renunciations, or vows.

Governmental Correspondence 14

June 24, 1533, from the city authorities in Brixen to the government in Innsbruck (summarized) [20]

In order to root out the Anabaptist sect, two spies were dispatched in the past weeks who were promised money if they were able to capture the leaders. One of them, Jörg Frue, was present at a fellowship meeting in Götzenberg and stayed there for two days. At his request, he got to know Jakob Hutter, Hans Tuchmacher, and other leaders. Then he slipped away and reported to the authorities in Schöneck and Michelsburg. These took trustworthy servants and ambushed the Anabaptists' camp but were unable to capture the leaders, who had been forewarned. Eight Anabaptists were captured. They are imprisoned at Michelsburg. Their testimonies are being sent to Innsbruck.

Governmental Correspondence 15

July 30, 1533, from Innsbruck to the authorities of several towns on the Inn River (summarized)[21]

The government has learned that the Anabaptists, whose possessions were confiscated and whose children were given over to the state authorities to raise, came secretly at night and took their children away to bring them to Moravia. In this way they carried off twenty-three children.

Therefore this command is going out: all outgoing ships should be searched for Anabaptists and their children. Those with children should be apprehended.

Governmental Correspondence 16

October 3, 1535, from Christoph Ochs, magistrate of Michelsburg, to the bishop's office in Brixen (summarized) [22]

He had thought that through his efforts the Anabaptists and those who desecrated the sacraments had been driven out. Then the magistrate of Schöneck, Peter Troyer of Nidervintl, sent him an urgent message to visit him. He told him in confidence that Jakob Hutter was back in Tyrol and had baptized up to twenty-five people on August 25, among them close relatives of his, meaning Troyer's daughter Anna and her husband Niclas Niderhofer.

Governmental Correspondence 17

October 10, 1535, from Brixen to Innsbruck (summarized) [23]

Several Anabaptists who had been driven from Moravia are said to be back in the Adige and Eisack valleys. They have held fellowship meetings and baptisms. Jakob Hutter and another leader are said to be among them. They should be hunted down so that the sect can be rooted out, as commanded by the royal mandates.

At the same time a message was sent to the bailiff of Rodeneck, informing him that Jakob Hutter had returned and some in his district had been baptized. They were all to be arrested.

Governmental Correspondence 18

October 15, 1535, from Peter Troyer, magistrate of Schöneck, to Brixen [24]

The [Anabaptist] leaders are not being housed in this valley but in Bozen or Sterzing; there are five or six of them. But around All Saints Day they are planning to hold a fellowship meeting of their sect here in this valley, either in the Taufers district or at Götzenberg. . . .

Jakob Hutter has his wife with him, who is very pregnant, expecting the child to be born any day – if it has not happened yet. She looked in two places here in the Schöneck district for a place for her confinement, but did not stay. It is necessary to write to the judges to ask around where a poor girl is lying in childbed, for wherever she is, he will also look for refuge.

Troyer then explained his difficulty: his son-in-law was an Anabaptist and would not recant. He took his daughter to a place where she could not cause any trouble. He would not bring her back in less than a year.

Governmental Correspondence 19

October 16, 1535, from Brixen to several towns (summarized) [25]

According to reports, five or six leaders of the sect are in the areas of Bozen and Sterzing. They are planning a conference in the Taufers district or Götzenberg. Jakob Hutter's wife is very pregnant. We assume she is in bed preparing for childbirth. Hutter is likely to visit her, and may be able to be apprehended there.

Governmental Correspondence 20

October 22, 1935, from Innsbruck to Brixen (summarized)[26]

Hutter and his team probably stay close to district borders so that if the authorities in one town learn of their presence they can quickly cross over into another. Innsbruck advises working together, between the townships that are under secular authority and those under the bishop, as well as between the various districts. Only in this way can they be sure of capturing the Anabaptists. This message is delivered to all the towns in the area.

Governmental Correspondence 21

November 20, 1535, from Innsbruck to several district authorities[27]

The government of Ferdinand I to the district judge in Sterzing, to Friedrich Franz von Schneeberg in Steinach, to Friedrich Fueger in Taufers, to the bailiffs of Altrasen, Toblach, Gufidaun, and on the Ritten, to the district judge in Gries and Bozen:

Faithful servant! Since we recently expelled the Anabaptists from our principality of Moravia out of Christian, honorable motives, we now report that these same Anabaptists, particularly their leaders, are back in our area, which is under your authority, and they are residing in other parts of our princely region of Tyrol, seducing our subjects, leading them away from our true Christian faith.

In order to duly punish them, we sincerely command you to work diligently in secret with persons whom you trust, as follows: The day after Saint Andrew's Day [November 30], before daybreak, break into all houses in your jurisdiction that you suspect of harboring Anabaptists. Search them thoroughly, especially for the leaders (who are the cause of this evil). Spare no effort. Arrest all suspects, guard them well, and interrogate them in depth. Notify us and report your findings to our Upper Austrian government as well as to our prince, the bishop in Brixen, and to the governors, mayors, and judges whose subjects the prisoners indicate. Send us a copy of the prisoners' statements and wait for further instructions.

In order that this remain more secret and secure, we command you as well to summon those whom you intend to use for this purpose the night before. Keep them with you and make them swear to obey and not to warn anyone or write to anyone, on pain of severe punishment.

In the meantime, until the date aforementioned, stop arresting suspects apart from the leaders so that they are not warned. Diligently guard all roads, bridges, and passes, especially on said night and day. Omit nothing that this necessity demands so that we are not obliged to punish you. We have given the same orders to the judges and governors of the districts neighboring yours, and the bishop of Brixen has commanded the same of those under his authority.

After this house search has taken place, summon all your subjects and, on our behalf, forbid them to take in or give lodging to any Anabaptists who may come to their homes. They should report them to you immediately so that they can receive their due punishment. If anyone is disobedient and takes in such Anabaptists or fails to report them, and we hear of it, we will be obliged to send in troops, at your cost, to remain until the Anabaptists are completely rooted out and unable to find lodging in the district.

Governmental Correspondence 22

December 1, 1535, from Brixen to Innsbruck[28]

The cleansing action against the Anabaptists and their leaders, planned in cooperation with the government in Innsbruck, took place on November 30. A report has just come in from the deputy captain[29] from Säben. He, along with the city judge of Klausen and some citizens, searched all suspect houses of the town without success. Finally, they searched the house of the former sexton in the Gufidaun district, bordering Klausen, and there found Jakob Hutter, the principal leader, his wife, and another girl. They arrested them all, including the hostess, and led them to Branzoll, where they are currently under guard.

We are aware of our agreement that if the king's officers should pursue such persons into our jurisdiction, they should arrest them and then inform the bailiff and administrator in whose district they were apprehended or discovered. Therefore, we are willing to assign these prisoners to the bailiff of Gufidaun and deliver them to him. However, it is crucial and essential to guard securely this Hutter as the principal leader and thoroughly investigate the whole truth regarding him. Due to our concern that the building in Gufidaun is not secure, as it is too open, offering too much liberty, we have not yet turned him over, in order that the rectitude and governance of the authorities in Gufidaun will remain unimpeached. We ask you kindly to act on this as soon as possible and reply by return post and let us know your thoughts, desire, and decision. We did not want you to be uninformed.

Governmental Correspondence 23

December 3, 1535, Klausen, interrogation questions for Katharina Hutter, Anna Stainer and Appolonia Praun at Branzoll [30]

First of all, inquire:

How did they join this sect, who introduced them?

Where and at what time were they baptized, and who was baptized with them?

When did they return from Moravia?

Which routes did they travel and who traveled with them?

With whom did they receive accommodations and meals,[31] and in which locations?

On which day did they arrive in the region of Tyrol, and subsequently in the Wipp Valley, Puster Valley, and Eisach?

Where have they resided until now?

And in particular, in the six to eight days prior to their arrest, where did they get their meals and accommodations?

Where had they planned to go after the day when they were arrested, and to whom?

In which locations have they held fellowship meetings up to this point, and since their arrival in this region?

Who was present or involved?

Have they planned for there to be another fellowship meeting in the near future, and at which locations and whom did they notify about it?

Are there still other leaders, treasurers, or others who have duties, who are here [in Tyrol], and what are their names, and where do they reside?

Was Niclas Niderhofer in the district of Schöneck part of their sect and was he baptized? Likewise for Hans Hueber with the Hulbens who are at Obervintl?[32]

Did they both stay there overnight and have discussions?

Did [Jakob] Hutter not have cash, silver, or the like in a secret repository? Where and with whom?

Also inquire about other circumstances, about which they, the women, can explain any further information.

Governmental Correspondence 24

December 4, 1535, from Brixen to the governor of the Adige (summarized) [33]

Response to the district commander's[34] demand that Jakob Hutter be delivered to him, because he was arrested within his jurisdiction, in the Gufidaun district. Since Hutter, as the principal leader, is so important to the king, the bishop, and the whole country, he has to be handled differently than other Anabaptists. For this reason he, his wife, and her maid are being held in Branzoll. Jakob Hutter will be transferred to Innsbruck still today, by the vice-marshal, Erasmus Offenhauser. This does not in any way infringe on the rights of the district commander.

Governmental Correspondence 25

December 7, 1535, from Innsbruck to the governor of the Adige [35]

We received your letter dated in Tyrol, the second of this month of December, regarding the arrest of Jakob Hutter, the Anabaptist leader, apprehended by our gracious lord, the bishop in Brixen's bailiff at Säben, and his princely and gracious city magistrates in Klausen, among others, who entered into the house of a sexton. But he was taken to Branzoll, out of the attending district of Gufidaun, under the auspices of the administration of the bishop of Brixen. There he was detained as a prisoner and shall not be made to give an account in the attending district of Gufidaun. Even though you and other residents in your district of Gufidaun have complained about this, this is a matter we have already examined.

We will not neglect to tell you that a few days ago we made an agreement with the bishop in Brixen, i.e., that a search shall be made on the same night of all suspect houses in the Puster Valley and other towns belonging to His Royal Majesty and all his attendees, and all possible effort should be spent to bring Hutter and other Anabaptists to prison, because we had reliable information that he was there. If [the troops of] one district capture him in another, that should be allowed without the authorities [in the district he was captured in] feeling their authority slighted. But after his arrest he should be transferred to the district he was captured in.

However, because this Hutter is not an insignificant leader of the Anabaptist sect (having misled a substantial number of people, causing their death and martyrdom), our gracious lord of Brixen had this Hutter and his fellow captives brought to Branzoll, because he is not an ordinary prisoner but a leader. Necessity demands that he be well guarded, and it is feared that the prison in Gufidaun is not secure enough. By his princely grace we were sent a report of the capture of Hutter and his companions and the matter awaits our decision, as you will see from his message.

As it indicates, he has no other motive than to ensure that the authority of Gufidaun, with its system of justice and governance, shall remain unimpinged. This is the only reason he acted as he did, and you should take it in that way. We surely would not like it, and it would not be appropriate, for His Royal Majesty or any other authority to deprive you of your rightful authority, whether much or even a little.

Following the bishop's report, we sent for Hutter to be brought to Innsbruck by the under-marshal. We will talk with him as need requires and punish him. We have written to Brixen to interrogate the other prisoners and send us their testimonies. When this has taken place, as we believe it has, we will see that you and the authorities in Gufidaun have nothing to complain about.

We did not want to withhold our friendly sentiment from you.

Governmental Correspondence 26

December 13, 1535, from Innsbruck to King Ferdinand [36]

Most serene Highness! We humbly inform your Majesty that after we heard several reports that the Anabaptist sect has again entered our land in several towns in the Puster Valley (Klausen, Bozen, Sterzing, and others) through Jakob Hutter, the principal leader, introducing their seductive teaching, we organized a raid, in cooperation with our gracious lord of Brixen, in suspect districts and towns where the Anabaptists find assistance and lodging. This took place on the past Saint Andrew's Day [November 30].

That night when the raid and house search took place in several towns, his grace the magistrate of Branzoll discovered Jakob Hutter as well as his wife and another woman during the night in a house bordering Klausen on the other side of the Eisack bridge, in the Gufidaun district. He arrested them and brought them to Branzoll Castle. When we learned of this from the bishop of Brixen, we had Jakob Hutter transferred here and immediately interrogated him without torture. In addition we had the preacher Dr. Gall instruct him with holy scripture three times consecutively, regarding his error, because he blasphemes and curses infant baptism.

But because he did not accept this instruction but only rebuked and cursed, we continued to interrogate him using some questions we had compiled. We are sending your Majesty his confession and testimony. We are doing all we can to root out this seductive sect of Anabaptism, as we have until now, not wanting to omit anything.

Because the bishop of Brixen also sent us the enclosed letter that Hans Tuchmacher, Anabaptist leader, and others had sent Jakob Hutter from Moravia, and because we learned by examining Hutter with and without torture that he rejects and condemns all Christian orders of the Church – confession, the holy sacrament, and others – we want to hear from your Majesty before we go any further. Since he is a bishop of the leaders and for a long time has been traveling in Moravia where he is well known and has been preaching, we would like to know if your Majesty would like to question him in detail regarding his activities in Moravia, or whatever else your Majesty would like.

He and the other leaders and members of the Anabaptist sect intend to force through their plans for spreading Anabaptism wherever they have success, to press on forcefully, and therefore we await notice from you before taking further action.

Furthermore, because the other leaders who should still be in Moravia – [Hans] Tuchmacher, Onophrius [Griesinger], [Jörg] Zaunring, and others – are well informed and know the way here, it is to be feared that when they learn that Hutter has been arrested, they will return secretly to our land and introduce their sect to the common people. Would your Majesty be so gracious as to give command in Moravia that these Anabaptist leaders be rooted out so that they do not come into this land again and sow their evil seed?

Governmental Correspondence 27

December 17, 1535, from Brixen to Innsbruck [37]

On the orders of the Innsbruck authorities they had Caspar Hueter[38] from Stegen, fisherman of the prince-bishop in Prags,[39] interrogated in depth by Captain Abrosius Vintler of Brixen. Caspar Hueter testified that about nine years ago Jakob Hutter worked for him in Stegen, practicing as a hatmaker.

Back then, they had been playing for money one time and Caspar won an eight off him. Jakob was very sad; he sighed and said, "God have mercy on me for playing away my money that I earned by such hard work. I could hang myself." At this, Caspar returned the eight that he had lost to him, and he was happy again.

But when Wölfl, the goatherd in Pflaurenz spread and preached his false teaching, Jakob Hutter became his follower. He bought himself a New Testament at the market in Bozen and began reading and preaching from it to Caspar and those in the house. Caspar forbade him and would not tolerate it. After that, Jakob Hutter left within a month. He left in indignation and never came back. He knows nothing more to tell about him.

Governmental Correspondence 28

December 24, from King Ferdinand to the government office in Innsbruck [40]

Highborn, noble, revered, learned, and dear faithful [servant],

We received and read your letter announcing how the principal leader of the seductive Anabaptist sect, Jakob Hutter, was arrested. It also established clearly how the first interrogation by preacher Dr. Gall proceeded, both with and without torture, with explanations regarding his error, as well as the copies of several letters written to him by the Anabaptists in Moravia.

We are pleased that after so much effort, Hutter, the ringleader of this seductive sect, has finally been caught. We are certain that his capture will serve toward the eradication and extermination of this sect.

We are firmly resolved that even if said Hutter should renounce his error, recant, and do penance, we will never pardon him. The punishment he deserves many times over will be carried out, for misleading many people in many districts in our principality and territories, to fall from the true holy Christian faith, lose the salvation of their souls, their honor, their lives, and their property.

On your offer to send us a copy of his testimony, we want to let you know what our will is. For a long time, up to eight or nine years, Hutter, as leader and head of this seductive sect, has been traveling, not only in our Margraviate of Moravia but also in Lower Austria and the mountains of Styria and Carinthia, up and down the Enns River. We have no doubt that wherever he went he has introduced his seductive sect.

Necessity demands that Hutter be questioned as to the following:

How did he come into this sect at the beginning?

In which counties of our principality did he establish this sect over the years, from one month to the next?

Specifically, which individuals of noble birth did he baptize?

Also, where was he given food and lodging?

Gather anything else that can be learned from him.

We have no doubt that you have decreed that the persons mentioned in the letter from Moravia – insofar as they are under your jurisdiction – will be imprisoned. We have commanded that in our Margraviate of Moravia the Anabaptist leaders who are still there should be hunted down and imprisoned so that this evil does not spread in our princely region of Tyrol or anywhere else.

We consider, as you do, that persons connected with this sect, now that their leader has been arrested, will want to win over the common people and incite evil. It is urgently necessary to prevent this as far as possible.

Therefore we command you to send the preacher Dr. Gall to the Adige and Puster valleys, to Bozen, and wherever else you deem necessary, to preach and warn the common people about this seductive error. You should see that the district authorities pass strict laws, and that they are more diligent so that further spread is prevented.

In one letter from the Anabaptist fellowship in Moravia addressed to Hutter, a cipher was discovered. See to it that Hutter is questioned under torture to explain this cipher and if it means something to let us know. Send us a thorough report as well as the original of the missive that contains the cipher.

In all this you will do our pleasure and will.
Vienna, December 24, 1535
Ferdinand

Governmental Correspondence 29

December 24, 1535, from Innsbruck to the bishop in Brixen (summarized) [41]

Jakob Hutter has not yet been interrogated using the list of the questions you sent, because the preacher Dr. Gall Müller is trying to convince him to turn from his Anabaptist error through holy scripture.

After the holy Christmas season is passed we will interrogate him and will report his answers to you.

P.S. In the meantime, we have received the report concerning Hutter, and what transpired with the fisherman from Prags.

Governmental Correspondence 30

January 1, 1536, from Innsbruck to the captain of Kufstein [42]

Until now we have instructed Jakob Hutter, the leader of the Anabaptist sect, through good Christian teaching, to renounce his error, without accomplishing anything. So we have decided that, as you have beaten other Anabaptists who were imprisoned in Kufstein with rods, you should attempt to see whether this would help, as it did with others.

Therefore, in the name of his gracious Majesty, we command you immediately to send the two soldiers who beat your imprisoned Anabaptists with rods. We will have them beat him. We would also like you to appear in person, if possible.

Governmental Correspondence 31

January 8, 1536, Innsbruck, entry in the account book [43]

Two court employees [*Gerichts Knechten*] from Kufstein whom the Knight Christoph Fuchs sent here on our command to convince, by torture, Jakob Hutter, leader of the Anabaptist sect, to renounce his seductive error; they are paid for their provisions in coming here and returning home with two horses.

Governmental Correspondence 32

January 21, 1536, from Innsbruck to the warden of Rodeneck [44]

It has been reported to us that the wife of Jakob Hutter, leader of the Anabaptist sect, who is currently being held in prison in Gufidaun, was released previously from Rodeneck prison, where she had been held because of the same Anabaptist sect. We request of you to report to us the conditions on which she was liberated from Rodeneck, in the name of his Royal Majesty, our gracious lord.

Governmental Correspondence 33

Interrogation questions for Jakob Hutter [45]

First: When he, Jakob Hutter, worked as a hatmaker in Braunegg and Stegen, whether, and in what town, in whose house or bathhouse did first start to preach and to baptize?

Who were the first people he baptized?

Are these persons known or still secret, alive or dead?

Where did they come from?

Is one or more present, and where do they live?

Did he, Jakob Hutter, at that time or now, have lodging or assistance in Dietenhaim, Luns, St. Georgen, Stegen, or the surrounding areas?

With whom or in which house?

Are such people connected to the sect or sympathize with it? He shall name these persons.

Particularly, how often did he stay in Neuhaus Castle and above it in Pfaffenbach? How often did he preach there, hold fellowship meetings, and baptize there?

Who was there and who was baptized?

Further, as he traveled back and forth, did he not have accommodation in St. Georgen with the Grembses, Jörg Rumer, Andrew Zimmerman, Oswald Schuster, and later with the wife of Andrew Zimmerman in Werdt, with the Breidlens, or anyone else?

Did he hold fellowship meetings there, preach, and baptize?

Who was present?

Who was baptized?

Are there still several secret brethren in St. Georgen?

Further: Previously or recently, didn't he stay in Stegen with Huber by the bridge, with Wuerer or someone else?

Wasn't he hidden nearby at the recent market in Stegen?

Doesn't he know that Huber recently went with the treasurer over Kosten to Welsberg?

What did they talk about?

Didn't he meet them and help them?

Further: About three years ago on Our Lady's Day [December 8] when the authorities of St. Michelsburg went to the mountain at St. Georgen with some servants, wasn't he in a small house above St. Georgen, in Breidlen's house or under the eaves?

Who else was there?

What did they do there or where did they go?

Further: When the Anabaptists held a fellowship meeting on Corpus Christi [sixty days after Easter] in 1533 in the woods above Ehrenburg, who helped them and gave them lodging?

Weren't they given provisions and food by Hueber, the two Ebners, Erspämer, or others in Götzenberg?

Since the former Hueber fled with his two children, hasn't Hutter been given lodging by the current Hueber?

Did he preach or baptize in the house?

Recently when he returned from Moravia didn't he hold another fellowship meeting in the woods at Hueber's in Götzenberg?

Who was present?

Did Hueber or his neighbors know about the fellowship meeting? Were they themselves present?

Did they provide food and lodging?

Who was it who during the holidays and at the recent fellowship meeting came into the woods with sidearms?

Whom did he baptize there? How long and how often were they together?

And who became members?

Was he given assistance or lodging, in former years or now, in Sonnenburg, Wässing, Lotten, Pflaurenz, or Ellen?

Did Walder or Pranger at Ellen give lodging or accommodation to him or his people?

Did this Walder or Pranger sympathize or associate with them or warn them?

Didn't they grind grain for them, bake bread, bring them meat or lard, or lend them household necessities?

Further: Didn't he know about the fellowship meeting held by Hans Tuchmacher in the woods above Kuelechen?

If he knew about it, ask him who was present, who was baptized, who gave them food?

Didn't Pranger give them food and other things?

Or was he there himself and knew about it ahead of time?

Further: Since he recently came from Moravia, how often was he at Hörschwang?

Who brought him there?

Who gave him food?

How often was he at Ober's at Hörschwang – whether in his cellar or in his house?

How often did he hold fellowship meetings there, preach or baptize? Who was present, and who was baptized?

Where was (or still is) their hiding place there?

How often, now or previously, was he at Underrainer, Mair, or Ebner at Hörschwang?

Is it true that a few years ago when a traveling merchant came through, he came to Michel Metzger in Braunegg and attended the sermon of the assistant preacher there, Herr Steffan? And after hearing the sermon, did he return to the inn and say, "The priest knows the truth but his mouth is gagged so that he cannot speak the truth." In the meantime a priest came by with the sacrament, and Hutter said to Michel Metzger, "What is he doing?" And didn't Metzger answer, "He is walking around with the sacrament, or our Lord"? And then he said, "Oh, where the devil did they get that idol?" What other words did he use?

Further: Weren't they also in Onach when Gregori Weber, the Anabaptist leader, was arrested there and executed in Brixen? And didn't someone have sanctuary and lodging on Kienberg?

In conclusion, he needs to be asked about the people in this region whom he brought into their sect, recently or formerly, whether they are alive, dead, have fled, or are in the region, openly or hidden, poor or rich. During the time that they were traveling in this region, who gave him, Jakob Hutter, or his fellow believers and relatives lodging, advice, and assistance?

Who fell to his teachings or, if they were not baptized, were sympathetic? These towns and individuals need to be named.

Also whether and where, since the beginning of their sect until now, they had their huts or campsites during winter and summer: above Neuhaus Castle, or in St. Georgen, in Götzenberg above Ellen, above Hörschwang, or anywhere else in the region, in the woods or meadows?

Are they still using those places? All such hideouts need to be investigated and destroyed.

Jakob Hutter shall tell everything he knows, whether it has been mentioned here or not.

Postscript:

He should also be asked whether in Brixen, Bruneck, Klausen, and the surrounding areas there are still people belonging to his sect who have been rebaptized. He should give their names and addresses, whether they reside in their home or not.

Who gave him food and lodging there?

It is known that common people in this land gave him a large amount of cash, silver, and jewelry. We suspect that he did not share it all among his brothers and sisters but kept some secretly for himself. Also, Hans

Tuchmacher wrote to him from Moravia that he should give greetings to the brothers and sisters in the Adige and Puster valleys, and he should be asked who these are.

Governmental Correspondence 34

January 26, 1536, from Innsbruck to the judge in Sonnenburg [46]

At the command of our gracious Royal Majesty, we have put together several questions to be asked Jakob Hutter, the leader of the Anabaptist sect, using torture. We earnestly request that you set a date for this interrogation. Let us know in time so that we can tell the messengers. You should also bring the scribes and other people whom you have used before for interrogations with torture. The questioning should begin around seven o'clock in the morning, when the prisoner is alert. You will find the interrogation questions at the office.

Governmental Correspondence 35

February 5, 1536, from Innsbruck to the warden of Gufidaun prison [47]

Faithful servant!

We received a copy of Simon of Permatin's letter that you sent to our Upper Austrian government on January 27, reporting that the wife of leader Jakob Hutter was pardoned and released from Rodeneck in 1533 on her recantation of the Anabaptist sect and recognition of her error. Since she has fallen into the error of Anabaptism again, we command that you yourself, or one or more sensible, devout men or women, whom you would bring to her in prison in your presence, try to convince her with good, Christian admonition and all possible diligence to renounce her error of Anabaptism again, and return to the old, true Christian belief of infant baptism and recognition of the revered sacrament of the altar.

Governmental Correspondence 36

February 26, 1536, Innsbruck, entry in the account book [48]

Dear lords of the chamber,

Jakob Hutter the Anabaptist was brought to the Roman emperor's prison here in the Kreuter House on 29 November 1535 (last year), and now on 25 February (this month) was taken out and executed – and rightly so. The time that Hutter was in prison amounts to eighty-seven days, and our servant Martin Hagler brought him food and drink all that time and he demands twelve kreuzer for every day. This comes to seventeen gulden and twenty-four kreuzer. Please see that Martin Hagler is paid 17 G 24 K. [49]

Governmental Correspondence 37

April 28, 1536, from Innsbruck to Brixen and Gufidaun (summarized) [50]

The wife of Jakob Hutter, the deceased Anabaptist leader, who remains in Gufidaun, persists in her stubborn opinion. Somebody who is educated, sensitive, and sensible, should be sent to instruct her and convince her of her error, thus bringing her back to the old Christian faith.

Anna Stainer should also be transferred to Gufidaun, where both she and Katharina would receive instruction in matters of faith from the priest.

Governmental Correspondence 38

August 2, 1536, from Innsbruck to Georg von Firmian [51]

We wrote last April 29 to the warden of Gufidaun, commanding that Anna Stainer, who is imprisoned at Branzoll, be transferred to Gufidaun. We have just heard from the council in Brixen that this has not yet happened. We are displeased with the warden of Gufidaun and seriously request, in the name of his Royal Majesty, that you order your warden of Gufidaun or his administrator that he take over Anna Stainer, through the deputy captain of Branzoll, and lead her to Gufidaun prison and deal with her according to our commands. She must be well guarded and secured so that she does not escape, as Jakob Hutter's wife did. In addition, in the name of his Royal Majesty we will punish whoever it was who let Hutter's wife escape. . . .

6

Additional Documents

Several important sources that do not fit easily into the other collections are provided below. They are arranged in roughly chronological order and include a eulogy for Jakob Hutter, a summary of his execution, stanzas from a ballad called *Das Vaterlied* (the hymn to our fathers), and a list of twelve congregational ordinances from 1529. Two relevant non-Hutterite letters that stem from the early years of the fellowship, from Brandhuber and Reublin, shed key insights on early developments of the community of goods, and on authority and leadership in Moravia. In two parts, document 7(a–b) presents the views of a Catholic polemicist (Fischer) and the Anabaptist leader, Gabriel Ascherham, concerning Hutter. Fischer's use of Ascherham's writing on Hutter served his purpose to discredit the entire Hutterite Brethren in the early 1600s. Ascherham's writing on Hutter stems from ca. 1540. Finally, the insights of modern historians, both the Catholic Johann Loserth and the founder of the Bruderhof, Eberhard Arnold, provide summaries of their views of Hutter and the Hutterite practice of community in previously unpublished writings.

Additional Document 1

Wolfgang Brandhuber to the fellowship in Rattenburg[1]

Brandhuber, executed in Linz in 1529, was an early Anabaptist leader who may have influenced Jakob Hutter. In the letter excerpted below he gives one of the first instructions regarding the practice of community.

For not everyone in the fellowship of God is a treasurer; the person to distribute the assets of both poor and rich is the one who was elected for this reason. But a disorderly lifestyle, offense, and scandals have arisen due to frivolous people, indeed, even in the Christian fellowship, contrary to God's word – they ramble about in hypocritical ways and contradict the life of Christ within his Christian fellowship, even contradicting the order which the dear apostles themselves taught and preserved. They are the ones John mentions who "went out from us, [but were not of us,]"[a] who are also mentioned in the epistles of Paul, Peter and Jude.[b]

Yet they state it is unjust, either that goods be held in common or for one to reveal to another in love what his assets are, and they don't want there to be servants of temporal affairs or for the elders to reach out a helping hand to those in need; rather, they want this to occur only with their knowledge, or that each person should be their own treasurer. But I state that is false. What should happen, to the extent that God permits or accommodates, is that all things which serve in praising God are to be held in common. For, as we partake communally in Christ of that which is greatest (that is, in the power of God), then why would we not much more partake communally in that which is lesser, that is, temporal goods. It does not mean that we should collect all our belongings and drag them into one big heap, for such would not be suitable in all places. But each head of the household and all those who partake of one faith shall work together, contributing to one treasury, whether they are the master, servant, wife, maiden, or another fellow believer; and even though each worker is due his daily wage, according to the word of Christ,[c] each

a 1 John 2:19.
b E.g., 1 Cor. 11:19; 1 Tim. 4:1; 2 Pet. 2:1; Jude 4.
c Luke 10:7.

worker who is worth his wage should himself also promote love toward others in the truest way, to place [his wages] into the treasury. Indeed it is love which shall behave in this way.[2]

Additional Document 2

Twelve ordinances from 1529 [3]

The ordinances given below were agreed to early on and provided the standard to which Jakob Hutter held his congregation.

First, when the fellowship assembles, we should ask God from our hearts for his grace to make his divine will known to us. When parting from one another, we should give thanks to God and intercede for all brothers and sisters of the whole Christian fellowship.

Second, as Christians we should admonish one another from our hearts to remain steadfast in the Lord. We should meet frequently, at least four or five times a week if possible.

Third, when a brother or sister does wrong publicly, one should be punished publicly before the fellowship with loving admonition. If it was done in secret, it should be disciplined privately, but in accordance with God's command.

Fourth, every brother and sister should be fully surrendered to the fellowship, with body and soul for God. All gifts received from God should be held in common, according to the practice of the original apostolic church and the fellowship of Christ, so that the needy in the fellowship can be supported as in the time of the apostles.[d]

Fifth, the servants chosen by the fellowship should look after the needs of the poor with great care and provide for their needs on behalf of the fellowship according to the commands of the Lord.[e]

Sixth, they should all conduct themselves respectfully toward everyone, and no one should behave frivolously in the presence of God's

d Acts 2:44–45; 4:32–37; 5:1–11.

e Acts 6:1–5.

fellowship, neither with words nor deeds, including with others outside of the fellowship.[a]

Seventh, at fellowship gatherings only one person should speak at a time, and the others should listen and discern what is being said; two or three should not stand up at once.[b] No one should curse or swear [oaths] or talk idly; this is to spare the weak.[c]

Eighth, at a gathering one should not eat or drink to excess but give thanks and be moderate with what God created for our nourishment, serving one or two dishes. After the meal, the tables should be cleared.

Ninth, matters that are dealt with and put right among brothers and sisters in meetings are not to be made known to the world. As for the sympathetic seeker, at the outset the gospel should be proclaimed and explained to them. If that person accepts the gospel with desire and love in their heart and is willing to live accordingly, they should be received by the fellowship as a member of Christ.

Tenth, daily we should await the Lord's action, and the cross. We have surrendered ourselves and confirmed that we are under his discipline. Everything he bestows upon us should be received with thanks and borne with patience; we should not be swayed by gossip or frightened by every wind that blows.

Eleventh, all those who are of one body and bread in the Lord and are of one mind should observe the Lord's Supper in memory of his death. At that occasion everyone should be admonished to be like the Lord in obedience to the Father.

Twelfth, as we have been taught and are admonished by the Lord, we should be watchful at all times and await his coming so that we may be worthy to go in with him and escape the evil that is to come upon the world.

---

a 1 Tim. 3:1–7.
b Cf. 1 Cor 14:26–33; Eph. 5:4.
c Ecclus. 23:1–15.

Additional Document 3

January 26, 1531, Wilhelm Reublin to Pilgram Marpeck [4]

Reublin, who was never fully accepted by the proto-Hutterites in Austerlitz, gave his side of the conflict of 1530–1531 in a letter to Pilgram Marpeck.

Since I have been accused I requested to be permitted to make a reply as would be right and in accordance with imperial and divine law. . . .

On the Monday following the New Year the elders took counsel with some of their men, and on Tuesday they demanded of me, Jörg [Zaunring], and Burkhart [of Ofen], that since we had labelled their elders as false teachers and false prophets we should now prove this before them. We replied: Since we have been accused before all the people we wish to make our reply before all the people, answering with the truth and with holy scripture, which would testify to and overcome that which we would speak. We requested only to appear before the people and the congregation. Therefore the congregation was summoned. On Wednesday I stood with my brethren, Jörg, David [Burda], and Burkhart, before the congregation in the yard and stated that Jakob [Wiedemann], Kilian [Volckhamer], and Franz [Intzinger] [Austerlitz leaders] together with their elders were false teachers and false prophets, unfaithful to God and his children, and that I would prove this by the truth of scripture and from living men.[5] They refuse to pay the blood-money and tax to Charles which would support the war, as Caspar also certainly heard, yet the Lord of Austerlitz himself, with great animosity, paid money to the state on behalf of the brethren. But as soon as Caspar arrived they became willing to pay this blood-money, without being required. Also for that reason David [Burda] made a public address against them, but they also acted against him falsely; in this way they have acted like utter hypocrites.[6]

Additional Document 4

Eulogy of Jakob Hutter from an early Hutterite codex[7]

The departure of the dear, faithful Brother Jakob Hutter, briefly summarized

The trials described above (which God Almighty allowed to come upon his people in order to prove and test their faith) weighed heavily on the believers, as it was ongoing, seemingly permanent. The authorities were searching persistently for Brother Jakob and were often heard to say, "If only they had Jakob Hutter . . ." – as if to say that then the others would soon allow themselves to be put under control and once again button their lips[8] as they had done previously. So the brethren and the whole fellowship had no other choice but to send Brother Jakob Hutter away from them and return to the region of Tyrol, to carry out the duty of his office and service there, according to the Lord and the rightful Chief Shepherd, Jesus Christ, to assist in gathering his own and all those predestined to eternal life, to strengthen, comfort, and build up the fellowship. He commended the fellowship of the Lord to the care of Hans Amon or Tuchmacher in his absence and traveled in the peace of God up to the region of Tyrol and the Adige Valley.

Then it came to pass as a divine calamity that the dear brother Jakob Hutter was arrested in Klausen in the Adige Valley in the home of the former sexton. Under arrest, he was set onto a horse, then a hat with a tuft of feathers was placed on his head, and a gag was bound in his mouth. They led him as a laughingstock through the villages and town squares[9] up to Innsbruck. There he had to suffer horrible torture and pain for the sake of the name of Jesus Christ and his divine truth, as follows: First, they put him in ice water, then pulled him out and took him into a heated room.[10] Then they carried out their wantonness by lacerating his back, pouring brandy into the wounds, and setting it on fire, letting it burn in the wounds. Not satisfied with such gruesome deeds, they had no peace until they had removed him from Earth. They sentenced him to the flames and burned him alive. Thus he gave his spirit up to God and sealed and confirmed his true faith as a Christian hero, and as a captain, knight, and warrior for the truth. The gates of hell could not overcome or overwhelm him.[a] He was a true example and model, a stimulus or act of discipleship for all believers who would surrender to God.

This took place on the Friday before the first week of Lent in the year of Christ in 1536.[11]

Additional Document 5

Summary of Jakob Hutter's execution.[12]
A short description from an early Hutterite codex.

Jakob Hutter, a servant of Jesus Christ and his holy fellowship in Moravia was arrested and executed at Innsbruck in the Inn Valley. His enemies mocked him and led him around with a tuft of feathers. In the cold of winter they placed him in ice water so that he froze and then put him in a hot room. They lacerated his body, poured brandy into the wounds, ignited it, and let it burn on him. After long and varied torture and agony they finally burned him. He was constant and upright before God in all his torture until the end, remaining a witness to Jesus Christ. Amen.

Additional Document 6

Stanzas from the Hutterite "Vaterlied"[13]

Hutterites today continue to pass on their history through song. The "Vaterlied" [song of the fathers] was begun by Georg Bruckmaier (d. 1585). With over a hundred stanzas, it tells of each of the early Hutterite bishops. Numbers 41 to 50 describe Jakob Hutter.

Original Text	**Poetic Paraphrase**
Die G'mein, die christlich Mutter,	The church, the Christian mother
Die hat viel Söhn verlor'n,	Lost many a valiant son –
Bis auf den Jakob Huter,	I sing of Jakob Hutter,

a Matt 16:18.

Den hat Gott auserkor'n,
Ein frommer Mann er ware,
Feind allem eignen Nutz,
Mit ihm ein kleine Schare,
Doch so war Gott ihr Schutz.

A brave and faithful one.
He tackled greed and envy
And shepherded his flock,
In face of persecution
Stood solid as a rock.

Translation: *The fellowship, the Christian mother, lost many sons before Jakob Hutter, who was chosen by God, a devout man, enemy of private property, with a small flock, with God as their protection.*

Er ward von Gottes G'meine
In solches Amt gestellt,
Nach Gottes Wort so reine,
Als ein christlicher Held,
Hat er das Volk des Herren
Versammelt und erbauet,
Lieb' und Frieden tun lehren,
Sein Volk auf Gott vertraut.

Chosen by his people
As the bishop they preferred,
Appointed and ordained
According to God's word,
He gathered them and taught them
To live in love and peace,
A holy church of God
His glory to increase.

Translation: *He was appointed to this office by the fellowship of God, according to God's pure word. As a Christian hero he gathered and edified the people of the Lord, teaching them love and to make peace, a people trusting in God.*

Sie richteten ins Werke
Die recht christlich G'meinschaft,
Darzu gab ihn' Gott Stärke,
Haben darneben g'straft,
Was sich's Unrechts erfande,
Kein Person nicht geacht,
Das Bös hat kein Bestande,
Jakob hätt fleissig Acht.

They organized and founded
Community of goods
And God gave him endurance
To fight for brotherhood.
With no regard of persons
Jakob practiced discipline
And evil could not prosper
When he confronted sin.

Translation: *They established in reality, the true Christian community. God gave them strength to do this. They used discipline, along the way, all persons being equally esteemed. Evil had no chance with Jakob diligently on guard.*

Es tät ihn der Herr segnen
Und auch sein Volk so schon,
Mit Gutem ihm begegnen,
Hätt täglich zu ihm tun.
Die Bösen weggereiten,
Welche verrunnen weit,
Aber die Frommen g'läutert
Mit trübseliger Zeit.

The Lord gave them his blessing –
His church, his holy bride,
And in God's name confessing
They grew and multiplied.
Those with evil motives
Left and ran away
While pain refined the faithful,
Those who chose to stay.

Translation: *The Lord blessed him and his people, each day providing them with what was needed. The wicked left and ran far away, while the devout were purified through hardship.*

Lang tät nicht aussen bleiben	But persecution followed
Der Trübsal, kam bereit,	With sorrow and distress
Dass man sie tät vertreiben	When soldiers came and chased them
Wohl auf die lichte Haid.	To the wilderness.
Jakob um Ursach' wegen	The church sent brother Jakob
Ward g'schickt ins Oberland,	Back to the Tyrol
Daselbst tät ihm begegnen	To flee the growing danger
Trübsal, Schmach, und auch Band.	And seek repentant souls.

Translation: *Trouble did not stay away long. They were driven out onto the open pasture. Because of this Jakob was sent to the mountains where he encountered affliction, shame, and also confinement.*

Beim alten Messner zware,	There in the town of Klausen
Zu Clausen war er z'letzt,	They caught him in the end,
Fing ihn Pilatus Schare,	In the former sexton's house –
Ward auf ein Ross gesetzt,	They thought he was a friend.
Ein Knebel ins Maul gebunden,	Pilate's sons arrested
Die antiochisch Brut,	Him with cruel force,
Ein Federbusch zu stunden	With mockery and jesting
Steckten's auf seinen Hut.	They set him on a horse.

Translation: *He was in the home of the former sexton in Klausen when Pilate's troops caught him. They put him on a horse, a gag in his mouth – the brood of Antiochus – and stuck a tuft of feathers in his hat.*

Ist mit solchem Gespötte	To Innsbruck thus they dragged him
Geführt worden gen Innsbruck,	With feathers in his hat,
Daselbst viel leiden täte,	They tied him up and gagged him,
Haben in seinen Rucken	Paraded him like that.
Viel tiefer Wunden g'schnitten,	They cut deep lacerations
Das antiochisch G'sind,	Across his aching back,
Täten Brandwein drein schütten	Poured brandy in and lit it –
Und darnach angezünd.	A spiteful, cruel attack.

Translation: *With such mockery he was taken to Innsbruck where he was made to suffer greatly. They cut deep wounds into his back – Antiochus' crowd – and poured brandy into them, setting it on fire.*

Geduldig hat er g'litten
Solichen Schmerzen gross,
Antiochi Knecht fortschritten,
Kühlten ihr Mütlein[14] bass,
Setzten ihn in ein Wasser,
Musst drin erfrieren schon
Und darnach also nasser
In ein heisse Stuben tan.

But Jakob bore it bravely
And never would complain
Though Antiochus' servants
Inflicted so much pain.
They set him in ice water,
A chilly, freezing bath,
Then in a steaming chamber,
Working their fierce wrath.

Translation: *He patiently suffered this terrible pain. The servants of Antiochus further unleashed their wrath, by setting him in water, where he was meant to freeze, and then they put him into a hot room.*

Noch konnten's nicht satt werden
Mit einer solchen Tat,
Er musst von dieser Erden
Hinweg nach Kaiphas Rat.
Durch Feuersflamm verscheiden
Im sechsunddreissigsten Jahr,
Ruht jetzt in grossen Freuden
Bei der Martyrer Schar.

But even all this torture
Failed to satisfy
The cruel bloodthirsty mob –
He was condemned to die.
He must be killed by fire,
The fate of heretics.
This came to pass in Innsbruck
In 1536.

Translation: *Not yet satisfied with what they had done, they sentenced him to death by Caiphas' council. He died by fire in 1536 and now rests in great delight among the crowd of martyrs.*

Aus dieser Welt verscheiden
Durch gross Marter und Pain,
Viel Kummer, Sorg' und Leide
Hat er genommen ein.
Wie man das wohl kann spüren
In sein Episteln zwar
Er tät die G'mein regieren
Bis in das dritte Jahr.

He left this world behind him,
The people he had known,
To join the throng of martyrs
Beneath the Father's throne.
His letters tell the story
Of his suffering and fears.
He led our congregation
For less than three short years.

Translation: *He left this world in much sorrow, anxiety, and suffering, as we can read in his epistles. He led the fellowship into its third year.*

Additional Document 7a

The Dovecote of the Hutterian Anabaptists by Christoph Andreas Fischer [15]

Fischer was a Jesuit priest and a fierce opponent of the Hutterites in Moravia. His descriptions of their life are based on personal observation.

The Dovecote of the Hutterian Anabaptists in which their manure, dung, and filth – that is, their stinking, filthy, abominable teaching on God, on Christ, on the holy sacraments and other articles of the Christian faith is explained briefly and truthfully, out of their own books, both printed and handwritten, with citations of where such can be found. Also, the life of the big dove, Jakob Hutter, from whom the Anabaptists take the name Hutterites.

By Christoph Andreas Fischer, priest in Feldsberg,
printed in the Ederisch printshop, Ingolstatt, 1607.

To the noble, highborn Maximilian von Dietrichstein,
baron of Hollenburg, Finkenstein, and Thalberg . . .

Noble and highborn gracious lord, I write as an old, admirable scribe. At the time of the blessed Emperor Theodosius many heretics arose, who submitted their articles of faith in writing to the emperor himself. When he received them he commanded that they be examined and compared with the teachings of the fathers, whether they are in accordance. If they were in agreement with the ideas of the holy fathers, they should be accepted, but if they were found to disagree, they and their followers should be thrown out and hunted down.

Without a doubt, the enlightened and noble princes in Austria, Charles V and Ferdinand, followed this blest and holy advice, both Kaiser and Margrave in Moravia . . . when (according to the Hutterian Anabaptist Chronicles in Brünn in Moravia) they executed Wilhelm Griesbacher and Thomas Balthasar, both Anabaptists, burning them at the stake. They did this because they saw that their beliefs opposed the teachings of the fathers and the fifteen-hundred-year-old church, and they persisted stubbornly in their error.

In the meantime the Anabaptists are in Moravia under [the protection of] practically all the feudal lords, feigning true religion – which is the custom of all heretics. They have become established and are now many thousand strong. They have taken the best properties, the most suitable places, the most stately houses, and make the greatest profit.

Because it is not a temporal matter, but it touches on the eternal, it would be well to take the advice of the blessed Emperor Theodosius: to study their writings and compare them to the teachings of the holy Catholic church and of the holy fathers.

Because for a long time your Grace has borne the great displeasure of this sect, to the shame of your government, and you are willing to drive them out, I have collected their outrageous teachings and blasphemies out of their own books, both handwritten and printed – as much as I have been able to obtain. I have summarized them concisely and accurately and dedicate it obediently to the honor of your Grace so that you, following the example of the highly praised Emperor Theodosius, may better examine their sect and compare their teachings with those of the Holy Catholic Church and the holy fathers.

I humbly beg your grace to accept my modest work and consider whether the advice of such a great and sublime emperor should be followed and set in action or not.

Your humble and obedient servant, Christoph Andreas Fischer
Feldsberg, September 1, 1605

To the Reader

The holy apostle and evangelist John saw in his Revelation a great and terrible animal which opened its mouth to blaspheme against God, against his name and his tabernacle, and against those who live in heaven.[a] Even if this animal represents older heretics and false teachers, who could better be understood by this than the Anabaptists? In all their writings there is nothing but blasphemy against God, against Christianity, against the holy sacraments, against the church, and against the saints who live in heaven.

a Rev. 13:5–6.

But so that no one should imagine that I am making this up, I have taken some of their blasphemies out of their own writings. I have compiled them into a small booklet, without falsifying anything. I have indicated briefly who poured out such blasphemies, who has disputed them, and how the holy, divine Scriptures repudiate them.

Whoever wants a full and complete report of the sect and their thorough arguments should read the book of the Hutterian Anabaptists entitled: *Rechenschaft unserer Religion, Lehre und Glaubens von den Brüdern so man die Hutterischen nennt* [confession of our religion, teaching and faith by the brothers called Hutterites].[16] This book is complete and, God willing, will soon go to press. There he will find everything that pertains to this matter. He will indeed see that this [is the] animal that pours out such blasphemies against God, against his name, against his tabernacle, and against his saints.

As I thought about putting this tract into print, I considered for a long time how to portray them. It then occurred to me that when I was traveling in Moravia their houses were like pigeon houses or dovecotes. I decided to call this book "Dovecote" because that is what their houses look like. I compare them to the doves themselves. They give the appearance of being simple, honest people. But I compare their terrible, stinking teachings to the doves' filth and manure. They have polluted all of Moravia – and not without reason. For the dovecotes have many small holes through which the doves fly in and out. In the same way, the Anabaptists' houses and communities are full of windows, and they look out of them like monkeys. A dovecote is filled with nests inside, where the doves live. They fill every corner with Anabaptists, up to the peak of the roof. The dovecotes are mostly out in the open, in the most convenient places. So too, the homes of the Anabaptists are in the best, most convenient towns, and in addition they are free of supervision, of forced labor, of tolls and war taxes, and the general requirements of the country. (This is not always to their advantage as often their cattle are driven off or their stately horses are let loose.)

I compare the Anabaptists to the doves themselves. Just as the doves fly out and bring foreign doves home with them, the Anabaptists send out their false apostles every year to seduce the people, both men and women, and bring them to their dovecote. It was reported to me that in the year 1604 they lured more than two hundred people out of the German empire and led them to their dovecote. Just as in the first days the newly caught doves are treated with wheat, honey, and other things until they have become accustomed, in the same way the Anabaptists give the newcomers boiled and fried [meat] and sweets. Later they are told, go and work and be satisfied with cabbage and beets. Just as the doves' flight feathers are plucked so that they can't fly away, the Anabaptists rob the newcomers of the money and possessions they brought with them into their synagogue – so that even if they wanted to they would not be able to leave later. The doves are fruitful and usually have a new brood every month. So too the Anabaptists have taken the command "Be fruitful and multiply"[a] so seriously that in a single school there are more than three hundred children, not to mention the infants. The doves take the best wheat and the best grain. The Anabaptists have the best fields and meadows, houses and farms, cows and horses. The doves fly over the fields that have been sown and cause great damage. The Anabaptists undercut the honest Christian craftsmen with their work, taking the bread out of their mouths. The doves stain and pollute the roofs of the houses and everything they sit on. So too, wherever the Anabaptists have been they leave signs of their false teaching and way of life so that it can hardly be rooted out. The doves are often not satisfied with a single mate but find a second. The Anabaptists do the same, and in addition to living with their spouse they permit harlotry, as recently Elisabeth Beck in Mascowitz and Peter Han in Stignitz testified.

But the filth and manure that emanates from the doves is their teaching. Dove manure is filthy, shameful, and it stinks. Their teaching also stinks and everyone finds it repulsive. The manure is rejected, and everyone turns their face away from it. So too the whole of Christendom, the fathers and teachers for sixteen hundred years have rejected and repulsed their false teachings. Since their shit and filth has always been discarded, who should seek it out now or buy it? During the siege of the city of Samaria a quarter of dove manure sold for five shekels.[b] But for all their filth and manure all of Christendom has not given a single penny.

---

a Gen. 1:28.
b 2 Kings 6:25

Rather, more than many thousand ducats have been spent to eradicate the filth, as happened in Münster.

A clever Anabaptist might answer this book of mine by saying, if their teaching is filth, why do I touch it? I answer that I have been and am repulsed by their filth and had made up my mind not to touch it. But I see that they present their shameful, filthy, repulsive, stinking manure to the common people as if it were a precious perfume. This has compelled me to read [their teachings] and compile them as an antidote so that everyone can see and smell for themselves. When they perceive the terrible odor and stink they will reject and condemn it with the whole of Christendom and the holy fathers.

[This book is] commended to God.[17]

Now follows the life of the great dove, that is, Jakob Hutter.

Additional Document 7b

Critique of Hutter by Gabriel Ascherham, 1542, as quoted by Christoph Andreas Fischer in his "Dovecote" [18]

The life of the great dove, that is, Jakob Hutter (after whom the Anabaptists name themselves "Hutterites"), as described by Gabriel Kirschner [Ascherham] from whom the Gabrielite Anabaptists originate, in his chronicle bearing the title: "What took place among the brethren who were driven out of all German lands for the sake of the faith and who therefore came at the same time to Moravia to reside there from 1528 until 1541." I will write (he says) what I myself have seen, heard and learned from genuine witnesses, which I can explain with a clear conscience.

First of all, this Jakob Hutter was a puffed up, ambitious man. Therefore, he shoved aside Sigismund Schützinger and was elected as elder in his place. But before he was elected he was not able to disguise his expectation and ambition, when he came forward and spoke to the people in great anger: "Am I not an apostle and pastor as well? Must I then be rejected by you in this way?" But the great outcomes that resulted from his tenure and establishing of a community was that he destroyed love and unity, and to the peoples who previously had unity he brought disunity.

Now one can sing songs and tell stories about this Jakob Hutter as he wishes, but I say that this Jakob Hutter was a bad man, because I saw through him clearly. Whether he indeed allowed himself to be of some use,[19] I know not what I'd say, for he failed to prove himself in this region. Indeed, he took vengeance on all who spoke up for Schützinger, and like a poltergeist he threatened the fellowship, saying: "See now whom you have praised, namely this villain, whom you regarded as devout, while you diminished me by stating that Schützinger should continue his tenure. Here you made a false judgment. Therefore repent for that."

Such is a true poltergeist, a person who seeks his own honor, which is not the spirit of Paul. It is the spirit of the children of Balaam,[a] meaning the children of fools. But when Jakob boasted so highly of himself and bragged that he had the spirit of Paul, one woman said to him, "You have the spirit of the devil."

At the time that the king [Ferdinand] wanted to expel the fellowships out of Moravia the Abbess at Brno sent her servants to Auspitz and drove Jakob with his people from the house. When, however, the captain of the province sent his servants to him and presented him with the royal command, then Jakob began to speak: "Oh, the bloodhound, the murderer! In the alpine regions he drove us from house and home, taking what belonged to us and murdering us! And now he wants to expel us here, too!" And he said to the servants of the captain, "Tell your master the following: We will not move away anywhere. If the bloodhound wishes to have our blood, let him come and we will wait for him."

The servants, however, said: "We cannot deliver such a message verbally." They said this because it was so full of statements and rebukes from Jakob that they could not retain it all. Thus he wrote it all in a letter [L-4], with much rebuke and slandering of the king. The sum of it was: We will wait for the king here.

When this letter was delivered, Jakob was pursued, but he quickly departed and would not let himself be found. Perhaps the whole matter became too much for him to wait there for the king, from which it can be

a Cf. Num. 22; 2 Pet. 2:15; Jude 11; Rev. 2:14.

concluded that he was only a man of words and nothing more. However, others in this region had to pay the price for his riotous behavior. This Jakob fled up country to the Adige Valley, but the king had notices sent out about him, and then he managed to have him burned in Innsbruck.

Thus Jakob perished, under the guise that it happened for the sake of the gospel, which however, was not the real reason in this case. Yet he would have had to die on account of his rebuke [of the King], even if he had twenty lives.

This is faithfully transcribed word for word, without any falsification, from the above mentioned chronicle of Gabriel Kirschner.

Additional Document 8

January 29, 1930, from Eberhard Arnold to Johann Loserth [20]

The Austrian Catholic church historian Johann Loserth (1846–1936) prepared the second volume of The Chronicle of the Hutterian Brethren *for publication. In 1929 he handed the project to Bruderhof founder Eberhard Arnold (1883–1935), who asked him to write an introduction.*

Today I renew my urgent and heartfelt request to you to write equally significant[21] introductions to the first and second parts [of the *Klein Geschichtsbuch*]. This would answer Elias Walter's question about the place of the Foreword, "Life and Work of Johannes Waldner." For the first part it would be of particular significance to have an appraisal from your pen of the outstandingly important founding years of the Hutterian Church. It should include the historical significance for Moravia, as well as the cultural, social, and ecclesiastical history, and should show the character of Hutterian faith and life in its essential features. The attempt could be made to treat the early history as a whole – the foundation period of Jakob Hutter and Peter Riedemann, the good and golden years, and the last great effort by Andreas Ehrenpreis to preserve Hutterianism inwardly and outwardly. On the other hand, the second part of the work would need an introduction in which you could show the loyal and desperate struggles of the elders and preachers of this period of decline and the inner and outer causes of collapse.

I know that this is a considerable request; but I dare to approach you at your advanced age, in deep respect, because we don't have anyone who could do this with the same knowledge and insight as you could.

Additional Document 9

Excerpts from Johann Loserth's introduction to the Klein Geschichtsbuch [22]

Unfortunately, due to circumstances in Germany in the 1930s, Arnold was unable to complete the publication of The Chronicle of the Hutterian Brethren, *vol. 2. But Loserth did draft an introduction, parts of which are included here that describe Jakob Hutter and the communities in Moravia.*

2. Jakob Hutter and the Hutterian doctrine of community

The difference between the Hutterian Church and the related religious confessions

The Anabaptist movement took root more deeply in Tyrol than in other regions of Austria.

1. It had followers already in 1526; Pilgram Marpeck joined it two years later – about whose life and teachings recent Anabaptist research has shed so much new light.

2. The fact that in distributing his major mandate against the "ecclesiastical renovators" of October 21, 1527, Ferdinand I sent to Tyrol no less than 1200 of the 2000 copies bound for the six territories of Austria, indicates the extent as well as the depth of the Anabaptist movement in this region, where the flames of execution were burning. Men and women, old and young on both sides of the Brenner Pass, were joining the new sect – people from all walks of life: farmers, miners, townspeople, and nobles.[23]

3. The centers of the movement were Sterzing, Hall, and Kitzbühel. No sooner were the prisons emptied than they were filled again and again with new followers, eager "to pluck the bloody rose for which the faithful heart longed."[24] In Jakob Hutter the movement soon gained a leader of enduring strength and great renown.

The *Chronicles* of the Anabaptists speak of him in tones reminiscent of the Bible: "At this time came a man by the name of Jakob, a hatmaker by trade, born in Moos (near St. Lorenzen in the Puster Valley), half a mile from Bruneck. He accepted the covenant of grace, of a good conscience in Christian baptism, to live in true surrender and live a godly life." After completing sufficient schooling in Bruneck, he came to Prags where he learned his trade and then settled in Spittal in Carinthia. He may have first become familiar with Anabaptism in Klagenfurt. The *Chronicles* report: "When it was felt that he had abundant gifts from God, he was chosen for and confirmed in the ministry of the gospel." In this role he traveled first through the Puster Valley. The small fellowship met in Welsberg, in the house of a relative Balthasar Hutter, or at the workshop of a scythe smith Andrew Planer. When he first began to baptize, ten individuals were baptized in one day. Soon the authorities were searching for him, and they arrested a number of Anabaptists – including Hutter himself, but he was able to escape. From the interrogations of the others they learned that he baptized "for money" – that is, each one who was baptized had to make a contribution to the communal purse. From this we can infer that community in the sense of the biblical account in Acts 2 to 4 was already being practiced.

The persecution of the devout in the land increased incessantly. Everywhere the blood of the martyrs flowed, the flames rose, and the prisons filled. Then the fellowship recalled that God had gathered a people in his name in Austerlitz in Moravia. This prompted them to send Jakob Hutter and Sigmund Schützinger to Austerlitz "to inquire into their activities." There they united with the fellowship in the name of the Tyrol fellowship. Upon return, Hutter reported that in Austerlitz he had seen the "fellowship of the saints," and all "those in Tyrol who had nowhere to go" were sent to Austerlitz. One group after another moved there with all their property, to live in community with the believers there. Although some of them found the sermons in the new land less edifying and comforting than at home, the union remained firm, and Hutter was the leader of the fellowship.

While he continued spending his energy caring for the fellowship in Tyrol, differences of opinion in Austerlitz threatened the fellowship, which ultimately split into two hostile camps: Austerlitz and Auspitz. So Hutter and Schützinger traveled again to Moravia to establish order. Once again, group after group traveled there, and the fellowship increased daily. At the same time, persecution in Tyrol was intensifying, and Hutter felt compelled to move the center of his activity to Moravia. The leaders there still clung to their private possessions, but, in the words of the *Chronicle*, Hutter established a considerable degree of order through the help and grace of God, "and for this reason we are still called Hutterites."[25]

Here let me point out the essence of this set of ordinances.[26] Although certainly the whole communal system, as it was established in the second half of the sixteenth century, developed gradually, the foundation of community was surely laid by Jakob Hutter – and for this reason the church bears his name. This doctrine was not of any interest to Balthasar Hubmaier. It is not mentioned in his numerous tracts. Quite the opposite for Hutter. For him this doctrine, based on the example of the early Christian church, was the center of the whole system. He practiced it himself in his words and by his example, and his followers taught it as a matter of principle. Anyone who does not recognize this teaching of community and does not wish to live accordingly is excluded from the Hutterian fellowship. It is this doctrine that distinguishes the Hutterian Church from related religious groups.

The Seven Articles of Schlatten am Randen[27] of February 24, 1527 speak of baptism, the ban, the breaking of bread, separation, the shepherds of the church, the sword, and swearing of oaths, but not of community.[28] To be sure, already in Hubmaier's time there was a group of Anabaptists who spoke of community: the followers of Jakob Wiedemann and Philip Jäger, "the community people." "They held meetings in one another's houses, welcomed pilgrims, guests, and strangers, and practiced community."[29] But this community had nothing to do with

Jakob Hutter's. It stemmed from purely outward motives, "for there was much disorder among [those they separated from] and guests and strangers were not welcomed."[30] Hutter's reform was aimed at a community of saints, as in the days of the apostles. Already in the first sermon he held when he arrived in Moravia for the second time, the topic was the true community of God. As in the time of the apostles, whoever joins is to present his temporal possessions to the church: money, linen, beds, chests, etc. Community is the criterion by which the true leader is recognized. Not everyone passed the test, for not everyone was willing to part with their possessions. For this reason Reublin and Schützinger were removed from the office of shepherd after a short time. By contrast, Hutter brought a small donation with him from Tyrol. It served to pay a debt that the fellowship had made in a time of need. Not everyone was able to place himself easily into this position. Jörg Fasser gave his possessions to the fellowship, but his wife withheld some of her and her children's money; she was severely admonished and disciplined by the whole fellowship.

The Hutterites held firmly to community. In the 1530s they built a number of houses – so-called "Haushaben" – in which they practiced community. Their communal lifestyle aroused the apprehension of the governing authorities. In order to allay this suspicion, they said in the manifesto they addressed to the Moravian landowners in 1545:[31] The reason people won't tolerate our communities is that they are afraid that if we are so many together, we would act like the Münsterites did – but that has never been our intention. A second reason is that we live according to the truth. To be sure, it has happened that people come to us in a superficial manner and then accuse us of taking all they had – even if they may not even have had enough to pay the costs of their journey to Moravia – while others gave up their possessions in order to support widows and orphans.

In the days of Hutter and his followers it was considered a serious sin to withhold even the smallest items of one's personal property. Take, for example, Hans Schmidt. Condemned to death, he sent his wife Magdalene his ear pick with the assumption that the brothers would have nothing against it.[32] Yet they all held so firmly to the community, for [the community] is what cares for them all. In [community], one of them said, the sick person has his doctor, the weak his security, the zealous his sermon, the hungry bread, and the thirsty drink. Another says: In the true community of saints, the sinful marks of finance and deceit, buying and selling, selfishness, greed, and usury are put aside. One cries out to those of other creeds, Why are there so many beggars among you? That is not a mark of the true church. Among us we have men who have been ordained to save money and goods in order to give help in times of need. A third one teaches that community means sharing everything out of love for our neighbor. All share everything with one another: both joy and sorrow. Only among the heathen does everyone have his own law, his own house, his own fields, his own kitchen, his own cellar, and his own table.

Another defends community against numerous opponents in a series of powerful antitheses:[33]

Community seeks the good of all; private property [seeks] private good.

Community takes care that children are raised according to scripture in order and discipline; private property does not do so.

In community, each one works and produces honestly and gives to the poor; private property gives rise to quarreling and discord, to extortion and demanding payment.

Community plants a unique, obedient, benevolent, and humble people; private property, an opinionated, obstinate, and stubborn people.

Community points out to the rich man the eye of the needle[a] and to the poor man, love for all; private property points the rich man toward the door to his barns[b] and the poor man toward narcissism. It continues in this tone. In a word: community is the solution to all problems of human society.

Eitel Hans Langenmantel, who was wealthy and came from noble ancestry, spoke these words: Nobody should say mine, mine, for it belongs to us all, including our brother.[34] Ulrich Stadler claims: In the house of the Lord there is no "mine," "yours," and "theirs," for love rules everywhere alike – the same worries, and the same distribution of goods.[35] And Peter Riedemann in his famous *Rechenschaft unserer Religion, Lehr*

a Matt. 19:24.
b Luke 12:18.

und Glaubens (account of our religion, teaching, and faith) dedicates an entire chapter to community as ordained according to the example of the apostles. He says: "Just as Christ has nothing for himself, since all he has is for us, so too, no members of Christ's body should possess any gift for themselves."[36] Niklas Geyersbühler praises his comrades before the court because they practice community,[37] and Leonard Dax teaches: "Anyone who has possessions and misuses them might well be damned, but whoever distributes them voluntarily according to God's command will be blessed."[38] Similarly the bishops of the Hutterian Church, on their deathbeds (for example Klaus Braidl) urge the fellowship: "Hold firmly to Christian community and fight with all your might against stinginess and selfishness."[39]

The last one to take a firm position on the doctrine of community is one of the most venerable leaders of the Hutterian Church: Andreas Ehrenpreis, whose voice we still want to consider here, even though it belongs to a period of the decline of Hutterite Anabaptism – but perhaps just for this reason rings more strongly.

He summed it up in a letter to Daniel Zwicker, a Socinian who learned of Hutterite teachings through Hans Martin, Jobst von Stein, and Leonhard Nadler and began corresponding with Andreas Ehrenpreis.[40] In his letter, Ehrenpreis writes that "our forebears and fellow brethren witnessed to community amid great tribulation, suffering, and death, against the world and its tyrants." Zwicker took offense at these words: "There can be nothing more damaging than to console oneself by quoting one's forebears." Ehrenpreis replied in a letter of September 1650, first presenting examples from the Bible of saintly persons who quoted their forebears, and then elucidating the text from Acts 2:44–45: "You know well that my entire letter is directed toward love and community, serving the poor and needy, and that I have quoted many scripture passages to prove this. Your letter, on the other hand, is directed toward declaring that community was not commanded and unnecessary. I wrote that we have many who are poor and old, widowed, orphaned, crippled, blind, and lame who we feed and care for, and for this reason cannot give everybody money to distribute among the poor of the world [outside of our community]. Yet some poor of the world receive more from our [community] houses as tangible donations than they receive from one or two entire villages. In spite of this, people who do not know us and wish us ill accuse us falsely. Yet we will not withdraw our hearts and hands, holding them back from the poor; we hold them open as is right and just. Even in times of famine, since the time that we were driven out of Moravia and experienced poverty through war and fire, we have sometimes had up to sixty, seventy, or eighty neighbors and children in our house, hoping for alms; none of them left empty-handed – although we did not give them money, only bread and sauce. Still today poor people come to the house, who cost us a significant amount. Once, when there was a great famine throughout Moravia, we baked bread for the poor that they could have for a small price (nine kreuzer, instead of the normal half guilder or thirty kreuzer or more). I heard that this was even entered into the Moravian state record, and many people, both rich and poor, recognized that without our help many people would have died of hunger. The people we helped were not even relatives or fellow believers.

"I'm telling you this," Ehrenpreis says, "not to brag but because of your accusations. You write that only our elders and those designated to give alms help the poor, but you should inform yourself before you write. The Lord or the Evangelists say in the New Testament, 'Sell what you have and give to the poor.'[a] That means nothing other than giving to the poor, the old, the sick, the widows and orphans in Christian community. This is the highest command:[b] Love of God and one's neighbor, the true way of perfection, a 'cunning deception'[41] in the face of human reason, understanding, and wisdom, yes, the treasure hidden in the field, which people walk the length and breadth of without finding it. Property is a spirit of enslavement; it is not the inheritance in the house of the heavenly Father, for they have been overcome by their love of possessions."

Ehrenpreis speaks in 1650 no different from Jakob Hutter, 120 years earlier. In his letter to Zwicker of March 16, 1654, he praises community in memory of the earlier suffering:

> When our fellowship was persecuted in tribulation and suffering in Moravia, Austria, and Hungary, when they had no houses or homes, they divided themselves into groups of twelve or fifteen, the stronger ones looking out

a Matt. 19:21.
b Cf. Matt. 22:34–40.

for the weaker ones, providing food and hiding in barns and hiding places during the day. It was necessary to admonish everyone to remember the poor. This tribulation lasted five years. Why fight over houses and homes, riches and property, when in any given year we were unsure if in a month's time we might be driven out, persecuted, and banished?

Appendix 1

Timeline for Jakob and Katharina Hutter

1529

Beginning of Jakob Hutter's ministry.

May 23: Raid of a group in Welsberg. Later interrogation reveals that Jakob Hutter had baptized some of them. He had been present at the gathering but escaped.[1]

September 6: Georg Blaurock is executed in Gufidaun, South Tyrol. His mantle falls on Jakob Hutter.

Hutter takes his first trip to Moravia, uniting with Jakob Wiedemann's group in Austerlitz, perhaps after the raid in May or after Blaurock's execution in September.[2]

December 1529: Hutter's sister Agnes is executed.[3]

1530

June: Georg Zaunring travels from Tyrol to Moravia.[4] Hutter probably sends his letter (L-1) with him.

Hutter's second trip to Moravia: Hutter and Simon Schützinger are summoned by the group in Moravia, perhaps late 1530, to settle a dispute between Wilhelm Reublin and Wiedemann. Hutter leaves Georg Zaunring in charge in Moravia.[5]

1532

Hutter's third trip to Moravia. "Around Easter" Hutter and Schützinger are summoned to Moravia again because of Zaunring's wife's unfaithfulness. Hutter leaves Schützinger in charge.[6]

Katharina Präst is baptized by Jakob Hutter.[7]

December 31: Katharina's employer, Paul Gall, is arrested with four others. She may have been one of them.[8]

1533

January: Katharina recants at Rodeneck.[9]

March 25: Katharina and three other women are arrested. She is held for two months and beaten with rods.[10]

June 25: Paul Gall is executed.[11]

Summer: Hutter is sent to Moravia by the fellowship in Tyrol because of repeated disorder in the Moravian fellowship.[12]

August 11: Hutter arrives in Moravia (his fourth trip) with a group of converts[13] (possibly Katharina among them).

October 12: After weeks of dissension, Hutter is appointed bishop in Moravia.[14]

1534

Throughout this year, Hutter lives in Auspitz, Moravia.

Bastel Glaser leads a group from Tyrol to Moravia; they are caught and held in Hohenwart. Hutter writes a letter (L-3) to them.[15]

Hutter and other leaders are imprisoned for a short time by the abbess at Brünn.[16]

1535

May 6, Ascension Day: Hutter's community is driven from Auspitz[17] and forced to camp in an open field. From here, Hutter writes to the governor of Moravia (L-4).

May 16, Pentecost: Date of Jakob and Katharina's wedding, according to her testimony in December.[18]

July: Jakob and Katharina return to Tyrol for the last time.[19]

October 3: The authorities become aware of Hutter's presence.[20]

Mid-October: Probable date of birth of Jakob and Katharina's child.

December 1: Arrest of Jakob and Katharina.[21] Jakob is brought to Innsbruck; Katharina remains in Gufidaun.

1536

February 25: Jakob Hutter is executed in Innsbruck.[22]

Sometime between April 28 and August 2, Katharina escapes from Gufidaun.[23]

1538

Presumed date of Katharina's execution.

Appendix 2

List of Codices

A large number of Hutterite codices have been preserved in archives and libraries across Europe.[24] For the most part, these were confiscated from the Hutterian communities in times of persecution. They contain historical accounts, doctrinal tracts, and letters written to or from those in prison or on mission journeys.

We have been able to study and compare a number of these codices (either physically or electronically) for the chapter containing Jakob Hutter's eight letters, and for the account of the division of 1533 in the "Chronicles" section, and assigned a number to each.

Codex 1: Rkp.zv.305 in the Central Library of the Slovak Academy of Sciences in Bratislava Lyceálna knižnica, (Kabinet historických fondov Ústrednej knižných Slovenskej akadémie vied), made available to us as a professional quality scan. 537 leaves, 191 x 151 mm, 1618.[25]

Codex 2: I 87.708 (Ms I 340) in the University Library in Vienna. 420 leaves, 151 x 101 mm, 1577.[26]

Codex 3: Rkp.zv.388 in the Central Library of the Slovak Academy of Sciences in Bratislava Lyceálna knižnica, (Kabinet historických fondov Ústrednej knižných Slovenskej akadémie vied), made available to us as a professional quality scan. 318 leaves, 150 x 100 mm, 1577.[27]

Codex 4: EAH 159 in Bruderhof Historical Archive, Walden, NY. A typed copy of a 1795 codex from Rockport, SD, 1932, bound in two volumes.

Codex 5: EAH 80 in Bruderhof Historical Archive, Walden, NY. 240 leaves, 100 by 165 mm, 50 mm thick, 1781.

Codex 6: EAH 82 in Bruderhof Historical Archive, Walden, NY. 147 leaves, 146 x 97 mm, 1617.

Codex 7: HAB.5 in Štátny archív v Bratislave in Bratislava. 405 leaves, 148 x 100 mm, 1570.[28]

Codex 8: HAB.6 in Štátny archív v Bratislave in Bratislava. 594 leaves, 155 x 103 mm, 1580/81.[29]

Codex 9: HAB.13 in Štátny archív v Bratislave in Bratislava. 426 leaves, 156 x 100 mm, 1593–95.[30]

Codex 10: HAB.17 in Štátny archív v Bratislave in Bratislava. 696 leaves, 205 x 150 mm, After August 28, 1576.[31]

Codex 11: HAB.9 in Štátny archív v Bratislave in Bratislava. 257 leaves, 152 x 97 mm, 1632.[32]

Codex 12: HAB.12 in Štátny archív v Bratislave in Bratislava. 279 leaves, 157 x 100 mm, 1592.[33]

Codex 13: HAB.16 in Štátny archív v Bratislave in Bratislava. 369 leaves, 150 x 97 mm, 1655.[34]

Codex 14: Ab 15 in Eötvös Loránd Tudományegyetem Könyvtára in Budapest. 181 leaves, 87 x 70 mm, after 1605.[35]

Codex 15: "Caspar Breitmichel Codex, " Estate of Reinhold Konrath, Conrad Grebel University College, Waterloo, Ontario. 260 leaves, possibly 1551.

Central Europe, ca. 1540

Münster
Wittenberg
HOLY
ROMAN
EMPIRE
Cologne
SILESIA
Prague
Worms
Nuremberg
BOHEMIA
MORAVIA
Strasbourg
Regensburg
SLOVAKIA
Augsburg
Munich
Vienna
Zürich
AUSTRIA
Salzberg
Bern
Innsbruck
Budapest
TYROL
HUNGARY
Geneva
Mohács
Milan
Venice
Modena
OTTOMON
EMPIRE
Florence
PAPAL
STATES
Rome

Tyrol today and ca. 1540

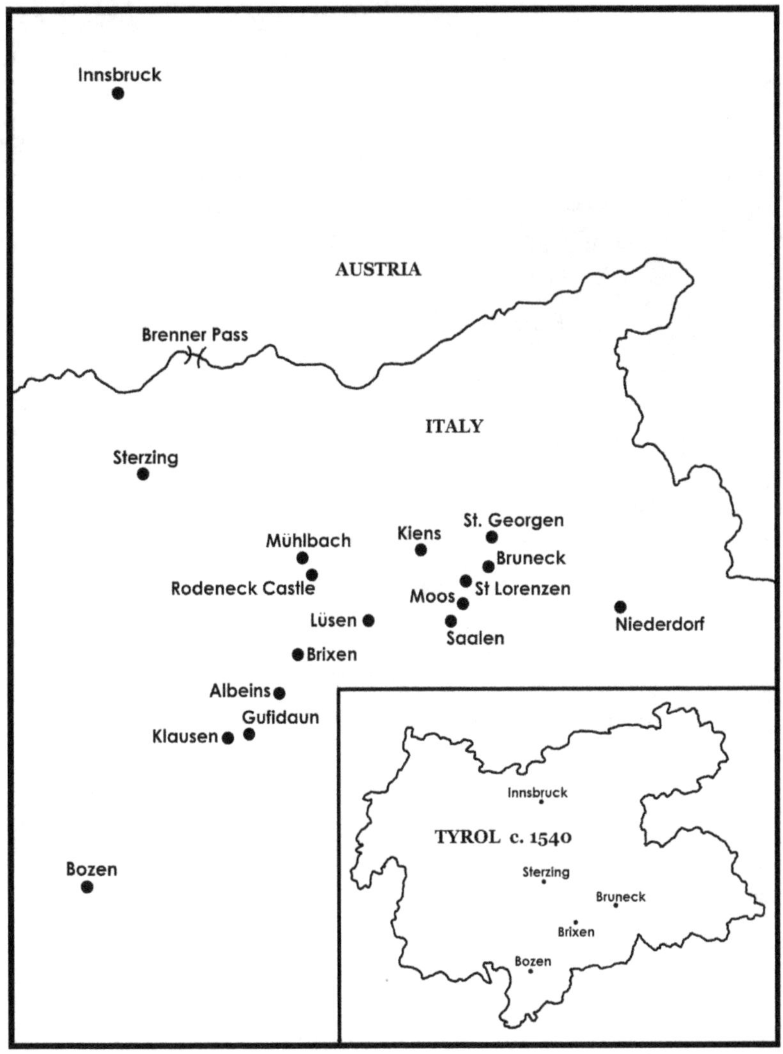

Moravia, ca. 1540

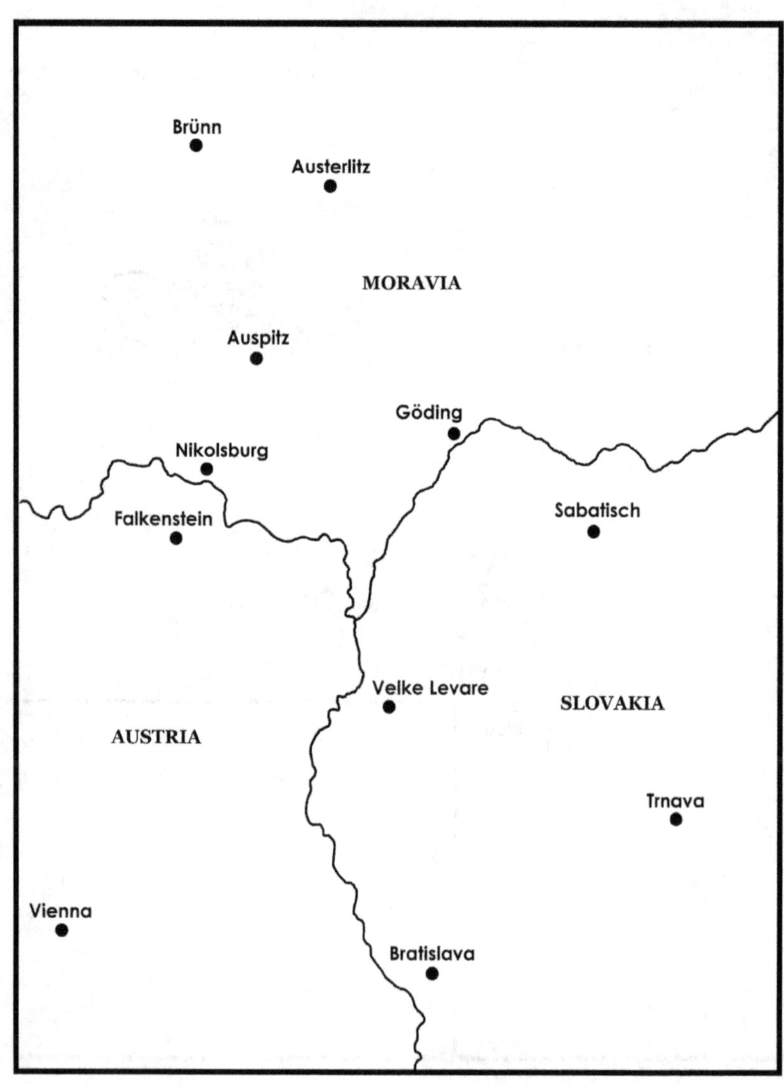

Acknowledgements

This book has been a project of many years, and I thank my co-editor, Jonathan Seiling, for helping me organize the material and for his thorough introduction which, for the first time, documents the life of Jakob Hutter.

I was inspired first of all by Eberhard Arnold's enthusiasm for the earliest Hutterites. Arnold, Plough's founding editor, had planned to publish Jakob Hutter's letters as well as a collection of other Hutterite documents, but due to the rise of Hitler and his own early death, he was unable to realize his plans.

My late husband Jake Maendel enthusiastically supported my research, and his memory has helped me persevere. He grew up Hutterite, and it was our common interest in Anabaptist history that drew us together after his first wife, Irene, died.

I thank my community, the Bruderhof, for making it possible for me to travel in Europe and visit various archives in Austria, Italy, Chechia, and Slovakia in pursuit of details relating to Jakob and Katharina's lives and deaths.

Special thanks to Dr. Manfred Rupert of the Tiroler Landesarchiv in Innsbruck. He went out of his way to help me find and decipher sixteenth century documents and interpret obscure phrases.

And thanks to many archives across Europe that welcomed and assisted me. And thanks to the Plough staff: Sam, Cameron, Coretta, Miriam, and Emily.

Emmy Barth Maendel

I am grateful to the Bruderhof and Plough Publishing House for inviting me to participate in this project with Emmy Barth Maendel, who has been a delight to work with and to learn from. Werner Packull first introduced me to the complex world of Moravian Anabaptism and Hutterite manuscripts and the worthwhile challenge of decoding handwriting that is nearly five centuries old, while trying to gain insight into the lives of those who formed communities around faith convictions they were willing to die for. I am also deeply grateful to Karin Packull, who generously offered me the her late husband's collection of Hutterite literature, which supported my scholarship in this field. Martin Rothkegel has also been a colleague who provided more insights than I could handle at times. I'm also grateful to Kenny Wollman for his careful review of the translation, and to Astrid von Schlachta for her constructive comments on the introductory essay. The staff at the library of Conrad Grebel University College were also very supportive, especially during the pandemic when it was more difficult to obtain materials. Grace Mennonite Church in St. Catharines, Ontario, provided office space which I also gratefully acknowledge.

Jonathan Seiling

Notes

Introduction

1. A. J. F. Zieglschmid, *Die älteste Chronik der Hutterischen Brüder: Ein Sprachdenkmal aus frühneuhochdeutscher Zeit* (Ithaca, NY: Cayuga Press, 1943), 89.
2. James Stayer highlighted the ascendant status of artisans as leaders in Anabaptism, paraphrasing Trotsky and speaking of the "leading role of the artisanry" in Anabaptism. He writes, "Artisan leaders of Anabaptism simply articulated the economic and religious ideals of pre-capitalist, pre-industrial rural and semi-rural commoners generally," and their leadership was not simply the "historicist cliché about thve rise of the middle class." James M. Stayer, *The German Peasants' War and Anabaptist Community of Goods* (Kingston, ON: McGill-Queen's University Press, 1991), 10.
3. While Pietism later strengthened the church-state relation, it would never return to pre-Reformation levels of stability.
4. For overviews of the German Peasants' War, see Stayer, *German Peasants' War;* and Michael G. Baylor, *The German Reformation and the Peasants' War: A Brief History with Documents* (Boston: Bedford/St. Martin's, 2012).
5. The capitals of these districts were: Bruneck (Pustertal), Brixen (Eisacktal), and Sterzing (Wipptal).
6. Stephan Vajda, *Felix Austria: Eine Geschichte Österreichs* (Vienna: Ueberreuter, 1980), 229–230. Ferdinand spent most of his time in Vienna, but he had an administrative office and castle in Innsbruck. Robert A. Kann, *A History of the Habsburg Empire 1526–1918* (London: University of California Press, 1974).
7. Werner O. Packull, *Hutterite Beginnings: Communitarian Experiments during the Reformation* (Baltimore: Johns Hopkins University Press, 1995), 169. Urban Regier (classically: Urbanus Rhegius), was one such son of a priest, and although his illustrious reforming career would span much of the German territories, he was briefly at Hall in Tyrol during 1522 as a substitute following the expulsion of Jakob Strauss. See Johann Loserth, *Anabaptism in Tyrol: Faithful Resilience through Persecution (1526–1626)*, trans. Hugo Brinkmann (St. Catharines, ON: Gelassenheit Publications, 2022).
8. This confusion of jurisdictional process would later play a significant role in the capture and execution of Jakob Hutter. Many communications between the religious office in Brixen and the secular office in Innsbruck regarding the arrest and punishment of Anabaptists are preserved in the archives in Innsbruck and Brixen. See, for example, GOV-4, 12, 14, 17, 27–29, 37–38.
9. On Gaismair's life and reform agenda, see Jürgen Bücking, *Michael Gaismair, Reformer, Sozialrebell, Revolutionär: Seine Rolle im Tyroler "Bauernkrieg" (1525/32)* (Stuttgart: Klett-Cotta, 1978); Josef Macek, *Der Tiroler Bauernkrieg und Michael Gaismair,* trans. Eduard Ullmann (Berlin: Deutscher Verlag der Wissenschaften, 1965); Walter Klaassen, *Michael Gaismair: Revolutionary and Reformer* (Leiden: Brill, 1978); Werner Legère, *Der gefürchtete Gaismair: Roman* (Berlin: Union Verlag, 1976); Ralf Höller, *Eine Leiche in Habsburgs Keller: Der Rebell Michael Gaismair und sein Kampf für eine gerechtere Welt* (Vienna: Otto-Müller, 2011).
10. Josef Innerhofer, *Taufers, Ahrn, Prettau: Die Geschichte eines Tales* (Val di Tures: Verlagsanstalt Athesia, 1980).
11. Packull, *Hutterite Beginnings,* 179.

12. Although peasants may have joined many of the radicals such as Gaismair and others, they maintained key trappings of the "Old Church" tradition, such as references to the "holy martyrs," "sacraments," and the Virgin Mary, leading one to believe the key issues of reform centered on those which Luther in fact rejected, most of which were shared, either by coincidence or by some means of influence, with the broader peasant uprisings throughout central Europe. In this case, the outcry of reform was directed not at some collection of verses from the writings of St. Paul, but against the abuse of power by the church and state.
13. Vajda, *Felix Austria*, 231.
14. "Hutterites attained the social goal of Michael Gaismair's Tyrolean peasants, a self-contained, relatively egalitarian society of commoners." Stayer, *German Peasants' War*, 12.
15. See Stayer, *German Peasants' War*; cf. Gretl Köfler, "Täufertum in Tyrol," in *Michael Gaismair e il Tyrolo del 500*, ed. Christoph von Hartungen and Guenther Pallaver (Bolzano: Comitato di Contatto per L'altro Tyrolo, 1983), 115, who determines only two or three of those who participated in Gaismair's uprisings had become Anabaptists. She also names members of Gaismair's family who became Anabaptists, but they had not participated in the violent uprisings. She notes however, Bartlmä Dill, had been part of the upper German peasants' wars (116).
16. In addition to Hans-Jürgen Goertz, *The Anabaptists* (New York: Routledge, 1996), he presents this thesis in Hans-Jürgen Goertz, *Antiklerikalismus und Reformation: Sozialgeschichtliche Untersuchungen* (Göttingen: Vandenhoeck und Ruprecht, 1995); Hans-Jürgen Goertz, "'What a Tangled and Tenuous Mess the Clergy Is!': Clerical Anticlericalism in the Reformation Period," in *Anticlericalism in Late Medieval and Early Modern Europe*, ed. Peter A. Dykema and Heiko A. Oberman (Leiden: Brill, 1993), 499–519.
17. Hans Hut's apocalyptic influences resonated strongly, and Melchior Hoffman's more prolific expositions also found an eager readership among the Hutterite fellowship. See Packull, *Hutterite Beginnings*.
18. See Walter Klaasen and William Klassen, *Marpeck: A Life of Dissent and Conformity* (Waterloo, ON: Herald, 2008), 47–51.
19. See John Oyer, "The Influence of Jacob Strauss on the Anabaptists: A Problem in Historical Methodology," in *The Origins and Characteristics of Anabaptism*, ed. Marc Lienhard (The Hague: Nijhoff, 1977), 62–82; Hans-Jürgen Goertz, "Brüderlichkeit – Provokation, Maxime, Utopie: Ansätze einer fraternitären Gesellschaft in der Reformationszeit," in *Gemeinde, Reformation und Widerstand: Festschrift für Peter Blickle zum 60. Geburtstag*, ed. Heinrich R. Schmidt, André Holenstein, and Andreas Würgler (Tübingen: Bibliotheca-Academica, 1998), 161–178; Hermann Barge, "Jakob Strauß: Ein Kämpfer für das Evangelium in Tyrol, Thüringen und Süddeutschland," *Schriften des Vereins für Reformationsgeschichte* 54(2), no. 162 (Leipzig: Heinsius, 1937); Hermann Barge, "Die gedruckten Schriften des evangelischen Predigers Jakob Strauß," *Archiv für Reformationsgeschichte* 32 (1935): 100–121, 248–252.
20. Jakob Strauss, *Von dem ynnerlichen vnnd ausserlichem Tauff* (Erfurt, 1523; Barge 7). See also Jakob Strauss, *Widder den Simonieschen Tauff* (Erfurt, 1523; Barge 8a).
21. Johann Fabri effectively made this argument in relation to Hubmaier and attempted to apply it to the entire Anabaptist movement. See Jonathan Seiling, "Johann Fabri's Justification Concerning the Execution of Balthasar Hubmaier," *MQR* 84, no.1 (Jan. 2010): 117–139; Mathilde Monge, "Une représentation catholique de l'anabaptism en 1528" (M.A. thesis, Université Paris 1, 2001), 187–90.
22. On the persecution of Anabaptists see Horst W. Schraepler, *Die rechtliche Behandlung der Täufer in der deutschen Schweiz, Südwestdeutschland und Hessen 1525–1618* (Tübingen: Fabian, 1957); Thomas Winkelbauer, "Die rechtliche Stellung der Täufer im 16. und 17.

Jahrhundert am Beispiel der habsburgischen Länder," in *Ein Thema – zwei Perspektiven: Juden und Christen in Mittelalter und Frühneuzeit*, ed. Eveline Brugger and Birgit Wiedl (Innsbruck: Studien, 2007), 34–66.

23. Original: "muss mit kaiserlicher Ungnade und schwerer Strafe rechnen."
24. Seiling, "Johann Fabri's Justification," 117–39.
25. Packull, *Hutterite Beginnings*, 192.
26. Loserth, *Anabaptism in Tyrol*, 32.
27. Loserth, *Anabaptism in Tyrol*, 39.
28. Willem de Bakker, Michael Driedger, and James Stayer, *Bernhard Rothmann and the Reformation in Münster, 1530–35* (Kitchener, ON: Pandora, 2009).
29. John S. Oyer, "Nicodemites among Württemberg Anabaptists," *MQR* 71, no. 4 (Oct. 1997): 487–514.
30. This can be seen, e.g., in WIT-2: "Jakob Hutter was there and others whom he didn't know"; WIT-7: "Jakob Hutter stays at a farmer's. . . . He doesn't know the farmer's name."
31. Similarly in Switzerland, relocation meant Anabaptists were forced out of the cities into the alpine regions and out of some professions, and many eventually relocated to the Palatinate.
32. Martin Rothkegel, "Anabaptism in Moravia and Silesia," in *A Companion to Anabaptism and Spiritualism, 1521–1700*, ed. James M. Stayer and John D. Roth (Leiden: Brill, 2007), 163–215.
33. Astrid von Schlachta, *Gefahr oder Segen? Die Täufer in der politischen Kommunikation* (Göttingen: Vandenhoeck & Ruprecht, 2009), 94–95.
34. Von Schlachta, *Gefahr oder Segen?*, 94–95.
35. See references for executions in the third wave of persecution, found in Rothkegel, "Anabaptism in Moravia and Silesia," 164n4. See also *Chronicle*, 295–318.
36. For an analysis of complex Hutterite musical developments see Helen Martens, *Hutterite Songs* (Waterloo, ON: Pandora, 2002).
37. See Jonathan Seiling, "Verfolgung," *MennLex V*, http://www.mennlex.de/doku.php?id=top:verfolgung. The chronicler Kirchmair wrote: "The trouble with the heretics, in particular with the Anabaptists, kept getting worse and worse, and I think that alone here in the county of Tyrol and Görtz a thousand people have been burned, beheaded, and drowned on account of it." Quoted in Loserth, *Anabaptism in Tyrol*, 62, who says that this number is too high. Claus-Peter Clasen, *Anabaptism: A Social History, 1525–1618: Switzerland, Austria, Moravia, South and Central Germany* (Ithaca, NY: Cornell University Press, 1972), Appendix D, 337; Claus-Peter Clasen, "Executions of Anabaptists, 1525–1618: A Research Report," *MQR* 47 (Apr. 1973): 115–52.
38. Hermina Joldersma and Louis Grijp, eds., *Elisabeth's Manly Courage: Testimonials and Songs of Martyred Anabaptist Women in the Low Countries* (Milwaukee: Marquette University Press, 2001); Brad Gregory, *Salvation at Stake: Christian Martyrdom in Early Modern Europe* (Cambridge, MA: Harvard University Press, 1997).
39. Matthias Schmelzer, "Jakob Huters Wirken im Lichte von Bekenntnissen gefangener Täufer," *Der Schlern* 63 (1989): 596–618.
40. In "The Five Articles of Faith" as given in *Chronicle*, the section on community is coupled with the idea of *Gelassenheit*: "Von der waren gelassenheit und Christlicher Gemainschafft der Güeter," Zieglschmid, *Chronik*, 285. See also Robert Friedmann, "Gelassenheit," GAMEO (1955), https://gameo.org/index.php?title=Gelassenheit&oldid=162946.
41. Schmelzer, "Jakob Huters Wirken," 607.

42. On Hussite separatism, see Murray Wagner, *Petr Chelcicky: A Radical Separatist in Hussite Bohemia* (Waterloo, ON: Herald, 1983).

43. Calvin Pater, *Karlstadt as the Father of Baptist Movements: The Emergence of Lay Protestantism* (Toronto: University of Toronto Press, 1984). See chapter 4, in which Pater traces the complex evolution of Karlstadt's views on baptism, from 1519 (a trivialization of the external rite and even rejection of the need for baptism – one "shall denounce and condemn the external signs," with an emphasis on the spiritual or "inner" baptism) through to 1523, when he became more explicit in advocating for adult baptism. On the broader development of "anti-baptism" arguments see also Albert Henry Newman, *A History of Anti-pedobaptism: From the Rise of Pedobaptism to A.D. 1609* (Philadelphia, PA: American Baptist Publication Society, 1896).

44. Christian Neff, "Blaurock, Georg (ca. 1492–1529)," GAMEO (1953), https://gameo.org/index.php?title=Blaurock,_Georg_(ca._1492-1529)&oldid=172015. Some historians call him Georg Jakobi, others Bleurond; Bullinger knows him as Weissmantel; Johannes Kessler speaks of a Georg von Huss and a Jakobs zu Bonaduz, considering them two separate persons besides Blaurock. He was popularly called "der starke Jörg."

45. *Chronicle*, 43–45.

46. Packull, *Hutterite Beginnings*, 181–82.

47. Packull, *Hutterite Beginnings*, 181–82.

48. Grete Mecenseffy, "The Origin of Upper Austrian Anabaptism," in *The Anabaptists and Thomas Müntzer*, ed. and trans. Werner Packull and James Stayer (Dubuque, IA: Kendall/Hunt, 1980), 152–53.

49. The town of Chiusani, 20 kilometers (12 miles) northeast of Bozen (Bolzano), South Tyrol.

50. G. H. Williams wrote of Hutter as "a kind of heir of the Tyrolese mission of Blaurock." G. H. Williams, *The Radical Reformation*, 1st ed. (Philadelphia, PA: Westminster, 1962), 234.

51. Packull, *Hutterite Beginnings*, 186.

52. Karl Kuppelwieser, "Die Wiedertäufer im Eisacktal" (doctoral diss., Leopold Franzen University, Innsbruck, 1949), 54–55.

53. Kuppelwieser, "Die Wiedertäufer," 56–57.

54. Kuppelwieser, "Die Wiedertäufer," 107.

55. In a warrant for his arrest on June 26, 1530, he was described as "average height, wearing a light brown coat, black pants, a 'coarse' hat [as opposed to a fine one], no beard and a small ring [*red*]." Original: "ainer mittelmässigen mannßlenge seye, trag ain liechten praunen rockh, ain swartz par hosen, ain groben huet, kain part und hab ain klaine red." *QGT XIII, 377*.

56. See translations of three writings by Schiemer in John D. Rempel, ed., *Jörg Maler's Kunstbuch*, *CRR* 12 (Kitchener, ON: Pandora, 2010), 203–268.

57. Werner O. Packull, *Mysticism and the Early South German-Austrian Anabaptist Movement 1525–1531* (Kitchener, ON: Herald, 1977), 106–117. Schlaffer was beheaded at Schwaz in February 1528.

58. See Schlaffer's reference to leaders like Wiedemann, in Lydia Müller, ed. *Glaubenszeugnisse oberdeutscher Taufgesinnter, GZOT I* (Leipzig: Hensius, 1938), 118; cf. Jonathan Seiling, C. J. Dyck, and John D. Rempel, "Hans Schlaffer and Leonhard Frick, A Simple Prayer, Confession of Sin and Open Confession of Faith," in *Jörg Maler's Kunstbuch*, ed. John Rempel (Kitchener, ON: Herald, 2010), 269–301.

59. On the tangential reception of the Schleitheim Articles and whether there is convincing evidence, see C. Arnold Snyder, "The Influence of the Schleitheim Articles on the

Anabaptist Movement: An Historical Evaluation," *MQR* 63 (1989), 323–344. Attempts to link Schiemer and Schlaffer's Hutian apocalypticism do not seem to warrant the assumption that these two made an imprint of separatism upon the Tyrolean scene, in terms of ecclesiology. Cf. Packull, *Mysticism*, 113, also 213n144. However, the writings by Schiemer in which he is said to advocate for "the establishment of separate brotherhoods" do not indicate anything regarding communal separatism. In Müller, *GZOT I*, the simple phrases "brüederlich gmainschaft der heiligen" (73) and "gmainschaft der heiligen" (79) are not adequate evidence of separatism, if there is any at all, to warrant speculation that he "made contact with Swiss Anabaptists."

60. For a general overview of sectarianism and the concept of *Absonderung* (separatism) in early Anabaptism see, Jonathan Seiling, "Absonderung," *MennLex V*, http://www.mennlex.de/doku.php?id=top:absonderung.

61. Jonathan Seiling, "Christoph Freisleben's *On the Genuine Baptism of John, Christ and the Apostles,*" *MQR* 81, no. 4 (Oct. 2007): 623–54.

62. Packull, *Mysticism*, 146.

63. Christian Neff and Robert Friedmann, "Eleutherobios, Stoffel and Leonhard (16th century)," GAMEO (2011), https://gameo.org/index.php?title=Eleutherobios,_Stoffel_and_Leonhard_(16th_century).

64. Packull, *Hutterite Beginnings*, 215–20; Müller, *GZOT I*, 118; Josef Beck, *Die Geschichts-bücher der Wiedertäufer in Oesterreich-Ungarn* (Nieuwkoop: De Graaf, 1967), 50n2. The wife of Wolfgang Brandhuber was Margreth Schernegker from Vilshofen, noted on February 6, 1528. Packull, *Hutterite Beginnings*, 339n45.

65. C. Arnold Snyder, *Anabaptist History and Theology: An Introduction* (Kitchener, ON: Pandora, 1995), 240; see 249nn17–18, referring to chap. 5.2 of Packull's unpublished manuscript, which later appeared as *Hutterite Beginnings*. See Packull, *Hutterite Beginnings*, 121, 355n85, arguing the reference to the Wolfgang Schernegker from Burghausen was Brandhuber himself, who conducted Gabriel's baptism. Packull refers to the source in *QGT XI*, 107.

66. C. Arnold Snyder, ed., *Sources of South German-Austrian Anabaptism* (Kitchener, ON: Pandora, 2001), 155. In *Mysticism*, 151, Packull states Brandhuber was a seamster from Linz, and Packull corrected his profession and place of origin in *Hutterite Beginnings*, 60.

67. Packull, *Mysticism*, 151–52.

68. Snyder, *Sources*, 156; see also Beck, *Die Geschichts-bücher*, 88–89; Packull, *Mysticism*, 151–52.

69. Stayer, *German Peasants' War*, 8–9, 122.

70. Packull, *Mysticism*, 152.

71. Packull, *Hutterite Beginnings*, 60; Müller, *GZOT I*, 137–43. On the establishment of the community of goods and of the ban, in relation to discipline, the text by Ulrich Stadler, "Cherished Instructions on Sin, Excommunication, and the Community of Goods," provides details as early as 1537, which likely reflect Hutter's thought and practice in these matters.

72. Braitmichel's *Chronicle*, 61, uses "church" as the translation of *Gmain*, which is here translated as "fellowship." See Zieglschmid, 65–66.

73. Cf. Stayer, *German Peasants' War*, 122, on Brandhuber belonging to the line of Müntzer and Hut. Packull suggests on the other hand, that by 1529 Brandhuber had come under the Austerlitz influence and is less a founding father of the community of goods as a "member and articulator of a form of Anabaptism under a mixed Swiss-Hut influence." Packull, *Hutterite Beginnings*, 60–61. While Packull himself attests that Brandhuber's letter is the first evidence of community of goods, it seems convoluted to argue that he came under the

influence of Austerlitz in this regard. Far more viable is the conclusion that Brandhuber formulated a version of the practice, which he exported to Moravia and in the course of his leadership in Tyrol, convinced Hutter to embrace, who then developed it further in coordination with leaders in Moravia. Stayer seems to maintain the earlier position that Packull refutes. Cf. Stayer, *German Peasants' War*, 122; James M. Stayer, "Swiss-South German Anabaptism, 1526–1549," in *A Companion to Anabaptism and Spiritualism, 1521–1700*, ed. James M. Stayer and John D. Roth (Leiden: Brill, 2007), 88.

74. Packull, *Mysticism*, 153.

75. Packull, *Mysticism*, 152.

76. See *Chronicle*, 164, and Robert Friedmann, "Riedemann: Anabaptist Leader," *MQR* 44 (Jan. 1970): 5–44.

77. According to Williams, *Radical Reformation*, 412, Ascherham led a group of two thousand from Silesia to Moravia, "having collected seven thousand guilders for the trip." His followers first established the community at Rossitz in 1527.

78. Werner O. Packull, *Peter Riedemann: Shaper of the Hutterite Tradition* (Kitchener, ON: Pandora, 2007), 14–15, 18. Packull suggests that Riedemann's Gmunden Confession is likely a reflection of Brandhuber's own teaching.

79. Packull notes that among Tyrolean Anabaptist documents and literature, no pacifist statement survives from the years 1527–29, allowing for "inconsistencies and ambivalences" in the presumed violence-affirming revolutionary movements of 1525–26 and the post-1529 rejection or absence of violent revolutionary proposals. Packull, *Hutterite Beginnings*, 174.

80. See Schmelzer, "Jakob Huters Wirken."

81. Williams, *Radical Reformation*, 418–19.

82. Although many of the first generation of Anabaptist leaders were from the intellectual classes or clerics, in the second-generation artisans and craftsmen outnumbered other classes in leadership roles. See Stayer, *German Peasants' War*, 10.

83. See CHR-1.

84. Packull, *Hutterite Beginnings*, 179. See also CHR-1.

85. Klaassen and Klassen, *Marpeck*, 50.

86. Schmelzer, "Jakob Huters Wirken," 597.

87. See Linda Huebert Hecht, "A Brief Moment in Time: Informal Leadership and Shared Authority among Sixteenth Century Anabaptist Women," *Journal of Mennonite Studies* 17, (1999), 65–66. Schmelzer writes:

> Apart from being at the castle [Wölfl] was in various houses in Gufidaun to proclaim the true faith. If asked, he was ready to preach in a church. Finally, Peter Binder (one of the Binder family in Klausen) took him to the Puster Valley where he preached in Pflauretz and Montal. In St. Lorenzen [in Widum] he spoke about his faith in the presence of the parish priest in the jurisdiction of Michelsburg. The district judge and his father also listened to what was said. He was taken to Bruneck by the town sexton, first preached at a miller's outside the town, and then at a stabling place for oxen in the town itself. Here eight priests came to hear him preach. In St. Georgen he preached at the Grembs's house. From there Anton von Wolkenstein invited him to Neuhaus Castle where he stayed for a week, read aloud from the Bible and held discussions. In Sand in Taufers he preached in the presence of the mine administrator (Hans Glöggl) and several priests. Everyone agreed with him except the district judge of whom Wölfl had already been warned in Innsbruck. Schmelzer, "Jakob Huters Wirken," 598.

88. See Schmelzer, "Jakob Huters Wirken," 614–17.
89. Packull, *Hutterite Beginnings*, 179.
90. See Klaassen and Klassen, *Marpeck*, 50.
91. Schmelzer, "Jakob Huters Wirken," 596.
92. Schmelzer, "Jakob Huters Wirken," 596.
93. Packull suggests the arrest of Wölfl along with the tension with Caspar Hueter may have prompted Jakob to depart from the Puster Valley. Packull, *Hutterite Beginnings*, 199.
94. It has also been suggested that it was Gamperer who baptized Hutter. Packull, *Hutterite Beginnings*, 199; GOV-1. See *QGT XIII*, 322–23, where Mecenseffy surmises Agnes Hutterin was Jakob's sister. From this we might further assume their father was also a hatmaker and the likelihood of Caspar Hueter, who was also a hatmaker, being a cousin or uncle of Jakob and Agnes. See GOV-27; cf. Packull, *Hutterite Beginnings*, 252.
95. Cf. Packull, *Hutterite Beginnings*, 177–79, 180–81, 199. Georg Weber and Gregori Weber are the same person in the *QGT* sources but appear as two individuals in Packull's account.
96. Loserth, *Anabaptism in Tyrol*, 44; Packull, *Hutterite Beginnings*, 199, 373n71; *QGT XIII*, 311–12.
97. Loserth, *Anabaptism in Tyrol*, 49.
98. *QGT XIII*, 238.
99. *QGT XIII*, 263.
100. Upper Puster Valley (at Rasen), Vintl, Rodeneck, Klausen, Gufidaun, Villnöß, the Sarn Valley, on the Breitenberg above Leifers, Grassstein, Sterzing, Pfitsch, Tulfer and Schmuders. Schmelzer, "Jakob Huters Wirken," 600.
101. Rattenberg, Brennerbad where eighty to ninety people were gathered, in the Eisack Valley near Sterzing, Lüsen, St. Andrä, Klausen, Gufidaun, and Villnöß, in the Sarn Valley, in the area round Leifers on the Breitenberg, at Rodeneck, and, of course, in the administrative district of St. Michelsburg.
102. Loserth, *Anabaptism in Tyrol*, 102. At the regional Diet of Znaim, Ferdinand I finally succeeded in forcing the Moravian estates to desist their practice of tolerating Anabaptists.
103. See Leonard Gross, *The Golden Years of the Hutterites*, rev. ed. (Kitchener, ON: Pandora, 1998).
104. Rothkegel, "Anabaptism in Moravia and Silesia," 163.
105. Rothkegel, "Anabaptism in Moravia and Silesia," 166.
106. E.g., the debate over real presence in the Lord's Supper. On the general background of this debate within Anabaptism, see John D. Rempel, "Anabaptist Theologies of the Eucharist," in *A Companion to the Eucharist in the Reformation*, ed. W. P. Wandel (Leiden: Brill, 2014), 115–137.
107. Hut's son Philipp was a member of the Hutterite fellowship in Moravia. Beck, *Die Geschichts-bücher*, 35.
108. Rothkegel, "Anabaptism in Moravia and Silesia," 177–78.
109. Rothkegel, "Anabaptism in Moravia and Silesia," 179–80.
110. Rothkegel, "Anabaptism in Moravia and Silesia," 180.
111. Rothkegel claims that "distinctive group theologies were apparently developed only after the groups had already separated," in "Anabaptism in Moravia and Silesia," 182. But, if we consider Brandhuber as being the more consistent line through which Tyrolean and then Moravian practice and theology developed, then there would be a clearer developmental

liaison with Wiedemann, Ascherham, Hutter, and Riedemann. While the documented evidence does not provide adequate textual proof that Riedemann's theology and practice conformed in detail to the earlier leaders' expression, Hutter and Riedemann do not take issue with Brandhuber, nor does Gabriel. However, it is worth proposing Brandhuber as the likely source of authority for the general current of the separatist-communitarian-nonresistant theological and practical guidelines that would initially become formulated in the Austerlitz and Auspitz communities and eventually become more concrete and finally codified under Riedemann as standard Hutterite practice.

112. Rothkegel suggests that the Hubmaier-Hut split arose from the incompatibility of their theologies among the separatist Anabaptists who left Nikolsburg for Austerlitz, but their internal debates were due more to "practical problems related to their commitments to community of goods and nonresistance, and from personal rivalries among leaders. Distinctive group theologies were apparently developed only after the groups had already separated." Rothkegel, "Anabaptism in Moravia and Silesia," 182.

113. No writings from Wiedemann survive, and there is little information about his death, except that he was executed in Vienna in 1535 or 1536.

114. Packull, *Hutterite Beginnings*, 55–66; Rothkegel, "Anabaptism in Moravia and Silesia," 180–81.

115. Zieglschmid, *Chronik*, 87; *Chronicle*, 81.

116. See Johann Loserth, "Zur kirchlichen Bewegung in Mähren im Jahre 1528," *Zeitschrift des deutschen Vereins für die Geschichte Mährens und Schlesiens* 23 (1919): 176; Rothkegel, "Anabaptism in Moravia and Silesia," 181.

117. Rothkegel, "Anabaptism in Moravia and Silesia," 181.

118. Letter from Jeronimus Käls, *Hutt.Epist.*, III, 116. See also https://gameo.org/index.php?title=Wideman,_Jakob_(d._1535/6).

119. *Chronicle*, 84.

120. *QGT XIII*, 319.

121. The date of Zaunring's departure is deduced from *QGT XIII*, 377 – namely, a report of June 26 that Zaunring had been in Hall (beyond Innsbruck) two weeks previously, heading to the Zillertal. Hutter's Letter 1 was presumably sent along with this group.

122. For another example of the life of a Tyrolean Anabaptist missionary, see Leonard Gross, "Nikolaus Geyersbühler, Hutterite Missioner to Tyrol," *MQR* 43, no. 3 (Oct. 1969): 283–92.

123. *Chronicle*, 86. Wilhelm Reublin (ca. 1480–1559) is something of an enigma. He was part of Zwingli's circle in Zurich in 1525, and in the following years his name appears in connection with numerous Anabaptist leaders including Michael Sattler, Hans Denck, and Pilgram Marpeck. He apparently withdrew from Anabaptism after being excommunicated by Jakob Hutter in 1531. Gustav Bossert Jr. and James M. Stayer, "Reublin, Wilhelm (1480/84-after 1559)," GAMEO (1989), https://gameo.org/index.php?title=Reublin,_Wilhelm_(1480/84-after_1559)&oldid=172017.

124. J. C. Wenger, "A Letter from Wilhelm Reublin to Pilgram Marpeck, 1531," *MQR* 23, no. 2 (Apr. 1949): 67–75, at 71–72. For further background see Packull, *Hutterite Beginnings*, 214–35.

125. For a detailed study of Reublin's own activities in relation to the Peasants' War and his position on the sword, see James M. Stayer, "Reublin and Brotli: The Revolutionary Beginnings of Swiss Anabaptism," in *The Origins and Characteristics of Anabaptism*, ed. Marc Lienhard (The Hague: Nijhoff, 1977), 83–102.

126. Manuscript is located at Nuremberg, Bayerisches Staatsarchiv, Markgrafentum Ansbach, Ansbacher Religionsakten 39, Bl. 129r–149v; 154r–172r. See Martin Rothkegel, "Ausbreitung und Verfolgung der Täufer in Schlesien in den Jahren 1527–1548," *Archiv für schlesische Kirchengeschichte* 61 (2003): 149–209; and the detailed description of the text in Martin Rothkegel, "Antihabsburgische Opposition und täuferischer Pazifismus: Die Auslegung von Römer 13 des David Burda aus Schweinitz 1530/31," *MGBL* 69 (2012): 23–29.
127. For further background on the origins of the schism, see Packull, *Hutterite Beginnings*, 214–35.
128. Wenger, "Letter from Wilhelm Reublin to Pilgram Marpeck," 72–74.
129. Packull, *Hutterite Beginnings*, 218.
130. Packull, *Hutterite Beginnings*, 220–21.
131. Zieglschmid, *Chronik*, 98; *Chronicle*, 91.
132. Zieglschmid, *Chronik*, 98; *Chronicle*, 91.
133. Zieglschmid, *Chronik*, 98; *Chronicle*, 91.
134. Packull, *Hutterite Beginnings*, 221.
135. Packull, *Hutterite Beginnings*, 218.
136. See Beck, *Die Geschichts-bücher*, 58.
137. Zaunring was later accepted back into the fellowship and later sent on a mission to Franconia, where he was then executed in Bamberg. Beck, *Die Geschichts-bücher*, 91–102; *Chronicle*, 93–94, 97.
138. *Chronicle*, 93. Although some sources give the date as Easter 1531 (see Beck, *Die Geschichts-bücher*, 101), it was most likely Easter 1532. See Packull, *Hutterite Beginnings*, 379n39. See also GOV-5, a report of March 10, 1532, that Hutter was on his way to Moravia.
139. Packull, *Hutterite Beginnings*, 221–22; *Chronicle*, 110.
140. In 1529 Plener led a group from Hesse and the Palatinate to lands near Auspitz, whose proprietor was the abbey, directed by Maria Saal. See Williams, *Radical Reformation*, 418.
141. John A. Hostetler, *Hutterite Society* (Baltimore: Johns Hopkins University Press, 1997 [1974]), 20. According to Hostetler, Ascherham was already established as senior leader in 1527 (17), a statement that is cited by several scholars from Williams, *Radical Reformation*, 421. Williams writes that in the period after Schützinger was appointed leader in place of Zaunring, the three communities at Rossitz/Auspitz each had leaders, but "Gabriel Ascherham himself was named bishop of the three groups." See also Beck, *Die Geschichts-bücher*, 69n2.
142. Packull, *Hutterite Beginnings*, 266–67.
143. Fischer, Hans. *Jakob Huter: Leben, Froemmigkeit, Briefe* (Newton, KS: Mennonite Publication Office) 1956, 30. Cf. *Hutt.Epist.*, II, 220. This letter is erroneously dated 1536 in *Hutt. Epist.*, II. Amon would later inherit Hutter's position of leadership, and we might guess that his level of attention to strict conformity was similar to that of Hutter, even as his letter in 1533 indicates an awareness of how Hutter's level of strictness might be perceived by others.
144. The English translation of the *Chronicle* devotes twelve entire pages to recount the debates between the erstwhile Tyrolean co-leaders, Schützinger and Hutter. *Chronicle*, 98–110.
145. See ADS-9, excerpt of a previously unpublished essay by Johann Loserth, in which he explains that the practice of community was central to Hutter's interpretation of a Christian life and the doctrine that distinguishes the Hutterian Church from other related religious groups.

146. *Chronicle*, 99.
147. *Chronicle*, 99.
148. Cf. translation in *Chronicle*, 99, i.e., fickle, selfish people; original: *aigennützige vnd leichttuertige hertzen,* in Zieglschmid, *Chronik*, 106.
149. *Chronicle*, 99; Zieglschmid, *Chronik*, 106.
150. *Chronicle*, 99–100.
151. *Chronicle*, 216.
152. *Chronicle*, 102.
153. *Chronicle*, 103.
154. *Chronicle*, 103–105.
155. *Chronicle*, 105.
156. *Chronicle*, 106.
157. Some sources give the date of Zaunring's death as 1538, but he does not appear in Hutterite sources after 1531.
158. Stadler's "Cherished Instructions" (ca. 1537) includes a passage that may reflect Hutter's approach to the matter of accepting someone who has sinned: "therefore, whoever proclaims and promises mercy to such a persistent sinner, who blasphemes the spirit of grace and treads the Son of God under foot, let him be answerable for himself rather than [maintaining] that God's spirit ever so testified." G. H. Williams, ed., *Spiritual and Anabaptist Writers: Documents Illustrative of the Radical Reformation* (Philadelphia, PA: Westminster, 1957), 275; see Müller, *GZOT I*, 215–221.
159. *Chronicle*, 110.
160. *Chronicle*, 136.
161. *Hutt.Epist.*, III, 116.
162. Robert Friedmann, "Philippites," GAMEO (1959), https://gameo.org/index.php?title=Philippites.
163. *Chronicle*, 164.
164. Riedemann's first letter regarding the schism is in the *Chronicle*, 164–65. In 1538 he visited scattered Philippites and restored brotherhood among them. *Chronicle*, 168–69. Later that year Hans Gentner, a Philippite leader, visited the fellowship in Moravia and joined them; as a result, Riedemann wrote a second letter explaining the schism. *Chronicle*, 177–81. Again in December 1539 some Philippites were visiting the Hutterite community in Steinebrunn in order "to find out on what basis the community was living." *Chronicle*, 188. They were among 150 who were arrested and taken to Falkenstein Castle and later marched down to Trieste. Similarly in 1545 a group of Gabrielites re-entered the Hutterian Church after investigating the accusations and counterarguments. *Chronicle*, 233–39.
165. After Hutter's departure from Auspitz, leadership of the early Hutterite fellowship was in the hands of Hans Amon until his death in 1542. Peter Riedemann would later expound upon these practices in his *Rechenschaft* (1540), available in English as John J. Friesen, ed., *Peter Riedemann's Hutterite Confession of Faith*, CRR 9 (Walden, NY: Plough, 2019). Riedemann had been ordained in 1529 and was made co-bishop starting in 1542, following Hans Amon's death. He would work alongside Leonhard Lanzenstiel. *Chronicle*, 216–17.
166. Rothkegel, "Anabaptism in Moravia and Silesia," 182.
167. *Chronicle*, 134; Zieglschmid, *Chronik*, 143.
168. *Chronicle*, 135; Beck, *Die Geschichts-bücher*, 116–17.

169. Packull, *Hutterite Beginnings*, 224–35; *Chronicle*, 134–35.
170. *Chronicle*, 135
171. *Chronicle*, 136.
172. *Chronicle*, 136
173. *Chronicle*, 138.
174. *Chronicle*, 141.
175. Katharina has been the subject of various studies. See Elfriede Lichdi, "Katharina Purst Hutter of Sterzing," in *Profiles of Anabaptist Women*, eds. Linda H. Hecht and C. Arnold Snyder (Waterloo, ON: Wilfrid Laurier University Press, 2001), 178–86; Astrid von Schlachta, "Huterin, Katharina Purst," *MennLex* V, https://www.mennlex.de/doku.php?id=art:huterin_katharina_purst&s[]=huter; Emmy Barth Maendel, "Research Note: Katharina Prast: Wife of Jakob Hutter," *MQR* 96, no. 3 (Jul. 2022): 438–58.
176. According to unpublished research by Manfred Rupert of the Tiroler Landesarchiv in Innsbruck, Katharina's maiden name was "Prast" (not Purst or Prust).
177. Schmelzer, "Jakob Huters Wirken," 610–11.
178. *QGT XIV*, 97.
179. *QGT XIV*, 115
180. Valtenin Luckner's testimony, *QGT XIV*, 169.
181. *QGT XIV*, 11, 123–24.
182. *Chronicle*, 135.
183. See Packull, *Hutterite Beginnings*, 240. Details are taken from the confessions of Katharina and others interrogated with her. *QGT XIV*, 296–303. (Wolf Zimmermann carried Hutter's Letter 6, according to some sources.)
184. Packull, *Hutterite Beginnings*, 242.
185. *QGT XIV*, 297.
186. Michel Walser carried the first letter, but then he was the one who helped Nändl escape a few weeks later – thus he must have returned.
187. It is possible the baby was born in prison a few months after Katharina's arrest, as Loserth and later historians have assumed. But in all court records referring to her during that time, there is no mention of her being pregnant. As a rule, a female prisoner's pregnancy was specifically stated in these records and torture was mitigated or delayed until after delivery.
188. *Chronicle*, 142.
189. The following year, Jeronimus returned to Tyrol to carry on the mission. He was caught and executed in Vienna two weeks before Easter 1536. *Chronicle*, 150. Emmy Barth, "For the Sake of Divine Truth: The Legacy of Jeronimus Käls, Michael Seifensieder and Hans Oberecker," *MQR* 81, no. 2 (Apr. 2007): 243–59.
190. Schmelzer, "Jakob Huters Wirken," 610–11. Schmelzer mistakenly gives the date as November 13, while citing *QGT XIV*, 368B, which states November 30.
191. See GOV-33.
192. Schmelzer, "Jakob Huters Wirken," 610. See also GOV-21.
193. This Jakob Steiner was likely a friend of Jakob Hutter's. In 1542 his fifteen-year-old son was "abducted" by Anabaptists. Unpublished paper by Christoph Gasser, Stadtarchiv Klausen, given to Emmy Barth Maendel, August 30, 2017.
194. It is noteworthy that the list of interrogation questions contains nothing about the political intentions of the movement, despite the charge that Anabaptism was de facto an act

of sedition; neither does it inquire whether Jakob Hutter planned a violent overthrow of existing authorities. The only concern, it seemed, was forcing Hutter to possibly recant and to extract from him the names of other leaders. Schmelzer, "Jakob Huters Wirken," 613–14.

195. *Chronicle*, 145.

196. Werner O. Packull writes: "Confusion surrounds the actual date of execution. Previous scholarship suggested February 25, 1536, but Hutter's jailor sought to collect for eighty-seven days from November 29, which would move the date of execution to the middle of March 1536." Packull, *Hutterite Beginnings*, 254; cf. GOV-36. However, a recalculation shows that February 25 is eighty-seven days after Hutter's arrival in Innsbruck. (From November 29 to December 29 is thirty days, to January 29 another thirty-one days, and to February 24 an additional twenty-six days, totaling eighty-seven days.) In addition, *Chronicle*, 145, reports that Hutter was executed "about the time of Candlemas, on the Friday before the first week of Lent, 1536." Easter was April 16 that year; Lent would have begun on Wednesday, March 1. The Friday before that was February 25. See also Fischer, III.48.

197. *QGT XIV*, 296–303

198. *QGT XIV*, 314

199. Klausen was under the jurisdiction of the prince-bishop in Brixen and Gufidaun under the secular authorities in Innsbruck.

200. However, Packull, *Hutterite Beginnings*, 255, says she remained in South Tyrol.

201. Loserth, 121. The original source for this date is probably a list of martyrs that includes Katharina's name although without any details, in Hab. 6 in the State Archive in Bratislava. The date is unclear. The entry reads simply: "Traindl Huetterin von Saal executed in Schöneck." Saalen is a hamlet in the municipality of St. Lorenzen.

202. See the story of Onophius Griesinger and Leonard Lochmair in the *Chronicle*, 169–72. Packull, *Hutterite Beginnings*, 269, writes: "Presumably [Onophrius's] mission included resumption of contacts with Hutter's last converts because Hutter's widow joined Onophrius's entourage after her escape from the Gufidaun prison."

203. Written of Christina Häring, a woman executed in Kitzbühel in 1533, whose story is not included in the *Chronicle*; taken from codex R 414 in the University Library in Wroclaw, 95–96. (See also Beck, 107, which includes the story but not this eulogy.)

204. Rothkegel, "Anabaptism in Moravia and Silesia," 184.

205. For Amon's letters, see *Hutt.Epist.*, I, 84–119; II, 195–99, 210–13; IV 452–60, 468–74. For Riedemann's letters see *Hutt.Epist.*, I, 145–53.

206. See Robert Friedmann, "Epistles, Anabaptist," GAMEO (1956), https://gameo.org/index.php?title=Epistles,_Anabaptist&oldid=143544.

207. Hutter's opponent Gabriel Ascherham argued this matter even after Hutter's death. See ADS-7b

208. Fischer, III.69.

209. Rothkegel, "Anabaptism in Moravia and Silesia," 184.

210. Williams, ed., *Spiritual and Anabaptist Writers*, 274–77.

211. In his *Hutterite Confession of Faith* Peter Riedemann describes the ban as a means of restoring a fallen member. Written less than ten years after the events just described, it likely reflects Jakob Hutter's practice: "When a person is excluded, we have no fellowship with that person until there is true repentance. . . . The church must perceive that the Lord has again drawn near to him, been gracious to him, and accepted him. When that is recognized, the church offers the hand of fellowship, as God has commanded us. The church reaccepts the

excluded person, who is once more considered a member of the church. Just as a person is first received into the church by a sign, the sign of baptism, so that person is received back into the church after separation due to sin by a sign, the sign of the laying on of hands.... It indicates that the repentant sinner once more has a share in God's grace and is rooted in it. When this has happened, that person is received back with complete love; all suspicion, complaint, and reluctance are removed. We should trust the reaccepted person as fully as we trust all other members of the church." Friesen, ed., *Riedemann's Hutterite Confession,* 152–54.

212. Luther's completed translation of the Bible first appeared in 1534.

213. Fischer, III.72.

214. Fischer, III.72–73.

215. The following section summarizes the analysis of Hutter's teaching by Matthias Schmelzer, based upon a close reading of interrogation records and government correspondence. See in general, Schmelzer, "Jakob Huters Wirken." The statements of the "witnesses" as found in Chapter 3 provide some of the texts which are referenced by Schmelzer.

216. While Hutter himself was not reported to have stirred up violence or destructiveness, Jakob Gasser, whom Hutter had baptized, reportedly seized the chalice from the priest and the consecrated wafer from the altar during Mass in the parish church of St. Andrew's at Brixen. After thrusting them behind the door, he trampled on the half wafer that he had torn from the priest's hand and flung it to the floor. He then fled, but was later arrested.

217. Schmelzer, "Jakob Huters Wirken," 606.

218. A more broadly defined "community of goods was at first an endeavour common to all Anabaptist groups." Stayer, *German Peasants' War*, 9. Diverse forms of the practice were more widespread than previously acknowledged, and furthermore, there is a strong connection to the lineage of those early political revolutionaries in the mid-1520s, who sought to reorganize socioeconomic distribution.

219. *German Peasants' War*, 12.

220. The existence of very early nonresistance expressions by future Anabaptists notwithstanding, if we allow for a dynamic trend within Anabaptism, in which those who had once promoted violent resistance now realized it was a failed position, and if we consider that they would have arrived at this point by considering both scripture and their own experience, it is unnecessary to ask whether a change in belief, practice, or reform-survival tactics renders their position "internally inconsistent," just as it is needless to assume they should have developed a static position on a deeply controversial matter that would determine their survival.

221. The system of communalist economics was uniquely shaped by the era and context in which it was developed, and therefore it is neither helpful nor accurate to apply the label of "communist" to Hutter's political-economic vision. See Leonard Gross, "Jakob Hutter: A Christian Communist," in Hans-Jürgen Goertz and Walter Klaassen, eds., *Profiles of Radical Reformers* (Scottdale, PA: Herald Press, 1982), 158–67. Gross praises Hutter's option of establishing "God's kingdom in the present world" instead of building upon "the spiritualistic idea of Austrian Anabaptism," while admitting he died too soon to "develop fully his views," and further claiming that "all the points of a kingdom-of-God Christianity, as developed at Schleitheim, were integral to Hutterianism from its inception" (165). However, such a denigration of what Gross calls the "spiritualistic idea" has been discarded with the extensive work by Werner Packull into the intellectual-theological movements at play in Tyrol and Moravia, which are also not inconsistent with what one might conjecture was the intent in the Schleitheim articles of 1527.

222. Rothkegel, "Anabaptism in Moravia and Silesia," 184.
223. Fischer, III.25–26.
224. Fischer, *Jakob Huter*, Vorwort, vii.
225. Z157–58; cf. *Chronicle*, 146.
226. Eberhard Arnold, "Das Glaubensleben und die alten Schriften" [The life of faith and the old writings], 1928, EA 28/12, Bruderhof Historical Archive, Walden, NY, https://www.eberhardarnold.com/archive/2020/04/24/20126079238.
227. Packull, *Hutterite Beginnings*, 255.
228. Johann Loserth, "Hutter, Jakob (d. 1536)," GAMEO (1959), http://gameo.org/index.php?title=Hutter,_Jakob_(d._1536)&oldid=145473.
229. Fischer, III.33.
230. Gross, "Jakob Hutter," 166.
231. Stayer, *German Peasants' War*, 12.
232. Kuppelwieser, "Eisacktal," 49.
233. Martin Rothkegel, "Die Chroniken der Gemeinde Gottes in Mähren: Historiographie und Martyrologie bei den Hutterischen Brüdern im 16. und frühen 17. Jahrhundert," in Konfessionelle *Geschichtsschreibung im Umfeld der Böhmischen Brüder (1500–1800): Traditionen – Akteure – Praktiken*, ed. Joachim Bahlcke, Jiří Just, and Martin Rothkegel (Wiesbaden: Harrassowitz, 2022), 321–75.
234. Thieleman J. Van Braght, ed., *The Bloody Theatre or Martyrs Mirror of the Defenseless Christians*, trans. Joseph Sohm (Scottdale, PA: Mennonite Publishing House, 1950), 440. The date of Zaunring's death is stated here as 1531, but elsewhere it is stated as 1538.

Chapter 1: Jakob Hutter's Letters

1. Robert Friedmann, "Hutterite Chronicles," GAMEO (1953), https://gameo.org/index.php?title=Hutterite_Chronicles&oldid=120292.
2. Josef von Beck's papers in the Moravian State Archive in Brno (G10 48)
3. This letter appears in COD. 1, PUB. 1, and PUB. 2 (II, 9–12; copied from PUB. 1).
4. In many of the manuscript collections of Hutter's letters, the letter is introduced with a paragraph summarizing the contents. This summary comes from the codex but is not part of Hutter's letter itself.
5. COD. 1 has *wachhafftig* while PUB. 1 has *wahrhaftig*.
6. Pentecost was June 5 in 1530. Saturday eight days prior was May 28.
7. Likely refers to the noble family Han von Hanberg. Schloss Hanberg is not far from Brixen (Bressanone).
8. Phrase omitted in PUB. 1 *und haben 9 heüsser umbsetzt*.
9. The word *lieben* is omitted in PUB. 1.
10. Original: *Zukunft*, i.e., future coming.
11. COD. 1 has *dem Waren Ertzhüertten, Christo*, while PUB. 1 has simply *dem Erzhirten*.
12. Georg Han was appointed to the service for temporal affairs in 1538 (*Chronicle*, 174) and died in Pergen in 1569 (*Chronicle*, 401).
13. Hans Platner was appointed to the service of the Word in 1547 (*Chronicle*, 298) and died 1552 (*Chronicle*, 317).
14. Names taken from COD. 1.

15. L-2 is included in the *Chronicle*; otherwise it was not widely disseminated. PUB. 1, PUB. 3, PUB. 4, and COD. 7 have been compared.
16. Phrase omitted in PUB. 1.
17. Original: *alleredelsten Trost;* COD. 7 has *alleredelsten schatz,* i.e., most noble treasure.
18. Evidently Hutter's earlier letters have been lost.
19. October 28.
20. Letter no longer extant.
21. Original: *Veyt.* Peter Voit was arrested later, in 1534, and his legs clamped so tightly that they had to be amputated. He lived to be seventy. See *Chronicle*, 132 and CHR-15.
22. Onophrius (or Offrus) Griesinger and Hans Amon (Tuchmacher) were Hutter's close assistants and continued his work after his death. Griesinger died a martyr's death in 1538. Hans Amon became Hutter's successor as Hutterian bishop until his death in 1542.
23. Valentin Luckner, see WIT-9.
24. COD. 7 has *Contzen* – possibly Kuntz Fichter; see *Chronicle*, 95.
25. Rüpel is probably Ruprecht Huber; see WIT-11, WIT-12. Stoffel is probably Christoph Schueknecht; WIT-10, WIT-12.
26. Phrase in COD. 7 only. The Stadler mentioned may be Ulrich Stadler.
27. Original: *Eingeschlossen,* i.e., included in the Anabaptist fellowship.
28. Original: *Freudenkranz*
29. Noteworthy is Hutter's confidence in speaking the word of God as a spiritual gift, without explicit reference to scripture.
30. Original: *der untuechtige Simon.* COD. 7 says *der schalckhafftig Sigmund.*
31. Omitted in PUB. 1, PUB. 3.
32. COD. 7 has *schweigen* (to be silent) instead of *schmiegen* (adulate).
33. Also known in the *Chronicle* as "the Bohemian," and identified as David Burda von Schweinitz.
34. Original: *alles irdische und zergängliche Leben und alles das das auf Erden und dahinten ist.*
35. *Diener* (ministers, attendants, servants, or possibly deacons in some contexts). Hutterite ministers were called *Diener des Worts.*
36. PUB. 4 has *leib* (body); PUB. 1 and PUB. 3 have *blut* (blood).
37. Possibly "Margareth Marpeck," the daughter of Anabaptist leader Pilgram Marpeck. Her mother, Sophia, presumably died late 1527 and Margareth was given into the care of guardians in January 1528. See Klaassen and Klassen, *Marpeck*, 103, 105.
38. Georg Fasser's wife had withheld money on entering the fellowship. See *Chronicle*, 103, and CHR-11. Fasser himself became a missionary and died a martyr. *Chronicle*, 161–62.
39. L-3 is included in COD. 2, COD. 4, COD. 5, COD. 6, COD. 8, COD. 9, COD. 10, PUB. 1, PUB. 2 (I, 37). The opening summary appears only in COD. 4 and PUB. 2.
40. Hohenwart is a parish in Lower Austria where Anabaptist refugees from Tyrol frequently stopped on the journey to Moravia. In 1534 Bastel Glaser, who was leading a company from Tyrol to Auspitz in Moravia, was seized there with his party. It is to them that Hutter wrote this letter. The prisoners were later transferred from Hohenwart to Eggenburg where they had their cheeks burned through and were then released. Several songs written by Bastel Glaser are preserved in the Hutterian songbook. He was martyred in 1537. See CHR-14.
41. COD. 4.

42. Omitted in COD. 5.
43. COD. 4, PUB. 2.
44. Omitted in COD. 6, PUB. 1.
45. PUB. 1 has *des heiligen Gottes*; all other sources have *des heiligen Geists.*
46. Original: *der heilige David.*
47. PUB. 1, COD. 8.
48. Omitted in PUB. 1, COD. 8.
49. Omitted in PUB. 1, COD. 8.
50. Omitted in PUB. 1, COD. 8.
51. Omitted in COD. 4, COD. 6, PUB. 2.
52. Omitted in PUB. 1.
53. Omitted in COD. 4, PUB. 2.
54. Omitted in PUB. 1.
55. Omitted in PUB. 1, COD. 8.
56. Phrase omitted in PUB. 1, COD. 8.
57. Omitted in PUB. 2.
58. PUB. 1, COD. 8.
59. PUB. 2 has *Petrus.*
60. Phrase omitted in COD. 6, PUB. 1.
61. COD. 4, PUB. 2 have *zeitlich* (temporal) instead of *leicht* (slight).
62. Omitted in PUB. 1.
63. *Fried* (peace), not *Freud* (joy) in COD. 2, COD. 4, COD. 5, COD. 6, COD. 9, COD. 10.
64. All sources (except PUB. 1 and COD. 8) have *Fried*, not *Freud.*
65. *Chronicle*, 132.
66. Probably Leonhard Schmerbacher and Wilhelm Griesbacher, both "ministers for temporal affairs" (See *Chronicle*, 100).
67. Hans Amon had come from Tyrol some time before Offrus Griesinger (Wolkan, 105). Leonhard Schmerbacher and Wilhelm Griesbacher were both ministers of temporal affairs in Auspitz and took an active part in Jakob Hutter's struggle with Gabriel and Philip in the fall of 1533. Wilhelm Griesbacher suffered a martyr's death in 1535 (Wolkan, 77–79; Beck, 119–20). Zieglschmid (1941) says Leonard Lanzenstiel instead of Schmerbacher (34).
68. COD. 4, COD. 5, PUB. 2.
69. In all sources except PUB. 1, COD. 8.
70. L-4 is the most often copied of Hutter's letters. It appears in COD. 1, COD. 2, COD. 3, COD. 5, COD. 6, COD. 11, COD. 12 as well as PUB. 1, PUB. 2 (III, 1), PUB. 3, PUB. 4, PUB. 5. (PUB. 5 used COD. 1; PUB. 1 copied from PUB. 3; PUB. 2 copied from PUB. 1.)
71. COD. 1.
72. COD. 2, COD. 3, COD. 5, COD. 6, COD. 11, COD. 12.
73. COD. 1, COD. 2, COD. 3, COD. 6, COD. 11, COD. 12.
74. COD. 2, COD. 3, COD. 6, COD. 12.
75. COD. 1, COD. 2, COD. 3, COD. 5, COD. 6, COD. 11, COD. 12.
76. COD. 1, COD. 2, COD. 3, COD. 5, COD. 6, COD. 11, COD. 12.

77. Omitted in PUB. 1, PUB. 2.
78. Omitted in COD. 1, COD. 2. COD. 3. COD. 6, COD. 11, COD. 12.
79. COD. 12.
80. COD. 3, COD. 6, COD. 12.
81. Omitted in COD. 1, COD. 2, COD. 3, COD. 5, COD. 6, COD. 11. COD. 1 has "It is nothing new." COD. 2 and COD. 12 have "We rejoice, for we know that we are wronged and it is not the truth."
82. COD. 1, COD. 2, COD. 3, COD. 6, COD. 11, COD. 12.
83. Omitted in PUB. 1, PUB. 2.
84. COD. 2, COD. 12; COD. 1 has "for the sake of God's truth."
85. COD. 1, COD. 4, COD. 5, COD. 9, COD. 10, COD. 11 (incomplete), PUB. 1, PUB. 2 (I, 23).
86. See PUB. 1 (I.38).
87. Summary in COD. 1, COD. 4, PUB. 2.
88. Omitted in COD. 1, COD. 4, COD. 5, COD. 9, COD. 10, COD. 11, PUB. 2.
89. Original: *Herzukunft*. We might more commonly use the word "incarnation" where Hutter spoke of the advent, or arrival, of Christ.
90. COD. 1, COD. 5, COD. 9, COD. 10, PUB. 2 have *teuren* instead of *treuen*. COD. 11 has *bitern*.
91. *Angenehm*.
92. Omitted in PUB. 1.
93. COD. 1, COD. 4, COD. 5, COD. 9, COD. 10, COD. 11, PUB. 2 have *ihr allerliebsten* where PUB. 1 has *ihr Auserwählten*.
94. Omitted in PUB. 1.
95. Omitted in PUB. 1.
96. Omitted in PUB. 1.
97. COD. 5.
98. Omitted in PUB. 1.
99. Omitted in PUB. 1.
100. Omitted in PUB. 1.
101. Omitted in PUB. 1, PUB. 2.
102. Omitted in PUB. 1.
103. Jeronimus Käls was a much-loved schoolmaster of the church in Moravia. He wrote teachings and prayers for the children. Johann Loserth, "Käls, Hieronymus (d. 1536)," GAMEO (1957), https://gameo.org/index.php?title=K%C3%A4ls,_Hieronymus_(d._1536)&oldid=145553; Wolkan, 119–23. In Tyrol he was one of Jakob Hutter's coworkers in the mission task. He suffered martyrdom and death for his faith. Brother Kränzler is mentioned again at the end of L-7 as one of those sending special greetings. All we know about him otherwise is that he was executed in 1536 (Beck, p. 131; *QGT XIV*, 325). He was arrested in May 1536.
104. Here the translation follows the text in the codices instead of PUB. 1.
105. "Holy, fiery" in COD. 4, PUB. 2.
106. See *Chronicle*, 142. They had to break up into groups of eight or ten.
107. The reference is unclear.
108. Omitted in PUB. 1.

109. Omitted in PUB. 1.
110. COD. 4 and COD. 9 have "Saint Paul" instead of "Saint Peter."
111. Omitted in PUB. 1.
112. Omitted in PUB. 1.
113. Omitted in PUB. 1.
114. Nändl is Anna Stainer. In L-7 Jakob Hutter describes how she was helped to escape. See Packull, *Hutterite Beginnings*, 246. Packull suggests that she may have been an old friend of Katharina's.
115. L-6 is included in COD. 1, COD. 2, COD. 4, COD. 9, COD. 10, COD. 11, PUB. 1, PUB. 3, PUB. 6. PUB. 6 used COD. 1 as the base text. COD. 2, COD. 4, COD. 11, PUB. 2 include a line at the end to say it was delivered by Wolf Zimmermann, although this fact does not appear in the letter itself.
116. In COD. 1, PUB. 1 the summaries of L-6 and L-7 were transposed. (L-6 speaks of two who were banned; L-7 tells of Nändl's release.) COD. 4, PUB. 2 have the summaries correctly placed.
117. Omitted in COD. 1.
118. Omitted in COD. 2, COD. 4, COD. 9, COD. 10, PUB. 2.
119. The reference is unclear. Perhaps he is noting this is the third time he has sent a letter to this particular fellowship.
120. *Ruhm.*
121. Most sources say *Mairegen*, but PUB. 1 (III.49) has *Morgenregen.*
122. This phrase is used in the apocryphal "Life of Adam and Eve."
123. Possibly Hutter is voicing his worry that the hue and cry will not stop until they have caught him.
124. Phrase found in COD. 2, COD. 4, COD. 9, COD. 10, COD. 11, PUB. 2, but not in PUB. 1.
125. COD. 4 has *Philler*; PUB. 2 (I, 62) has *Phüller*; PUB. 6 has *Bühler.*
126. Today Vipiteno in South Tyrol, 18 kilometers (11 miles) south of the Brenner Pass.
127. Omitted in COD. 2, COD. 9, COD. 10.
128. L-7 appears in COD. 1, COD. 4, COD. 6 (incomplete), COD. 10, COD. 11, PUB. 1, PUB. 2 (I, 45). It was carried by Christel Schmid (as stated in the letter).
129. In COD. 1, PUB. 1 the summaries of L-6 and L-7 were transposed. (L-6 speaks of two who were banned; L-7 tells of Nändl's release.) COD. 4, PUB. 2 have the summaries correctly placed.
130. COD. 4, COD. 10, PUB. 2.
131. COD. 4, COD. 10, COD. 11, PUB. 2.
132. Omitted in PUB. 1.
133. Omitted in COD. 1, PUB. 1.
134. COD. 4, PUB. 2; omitted in COD. 1, PUB. 1.
135. Omitted in COD. 1, PUB. 1.
136. Phrase omitted in COD. 1, COD. 10, PUB. 1.
137. All sources say Mayer, but it was Troyer. See archival records, October 15. Packull also explains this story in *Hutterite Beginnings*, 245.
138. This was Katharina Tagwericher; see WIT-14.
139. Spelled Greiffenwerckh, Greiffenberg, Greisenwick, or Greiffenwink in various manuscripts.
140. See *QGT XIV*, 336. She was given over to her brother Paul Troyer. Niclas and Anna Niderhofer recanted at least twice. See also Packull, *Hutterite Beginnings*, 256–57.

141. See *QGT XIV*, 315, #381. Niclas Niederhofer and wife recant.
142. Omitted in COD. 1, PUB. 1.
143. Omitted in PUB. 1
144. COD. 6, COD. 11.
145. The three traditional temptations in Western Christian theology, often renounced in baptismal vows, are not directly biblical, but they reflect the temptations of Jesus in the wilderness (Matt. 4:1–11) and are also presented in Eph. 2:1–3.
146. Original: *entschlafen* is a euphemism for "passed away" but literally means to fall asleep or "to go into dormition." Some Anabaptists held to the notion of the "sleep of the soul," of which this is an example. It was seen as a means of accounting for the location of souls who had passed from this life and would remain in a neutral state until the final Day of Judgment, without affirming the teaching of purgatory. See the extensive treatment of "psychopannychism" in Williams, *Radical Reformation*. The *Chronicle* frequently uses the phrase *im Herrn entschlafen* (fell asleep in the Lord).
147. Hutter's wife, Katharina, is mostly referred to by the abbreviated form of her name, Traindel.
148. Omitted in COD. 4, COD. 10, PUB. 2. The same phrase is used as an opening greeting in COD. 4, COD. 10, COD. 11, PUB. 2
149. Postscript found in *Hutt.Epist.*, I, 55.
150. Postscript found in PUB. 1 (III.61).
151. L-8 is included in COD. 1, COD. 2, COD. 4, COD. 6, COD. 10, COD. 11, PUB. 1, PUB. 2 (I, 64), and PUB. 6. PUB. 6 used COD. 1 as its source.
152. COD. 1.
153. COD. 4, PUB. 2. The same phrase is used at the beginning of L-7 in COD. 4, COD. 10, COD. 11, PUB. 2.
154. PUB. 1 (III.62) has *allenthalben*; all other sources have *in allen Ländern.*
155. COD. 2 has *der euch darzu berufen*; all other sources have *der mich darzu.* PUB. 1 has neither.
156. Original: *treu*, i.e., faithful, true.
157. All sources have *in vielen denen ers durch mich* where PUB. 1 (III.62) has *den Willen den er mich.*
158. Hutter is employing a key notion from the late mediaeval German mystic tradition, the attachment to created beings over that which is divine, and beyond space and time. Tribulation is seen as a means of shaking our grip upon creaturely things, whereby we are freed or purified of our need to cling to that which is temporal, earthly, or fleshly, in favor of that which is eternal.
159. Original: *Kundschaft.*
160. PUB. 1 has *und ihm allein dienen* where other sources have *in allen dingen.*
161. Linda Hubert A. Hecht, "Anabaptist Women in the Tyrol who Recanted," in *Profiles of Anabaptist Women: Sixteenth-century Reforming Pioneers*, ed. Linda Hubert A. Hecht and C. Arnold Snyder (Waterloo, ON: Pandora, 1996), 156–63; Hans Hermann Theodor Stiasny, *Die strafrechtliche Verfolgung der Täufer in der freien Reichsstadt Köln: 1529 bis 1618* (Münster: Aschendorff, 1962); Nicola M. Sutherland, "Persecution and Toleration in Reformation Europe," in *Persecution and Toleration*, ed. William J. Sheils (Oxford: Basil Blackwell, 1984), 153–62.
162. Phrase omitted in PUB. 1.
163. Omitted in COD. 10.

Chapter 2: Chronicle Sources

1. For an analysis of early Hutterite historical accounts, see Rothkegel, "Die Chroniken der Gemeinde Gottes in Mähren," 321–75.
2. Kirchmayr (1481–1554), also spelled "Kirchmair," became the financial administrator at the monastery in Bruneck in 1517 and in 1519 was appointed as the court judge. In this context he experienced the peasants' revolt first-hand, and his observations about Tyrol and imperial-ecclesiastical politics until the 1550s make his writings an invaluable source collection, which appears in Theodor Georg v. Karajan, ed., "Georg Kirchmair's Denkwürdigkeiten seiner Zeit: 1519–1553," *Fontes rerum Austriacarum* I, (Vienna, 1855), 417–534. A selection of texts is also made available with commentary in Franz-Anton Sinnacher, ed., *Beyträge zur Geschichte der bischöflichen Kirche Säben und Brixen,* vol. II (Brixen, 1830).
3. *Raths-Protokol.,* I, 759, in Sinnacher, *Beyträge zur Geschichte*, 260.
4. Plate used during Mass.
5. Meaning unclear. Sinnacher, *Beyträge zur Geschichte*, 260–61.
6. For the arrest of Ulrich Müllner and Gilg Paderinn, see also QGT XIII, 42.
7. Sinnacher, *Beyträge zur Geschichte*, 262.
8. Text found in Josef Beck, *Die Geschichts-bücher der Wiedertäufer in Oesterreich-Ungarn* (Nieuwkoop: De Graaf, 1967), 79–81.
9. On the origins of the nickname "Blaurock" (or bluecoat in English), see the *Chronicle*, 44. His birth name, Cajacob, was a Latinized form of the Hebrew term "from the house of Jacob." Elsewhere he is known as Georg von Chur, the town in Switzerland, where he had served as a vicar prior to the Reformation. But Anabaptist history has usually referred to him by his nickname, Blaurock (sometimes spelled "Blabrock" in old texts).
10. *Holschranen:* meaning unknown.
11. In Luke 19:11–27, the parable of the ten coins (minas or talents) tells of the master who gives ten coins to his ministers, one of whom invested it and it grew (Luke 19:23). Froschauer's translation reads: *Warumb hast du dann mein gelt nit in den wächsselbanck gegeben? und wenn ich kommen wäre, hette ichs mit wucher geforderet.*
12. Beck, *Die Geschichts-bücher*, 81.
13. These are locations in modern-day Italy that maintain the use of these German names but today are additionally referred to by Italian names: Klausen = Chiusa, Brixen = Bressanone, Sterzing = Vipiteno, Bozen = Bolzano, Neumarkt = Egna, Kaltern = Caldaro, Terlan = Terlano, Kuntersweg = Via Kunter.
14. These locations are in Austria, northern Tyrol, along the Inn River.
15. Beck, *Die Geschichts-bücher*, 82–84.
16. For Georg Frey, see GOV-11 and GOV-13 (there called Jörg Frue).
17. Also spelled "Pranger," which translates as "pillory," i.e., the person who would imprison and shame a criminal in a public square.
18. I.e., refusing to carry swords but only a staff as a means of self-defense.
19. Cf. *Chronicle*, 129–30.
20. Beck, *Die Geschichts-bücher*, 84–86. The first brief paragraph uses key terms that provide insight into the nature of the first encounter of Hutter and the Austerlitz fellowship, particularly in terms of the implications of leadership. The subsequent texts in this section, taken from other manuscripts, provide further detail into the nature of Hutter's leadership in 1529.
21. The German term "verainigt" means "unified," and this term is the same that was used for the union that was formed at Schleitheim, the title of that document being the "Union of

Brethren" (*Brüderlich Vereinigung*). The above text implies the same sort of quasi-denominational unity was formed between Hutter's Anabaptists and those at Austerlitz.

22. Cf. *Chronicle*, 83–84.
23. Original: *erwelt und bestätigt*.
24. Original: *aller Handlung*.
25. Reublin had been one of the first opponents of infant baptism in Zurich in 1524.
26. This section is a revision of the translation found in *Chronicle*, 82–94; cf. Zieglschmid, *Chronik*, 89–102.
27. Present day Český Krumlov in the Czech Republic.
28. Cf. Reublin's letter to Pilgram Marpeck, ADS-6.
29. Beck, *Die Geschichts-bücher*, 91n1. Cf. Braitmichel's alternative version of this event in Zieglschmid, *Chronik*, 93–94; *Chronicle*, 87–88; CHR-6.
30. Original: *Diener*, i.e., Servants of the Word, translated throughout as ministers.
31. David Burda von Schweinitz; cf. Martin Rothkegel, "Antihabsburgische Opposition," 7–44.
32. Original: *ausgeschlossen*, also translated as "excluded" or "shunned" or "banned" in various Anabaptist traditions.
33. Karajan, "Georg Kirchmayr," 491–92.
34. Beck, *Die Geschichts-bücher*, 113. This is a brief summary of the detailed account given in CHR-11 below.
35. Manuscript D states Hutter's arrival as August 11; the other manuscripts state August 12.
36. Beck notes the textual locations. Beck, *Die Geschichts-bücher*, 113n1.
37. The account given below comes from several codices but has never been published. Written in the first person, it is evidently the basis for the official *Chronicle* account. Robert Friedmann, with Adolf Mais, eds., *Die Schriften der Huterischen Täufergemeinschaften: Gesamtkatalog ihrer Manuskriptbücher, ihrer Schreiber und ihrer Literatur, 1529–1667* (Austria: Böhlaus, 1965), 107, 175, attributes it to Caspar Braitmichel, but according to Martin Rothkegel, there is no basis for this assumption. We have looked at six codices for the translation of this text. Not one of them includes the entire account as given here. We note significant variances and omissions but not differences in individual words or phrases. HAB.5 (COD.7), HAB.12 (COD.12), HAB.16 (COD.13), AB.15 (COD.14), I 87.708 (COD.2), and "Caspar Breitmichel Codex" (COD.15).
38. This phrase only in COD.7.
39. August 11 in COD.7, COD.12, and in the *Chronicle*; August 12 in COD.13, COD.14, COD.2.
40. Phrase omitted in COD.13, COD.14, COD.2.
41. Phrase in COD.13, COD.14, COD.2 only.
42. COD.13, COD.14, and COD.2 have "But if they needed him, he would serve them and the Lord, wherever the Lord sent him."
43. Beginning of section missing in COD.12 – evidently a missing page.
44. End of section missing in COD.12.
45. Philip's community, like Simon Schützinger's, was in Auspitz. Rossitz (Gabriel's community) is about 45 kilometers (28 miles) away.
46. The next paragraphs are missing in COD.13, COD.14, COD.2.
47. To here, previous paragraphs missing in COD.13, COD.14, COD.2.
48. Phrase missing in COD.7.

49. Section in parentheses missing in COD.12.
50. Section missing in COD.12.
51. Jörg Fasser is mentioned in Sigmund of Kien's testimony, WIT-1 (there Georg Vasser). He was later imprisoned with Leonhard Seiler (see their correspondence with Hans Amon, HEP-2, HEP-3, HEP-4, HEP-5, HEP-6, HEP-7) and executed in 1537 (*Chronicle*, 161).
52. Omitted in COD.13, COD. 4, COD.2.
53. Starting here, two pages are missing in COD.15.
54. End of section is missing in COD.15.
55. The following section is missing in COD.13, COD.14, COD.2.
56. Phrase in COD.12 only.
57. Section is missing in COD.13, COD.14, COD.2.
58. "Bohemian" David Burda.
59. Next section is missing in COD.14.
60. Missing in COD.14.
61. The next section missing in COD.13, COD.14, COD.2.
62. The author of this report is possibly referring to himself here.
63. Hans Both; see *Chronicle*, 126–28; CHR-15 below.
64. The previous paragraphs are missing in COD.13, COD.14, COD.2.
65. COD.7 ends the account here.
66. Continuation of the account given as CHR-11.
67. In COD.14 only.
68. Missing in COD.12, COD.13.
69. In COD.12 only.
70. Missing in COD.4.
71. COD.14 ends the account here.
72. Continuation of CHR-11 and CHR-12.
73. The following paragraphs are in COD.12 and COD.15 only.
74. From here to the end is included in COD. 12 and 15 and partially in COD.2 and COD.13 as well, though with some phrases omitted.
75. Conclusion in COD.12.
76. Conclusion in COD.2.
77. Conclusion in COD.13. This is an indication that at the time of this writing, 1570, Braitmichel was still writing.
78. Beck, *Die Geschichts-bücher*, 116.
79. This section is a revision of the translation found in *Chronicle*, 126–37; Zieglschmid, *Chronik*, 138–49.
80. A similar account is found above in CHR-4.
81. See L-3.
82. Karajan, "Georg Kirchmayr," 492.
83. Beck, *Die Geschichts-bücher*, 122–23.
84. Original: *schaidterhauffen,* i.e., a pile of wood centered on a stake.
85. By this account, the fellowship of God, in this case meaning the Hutterite Church, was founded in 1533, which concurs with the statement above, from Beck, *Die Geschichts-bücher*,

113, stating Hutter's role in the conflict between Gabriel and Philip was the reason why they are called Hutterites.

86. Cf. translation in *Chronicle*, 141–46; Zieglschmid, *Chronik*, 154–58.
87. Also called Leonhard Lanzenstiel.
88. See L-8
89. MSs.A.–L. include the following summary, as reprinted in Beck, *Die Geschichts-bücher*, 123n2.

Chapter 3: Witnesses

1. *QGT XIV*, 20–22.
2. This seems to indicate that the interrogator wanted to know if Sigmund heard Hutter denouncing the veneration of Mary. They evidently did not reject the veneration of Mary. However, there is not enough clarity in this passage to determine this issue definitively.
3. *QGT XIV*, 22–23.
4. Original: *sei gleich ein ding.*
5. *QGT XIV*, 24–25.
6. Original: *Secklmeister.*
7. *QGT XIV*, 71–73.
8. *QGT XIV*, 90–93. See also Werner O.Packull, *Hutterite Beginnings: Communitarian Experiments during the Reformation* (Baltimore: Johns Hopkins University Press, 1995), 197–98.
9. Original: *wenn es zu Jahren und Verstand gekommen sei.*
10. Implied is the notion that the long-awaited General Council would deal with such matters in the near future and that, until then, executions due to heresy should be suspended. The Council never materialized in a "general" sense, but the Catholic Church embarked on the Council of Trent in 1545, resulting in a formalization of Catholic doctrine and practice.
11. Reference unclear. *Fronbote* can mean a "holy messenger," an angel, but it is uncertain whether this simply refers to someone whose name was Fronbote.
12. Original: *Junker.*
13. See WIT-9.
14. Original: *Gantmauer*, a pile of rocks.
15. *QGT XIV*, 104–105.
16. Urscher's wife was also executed. They left seven small children, the oldest being twelve years old. See *QGT XIV*, 135.
17. Hartmann Ammann, "Die Wiedertäufer in Michelsburg im Pusterthale und deren Urgichten," *XLVI, Programm des K. K. Gymnasiums zu Brixen* (A. Weger's Hofbuchdruckerei, 1896), 21.
18. *QGT XIV*, 157–61.
19. Hans Beck was one of seven brothers executed in Gufidaun in 1533; their story is in *Chronicle*, 97–98. A copy of his letter is printed in *Hutt.Epist., II*, 240–42. The phrase in question: *Weiter, ihr geliebten Brüder, es grüssen euch die Brüder, ein jeder in Sonderheit, zu vielen tausend Malen mit dem Frieden unseres Herrn Jesu Christi und mit dem Kuss heiliger, göttlicher Liebe. In Sonderheit dich, Jakob Hutter, Hans Amon, Valtin, Hansel Mayer, auch die Justina, Paul Rumer und die Geschwister, wo der Eichhorn zum Fenster hinaus life.* (Beloved brothers, we greet each one individually many thousand times with the peace of

our Lord Jesus Christ and the kiss of holy, divine love, particularly you, Jakob Hutter, Hans Amon, Valtin, Hansel Mayer, Justina, Paul Rumer, and the brothers and sisters where the squirrel ran out the window.)

20. *QGT XIV*, 165–72.
21. government spy.
22. *QGT XIV*, 173–75.
23. *QGT XIV*, 176–77.
24. *QGT XIV*, 181–82.
25. *QGT XIV*, 216–19.
26. It was customary for the owner of a castle to live elsewhere and leave the administration of the castle and surrounding lands to a *Pfleger.*
27. *QGT XIV*, 287–89.
28. *QGT XIV*, 287–89.
29. Historically located in the district of Schoeneck, currently named Terento in South Tyrol, northern Italy, located about 50 kilometers (31 miles) northeast of Bolzano.
30. Approximately April 1533.
31. See WIT-1 for Sigmund of Kiens's testimony.
32. Present day San Lorenzo di Sebato, South Tyrol, Italy.
33. Approximately August 17, 1535.
34. *Loden* is a thick water-resistant woolen material produced by peasants in Tyrol.
35. Niclas Niderhofer was also interrogated, by orders of the bishop, who wished to learn from him where he was baptized, by whom, the names of other Anabaptists, and where they were staying. *QGT XIV*, 289–90.
36. Present day Selva dei Molini, South Tyrol, Italy.
37. *QGT XIV*, 297–98.
38. Original: *Wappenrockh.*
39. Located in present-day Latsch/Laces, Bolzano, South Tyrol, Italy.
40. This is the Nändl mentioned in Hutter's letters. In her testimony, she is careful only to give the names of individuals who are safe in Moravia. *QGT XIV*, 299–300.
41. *QGT XIV*, 299–300.
42. *QGT XIV*, 300–301.
43. Original: *eelicher brueder und mann.*
44. Pustertal, St. Lorenz, South Tyrol, Italy.
45. *QGT XIV*, 302. Anna Stainer was later to be released on paying a fine (letter from Innsbruck authorities, December 8, *QGT XIV*, 309). Those whose names were given by the defendants were also interrogated. Andrew Prader admitted to giving lodging to Jeronimus and another. His wife, Barbara, had been baptized, but she now recanted (302–303).
46. Reprint from Emmy Barth, "For the Sake of Divine Truth: The Legacy of Jeronimus Käls, Michael Seifensieder and Hans Oberecker," *MQR* 81, no 2 (Apr. 2007): 243–59 (used with permission).
47. *Chronicle*, 147–50.
48. A reference to Paul's conversion.

49. See Adolf Mais, "Gefängnis und Tod der in Wien hingerichteten Wiedertäufer in Ihren Briefen und Ledern," *Jahrbuch des Vereins für Geschichte der Stadt Wien,* 19–20 (1963): 87–182; see also Barth, "For the Sake of Divine Truth," 247–48.
50. He is called Hans Oberecker in the *Chronicle.*
51. Meaning unclear.
52. Arrested in Bavaria in 1560 and executed early the following year. *Chronicle*, 372–78; *Hutt. Epist. II*, 279, q.v. Wolkan, 311; Codex I 87.708 in Universitätsbibliothek, Vienna.
53. *Chronicle*, 376.

Chapter 4: Hutterian Epistles

1. *Hutt.Epist.* I–IV.
2. *Hutt.Epist.* II, 220. There dated 1536, but it must be 1533. See Packull, 223 and 38 on 53. Schmerbacher did speak up for Hutter; see *Chronicle*, 100–102.
3. Original: *du wollest dir ihn lassen befohlen sein.*
4. *Hutt.Epist.* I, 93; COD. 4, 315; COD. 10, 523. See *Chronicle*, 152.
5. *Hutt.Epist.* I, 85; *Hutt.Epist.* IV, 453; COD. 10, 513v.
6. Executed in 1536. *Chronicle*, 147.
7. *Hutt.Epist.* IV, 458; COD. 10, 430.
8. Meaning his wife, Katharina. Kaspar Kränzler had accompanied Jakob Hutter on his final mission trip.
9. *Hutt.Epist.* I, 262.
10. In another letter he writes of *unsere Schwachheit . . . die wir noch in unsern sterblichen Hütten tragen* (270) and *unsere fleischliche Hütte ablegen* (272).
11. *Hutt.Epist.* I, 280. Jörg Fasser and Leonard Seiler were later released, but at the time of writing this letter they evidently thought they would soon be killed.
12. *Hutt.Epist.* I, 289; COD. 10, 499v.
13. *Hutt.Epist.* III, 111–12; COD. 10, 410 r–v.
14. See WIT-20 for Käls's confession of faith and WIT-21 for Oberecker's testimony.
15. *Hutt.Epist.* III, 105; COD. 10, 404v.
16. Adolf Mais, "Gefängnis und Tod der in Wien hingerichteten Wiedertäufer in ihren Briefen und Liedern," in *Jahrbuch des Vereins für Geschichte der Stadt Wien,* 19–20 (1963): 87–182. This is a more accurate source of Jeronimus Käls's letters than *Hutt.Epist.* Cf. Mais, 115–16; COD. 10, 414v. (The letter is included in *Hutt.Epist.* III, 113–119, but the paragraphs given here were omitted.)
17. *Hutt.Epist.* II, 143.

Chapter 5: Governmental Correspondence

1. *QGT XIII*, 263–65.
2. Note: "baptized for money." Hutter preached community of goods, and those whom he baptized gave what they owned to the elders, to be distributed among the believers.
3. *QGT XIII*, 265.
4. *QGT XIII*, 311–12. Agnes Hutter was Jakob Hutter's sister.
5. *QGT XIII*, 319.
6. Original: *Seckelmeister.*

7. *QGT XIV*, 37.
8. Original: *Jacob Huetter von Welsperg genannt, so ain praune person, ainen schwartzen part hat, beclaidt mit ainem schwartzen lodein wappenrockh, ainem plaben wammas, weissen hosen, ainem schwartzen huet und der ain häckl am arm tregt.* This description of Hutter has been the subject of much discussion; in particular the *wappenrockh* and *häckl* have been understood as an indication that Hutter had taken part in the Peasants Revolt of 1525. The English translation is based on the interpretation of archivist Manfred Rupert of the Tiroler Landesarchiv (Manfred Rupert to Emmy Maendel, Innsbruck, Jul. 23, 2020). A *wappenrockh* is a surcoat (a medieval outer garment, often sleeveless); a *häckl* is a small axe or hatchet that can be carried on one's arm, a tool for working with wood or cutting meat.
9. Original: *so kainen vorsprecher, auch nit borgschafft haben.*
10. *QGT XIV*, 44–45.
11. *QGT XIV*, 84–86.
12. *QGT XIV*, 52–53.
13. *QGT XIV*, 96–97. It is possible that Katharina Prast, later Hutter's wife, was one of the "adult women" mentioned and that she recanted at this time.
14. *QGT XIV*, 110–11.
15. Original: *Urfehd*, i.e., a legal oath, something that most Anabaptists rejected in principle.
16. Original: *Gertten*, i.e., twigs and branches bound together to fashion a sort of whip.
17. Tiroler Landesarchiv (hereafter TLA), *Causa Domini* (hereafter *CD*), 1532–36, Bd 4, 100; summarized in *QGT XIV*, 113.
18. *QGT XIV*, 122.
19. *QGT XIV*, 123.
20. *QGT XIV*, 131.
21. *QGT XIV*, 139.
22. *QGT XIV*, 276.
23. *QGT XIV*, 277.
24. Diözesanarchiv Brixen, Fasz. 6428, summarized in *QGT XIV*, 277–78. See also L-7. Peter Troyer sent his daughter to Greifenburg in Carinthia into the care of her brother.
25. *QGT XIV*, 278–79.
26. *QGT XIV*, 279–81.
27. *QGT XIV*, 285–87.
28. *QGT XIV*, 292–93.
29. Original: *Unterhauptmann.*
30. *QGT XIV*, 296–97.
31. Original: *Zukher.*
32. Present-day Vandoies di Sopra, Italy.
33. *QGT XIV*, 306.
34. Original: *Landeshauptmann*
35. *QGT XIV*, 306–308.
36. *QGT XIV*, 312–13.
37. *QGT XIV*, 314.
38. Evidently the name of Caspar Hueter came up in Jakob Hutter's interrogation, and he too was questioned.

39. Prags is a village not far from Bruneck.
40. TLA, O.Ö. Regierung, von der fürstlichen Durchlaut, 1532–37, Bd.6, 314v–316.
41. *QGT XIV*, 316.
42. TLA, *CD*, 1532–1536, Bd.4, 299; summarized in *QGT XIV*, 317. Kufstein is a city about 80 kilometers (50 miles) to the northeast.
43. TLA, O.Ö. Kammer Raitbuch, 1536, Bd.82, 412; summarized in *QGT XIV*, 317.
44. TLA, *CD*, 1532–1536, Bd. 4, 307; summarized in *QGT XIV*, 319.
45. *QGT XIV*, 303–306.
46. TLA, *CD*, 1532–1536, Bd.4, 311v; summarized in *QGT XIV*, 319.
47. TLA, *CD*, 1532–1536, Bd.4, 335v; summarized in *QGT XIV*, 319.
48. TLA, O.Ö. Kammer Kopialbücher Entbieten, 1536, Bd. 151, 449v.
49. Although Packull, 254, questions February 25, 1536, as the date for Hutter's execution, the calculation given here confirms it. The *Chronicle* (n145) gives the jailer's name as "Hayler," based on Loserth. However, Manfred Rupert at the TLA points out that it is "Hagler."
50. *QGT XIV*, 323. Innsbruck had written several times for Anna Stainer to be transferred to Gufidaun, but she was still being held in Brannzol.
51. TLA, *CD*, 1532–1536, Bd. 4, 407v–408.

Chapter 6: Additional Documents

1. Müller, *GZOT* I, 137–38; cf. translation in Snyder, *Sources*, 157–58. The *Chronicle* writes the following concerning Brandhuber: "In 1529 brother Wolfgang Brandhuber of Passau and Hans Mittermaier, both servants of God's word and Christ's gospel, were captured with many believers at Linz in Upper Austria and condemned to die for the sake of divine truth. Altogether over seventy believers were executed by fire, water or the sword. Wolfgang Brandhuber faithfully held and taught Christian community: in the church no one should be the steward of his own purse. The property of poor and rich should be distributed by the one chosen by the church [*Gmain*, i.e., fellowship] and everything should be held in common to serve God's glory whenever and wherever God granted it. He led his people to reject worldly splendor, idolatrous images, buying and selling, taking vengeance and doing military service. But governing authorities should be obeyed in everything not opposed to God. He held true Christian baptism and the true Lord's Supper, rejecting infant baptism, the Mass, and other antichristian abominations, as we can still see in his writings." *Chronicle*, 61–62. Brandhuber's death is also included in the account of martyrs in Codex 330, 141r.
2. Müller, *GZOT* I, 137–38; cf. translation in Snyder, *Sources*, 157–58.
3. *Chronicle*, 77–79.
4. Reublin arrived in Austerlitz in early 1530 but was not recognized as a preacher (see CHR-6). Consequently, like Burda, he would harshly criticize the authoritarianism of the community's leadership and the injustice of the same individuals living in such excess while others were without basic needs. Jacob Wiedemann, the central leader at Austerlitz, announced that only a certain few people, Reublin excluded, were permitted to preach, effectively silencing those who might use the pulpit as a platform to criticize the leaders. Feeling unjustly silenced by Wiedemann, Reublin appealed to "imperial and divine law" as he wrote to Marpeck. It seems that between Reublin and Marpeck there may have been an understanding that an appeal for justice to either the civil authorities or to a notion of divine justice as supported in scripture was certainly their prerogative as Anabaptists. Reublin

describes the course of events in his letter to Marpeck. In Reublin's defense against these impositions, David von Schweinitz would also stand in defiance of these demands although Zaunring defended Wiedemann at that time. Wenger, "Letter from Wilhelm Reublin to Pilgram Marpeck," 71–72. For further background see Packull, *Hutterite Beginnings*, 214–35.

5. Wenger, "Letter from Wilhelm Reublin to Pilgram Marpeck," 72.
6. Cornelius, *Geschichte des Münsterischen Aufruhrs*, 257. Cf. Wenger, "Letter from Wilhelm Reublin to Pilgram Marpeck," 73. Here we have provided our own translation, which differs from Wenger's.
7. COD. I, 222–23. Cf. Müller, *GZOT* I, 189–90.
8. Original: *stillschweigen.*
9. Original: *gericht.*
10. Original: *ein warme stuben*. This could translate simply as "a warm room"; however, it is a term that was historically used for a homeless shelter or a calefactory, the latter being a boiler room, which would be extremely hot. This, not simply a "warm room," is the more likely meaning.
11. This date corresponds to the date given by the jailer Hagler (in archival sources). Easter was April 16 that year, Ash Wednesday was March 1, and the Friday before that was February 25.
12. Fischer, III.74, from COD. VIII g 39 Folio 411/412; Sammlung Beck folio 150/162.
13. The stories of many Hutterian martyrs have been preserved in songs that Hutterian school children are still required to memorize. The *Vaterlied* begins with the kings of Israel and summarizes briefly the life of Christ, the apostles, and the persecutions of the first Christians. Then, beginning with Jakob Hutter, it names each of the Hutterian bishops, ending with Andreas Ehrenpreis who was elected in 1639. The first 76 of the 105 stanzas of the *Vaterlied* are attributed to Georg Bruckmaier, who was executed in Ried, Bavaria, in 1585. Cf. translation in the *Chronicle*, 503–505. We include here the ten stanzas that tell Hutter's story (numbers 41–50). See, *Die Lieder der Hutterischen Brüder* (Caley, Alberta: Hutterischen Brüder, 1962), 774–75.
14. An expression meaning "to release one's rage."
15. Christoph Andreas Fischer, *Der Hutterischen Widertauffer Taubenkobel* (Ingolstadt, 1607), 55–57. Cf. James M. Stayer, "Appendix B: Fragment of the Lost Chronicle of Gabriel Ascherham," in *German Peasants' War and Anabaptist Community of Goods* (Montreal: McGill-Queen's University Press, 1991), 170–71.
16. John J. Friesen, ed. and trans., *Peter Riedemann's Hutterite Confession of Faith* (Walden, NY: Plough, 2019).
17. This is followed by fifty-five pages of quotations from Anabaptist literature and a response based on scripture, under such headings as, "What the Anabaptists believe about scripture," "What the Anabaptists believe about original sin," "Whether children are condemned through original sin," and "What the Anabaptists believe about baptism."
18. Ascherham's original text is no longer extant. Christoph Andreas Fischer reproduced it in his *Der Hutterischen Widertauffer Taubenkobel* (Ingolstadt, 1607).
19. Original: *er habe sich gleich sieden und braten lassen.*
20. In a letter from Eberhard Arnold, April 8, 1929, he introduced himself to Loserth, and subsequently in June 1929, Arnold visited Loserth in Graz: "the great joy, heartfelt gratitude, and sincere respect with which I look back on the unforgettable days I spent in working companionship with you."

21. I.e., as compared to *Der Anabaptismus in Tyrol.*
22. Johann Loserth, unpublished manuscript, Bruderhof Historical Archive, Walden, NY, Coll. 0300_01, Box 28, Folder 1.
23. Loserth notes, "Loesche, Tyrolensia. Jahrbuch für Geschichte des Protestantismus in Oesterreich. 47. Bd."
24. Georg Loesche, *Geschichte des Protestantismus in Oesterreich in Umrissen* (Leipzig: Mohr, 1902), 130.
25. CHR-10: "Afterwards, brother Jakob Hutter, through the help and grace of God, brought the true community into order. For this reason we are still called Hutterites." Beck, *Die Geschichts-bücher*, 113–14.
26. See Johann Loserth, "Der Kommunismus der mährischen Wiedertäufer im 16. und 17. Jahrhundert," *Archiv für österr. Geschichte*, 81 (1894):135–322. See also *Zeitschrift für Social- und Wirtschaftsgeschichte*, 3 (1895): 61–92; Lydia Müller, *Der Kommunismus der mährischen W.T.* (Leipzig, 1929). *The Chronicle of the Hutterian Brethren* 1 discusses the doctrine of community. See Wolkan, 219–26.
27. Schleitheim in Canton Schaffhausen is now generally accepted as the birthplace of the Seven Articles, although Schlatten am Randen, located in southern Baden, was understood earlier as the location named in the original publication. See Werner Pletscher, "Wo entstand das Bekenntnis von 1527?" *MGBL*, V (1940): 20–21.
28. The "Congregational Order," assumed to have been written at the same time as the Schleitheim Confession, does speak of community. Point 5: "Of all the brothers and sisters of this congregation none shall have anything of his own, but rather, as the Christians in the time of the apostles held all in common, and especially stored up a common fund, from which aid can be given to the poor, according as each will have need, and as in the apostles' time permit no brother to be in need." See http://www.anabaptistwiki.org/mediawiki/index.php/Schleitheim_Confession_(source)#Congregational_Order/.
29. Beck, *Die Geschichts-bücher*, 72.
30. Beck, *Die Geschichts-bücher*, 73.
31. *Hutt.Epist.*, I, 75–83, there (erroneously) attributed to Jakob Hutter. It was probably written by Peter Riedemann. See Werner O. Packull and Bruno Fast, "An Index of Peter Riedemann's Epistles," *MQR* 65, no. 3 (Jul. 1991): 340–51.
32. Hab 17, 245v: *Sunst schickh ich dir meinen Orlöffel, den behalt von meinetwegen, ich hoff die Brüeder werden nicht darwider haben.*
33. Josef Hauser, "Dass die Gemeinschaft der zeitlichen Güter eine Lehr des Neuen Testaments sei und von allen Gläubigen erfordert werde." *Hutt.Epist.*, IV, 418–20.
34. Bratislava, Lyceálna kniznica, Rkp.zv.305, 81v: *"So muess es ye auch mit dem zeitlichen guett also sein, daran die Lieb erkannt werde / und nit sagen, Mein, sonder auch seines Brueders sein,"* in "Ein kurze Rede von der waren Gemeinschaft."
35. Eine liebe Unterrichtung Ulrich Stadlers (ca. 1539): Von wahrer Gemeinschaft der Heiligen, cited in J. Loserth, "Der Communismus der Huterischen Brüder in Mähren im XVI. und XVII. Jahrhundert," *Zeitschrift für Social- und Wirthschaftsgeschichte* 3, no. 1 (1895): 61–92.
36. Friesen, *Peter Riedemann's Hutterite Confession of Faith*, 119.
37. Beck, *Die Geschichts-bücher*, 249–51. A copy of Geyersbühler's testimony is preserved in Bratislava, Lyceálna kniznica, Rkp.zv.305, 430–34.
38. *Hutt.Epistl*, III, 552.

39. *Chronicle*, 593.
40. Beck, *Die Geschichts-bücher*, 488–90. Ehrenpreis's letter is published in *Hutt.Epist.*, III, 417–26.
41. Original: *verdeckt Essen*, literally "a covered meal," but the expression means something that appears different on the outside than the inside.

Appendices

1. *QGT XIII*, 238, 263.
2. *Chronicle*, 83.
3. *QGT XIII*, 311.
4. *QGT XIII*, 377. However, the *Chronicle* places the dispute (Reublin/Zaunring) at the end of 1529. Zieglschmid, *Chronik*, 93.
5. *Chronicle*, 91. Zieglschmid, *Chronik*, 93: *Nun im 1530 Jar im anfang desselben*. It has to be after Zaunring's arrival.)
6. *Chronicle*, 91. Zieglschmid, *Chronik*, 93: *Nun im 1530 Jar im anfang desselben*. It has to be after Zaunring's arrival.)
7. At her trial in December 1535 she says three years ago.
8. *QGT XIV*, 96–97
9. *QGT XIV*, 319, states that she had recanted at Rodeneck in 1533. Since her employer Paul Gall was being held at Rodeneck at this time, it stands to reason that she is one of the women arrested with him.
10. *QGT XIV*, 110–11.
11. *QGT XIV*, 125.
12. *QGT XIV*, 158, testimony of Paul Rumer.
13. *Chronicle*, 98.
14. *Chronicle*, 105.
15. *Chronicle*, 131.
16. *Chronicle*, 132.
17. *Chronicle*, 134.
18. *QGT XIV*, 300. It is feasible that the marriage took place earlier. See Maendel, "Katharina Prast: Wife of Jakob Hutter," *MQR* 96, no. 3 (Jul. 2022): 438-458, at 443–444.
19. *QGT XIV*, 300. Katharina's testimony: Saint James' Day [July 25] they arrived in Tyrol.
20. *QGT XIV*, 276.
21. *QGT XIV*, 292.
22. Several sources verify this date.
23. *QGT XIV*, 323.
24. See Matthias H. Rauert and Martin Rothkegel, compilers, *Katalog der hutterischen Handschriften und der Drucke aus hutterischem Besitz in Europa*, edited by Gottfried Seebass, *Quellen zur Geschichte der Täufer*, vol. XVIII, parts 1 and 2 (Gütersloh, Germany: Gütersloher Verlagshaus, 2011).
25. Described in full in Rauert and Rothkegel, *Katalog*, 421. This codex was the basis for Lydia Müller, *Glaubenszeugnisse oberdeutscher Taufgesinnter (*GZOT*)*, I (Leipzig: Hensius Nachfolger, 1938), vol. 1, *QGT* 3.

26. See Rauert and Rothkegel, *Katalog*, 1238.
27. See Rauert and Rothkegel, *Katalog*, 460.
28. See Rauert and Rothkegel, *Katalog*, 169
29. See Rauert and Rothkegel, *Katalog*, 181.
30. See Rauert and Rothkegel, *Katalog*, 255
31. See Rauert and Rothkegel, *Katalog*, 314.
32. See Rauert and Rothkegel, *Katalog*, 240
33. See Rauert and Rothkegel, *Katalog*, 251
34. See Rauert and Rothkegel, *Katalog*, 308.
35. See Rauert and Rothkegel, *Katalog*, 708

Archives Consulted

Austrian National Library (Österreichische Nationalbibliothek) in Vienna, Austria

Austrian State Archive (Österreichisches Staatsarchiv) in Vienna, Austria

Bratislava State Archive (Štátny archív v Bratislave), Slovakia

Bruderhof Historical Archive, Walden, NY

Central Library of the Slovak Academy of Sciences (Lyceálna knižnica, Kabinet historických fondov Ústrednej knižných Slovenskej akadémie vied) in Bratislava, Slovakia

Conrad Grebel University College, Waterloo, Ontario

Diocesan Archive (Diözesanarchiv) in Brixen (Bressanone), Italy

Eötvös Loránd Tudományegyetem Könyvtára (Eötvös Loránd University Library) in Budapest, Hungary

Chiusa Klausen City Archive (Stadtarchiv Klausen), Italy

Moravian State Archive (Moravský zemský archive) in Brno, Czechia

Styria Provincial Archive (Landesarchiv Steiermark) in Graz, Austria

Tyrol Provincial Archive (Tirolerlandesarchiv) in Innsbruck, Austria

University Library (Universitätsbibliothek Wien), Vienna, Austria

University Library (Biblioteka Uniwersytecka), Wroclaw, Poland

Bibliography

Ammann, Hartmann. "Die Wiedertäufer in Michelsburg im Pusterthale und deren Urgichten." *XLVI. Programm des K. K. Gymnasiums zu Brixen*. A. Weger's Hofbuchdruckerei, 1896.

Bakker, Willem de, Michael Driedger, and James Stayer. *Bernhard Rothmann and the Reformation in Münster, 1530–35*. Kitchener, ON: Pandora, 2009.

Barge, Hermann. "Die gedruckten Schriften des evangelischen Predigers Jakob Strauß." *Archiv für Reformationsgeschichte* 32 (1935): 100–121, 248–252.

Barge, Hermann. "Jakob Strauß: Ein Kämpfer für das Evangelium in Tyrol, Thüringen und Süddeutschland." *Schriften des Vereins für Reformationsgeschichte* 54(2), no. 162. Leipzig: Heinsius, 1937.

Barth, Emmy. "For the Sake of Divine Truth: The Legacy of Jeronimus Käls, Michael Seifensieder and Hans Oberecker." *MQR* 81, no 2 (Apr. 2007): 243–59.

Baylor, Michael G. *The German Reformation and the Peasants' War: A Brief History with Documents*. Boston: Bedford/St. Martin's, 2012.

Beck, Josef. *Die Geschichts-bücher der Wiedertäufer in Oesterreich-Ungarn*. Nieuwkoop: B. De Graaf, 1967.

Bossert, Gustav, Jr., and James M. Stayer. "Reublin, Wilhelm (1480/84-after 1559)." GAMEO. 1989. https://gameo.org/index.php?title=Reublin,_Wilhelm_(1480/84-after_1559)&oldid=172017

Braght, Thieleman J. van, ed. *The Bloody Theatre or Martyrs Mirror of the Defenseless Christians*. Translated by Joseph Sohm. Scottdale, PA: Mennonite Publishing House, 1950.

Bücking, Jürgen. *Michael Gaismair, Reformer, Sozialrebell, Revolutionär: seine Rolle im Tyroler "Bauernkrieg"* (1525/32). Stuttgart: Klett-Cotta, 1978.

Clasen, Claus-Peter. *Anabaptism: A Social History, 1525–1618: Switzerland, Austria, Moravia, South and Central Germany*. Ithaca, NY: Cornell University Press, 1972.

Clasen, Claus-Peter. "Executions of Anabaptists, 1525–1618: A Research Report." *MQR* 47 (Apr. 1973): 115–52.

Fischer, Christoph Andreas. *Der Hutterischen Widertauffer Taubenkobel*. Ingolstadt, 1607.

Fischer, Hans. *Jakob Huter: Leben, Froemmigkeit, Briefe*. Newton, KS: Mennonite Publication Office, 1956. Fischer used Josef von Beck's papers in Brno,

GIO 48, folder 31 as his source. His edition of the eight letters appears in Part III of the book, restarting the pagination. Therefore, even though the book is a single volume, the abbreviated references in footnotes will appear as "Fischer, III.5" for page 5 of Part III, where the letters are reprinted: L-1 – L-8.

Friedmann, Robert. "Gelassenheit." GAMEO. 1955. https://gameo.org/index.php?title=Gelassenheit.

Friedmann, Robert. "Philippites." GAMEO. 1959. https://gameo.org/index.php?title=Philippites.

Friedmann, Robert. "Riedemann: Anabaptist Leader." *MQR* 44 (Jan. 1970): 5–44.

Friedmann, Robert, with Adolf Mais, eds. *Die Schriften der Huterischen Täufergemeinschaften. Gesamtkatalog ihrer Manuskriptbücher, ihrer Schreiber und ihrer Literatur, 1529–1667.* Austria: Hermann Böhlaus Nachfolger, 1965.

Friesen, John J., ed. and trans. *Peter Riedemann's Hutterite Confession of Faith.* CRR 9. Walden, NY: Plough, 2019.

Goertz, Hans-Jürgen. *The Anabaptists.* New York: Routledge, 1996.

Goertz, Hans-Jürgen. *Antiklerikalismus und Reformation: Sozialgeschichtliche Untersuchungen.* Göttingen: Vandenhoeck und Ruprecht, 1995.

Goertz, Hans-Jürgen. "Brüderlichkeit – Provokation, Maxime, Utopie: Ansätze einer fraternitären Gesellschaft in der Reformationszeit." In *Gemeinde, Reformation und Widerstand: Festschrift für Peter Blickle zum 60. Geburtstag*, ed. Heinrich R. Schmidt, André Holenstein, and Andreas Würgler, 161–78. Tübingen: Bibliotheca Academica Verlag, 1998.

Goertz, Hans-Jürgen. "'What a tangled and tenuous mess the clergy is!': Clerical Anticlericalism in the Reformation Period." In *Anticlericalism in Late Medieval and Early Modern Europe*, ed. Peter A. Dykema and Heiko A. Oberman, 499–519. Leiden: Brill, 1993.

Gregory, Brad. *Salvation at Stake: Christian Martyrdom in Early Modern Europe.* Cambridge, MA: Harvard University Press, 1997.

Gross, Leonard. *The Golden Years of the Hutterites*, rev. ed. Kitchener, ON: Pandora, 1998.

Gross, Leonard. "Nikolaus Geyersbühler, Hutterite Missioner to Tyrol." *MQR* 43, no. 3 (Oct. 1969): 283–92.

Hecht, Linda A. Huebert. "A Brief Moment in Time: Informal Leadership and Shared Authority among Sixteenth Century Anabaptist Women." *Journal of Mennonite Studies* 17 (1999): 52–74.

Hecht, Linda A. Huebert. "Anabaptist Women in the Tyrol who Recanted." In *Profiles of Anabaptist Women: Sixteenth-century Reforming Pioneers*, edited by Linda A. Huebert Hecht and C. Arnold Snyder, 156–63. Waterloo, ON: Pandora, 1996.

Höller, Ralf. *Eine Leiche in Habsburgs Keller: der Rebell Michael Gaismair und sein Kampf für eine gerechtere Welt.* Vienna: Otto-Müller-Verlag, 2011.

Hostetler, John A. *Hutterite Society.* Baltimore: The Johns Hopkins University Press, 1997 (1974).

Hutterian Brethren, trans. and ed., *Chronicle of the Hutterian Brethren, The.* vol. 1, Rifton, NY: Plough, 1987.

Hutterischen Brüder, ed., *Die Lieder der Hutterischen Brüder.* Caley, Alberta: 1962.

Hutterite Brethren in America, ed., *Die Hutterischen Episteln: 1525 bis 1767.* 4 vols. Elie, MB: James Valley Book Centre, 1986–91. The sources for the epistles published in these volumes are not given. Some come from codices in the possession of Hutterites in the United States and Canada (see preface to volume III), but published works are also reprinted in these volumes. Vol. I: L-3, L-5, L-6, L-7, L-8; vol. II: L-1; vol. III: L-4.

Innerhofer, Josef. *Taufers, Ahrn, Prettau: Die Geschichte eines Tales.* Val di Tures: Verlagsanstalt Athesia, 1980.

Joldersma, Hermina, and Louis Grijp, eds. *Elisabeth's Manly Courage: Testimonials and Songs of Martyred Anabaptist Women in the Low Countries.* Milwaukee: Marquette University Press, 2001.

Kann, Robert A. *A History of the Habsburg Empire 1526–1918.* London: University of California Press, 1974.

Karajan, Theodor Georg v., ed. "Georg Kirchmair's Denkwürdigkeiten seiner Zeit: 1519–1553." *Fontes rerum Austriacarum* I, 1, 417–534. Vienna, 1855.

Klaassen, Walter. *Michael Gaismair: Revolutionary and Reformer.* Leiden: Brill, 1978.

Klaassen, Walter, and William Klassen. *Marpeck: A Life of Dissent and Conformity.* Waterloo, ON: Herald Press, 2008.

Köfler, Gretl. "Täufertum in Tyrol." In *Michael Gaismair e il Tyrolo del 500*, edited by Christoph von Hartungen and Guenther Pallaver, 112–22. Bolzano: Comitato di Contatto per L'altro Tyrolo, 1983.

Kuppelwieser, Karl. "Die Wiedertäufer im Eisacktal." Doctoral diss., Leopold Franzen University, Innsbruck, 1949.

Legère, Werner. *Der gefürchtete Gaismair: Roman* (the dreaded Gaismair: a novel). Berlin: Union Verlag, 1976.

Lichdi, Elfriede. "Katharina Purst Hutter of Sterzing." In *Profiles of Anabaptist Women*, edited by Linda H. Hecht and C. Arnold Snyder, 178–86. Waterloo, ON: Wilfrid Laurier University Press, 2001.

Loesche, Georg. *Geschichte Des Protestantismus in Oesterreich in Umrissen.* Leipzig: Mohr, 1902.

Loserth, Johann. *Anabaptism in Tyrol: Faithful Resilience through Persecution (1526–1626)*, trans. Hugo Brinkmann. St. Catharines ON: Gelassenheit Publications, 2022.

Loserth, Johann. "Der Kommunismus der mährischen Wiedertäufer im 16. und 17. Jahrhundert." *Archiv für österr. Geschichte* 81 (1894): 135–322.

Loserth, Johann. *Zeitschrift für Social- und Wirtschaftsgeschichte.* 1895.

Loserth, Johann. "Zur kirchlichen Bewegung in Mähren im Jahre 1528." *Zeitschrift des deutschen Vereins für die Geschichte Mährens und Schlesiens* 23 (1919): 176.

Macek, Josef. *Der Tyroler Bauernkrieg und Michael Gaismair.* Berlin: Deutscher Verlag der Wissenschaften, 1965.

Maendel, Emmy Barth. "Katharina Prast: Wife of Jakob Hutter." *MQR* 96, no. 3 (Jul. 2022): 438–58.

Mais, Adolf. "Gefängnis und Tod der in Wien hingerichteten Wiedertäufer in Ihren Briefen und Liedern." *Jahrbuch des Vereins für Geschichte der Stadt Wien* 19–20 (1963): 87–182.

Martens, Helen. *Hutterite Songs.* Waterloo, ON: Pandora, 2002.

Mecenseffy, Grete. "The Origin of Upper Austrian Anabaptism." In *The Anabaptists and Thomas Müntzer*, edited and translated by Werner Packull and James Stayer, 152–53. Dubuque, IA: Kendall/Hunt, 1980.

Mecenseffy, Grete, ed. *Quellen zur Geschichte der Täufer. XI Band. Österreich* I. Gütersloh, Germany: Verlagshaus Gerd Mohn, 1964.

Mecenseffy, Grete, ed. *Quellen zur Geschichte der Täufer. XIII Band. Österreich II.* Gütersloh, Germany: Verlagshaus Gerd Mohn, 1972.

Mecenseffy, Grete, ed. *Quellen zur Geschichte der Täufer. XIV Band. Österreich III*. Gütersloh, Germany: Verlagshaus Gerd Mohn, 1983.

Monge, Mathilde. "Une représentation catholique de l'anabaptism en 1528." M.A. thesis, Université Paris 1, 2001.

Müller, Lydia. *Der Kommunismus der mährischen W.T.* Leipzig, 1929.

Müller, Lydia, ed. *Glaubenszeugnisse oberdeutscher Taufgesinnter*, 1. Leipzig: Hensius Nachfolger, 1938. Müller's edition was based on COD. 1, listed above: L-4, L-8.

Neff, Christian. "Blaurock, Georg (ca. 1492–1529)." GAMEO. 1953. https://gameo.org/index.php?title=Blaurock,_Georg_(ca._1492-1529)&oldid=172015.

Neff, Christian and Robert Friedmann, "Eleutherobios, Stoffel and Leonhard (16th century)." GAMEO. 2011. https://gameo.org/index.php?title=Eleutherobios,_Stoffel_and_Leonhard_(16th_century).

Newman, Albert Henry. *A History of Anti-pedobaptism: From the Rise of Pedobaptism to A.D. 1609*. Philadelphia, PA: American Baptist Publication Society, 1896.

Oyer, John. "The Influence of Jacob Strauss on the Anabaptists: A Problem in Historical Methodology." In *The Origins and Characteristics of Anabaptism*, edited by Marc Lienhard, 62–82. Den Haag, 1977.

Oyer, John S. "Nicodemites among Württemberg Anabaptists." *MQR* 71, no. 4 (Oct. 1997): 487–514.

Packull, Werner O. *Hutterite Beginnings: Communitarian Experiments during the Reformation*. Baltimore: The Johns Hopkins University Press, 1995.

Packull, Werner O. *Mysticism and the Early South German-Austrian Anabaptist Movement 1525–1531*. Kitchener, ON: Herald, 1977.

Packull, Werner O. *Peter Riedemann: Shaper of the Hutterite Tradition*. Kitchener, ON: Pandora, 2007.

Packull, Werner O., and Bruno Fast, "An Index of Peter Riedemann's Epistles." *MQR* 65, no. 3 (Jul. 1991): 340–51.

Pater, Calvin. *Karlstadt as the Father of Baptist Movements: The Emergence of Lay Protestantism*. Toronto: University of Toronto Press, 1984.

Pletscher, Werner. "Wo Entstand das Bekenntnis von 1527?" *MGBL*, V, 1940, 20–21.

Rauert, Matthias H., and Martin Rothkegel, compilers. *Katalog der hutterischen Handschriften und der Drucke aus hutterischem Besitz in Europa*.

Edited by Gottfried Seebass. *Quellen zur Geschichte der Täufer*, vol. XVIII, parts 1 and 2. Gütersloh, Germany: Gütersloher Verlagshaus, 2011.

Rempel, John D., ed. *Jörg Maler's Kunstbuch*. Walden, NY: Plough, 2019.

Rothkegel, Martin. "Anabaptism in Moravia and Silesia." In *A Companion to Anabaptism and Spiritualism, 1521–1700*, ed. James M. Stayer and John D. Roth. Leiden: Brill, 2007.

Rothkegel, Martin. "Antihabsburgische Opposition und Täuferischer Pazifismus: Die Auslegung von Römer 13 des David Burda aus Schweinitz 1530/31." *MGBL*, 69 (2012): 7–44.

Rothkegel, Martin. "Ausbreitung und Verfolgung der Täufer in Schlesien in den Jahren 1527–1548." *Archiv für schlesische Kirchengeschichte* 61 (2003): 149–209.

Rothkegel, Martin. "Die Chroniken der Gemeinde Gottes in Mähren. Historiographie und Martyrologie bei den Hutterischen Brüdern im 16. und frühen 17. Jahrhundert." In *Konfessionelle Geschichtsschreibung im Umfeld der Böhmischen Brüder (1500–1800): Traditionen – Akteure – Praktiken*, edited by Joachim Bahlcke, Jiří Just, and Martin Rothkegel, 321–75. Wiesbaden: Harrassowitz Verlag, 2022.

Schlachta, Astrid von. *Gefahr oder Segen? Die Täufer in der politischen Kommunikation*. Göttingen: V&R, 2009.

Schlachta, Astrid von. "Huterin, Katharina Purst." *MennLex* V. https://www.mennlex.de/doku.php?id=art:huterin_katharina_purst&s[]=huter.

Schmelzer, Matthias. "Jakob Huters Wirken im Lichte von Bekenntnissen gefangener Täufer." *Der Schlern* 63 (1989): 596–618.

Schraepler, Horst W. *Die rechtliche Behandlung der Täufer in der deutschen Schweiz, Südwestdeutschland und Hessen 1525–1618*. Tübingen: E. Fabian-Verlag, 1957.

Seiling, Jonathan. "Absonderung." *MennLex* V. http://www.mennlex.de/doku.php?id=top:absonderung.

Seiling, Jonathan. "Christoph Freisleben's *On the Genuine Baptism of John, Christ and the Apostles*." *MQR* 81, no. 4 (Oct. 2007): 623–54.

Seiling, Jonathan. "Johann Fabri's Justification Concerning the Execution of Balthasar Hubmaier." *MQR* 84, no.1 (Jan. 2010): 117–39.

Seiling, Jonathan. "Verfolgung, " *MennLex* V. http://www.mennlex.de/doku.php?id=top:verfolgung.

Seiling, Jonathan, C. J. Dyck and John D. Rempel. "Hans Schlaffer and Leonhard Frick, A Simple Prayer, Confession of Sin and Open Confession of Faith." In *Jörg Maler's Kunstbuch*, edited by John Rempel, 269–301. Kitchener, ON: Herald, 2010.

Sinnacher, Franz-Anton. *Beyträge zur Geschichte der bischöflichen Kirche Säben und Brixen in Tyrol.* Brixen: Weger, 1821–34.

Snyder, C. Arnold. *Anabaptist History and Theology: An Introduction*. Kitchener, ON: Pandora, 1995.

Snyder, C. Arnold. "The Influence of the Schleitheim Articles on the Anabaptist Movement: An Historical Evaluation." *MQR* 63 (1989): 323–44.

Snyder, C. Arnold, ed. *Sources of South German-Austrian Anabaptism*. Walden, NY: Plough, 2019.

Stayer, James M. *The German Peasants' War and Anabaptist Community of Goods*. Kingston: McGill-Queen's University Press, 1991.

Stayer, James M. "Reublin and Brotli: The Revolutionary Beginnings of Swiss Anabaptism." In *The Origins and Characteristics of Anabaptism*, edited by Marc Lienhard, 83–102. The Hague: Nijhoff, 1977.

Stayer, James M. "Swiss-South German Anabaptism, 1526–1549." In *A Companion to Anabaptism and Spiritualism*, 1521–1700, edited by James M. Stayer and John D. Roth, 83–117. Leiden: Brill, 2007.

Stiasny, Hans Hermann Theodor. *Die strafrechtliche Verfolgung der Täufer in der freien Reichsstadt Köln: 1529 bis 1618*. Münster: Aschendorff, 1962.

Strauss, Jakob. *Von dem ynnerlichen vnnd ausserlichem Tauff.* Erfurt, 1523.

Strauss, Jakob. *Widder den Simonieschen Tauff.* Erfurt, 1523.

Sutherland, Nicola M. "Persecution and Toleration in Reformation Europe." In *Persecution and Toleration*, edited by William J. Sheils, 153–62. Oxford: Basil Blackwell, 1984.

Vajda, Stephan. *Felix Austria: Eine Geschichte Österreichs*. Vienna: Ueberreuter 1980.

Wagner, Murray. *Petr Chelcicky: A Radical Separatist in Hussite Bohemia*. Waterloo, ON: Herald, 1983.

Wenger, J. C. "A Letter from Wilhelm Reublin to Pilgram Marpeck, 1531." *MQR* 23, no. 2 (Apr. 1949): 67–75.

Williams, G. H. *The Radical Reformation*, 1st ed. Philadelphia, PA: Westminster, 1962.

Williams, G. H., ed., *Spiritual and Anabaptist Writers: Documents Illustrative of the Radical Reformation*. Philadelphia, PA: Westminster, 1957.

Winkelbauer, Thomas. "Die rechtliche Stellung der Täufer im 16. und 17. Jahrhundert am Beispiel der habsburgischen Länder." In *Ein Thema – zwei Perspektiven: Juden und Christen in Mittelalter und Frühneuzeit*, edited by Eveline Brugger and Birgit Wiedl, 34–66. Innsbruck: Studien Verlag, 2007.

Wolkan, Rudolf ed. *Das grosse Geschichtsbuch der Hutterischen Brüder* (Standoff Colony, Macleod, AB., Canada, 1923) Abbreviated as: Wolkan: L-2, L-4.

Zieglschmid, Andreas Johannes Friedrich. *Die älteste Chronik der Hutterischen Brüder: Ein Sprachdenkmal aus frühneuhochdeutscher Zeit*. Ithaca, NY: Cayuga Press, 1943. Abbreviated as: Zieglschmid, *Chronik*: L-2, L-4.

Zieglschmid, Andreas Johannes Friedrich. "Unpublished Sixteenth Century Letters of the Hutterian Brethren." *MQR* 15 (1941): 5–25, 118–140. Zieglschmid's edition was based on COD. 2, listed above: L-3, L-6.

Index of Names and Places

I

J

K

Scripture Index

Old Testament

Jude

Revelations

The Editors

EMMY BARTH MAENDEL is a member of the Bruderhof communities and a senior archivist for the Bruderhof's historical archives. She is the author of *An Embassy Besieged: The Story of a Christian Community in Nazi Germany* and *No Lasting Home: A Year in the Paraguayan Wilderness.* Emmy's first husband, Jake Maendel, died in 2017. In 2023, she married Brian Trapnell.

JONATHAN SEILING, PhD, is a translator and editor of texts from several European languages, in particular those from the Anabaptist tradition. Raised in the Mennonite Church in Canada, his areas of research have included pacifism (particularly in the early Reformation, and in modern Canadian history), ecumenism, and religious philosophy (especially the traditions of Spinoza and sophiology in Russia). He is also the founder of Gelassenheit Publications, which publishes translations, studies, and literature related to Mennonite history.

Printed in the USA
CPSIA information can be obtained
at www.ICGtesting.com
JSHW010921080424
60678JS00006B/3